Chinese Healing Exercises

Chinese Healing Exercises

The Tradition of Daoyin

Livia Kohn

A Latitude 20 Book
University of Hawai'i Press
Honolulu

13 12 11 10 09 08   6 5 4 3 2 1

Library of Congress Cataloging-in-Publication Data

Kohn, Livia, 1956–
  Chinese healing exercises : the tradition of Daoyin / Livia Kohn.
    p. cm.
  Includes bibliographical references and index.
  ISBN 978-0-8248-3234-6 (alk. paper) — ISBN 978-0-8248-3269-8 (pbk. : alk. paper)
  1. Dao yin. 2. Breathing exercises—Therapeutic use. 3. Hygiene, Taoist. I. Title. II.
Title: Tradition of Daoyin.
  RA781.85.K64 2008
  615.8'36—dc22
                        2008009183

Designed by University of Hawai'i Press production staff

Printed by The Maple-Vail Book Manufacturing Group

Contents

List of Illustrations

Acknowledgments

This work grew over many years of study and practice, both academically and in various exercise traditions. I am indebted to many teachers, supporters, and fellow seekers.

First, I would like to thank qigong masters Roger Jahnke, Michael Winn, Karin Sörvik, Frank Yurasek, and Paul Gallagher as well as taiji quan master Bede Bidlack for providing pertinent instruction in Chinese physical practices—both traditional and modern—in a large variety of media: in person, through video, on audiotapes and CDs. Their work over a number of years greatly increased my personal experience of the Chinese modality of physical healing and enhanced my understanding of qigong and taiji quan in a way that books never could.

Next, I am deeply grateful to my many yoga teachers over the years, most notably Patricia Walden and Annie Hoffman, who provided thorough instruction in the Iyengar method and raised my awareness of the works of B. K. S. Iyengar, an invaluable resource for understanding the medical benefits of body bends and stretches. I would also like to thank my teachers Yoganand Michael Carroll and Martha Abbot, as well as other staff members of the Kripalu Center for Yoga and Health, for the in-depth training in yogic thinking, the thorough exposition of anatomy and physiology, and the compassionate assistance in actual practice they provided during my yoga teacher training at Kripalu in 2002. More recently, I would like to acknowledge Ana Forrest, yoga master extraordinaire, for her outstanding work in transforming bodies with apparently simple moves—something her yoga has much in common with the Daoyin practices studied in this book.

On a third level, I wish to thank John Loupos, healer and martial arts instructor of Cohasset, Massachusetts, for not only helping me with a bursitic shoulder but in the process introducing me to Hanna Somatics, thereby opening a completely new way of looking at exercise and the body that has pervaded the work on this book. By extension, I am much indebted to the late Thomas Hanna and his extraordinary work on the body. Not only transforming my own practice, his guidance—in his book and in numerous patiently recorded audio sessions— has helped to create a clearer image of what needs to be done to a body to effect relaxation and healing. His theory of the three key reflexes has been essential to my understanding of why Chinese practitioners do what they do and how they come to claim specific results for certain practices.

In a more academic and theoretical vein, I would like to thank several of my graduate students for doing outstanding work and raising my awareness and understanding of different aspects of physical practice and healing. Stephen Jackowicz, highly gifted acupuncturist and graduate of Boston University in 2003, did outstanding work on the absorption of *qi*, successfully applying information from medieval Daoist materials to a twentieth-century patient. His in-depth analysis of how medieval Chinese understood the workings of the inner body and his thorough medical and therapeutic analysis of the process of *qi*-absorption have greatly influenced my interpretation of this rather advanced aspect of Daoyin practice.

Another graduate student whose work and help were invaluable was Shawn Arthur, who graduated from Boston University in 2006. His dissertation is on the dietary and fasting techniques of Daoists and modern qigong practitioners, examining them both on the basis of traditional concepts and in terms of modern physiology and pharmacology. His work on fasting and the replacing of ordinary food and drink with *qi* provided me with great insights into the Chinese understanding of the body's structure and the role of breathing and diet in the context of healing exercises. Besides aiding this project with his knowledgeable expertise, Shawn has also been invaluable in assisting the actual manuscript preparation.

A third graduate student who provided knowledge and inspiration is Heidi Nugent at the Union Institute, Ohio. She has just completed a pathbreaking dissertation on breath, its understanding in different cultures, and the various ways people use (and abuse) it to create health or sickness. As she moved along in her in-depth study, she has greatly increased my understanding and awareness of breathing physiology and the role it plays in traditional forms of healing.

Beyond the background practice and information necessary for the completion of this book, I also received enormous support and encouragement in the course of manuscript preparation. First, in the summer of 2005, I was given the great chance to present my findings on Chinese healing exercises to experts at the annual convention of the National Qigong Association (NQA) in Boulder, Colorado. During a whole-day workshop on Daoyin and a two-hour seminar on Animal Forms, participants in good cheer actually performed the exercises I had translated from ancient texts. In subsequent discussions, they provided extensive feedback and substantive insights into the effects of the exercises, the connection to modern practices, and the best terminology to use. Until then I had, in imitation of European scholars, translated the term *daoyin* as "gymnastics," but workshop participants made it very clear that in the United States the word has too much of an athletic connotation to be appropriate for the Chinese tradition. I have since changed my rendition to "healing exercises," and thus the very title of this book is due to the great help and support of the U.S. qigong community. I am much indebted to them all.

Next, in the spring of 2006, I was kindly invited by Joseph Alter of the University of Pittsburgh and Geoffrey Samuels of the University of Cardiff, Wales, to speak at the annual meeting of the International Association for the Study of Traditional Asian Medicine (IASTAM), held in Austin, Texas. This gave me an opportunity to present my understanding of Chinese subtle body techniques in an academic setting and to connect to scholars with similar interests. Both audience and fellow panel members provided insightful comments and encouraged my work in the wider framework of the comparative study of body techniques—a growing field with an increasing influence on U.S. health services. I met numerous new people who have since become friends and would much like to thank all the IASTAM members for their good work, kindly welcome of newcomers, and generous support of all related research.

Third, at the Third International Conference on Daoism, held on the Fraueninsel near Munich in May 2006, I had a chance to present both on the possible application of Daoyin for stress relief along the lines of Hanna Somatics and on the state of the field of *yangsheng* or Chinese longevity studies. Again, I received helpful comments and suggestions from participating colleages, notably Ute Engelhardt, Catherine Despeux, and Sakade Yoshinobu. I also greatly enjoyed meeting both scholars and practitioners who encouraged continued efforts in this area. I am very grateful to the organizers of the conference and the participants for providing such a comfortable forum that made stimulating discussion possible.

Last and most important, I had great help with writing the actual book. Vivienne Lo, professor at the Wellcome Center for Applied Healing in London, kindly read parts of the manuscript, especially on the early period, and very generously shared her printed articles and her draft translation of the *Yinshu* with me. The articles raised my awareness of the role of healing exercises in the greater picture of ancient Chinese medicine and longevity techniques, and her translation was a tremendous help in clarifying several obscure passages of the ancient manuscript. Having only first met her at the IASTAM conference, I am very, very grateful indeed for her instantaneous friendship and overarching goodwill toward my project.

By far the most help on the actual manuscript I received from J. Michael Wood, qigong master and healer in Nashville, Tennessee. He participated in the workshop at the NQA meeting in Boulder and proposed many suggestions as to the actual workings of the practices, then generously offered to read the technical translations of exercises and provide suggestions on how they might be best interpreted in terms of modern physiology and Chinese medicine. As I continued to write and revise, he presented numerous powerful suggestions on how the exercises would affect the body in therapy, chiropractic, and medical qigong. I greatly appreciate the effort and work he invested in this project and wish to thank him, as much as all my teachers, friends, students, and supporters, from the bottom of my heart.

Introduction

Human beings are by nature embodied creatures. The very foundation of our life is the concrete, material reality into which we are born and which we shape. As the basis of our existence, the body is a source of great pleasure and overwhelming pain, a giver of deep satisfaction and utter misery, the root of potential perfection and dismal failure.

The Chinese have realized this fact and, over several millennia, have made the body the foundation of the great human endeavor of perfection: the perfection of health and well-being, the perfection of long life in youthful vigor, and the perfection of spirit in transcendence to an otherworldly realm. They have always understood the elementary need for accepting one's basic inborn qualities while yet working to live up to one's full potential, caring for and cultivating the body to the best of one's abilities. To this end, they have developed a plethora of methods, called longevity techniques, that can restore health, enhance the quality of life, prolong life expectancy, and even aid in the ultimate goal of spiritual transcendence.

Healing exercises, called Daoyin, constitute one form of these techniques. Documented already in Chinese antiquity, they have evolved and expanded over the centuries, are popular in China in their current forms of qigong (also chi kung) and taiji quan (also tai chi ch'üan), and have recently made inroads in Western health and spiritual circles. What, then, is the fundamental understanding of the human body in Chinese culture? What exactly are "longevity techniques" and how do they work? What is Daoyin, how is it done, where does it come from? And, finally, are there comparative methods in other cultures and the modern West that may be more familiar and thus help us explore the exact workings of the practice?

The Body and the Dao

The body in traditional China is closely connected to and even a replica of the Dao 道. The Dao is at the base of all creation; it is the fundamental productive power of the universe that causes things to come into existence and maintains them throughout. There is only one Dao, and all beings are part of this Dao, although most are not aware of it. People, the ancient texts say, are in the Dao like fish are in water.

Like water, the Dao is everywhere—around us, in us, with us. It flows naturally along its channels—in the body, in nature, in society. It is steady, fluid, easy, soft and weak; it never pushes, fights, or controls but is powerful by merely going along. People do not know it, but it the Dao always there, always sustaining, like a mother— the mother of the universe, the mother of all existence, the mother of all of us. It brings forth and nurtures; it cares and raises; it supports and moves along. Whatever we do, whoever we are, whatever we become, it is always part of the Dao.[1]

These two metaphors of water and mother express the nature of the Chinese universe as beneficent: soothing, protecting, generative. Both water and mother, of course, can be threatening. There are overpowering mothers whom one would not dare cross; there are mythical mothers who devour their children. And there are floods and droughts, when water can become a life-threatening force. However, in most people's experience and in their ideal understanding, water and mother tend to be generous and supporting. These metaphors thus reveal a sense of being in the world that involves feeling at home; moving with the flow in non-action (*wuwei* 無爲); being at ease and well protected, nurtured, and supported; and having a place and a direction that is natural. The body as the Dao is thus our most elementary home, the root from which we act and on which we rely at all times and in all our endeavors.

The natural place and direction presented in the body through the Dao is there for everyone, but it is also different for everyone. Just as in the natural world every species has its own habitat and specific characteristics, and each animal within its group has its role and position, so people have their unique physical characteristics, their special abilities and tendencies. Exploring and developing these, they ideally find a way of being in the world that is just their own—a role that is perfect for them, a home that completely matches their personality and abilities, a place from which they can live a long and healthy life and which can become the starting point for spiritual transcendence.

Vital Energy

The Chinese talk about people's inherently individual yet cosmically connected nature in terms of a vital energy known as *qi* 氣. *Qi* is the material and tangible aspect of the Dao. It can be described as a bioenergetic potency that causes things to live, grow, develop, and decline. People as much as the planet are originally equipped with prenatal or primordial *qi* that connects them to the greater universe, but they also work with postnatal or interactive *qi,* which can

---

1. Mother and water are both metaphors that already appear in the ancient *Daode jing*. For a study of the mother image, see Chen 1974. For a discussion of both in later Daoist thought, see Kohn 1991, 131–133.

enhance or diminish their primordial energy. *Qi* is the basic material of all that exists. It animates life and furnishes the functional power of events. *Qi* is the root of the human body; its quality and movement determine human health. *Qi* can be discussed in terms of quantity, since having more means stronger metabolic function. This, however, does not mean that health is a by-product of storing large quantities of *qi*. Rather, there is a normal or healthy amount of *qi* in every person and every aspect of nature, and health manifests in its overall balance and harmony, in the moderation and smoothness of flow.[2]

Just as the Dao is compared to water, the flow of *qi* is envisioned as a complex system of waterways both in nature and in the human body. In the latter, the "Ocean of *Qi*" is in the abdomen; rivers of *qi* flow through the upper torso, arms, and legs; springs of *qi* sprout at the wrists and ankles; and wells of *qi* are found in the fingers and toes. In both nature and the body, even a small spot in this structure can thus influence the whole, so that overall balance and smoothness are the general goal.

Seen in its most general terms, human life is the accumulation of *qi*; death is its dispersal. After receiving a core potential of primordial and prenatal *qi* at birth, people throughout life need to sustain it. They do so by drawing postnatal *qi* into the body from air and food, as well as from other people through sexual, emotional, and social interaction. But they also lose *qi* through breathing bad air, living in polluted areas, overburdening or diminishing their bodies with food and drink, or getting involved in negative emotions and excessive sexual or social interaction. Health and long life come through working with *qi* to the best of one's ability, attaining a state of perfect balance, utmost harmony, and complete self-fulfillment.

Rather than the mere absence of symptoms and ailments, health in this vision is thus a fundamental alignment with the Dao as it manifests in one's personal physical and psychological characteristics and as it opens paths to higher self-realization and spiritual unfolding. It means the presence of a strong vital energy and of a smooth, harmonious, and active *qi*-flow that moves in a steady alteration of yin and yang, two aspects of the continuous flow of creation: the rising and falling, growing and declining, warming and cooling, beginning and ending, expanding and contracting movements that pervade all life and nature. Yin and yang continuously alternate and change from one into the other. They do so in a steady rhythm of rising and falling, visible in nature in the rising and setting of the sun, the warming and cooling of the seasons, the growth and decline of living beings.

---

2. There are many works that discuss *qi* and its nature, mostly in Chinese medicine. Examples include Porkert 1974, Reid 1989, Johnson 2000, Kaptchuk 2000. For a more detailed outline of the Chinese energy and body system, see Kohn 2005. The latter forms the basis of the following presentation.

Phases and Energy Channels

This flow of *qi* in undulating waves is further systematized into a system of the so-called five phases (*wuxing* 五行), which are in turn symbolized by five material objects: minor yang is symbolized by wood; major yang, fire; yin-yang, earth; minor yin, metal; and major yin, water. These five continue to produce each other in a harmonious cycle in the order presented here. *Qi* that flows in this order and in the right amount is known as *zhengqi* 正氣 or "proper *qi*." In addition to personal health, this is also manifest by harmony in nature, defined as regular weather patterns and the absence of disasters, and as health in society, the peaceful coexistence among families, clans, villages, and states. This harmony on all levels, the cosmic presence of a steady and pleasant flow of *qi,* is what the Chinese call the state of Great Peace (*taiping* 太平), a state venerated by Confucians and Daoists alike.

The opposite of *zhengqi* is *xieqi* 邪氣 or "wayward *qi,*" *qi* that has lost the harmonious pattern of flow and no longer supports the dynamic forces of change. *Xieqi* is disorderly and dysfunctional, and creates change that violates the normal order. When it becomes dominant, the *qi*-flow can turn upon itself and deplete the body's resources. Thus, any sick person, decimated forest, or intrusive construction no longer operates as part of a universal system and is not in tune with the basic life force.

Whether proper or wayward, *qi* flows through and animates all the different systems of the human body, which are not classified according to skeletal, muscular, or hormonal, but in terms of yin organs that store *qi* and center the body's functioning; yang organs that move *qi* and take care of digestion and respiration; body fluids that moisturize the body including the lymph and sweat glands; building blocks that make the body come together; senses that connect it to the outside world; emotions that characterize negative reactions to the world; and virtues that enhance positive attitudes.

The full inner-body correspondence system is shown in table 1. The same system of the five phases also connects the body to the outside world, to the seasons, directions, colors, and other aspects of nature, creating a complex network of energetic pathways that work closely together and are intimately interconnected.

Within the body, moreover, the organs are the key storage and transforma-

TABLE 1. INNER-BODY CORRESPONDENCE SYSTEM

Phase	Yin organ	Yang organ	Body fluid	Building block	Sense	Emotion	Virtue
wood	liver	gallbladder	tears	joints	vision	anger	benevolence
fire	heart	small intestine	sweat	blood vessels	touch	agitation	propriety
earth	spleen	stomach	oral mucus	muscles	taste	worry	honesty
metal	lungs	large intestine	nasal mucus	skin	smell	sadness	righteousness
water	kidneys	bladder	saliva	bones	hearing	fear	wisdom

tion centers of *qi*. They connect to the extremities through a network of energy channels called meridians. There are twelve main meridians that run on both sides of the body. They include ten channels centered on the five yin and five yang organs, plus two added for symmetry: the Triple Heater (yang), a digestive organ that combines the *qi* from food and from air and transports it to the heart; and the pericardium (yin), a supplementary organ to the heart.

There are also eight extraordinary vessels that run along only one line in the body. They are considered primary and more elemental than the twelve matching channels, carrying a deeper blueprint of the human being and connecting us more intimately to the cosmic course. They include four lines that run along the arms and legs, supporting the basic yin and yang structure of the body, plus two that create a cross inside the torso: the Belt Vessel (*daimai* 帶脈), which encircles the waist horizontally, and the Penetrating Vessel (*chongmai* 沖脈), which runs vertically straight through our center from the head to the pelvic floor. The remaining two extraordinary vessels are the Governing Vessel (*dumai* 督脈; yang) and the Conception Vessel (*renmai* 任脈; yin), which run along the back and front of the torso, both originating near the base of the spine and ending around the mouth. They form an essential energy circuit along the torso and are used both in medical and meditative body cultivation.

Organs and, through them, the *qi*-flow of the body are accessed through points along the channels where the energy line comes closest to the surface of the body, the so-called acupuncture points. Each channel has a certain number of points, the longest being the Bladder meridian, which runs through several parallel lines along the back of the body. The points are stimulated with needles in acupuncture, with the burning of mugwort *(Artemisia vulgaris)* in moxibustion or cautery, and with the fingers in acupressure and Anmo massage. The overall *qi*-flow in the channels, moreover, is subject to the action of the longevity techniques: it can be regulated with food and herbs in dietary techniques, with respiration in controlled breathing practice, with body movements in healing exercises, and with the mind in meditation.

The Mind

The mind in this system is another aspect of *qi*, albeit one that vibrates at a much subtler level. As a result, medical and Daoist texts do not show a separation of mental from bodily symptoms but take both as indications of disharmony. According to them, the word "mind" (*xin* 心) has two meanings: it is a general term for all the various aspects of consciousness and mental activity, in which sense it is close to spirit (*shen* 神); and it is also a more specific term for the evaluation of the world in terms of good and bad, likes and dislikes, based on sensory stimuli, emotions, and classificatory schemes. In both forms it is closely linked with the inner organ of the heart, also called *xin,* and represents different aspects of consciousness—one evaluative and critical, essential for day-to-day survival in the ordinary world, the other flowing smoothly and open to all stimuli, the manifestation of the Dao within.

In a more subtle analysis, moreover, the mind, as outlined in the medical classic *Huangdi neijing* 黃帝內經 (Yellow Emperor's Inner Classic), divides into five different forms, associated with the five inner organs:

> Blood is stored in the liver—the residence of the spirit soul.
> Constructive energy is stored in the spleen—the residence of the intention.
> The pulse is stored in the heart—the residence of the spirit.
> *Qi* is stored in the lungs—the residence of the material soul.
> Essence is stored in the kidneys—the residence of the will. (*Huangdi neijing suwen,*
>   ch. 2)

Each inner organ, therefore, has its own particular body fluid or form of *qi* and also its specific mental or psychological energy. They each transform and mutate into one another, according to the cycle of the five phases (Ishida 1989, 59). As waves of the various energetic fluids move around the body, so the different aspects of the mind flow along all its parts, creating an integrated network of consciousness.[3]

The body-mind in Chinese culture, therefore, is an integrated energetic organism that consists of dynamic flows of *qi* at various levels of subtlety and is represented metaphorically as a system of waterways and undulating channels. The body is a microcosm of the universe: it reflects the landscape of the planet and is the home of celestial entities and starry palaces. Whatever we do in our bodies is accordingly never isolated from the rest of the world, and the world is part of who we are. Cultivating the body thus creates strong life in the person, harmony in society, and great potential for spiritual unfolding. As much as taking care of the body empowers the self, it also enhances the universal Dao—to the point where some Daoist thinkers see body cultivation as the foremost condition for ruling the empire.[4]

Longevity

The body being originally part of the Dao, the Chinese claim that it should be healthy and strong and function perfectly to the completion of the natural human

---

3. For more on Chinese body-mind concepts, see Chiu 1986, Ishida 1989. For a comparison of early Chinese medical thought with that of ancient Greece, see Kuriyama 1999.
4. The most important thinker in this context is Heshang gong, an early Han-dynasty commentator to the *Daode jing.* See Chan 1991.

life span of 120 years. Most people, however, tend to make it only to about half this period, undergoing several phases of body development that occur in an eight-year cycle in males and a seven-year cycle in females. As the *Huangdi neijing* says,

> When a girl is 7 years of age, the kidney *qi [jing]* becomes abundant. She begins to change her teeth and the hair grows longer. At 14, she begins to menstruate and is able to become pregnant. The movement of the great pulse is strong. The menses come regularly, and the girl is able to give birth.
>
> At age 21, the energy is steady, the last tooth has come out, and she is fully grown. When she reaches the age of 28, her tendons and bones are strong, her hair has reached its full length, and her body is flourishing and fertile. At 35, her yang brightness pulse begins to slacken, her face begins to wrinkle, her hair starts falling out.
>
> When she reaches the age of 42, the pulse of the three yang regions deteriorates in the upper part of her body, her entire face is wrinkled, and her hair turns gray. At age 49, she can no longer become pregnant, and the circulation of the great pulse is decreased. Her menstruation is exhausted, and the gates of blood are no longer open. Her body declines, and she is no longer able to bear children. (*Huangdi neijing suwen*, ch. 1; Veith 1972, 99)

The key factor in this development is a form of *qi* called essence (*jing* 精). It transforms naturally from primordial *qi*, stored in the Ocean of Qi (*qihai* 氣海; abdomen) in men and the Cavern of Qi (*qixue* 氣穴; chest) in women, through a sinking process that leads to the formation of semen in men and of menstrual blood in women. Both are emitted from the body more or less regularly, leading to the gradual decrease of primordial *qi*.

According to Daoists and Chinese doctors, it is natural to activate and lose essence regularly, thus coming eventually to physical decline and death. At the same time, it is also possible to regulate and slow down the process by controlling the emission of essence and consciously replenishing *qi*. They have accordingly developed practices that allow people to retain and strengthen their essence while reverting back to its original form of *qi* and thus renewing their life and enhancing their health. These practices serve to stimulate the fundamental blueprint of the person stored in the eight extraordinary vessels, to create an openness of flow in the body's channels and support mental states of stress-free tranquility that ensure continued health and long life.

Known as longevity techniques or methods for nourishing life (*yangsheng* 養生), these practices were originally part of preventive medicine that helped people recognize and rectify early signs of wayward *qi* and thus maintain a high level of well-being into extended old age. Undertaken by people on all levels of

Chinese society, they were soon integrated into religious and specifically Daoist regimens and have remained an important part of Chinese life. Longevity techniques work through lifestyle modification in many different ways: diet, herbal remedies, sexual hygiene, deep breathing, physical movements, and mental purification. They are used in various dimensions: to heal people from diseases, to help them maintain health and recover youth, and to assist them in attaining transcendent, spiritual states of immortality.

Levels of Practice

Although the domain of different kinds of practitioners—physicians, longevity masters, and Daoist masters—in traditional Chinese understanding, healing, longevity, and immortality were three stages along the same continuum of the *qi*-household of the human body. People's body-mind consists of *qi*, which functions through the continuous interchange of inborn primordial and prenatal *qi*, which connects the person to the cosmos, with earthly or postnatal *qi*, which is taken in through breath, food, and human interaction. The terms of this interchange are thus that primordial *qi* is lost as and when earthly *qi* is insufficient, and earthly *qi* becomes superfluous as and when primordial *qi* is complete (as in the case of the embryo in the womb).

As people interact with the world on the basis of passions and desires, sensory or sexual exchanges, and intellectual distinctions, they activate their essence and begin to lose their primordial *qi*. Once they have lost a certain amount, they decline, experience sickness, and eventually die. Healing, then, is the recovery of essence and replenishing of *qi* with medical means such as drugs, herbs, acupuncture, massage, and so on, from a level of severe deficiency to a more harmonious state.

Longevity comes in as and when people have become aware of their situation and decide to heal themselves. Attaining a basic state of good health, they proceed to increase their primordial *qi* to and even above the level they had at birth. To do so, they follow specific diets, supplement their food with herbs and minerals, and undertake breath control, healing exercises, self-massages, sexual hygiene, and meditation. These practices not only ensure that people attain their natural life expectancy but also lead to increased old age and vigor.

Immortality raises the practices to a yet higher level. To attain it, people have to transform all their *qi* into primordial *qi* and proceed to increasingly refine it to ever subtler levels. This finer *qi* will eventually turn into pure spirit, with which practitioners increasingly identify to become transcendent spirit-people or immortals (*xian* 仙). The practice that leads there involves intensive meditation and trance training as well as more radical forms of diet, healing exercises, and the mental guiding of *qi*. In contrast to health and long life, where the body's system remains fundamentally unchanged and is perfected in its original nature, immortality means the overcoming of the natural tendencies of the body and its transformation into a different kind of energetic constellation. The result is a bypassing of death—since the end of the body has no effect on the continuation of the spirit-person—the attainment of magical powers, and residence in the paradises of Penglai 蓬萊 or Kunlun 崑崙.

Practitioners on all three levels, moreover, make use of the same practices but with slight differences. For example, diets on the medical and health levels involve abstention from heavy foods such as meat and fat, as well as from strong substances such as alcohol, garlic, and onions. Instead, practitioners are encouraged to eat small portions of light foods. As their *qi* increases, they will need less and less food, until—in immortality practice—all main staples can be cut out and food is replaced by the conscious intake of *qi* through breath. This technique is called "avoiding grain" (*bigu* 辟穀) and is still undertaken today.

Similarly, healing exercises as first depicted in Han-dynasty manuscripts serve to stretch and loosen muscles, stimulate the circulation, and aid the smooth flow of *qi* in the body. They are never strenuous, but change in nature as people proceed from the longevity level to the immortality level, becoming more cosmic in pattern, more counterintuitive, and more internally focused. Similarly, breathing for health and long life involves inhaling all the way to the diaphragm, which expands upon inhalation. Breathing for immortality, on the other hand, is called "reversed breathing," and uses the diaphragm the opposite way, contracting it on inhalation. The breath may even become imperceptible and be stopped for extended periods, allowing the person to become one with the purer energies within.

Sexual techniques, too, are used on all levels, first with a partner, later celibately and within the practitioner. In all cases, sexual stimulation is experienced, but then the rising *qi* of arousal (essence) is reverted upward along the spine with the help of meditation and massage instead of being lost through ejaculation or menstruation. This is called "reverting essence to nourish the brain" (*huanjing bunao* 還精補腦) and is supposed to have strong life-extending effects. In more technical Daoist practice of later centuries, it might even lead to the gestation of an immortal embryo.[5]

In all cases, the same understanding of the fundamentally energetic nature of the human body-mind pervades all three levels and the same practices are used in various forms, depending on whether the goal is health, extended longevity, or complete transcendence of this world.

---

5. On Daoist diet, see Reid 1989, Arthur 2006. On breathing and exercises, see Berk 1986; on sexual practices, see Wile 1992, Chu 1993.

The Tradition

The various longevity techniques thus form an essential aspect of Chinese culture. Described in a variety of Han-dynasty manuscripts as well as many later texts, in both religious and medical collections, they occupy a middle ground between healing and immortality and can be usefully applied on either level. They can be described as the culmination of healing and the foundation of immortality; they are the ultimate path to perfect health and the entryway to Daoist perfection. Placed between two completely different dimensions yet connected to both, they represent a separate tradition that originally developed as part of preventive and antiaging medicine but were soon adopted by Daoists, who found the practices helpful to open themselves to the higher powers.

Thus, the earliest traces of a more internalized awareness of energies, an important feature of Chinese medicine, appears first in longevity texts (Lo 2000, 22). The first metaphorical nomenclature for parts of the body, essential in Daoist practice, is found in Han-dynasty long-life materials on sexual massage (Lo 2001b, 36). Yet despite its importance historically and in modern life, the longevity tradition neither forms part of mainstream Chinese medicine nor is it originally or even essentially Daoist.

Placed at the intersection of fields, the longevity tradition has rarely been the subject of specialized studies. Only a few dedicated scholars, such as Sakade Yoshinobu, Catherine Despeux, Ute Engelhardt, and Vivienne Lo, have contributed significantly to its understanding, and there are only two edited volumes in English that deal specifically with it (Kohn 1989c, 2006a). It has so far remained largely unrecognized for the powerful impact it had on many aspects of Chinese culture.

It is a major purpose of this book, therefore, to present a preliminary history of the longevity tradition as seen through the lens of healing exercises. This history serves two purposes: raising academic awareness of the tradition and thereby encouraging further forays into this field, and providing practitioners with a documented history that provides depth and cultural context to their practice. The following chapters accordingly present the worldview and practice of healing exercises in a chronological survey, beginning with medical manuscripts from the second century B.C.E.; moving on through the fourth century, when the practices were first integrated into Daoist practice, and the Tang dynasty, when they formed an important step in the formal attainment of immortality; to late imperial and modern China, when patterns emerged that are still prevalent today. In all cases the book places the exercises into the social context of the different periods, asking who their practitioners were and what kind of lifestyle they sought to realize.

Before we embark on the detailed history, however, let us briefly look at the nature and background of Chinese healing exercises and examine comparative systems that aid in our better understanding of their workings.

Healing Exercises

Chinese healing exercises are traditionally called Daoyin 導引.[6] According to the Web site of the Chinese Olympic Committee, this indicates "a form of calisthenic exercise that combines breathing with body movements mimicking animals. *Dao* means to regulate *qi* or vital energy by guiding its flow in the body. *Yin* means to limber up the body and limbs through physical movement" ("Daoyin: An Ancient Way of Preserving Life"; http://en.olypmpic.cn).

Indeed, the term *dao* essentially means "to guide" or "to direct," and appears originally in a political and cultural context in the sense of "leading" the people in a certain direction. The character consists of two parts, the word Dao 道 for "way," which is often also used in the sense of "to guide," and the word *cun* 寸 for "inch," which indicates a small distance. Guiding the *qi* in a concrete, physical way means thus that one makes a conscious effort to establish harmony with the Dao in the body, realizing the inherent polarity of yin and yang and aligning oneself with the cosmos (Ikai 2003, 34).

The second word of the compound is *yin*. It originally means "to draw a bow" and indicates the pulling and activating of strength and inner tension as well as the opening of a space between the bow and the string. Often short for *daoyin*, it can stand for breathing and exercises in general and be used as a generic term for "nourishing life." *Yin* may mean to limber up muscles, release joints, or stretch limbs (Ikai 2003, 33). The earliest manuscripts on healing exercises consistently use *yin* in a general sense for *daoyin*, meaning the practice of exercises.

More technically, the texts apply the term *yin* in conjunction with a pain or a problem, meaning "to pull out [the pain]" or "to release," as for example in "releasing blockages" or "releasing yin." This reflects the idea that one can pull the *qi* out from an ailing part and move it either to or from a specific area in the body. Stretching, another classical translation of *yin*, is one way of doing this. In this sense the term is applied most commonly when used as a supplement to descriptive or fanciful names, such as Eight Extraordinary Vessels Stretch or Tiger Stretch. In addition, *yin* may also indicate the stimulation of a certain meridian

6. A common English translation for Daoyin traditionally has been "gymnastics" (Kohn 2005, 177), a term that matches words used in French and German. However, while the term in these languages indicates a general physical workout that can range from highly acrobatic to very mild, in English "gymnastics" tends to invoke images of superior feats and Olympic training. To avoid this image, *daoyin* in this work has been rendered "healing exercises."

or yin-yang aspect of the body and the enhancement of *qi* in certain places. Translation of *yin* accordingly varies among "healing exercises," "stretch," "stimulate," "release," and "relieve" (Engelhardt 2001, 217).

Taken together, Daoyin is a physical exercise practice that purports to drive all evil out of the body. As the seventh-century medical handbook *Zhubing yuanhou lun* 諸病源候論 (Origins and Symptoms of Medical Disorders)[7] says: "The practice consists of drawing together in one's body all the bad, the pathogenic, and the malevolent forms of *qi*. Then one follows them, pulls them in, and guides them to leave forever. This is why it is called Daoyin" (22.1512; Despeux 1989, 239).

The Practice

More specifically, Daoyin involves gentle movements of the body in all kinds of different positions together with deep breathing and the focused mental guiding of *qi* around the channels. The oldest sources, manuscripts from the early Han dynasty (ca. 200 B.C.E.), tend to describe a large range of standing moves with only few seated and lying poses. After that, the most common posture for Daoyin is kneeling with heels tucked under the buttocks. This was the proper and most formal way of sitting in ancient China, where chairs were only gradually introduced from Central Asia under the influence of Buddhism (see FitzGerald 1965, Holzman 1967).

In addition to the cross-legged way of sitting on the floor, Buddhism also brought the first seating furniture, a folding chair or camp stool, known initially as the barbarian chair (*huchuang* 胡床; Kieschnick 2003, 231). It was soon superseded by the corded chair (*shengchuang* 繩床), a flat, low meditation chair with a simple back that allowed the legs to stretch. However, the Chinese were so used to being on the floor that they resisted having their legs hang down and used it as a platform for cross-legged sitting (Kieschnick 2003, 237). Chairs in our sense with a proper back only appeared in China from the tenth century onward and did not get used in healing exercises until very recently.

Other basic poses include squatting and sitting with legs straight out forward or spread fan-shaped out to the side. These postures were considered quite rude in traditional China and were associated with demons and exorcism (Kieschnick 2003, 225; Harper 1985b, 467). Their use in healing exercises, aside from opening the hips and strengthening the legs, shows the intentional separation

---

7. The text was compiled upon imperial command by Chao Yuanfang et al. and dates to 610. It is the first Chinese medical text to include longevity methods for various diseases, which are classified according to symptoms. See Ding 1993, Despeux and Obringer 1997.

from common social norms and patterns and is indicative of the thrust toward self-realization. Less frequently applied poses are lying on one's back, side, or belly, although various forms of meditative *qi*-guiding are executed in this position, including an entire group of practices called "sleep exercises."

The full range of postures is as follows (Ding 1993, 7):

Sit or kneel (*zhengzuo* 正坐, *duanzuo* 端坐, *pingzuo* 平坐)	Sit on buttocks or kneel with either heels or big toes touching.
Squat (*ju* 距, *dun* 蹲, *kua* 跨)	Crouch down on flat feet with knees outward and thighs wide, buttocks not touching the ground.
Wide seat (*ji* 箕)	Crouch or sit with legs spread wide, like a winnowing basket.
Cross-legged (*juzuo* 距坐)	Sit with knees bent and slightly raised, thighs and buttocks touching the floor.
Lotus posture (*jiafuzuo* 跏趺坐, *panxi zuo* 盤膝坐)	Sit cross-legged, with feet on opposite thigh, buttocks on the floor; can be executed half or full.
Lie down (*yanwo* 偃臥, *zhengwo* 正臥)	Lie flat on back using a mat or bed for support.
Lie on the side (*zewo* 側臥)	Lie on one side with arms and knees either bent or straight.
Belly down (*fuwo* 伏臥, *fuwo* 覆臥)	Lie flat on the stomach, head turned to one side.
Standing (*zhanli* 站立)	Stand up straight, feet flat on the floor, or maybe lean against a wall for support.
Tall kneel (*gui* 跪)	Kneel with the tops of feet, thighs, and knees touching the floor, but the torso lifted up.
Barbarian kneel (*hugui* 胡跪)	Kneel as in tall kneel, but with the right knee touching the floor and the left knee upright.
Dignified kneel (*weizuo* 危坐)	Kneel with one knee touching the floor, buttocks on right thigh, the other knee upright, spread open from the hips.
Lofty pose (*junzuo* 峻坐)	Wide-angled kneel, with thighs stretched to the sides.[8]

---

8. A further description is found in the Tang dynasty: "If you sit in the lotus posture when it is cold, you will warm up but then your legs will go to sleep. Sit lofty by opening the thighs into a character *ba* position [wide apart]. This will drive out the cold and alleviate the five kinds of piles" (*Ishinpō* 27).

Ancient Traces

Chinese healing exercises are very old, and references to physical self-culti-vation and breathing go back as far as the third century B.C.E., when the ancient Daoist text *Zhuangzi* 莊子 (Book of Master Zhuang) has the following:

> To huff and puff, exhale and inhale, blow out the old and draw in the new, do the "bear-hang" and the "bird-stretch," interested only in long life—such are the tastes of the practitioners of Daoyin, the nurturers of the body, Grandfather Peng's ripe-old-agers. (ch. 15; Graham 1986, 265)

While showing that the practices existed at the time, the text seems cynical about mere physical efforts toward self-perfection. On the other hand, it takes breath-ing exercises very seriously:

> The perfected of old slept without dreaming and woke without worrying. They ate without delighting in the taste and breathed very deep. In fact, the perfected breathe all the way to their heels, unlike ordinary folk who breathe only as far as their throats. Bent and burdened, they gasp out words as if they were retching. Involved deeply with passions and desires, their connection with heaven is shallow indeed. (ch. 6; Watson 1968, 77–78)

The image here is that one who works with these methods has the mind set com-pletely on the Dao and allows the cosmic energy to flow freely all the way to the heels. He or she has gone beyond passions and desires and is liberated from the concerns and worries of ordinary life. Physical bends and stretches pave the way for the internal openness required for such advanced stages.

As for specific practice instructions, the earliest known reference to healing exercises is an inscription on a dodecagonal jade block of the Zhou dynasty that dates from the fourth century B.C.E. The original function of the block remains uncertain (Chen 1982), but the inscription in forty-five characters has been stud-ied by several scholars (Wilhelm 1948; Engelhardt 1996, 19; Li 1993, 320–323). It reads as follows:

> To guide the *qi*, allow it to enter deeply [by inhaling] and collect it [in the mouth]. As it collects, it will expand. Once expanded, it will sink down.
>
> When it sinks down, it comes to rest. After it has come to rest, it becomes stable.
>
> When the *qi* is stable, it begins to sprout. From sprouting, it begins to grow. As it grows, it can be pulled back upwards. When it is pulled upwards, it reaches the crown of the head.

It then touches above at the crown of the head and below at the base of the spine. Who practices like this will attain long life. Who goes against this will die. (Harper 1998, 126)

This describes a fundamental *qi* practice commonly undertaken as part of Daoyin from the middle ages onward. People inhale deeply, allow the breath to enter both the chest and the mouth, and in the latter mix it with saliva, another potent form of *qi* in the body. Moving the tongue around the mouth, they gather the saliva and gain a sense of fullness, then swallow, allowing the *qi* to sink. They feel it moving deep into the abdomen, where they let it settle in the central area of gravity, known in Chinese medicine as the Ocean of *Qi* and in Daoism as the cinnabar or elixir field (*dantian* 丹田). There the *qi* rests and becomes stable.

As adepts repeat this practice, the *qi* accumulates and becomes stronger. Eventually it does not remain in the lower abdomen but begins to spread through the body or, as the text says, it "sprouts." Once this is felt, adepts can consciously guide it upward—a technique that usually involves pushing it down to the pelvic floor and then moving it gradually up along the spine, both in close coordination with deep breathing. Not only like the modern qigong and inner alchemical practice of the Microcosmic Orbit (*xiao zhoutian* 小周天), this is also the pattern of circulation recommended in the early medical manuscript *Maifa* 脈法 (Vessel Models) and has a counterpart in breath cultivation verses found in the manuscripts *Shiwen* 十問 (Ten Questions) and *He yinyang* 和陰陽 (Harmonizing Yin and Yang) (Harper 1998, 125). Yet another text describes a related practice called the Buttock Pull, a tightening of the pelvic muscles and the perineum:

> Rise at dawn, sit upright, straighten the spine, and open the buttocks. Suck in the anus and press it down. This is cultivating *qi*. When eating and drinking, to relax the buttocks, straighten the spine, suck in the anus, and let the *qi* pass through. This is moving the fluid. (Harper 1998, 430)

Moving all the way up the back, the energy eventually reaches the top of the head. When the entire passage between the head and the pelvic floor is opened, the Penetrating Vessel is activated, the first energy line in the human embryo, the central channel to connect people to the Dao. With this pervading line open, long life can be attained and one can reach for transcendence.

Classical Patterns
Both the emphasis on breathing and the conscious guiding of *qi*, often expanded into visualization, play an important part in the entire tradition of

Daoyin. They tend to be combined with specific forms of body movements and stretches that range from simple, repetitive moves, such as lifting and lowering the toes, through semiacrobatic feats, such as hanging head down from a rope, to complex integrated sequences that take the body through various postures and open, lengthen, and vitalize all different parts: muscles and joints, tendons and channels.

A typical Daoyin session should be undertaken during the early morning hours, when the yang-*qi* of the Sun is on the rise; practitioners should find a quiet, secluded, warm, and clean space where they can be undisturbed for the duration; they should relieve themselves and loosen any restrictive clothing. Then they begin with mental concentration and deep breathing, allowing body and mind to calm and be ready for the practice. Initial formalities may also include the invocation of protective deities or the formal chanting of invocations.

As in Daoist ritual, many Daoyin sessions involve clicking the teeth and beating the heavenly drum (snapping fingers against the back of the head while placing the palms over the ears) to stimulate internal vibrations and connect to the subtler levels of *qi*. Often self-massages of the face, eyes, and ears accompany the practice, stimulating the *qi*-flow in these areas; and many times a practice called Dry Wash (today known as Marrow Washing) is recommended; this involves passing the hands over the entire body along the lines of the energy channels, again to stimulate and balance the flow of *qi*.

The specific needs of the practitioner determine which practices are then chosen. Numerous simple techniques can improve specific areas of the body; they relieve pains, relax tensions, and open *qi* blockages. Many easy sets warm up and energize the body, moving all the different joints from feet to head, without focusing on specific symptoms or areas of the body. A number of set sequences serve to increase *qi*-flow and enhance health and long life. Other practices are more internally focused: using very little body movement, they emphasize holding the breath or guiding the *qi* through the different regions of the body, in some cases visualized in a wide spectrum of colors and as splendid palaces and passageways. Sessions can last from ten or twenty minutes to an hour or more, involving also meditations and ecstatic communications with the gods.

Whatever the case, Daoyin serves to increase practitioners' internal awareness of health and enhances their urge for balance and harmony, making it easy and even essential to practice an overall moderation that pervades all aspects of life and includes the various other longevity techniques. The practice activates the energy flow in the deep extraordinary vessels and deepens the self-conscious knowledge of how one's being in the body influences both one's internal well-being and the level of tension or ease one brings into the family and into the world.

Comparative Practices

While Daoyin is uniquely Chinese, practices in other cultures also engage the body in conjunction with breathing and mental awareness to create greater health and overall harmony in the person. The most obvious comparison is with Indian yoga, widespread and well known in the West; less obvious are matches with contemporary movement therapies that utilize similar moves. They help our understanding of why Daoyin is practiced the way it is practiced, how it affects the body and mind, and why it can be effective for healing and the creation of balance and harmony.

Yoga

The most popular and best known traditional body practice in the West today is yoga, an ancient Indian technique that has spread since the first presentation of Hindu concepts at the World Parliament of Religions in Chicago in 1893. While very similar to Daoyin in its integration of body, breath, and mind as well as in many of its specific moves and postures, in terms of worldview, goals, and history, yoga could not be more different.[9]

Although yogis, like Daoyin followers, emphasize alignment with the fundamental energies of the cosmos and see the body in energetic terms as consisting of five sheaths *(kośa),*[10] the fundamental worldview and ultimate goal of yoga connect the practitioner to the true self or eternal soul (atman), which is one with the creative power of the universe *(brahman).* Firm, fixed, permanent, and eternal, this true self is the person's ultimate identity. Originally one with the deepest transcendent ground of all, human beings have forgotten this identity through their karmic involvement with the world and sensory experiences. Through yoga, the "royal road home," they can recover the innate stability, wholeness, and permanence of the cosmos within and return to the essential substance of their being (Cope 2000, xiii; Farhi 2003, 7).

The Chinese, in contrast, see all reality as being in constant flux and do not acknowledge the existence of a true, permanent, and stable underlying entity either in oneself or in the universe. They also, in their basic practice of Daoyin—with the exception of some applications in Daoism—avoid references to religious or devotional aspects. In yoga, on the other hand, divine grace and devotion to a

---

9. For a more detailed description of yogic worldview, history, and practices in comparison to Daoyin, see Kohn 2006b.
10. The five sheaths are the physical body that is nourished by food; the etheric body that exists through vital energy or *prāṇa*; the astral body made up of thoughts and intentions; the causal body consisting of pure intellect and knowledge; and the ultimate bliss body, true self, or atman. See Worthington 1982, 23; Mishra 1987, 49; Cope 2000, 68.

deity are key factors for success, so that and *īśvara praṇidhāna,* or "refuge in the lord," is one of the five *niyamas,* the mental attitudes to be cultivated as the foundation of the practice, which also include purity, contentment, austerity, and self-study. The lord, *īśvara,* is innate cosmic enlightenment, coessential with the innermost self, the personified power that creates, upholds, and withdraws. Yoga is, therefore, essentially theistic (Eliade 1969, 16).

Matching this fundamental outlook toward the divine versus alignment with nature, Daoyin historically began as a part of preventive medicine and served an aristocratic class within society, while yoga grew from the ancient Indian hermit tradition that "rejected the world as it is and devalued life as ephemeral, anguished, and ultimately illusory" (Eliade 1969, 18). Whereas early documents on Daoyin are clearly dated and contain detailed practical instructions, the earliest documents on yoga are only vaguely dated and in contents tend to be philosophical. They are the *Yogasūtras* of Patañjali, who may or may not be identical with a well-known Sanskrit grammarian who lived around 300 B.C.E.; the text seems to be later than the *Upanishads* and early Buddhism and may even have come after the *Bhagavad Gita* (Worthington 1982, 55). It is divided into four main sections—Yogic Ecstasy, Discipline, Miraculous Powers, and Isolation (Eliade 1969, 12)—and consists of 196 sutras or short half-sentences that are more mnemonic aids than clarifying explanations (Taimni 1975, viii). It does not contain any practical instructions.

Details on yoga poses or asanas only emerge in writing when the hermit practice was adopted by larger segments of the population. This version, called hatha yoga, goes back to a group known as the Nath yogis who flourished in northern India from the tenth century onward. Founded by Goruksanatha, this group placed great emphasis on physical fitness, developed various forms of martial arts, and engaged in psychic experiments. Rather than remain aloof from society, they made attempts at reform, treating women and outcasts as equals and trying to unite Hindus and Buddhists (Worthington 1982, 129).

The main document of the Nath yogis is the *Hathayoga pradīpikā* (Light on Hatha Yoga), which was compiled in the fifteenth century on the basis of the notes and instructions of earlier masters by Svatmarama Swami. Arranged in five sections, it is written like the *Yogasūtras* in a series of short instructions that need further personal instruction (Worthington 1982, 129). Yet it is also quite different in that it places greater emphasis on physical and breath cultivation rather than meditation and trance states and in that it describes specific postures and movements, creating the foundation of modern yoga.

In the wake of the Nath yogis, various twentieth-century practitioners formulated yogic systems, experimented with the health benefits of yoga, and adapted the practice to modern life.[11] Most important among them is B. K. S. Iyengar. Born in 1918 in a small village in Karnataka, he suffered from various severe illnesses and malnutrition in his youth and, after the death of his father, went first to live with an uncle, then, at age fifteen, with the sister of T. Krishnamacharya, the leader of a yoga school in Mysore. There he trained with much difficulty but persevered and gained health and flexibility. In 1937, he was asked to teach yoga in a school in Pune, where he had to overcome more difficulties, both social and physical.

He gradually became an expert, especially in the medical application of the practice, and his fame spread beyond India when in 1952 he met the violinist Yehudi Menuhin, who arranged for him to teach in other countries. In 1966, he published *Light on Yoga*, which became an instant classic. Patterned in title and structure on the *Hathayoga pradīpikā*, it sets the tone for much of modern practice—detailing the exact performance of postures, the breathing patterns associated with them, and the medical and psychological benefits of practice. In 1975 he succeeded in establishing his own school in Pune, which has since become the major training center for Iyengar practitioners. He retired from active teaching in 1984 but still continues to run medical workshops and supervise the education of future teachers. His daughter, Geeta Iyengar, has become the de facto leader of the school.

For our purposes, Iyengar's work is particularly helpful in that it explains how certain poses and moves in Daoyin affect the body and why they are beneficial for practitioners' health. It is an important comparative resource for the study of Chinese healing exercises and provides insights into the comparative evaluation of the practices.

Movement Therapies

Another important comparative perspective, complete with neurophysiological explanations, is found in modern movement therapies that were developed to counteract the stress response, a ubiquitous hazard to health in modern societies. These therapies serve to loosen tight muscles and create an increased awareness of the inner function of the body as a living organism.

One example is Feldenkrais Therapy, developed by Israeli physicist Moshe Feldenkrais (1904–1984). A student of Asian martial arts, he injured his knee in an accident in 1936 and was told he would never walk again without a limp. He

---

11. As a result of this development, yoga practices today are available in three major types: meditative and restful with mostly seated and reclining poses (Restorative Yoga, Yin Yoga, Acu-Yoga); moderately strenuous with poses in all body postures and a strong emphasis on alignment and holding (Iyengar, Kripalu, Forrest, Viniyoga); and serious workouts undertaken in a flow of poses (*vinyasa*), working all major muscle groups in the body (Ashtanga, Bikram, Baptiste, Power Yoga). For an overview of the various schools of yoga, see McCall 2007, 102–114.

refused to listen to medical advice and cured himself by consciously noting what helped and by giving appropriate exercise and rest to his body, learning new ways of movement and the importance of close awareness in the process. As a result, he developed a new system of body integration, documented in his book *Body and Mature Behavior* (1949; see also Feldenkrais 1972).

In his wake, Thomas Hanna (1928–1990), a philosophy professor turned healer, created Hanna Somatics, a system of easy bends and stretches that relieves core muscles most likely to be stiff in modern people (Knaster 1989, 47–48). His starting point is to see people as conscious, self-regulating beings whose bodies are not outside them but are perceived and regulated from within. He calls this kind of body by the Greek word "soma" and defines it as a constantly flowing array of sensing and actions that occur in the experience of each of us. In contrast to the fact that everyone is equipped with a soma, people today suffer from proprioceptive illiteracy: they focus only on the external world and take the body out of the self (Hanna 1988).

His key concept to describe this proprioceptive illiteracy is "sensory-motor amnesia" (SMA), which means that people through years of stress-induced muscular contractions have forgotten how it feels to be relaxed (Hanna 1990, 7). The ability to control a certain muscle group is surrendered to subcortical reflexes and becomes automatic in the worst possible way. As a result, people live with chronically contracted muscles at 10, 30, or even 60 percent. These muscles become sore and painful, tense with constant exertion, and too strong for their own good. They cause clumsiness, represent a continuous energy drain, and create postural distortions such as scoliosis (sideward spinal leaning), swayback, hunchback, or flat back (with protruding belly).

Physicians, faced with an epidemic of lower back pain, headaches, muscle tension, and heart disease, have no good explanation and no cure. They prescribe painkillers and other symptomatic remedies—at worst suggesting surgery to replace joints—calling the syndrome "regional muscular illness" and putting it down to the "natural" effects of aging (Hanna 1990, 8).

Hanna, then, distinguishes three major reflexes that tend to lead to sensory-motor amnesia:

> The Red Light Reflex, also known as the Startle Reflex. A stress response, it works through abdominal contraction and shallow breathing. It says "Stop!" and halts all body activity.
>
> The Green Light Reflex, also called the Landau Reflex. An arousal response, it activates the lower back muscles. It says "Go!" and sets the body up for action.
>
> The Trauma Reflex. A reaction of cringing and pain avoidance, it affects the sides and the waist. Often originally caused by an accident or operation, it says "No!" to pain and causes the body to remain in a twisted, tense state (Hanna 1988; 1990, 8).

To alleviate the effects of these reflexes, Hanna Somatics works with simple bends, stretches, and twists that change the way the brain processes movement and that in many cases are similar to Daoyin moves. Disagreeing with the popular practice of intense stretches, Hanna finds that actively stretching a chronically tight muscle only makes it tighten further. He thus encourages conscious contraction in combination with slow, deep breathing; a deep, conscious awareness; and a very, very slow release—thus teaching the muscle that it can actually let go. The key to all this is, as he says, "our sensory-motor ability to control ourselves. I can contract here, I can release here. As I relax those muscles, what do I feel? I feel a flowing movement right down my body. I am creating that ability to relax and I open up" (Knaster 1989, 53).

Beyond the relief of back pain and various ailments, the ultimate goal of Hanna's system—not unlike the Chinese tendency to expand health practices into longevity and immortality—is the freedom, independence, and autonomy of the individual as described in his book *Bodies in Revolt* (1970). He sees body cultivation as a major way for people to become totally autonomous—self-determining, self-balancing, self-healing, self-regulating, self-correcting—not only physically but psychologically and in life in general. He also says—again in agreement with traditional Chinese practitioners—that aging is a myth; in fact, his most basic series of audio cassettes is called "The Myth of Aging." For him, the typical signs of aging are nothing but the effect of long-term muscular tension, forced immobility, and the resulting sensory-motor amnesia and proprioceptive illiteracy. They are learned responses and they can be unlearned, and he himself has brought about some amazing "cures" just by teaching people to be in their bodies more effectively. His work on the deeper understanding of the production and effects of stress in the body and the importance of becoming self-determining through internal awareness thus brings another comparative explanation to our understanding of Daoyin.

Theoretical Perspectives

Beyond contemporary practices that bear a distinct similarity to Daoyin and serve to place its methods into a comparative context, there are also several areas in which modern concepts and scientific analysis help one to see the practice in a more actual and relevant context. I will focus here on three: the modern understanding of breathing and its importance for health and well-being; the new advances in physics, biology, and other natural sciences that have led to the establishment of a new branch of science called energy medicine; and the use of simple exercises and self-massages as well as tapping protocols based on acupuncture channels in the emerging field of energy psychology.

Breathing

Breathing is a key function in the maintenance of the body, and it is also closely correlated with the mind. Typically, any tension, mental or physical, results in a short and shallow breath; any relaxation tends to make it longer and deeper—and vice versa: if one intentionally breathes shallowly, one gets tenser and more nervous; if one consciously breathes more deeply and slows the respiration down, one becomes more relaxed.

Breathing is closely connected with the autonomic nervous system, which has two branches: the sympathetic and the parasympathetic. The sympathetic nervous system is the energizing part. It puts people into a state of readiness to meet challenges or danger, causing nerve endings to emit neurotransmitters that stimulate the adrenal glands to secrete powerful hormones (adrenaline) that increase the heartbeat and the rate of breathing. They also influence our digestion, speeding up the metabolic function through increased acid secretion in the stomach. The parasympathetic nervous system, on the other hand, activates neurotransmitters such as acetylcholine that lower the pulse and breathing rate. Its responses are comfort, relaxation, and sleep. Any relaxation method will stimulate the parasympathetic nervous system and thus slow down the breath.[12]

If the sympathetic nervous system is "on," the parasympathetic is "off," and vice versa. Both, moreover, are linked closely with the endocrine system, which manages the hormones that control growth, activity levels, and sexuality. It secretes hormones known as endorphins and encephalins, which modulate reactions to stress and pain, affect moods and appetite, and support abilities of learning and memory. The more one is in the parasympathetic mode, the better the endocrine system can do its work. The same holds also true for the immune system. Failure to relax it efficiently thus causes many stress-related ailments.

Stress activates the sympathetic nervous system in reaction to a perceived threat. The emphasis here is on "perceived." Originally built into the organism as the "flight or fight" response, this reaction put the body on high alert when primitive man was confronted with a life-threatening situation. It enabled him to marshal all the body's powers into one focus, to become stronger than usual, more alert, and with higher endurance. Running for his life, he was using every part of the nervous system, increasing the force and the rate of the heart, looking with pupils wide open, and quieting the bladder and the digestive system.

Today, people react to ordinary problems as if they were life threatening. The

---

12. For an accessible description of the human nervous system, see Nathan 1969. Modern scientific studies and evaluations of breathing are found in Fried 1999, Miller 2000. For breathing methods and their effects within the system of yoga, see Yasudian and Haich 1965, Loehr and Migdow 1986, Farhi 1996, Khalsa and Stauth 2001.

mind perceives threats as more dangerous than they are, and people go into high alert. Worse than that, they get used to being in high alert, with its increased adrenaline rush and intense mental capabilities. The moment the high lets off, they obtain some caffeine or similar stimulant to artificially prolong the stressful state. Then, after a day's work, they find they cannot relax and over the long run become prone to all sorts of ailments.

Every time human beings perceive a situation as stressful, the breathing becomes shallow and short. Modern people, surrounded by situations perceived as stressful, have come to accept shallow chest breathing as the normal state of affairs. They no longer breathe naturally and deeply, filling the lungs all the way and engaging the diaphragm so that the abdomen expands upon inhalation and contracts upon exhalation. Instead, they gasp out air as if they were pushing a heavy load, no longer using the deeper and side parts of the lungs, where the blood-flow rate is faster and the renewal of energy greatest.

Breathing only as deeply as the chest speeds up the breathing process. Instead of ten deep and relaxed breaths per minute, people often take sixteen or more. The heart accordingly beats that much faster; it begins to work overtime and comes to wear out that much sooner. Heart disease and cardiopulmonary conditions are the eventual result. By breathing in this manner, people also prevent sufficient amounts of oxygen from reaching the cells. Instead of exchanging fresh oxygen for old carbon dioxide in the lungs and thereby giving new energy to the system, they release only a little and maintain an unhealthy amount of gaseous toxins within. This in turn causes the blood to become more acidic and tension to build up. The hypothalamus and pituitary glands are stimulated, and stress hormones such as cortisone and adrenaline are released to further fuel the sense of urgency, tension, and anxiety. Then, of course, breathing becomes even shallower and more rapid. It is a vicious circle that has no escape—until one gets sick and is forced to rest or decide that enough is enough and make some changes.

On the positive side, and strongly encouraged by yogis, movement therapists, and Daoyin practitioners, people can learn to become aware of their breathing and begin to control it. Doing so, they can balance the nervous system and return to a healthier overall constitution. They realize the inherent truth in the key rule about breath and stress: "It is physiologically impossible to breathe deeply and be stressed at the same time." Gentle body movements in conjunction with deep and slow breathing—as well as the controlled intake, release, and holding of breath—thus form a central pillar of all health practices and appear in a variety of unique forms in Daoyin practice, from the very beginning to its modern adaptations. Modern scientific explanations of the connection of breathing to stress and health thus help us understand why Daoyin adepts do what they do.

Energy Medicine

Another modern field that helps our understanding of Daoyin is the emerging trend toward energy medicine. Recent research in biology, physiology, and physics has opened up many new ways of looking at body functions and healing. These branches of science are beginning to create a language that will eventually allow Western science to integrate Chinese concepts, demystify the phenomenon and experiences of *qi,* and make Asian perspectives more widely accessible to the general public.

The most important new concepts emerging from this research are measurable biomagnetic fields and bioelectricity. Biomagnetic fields are human energy centers that vibrate at different frequencies, storing and giving off energies not unlike the inner organs in the Chinese system. Their energetic output or vibrations can be measured, and it has been shown that the heart and the brain continuously pulse at extremely low frequencies (ELF). It has also become clear through controlled measurements that biomagnetic fields are unbounded so that, for example, the field of the heart vibrates beyond the body and extends infinitely into space, verifying the Chinese conviction that people and the universe interact continuously on an energetic level.[13]

Similarly, bioelectricity manifests in energy currents that crisscross the human body and are similar to the meridians of acupuncture. Separate from and, in evolutionary terms, more ancient than the nervous system, these currents work through the so-called cytoskeleton, a complex net of connective tissue that is a continuous and dynamic molecular webwork. Also known as the "living matrix," this webwork contains so-called integrins or transmembrane linking molecules that have no boundaries but are intricately interconnected. When touching the skin or inserting an acupuncture needle, the integrins make contact with all parts of the body through the matrix webwork. Given this evidence, wholeness, which sees "the body as an integrated, coordinated, successful system" and accepts that "no parts or properties are uncorrelated but all are demonstrably linked" (Oschman 2000, 49, citing E. F. Adolph), is becoming an accepted concept.

The body as a living matrix is simultaneously a mechanical, vibrational, energetic, electronic, photonic, and informational network. It consists of a complex, linked pattern of pathways and molecules that forms a tensegrity system. A term taken originally from architecture, where it is used in the structural description of domes, tents, sailing vessels, and cranes, "tensegrity" indicates a continuous tensional network (tendons) connected by a set of discontinuous elements (struts), which can also be fruitfully applied to the description of the wholeness of the body:

---

13. The most important works in this context are Becker and Sheldon 1985; Gerber 1988; Seem 1987, 1989; Targ and Katra 1999. A good summary of recent findings appears in Oschman 2000.

> The body as a whole, and the spine in particular, can usefully be described as tensegrity systems. In the body, bones act as discontinuous compression elements and the muscles, tendons and ligaments act as a continuous tensional system. Together the bones and tensional elements permit the body to change shape, move about, and lift objects. (Oschman 2000, 153)

Similarly, from the perspective of quantum physics, the body is constantly vibrating and forms part of a universal pattern. The muscles and flesh are made of highly ordered, crystalline material consisting of tiny atoms vibrating in groups along coiled molecules. The patterns are constant, rapid, and orderly. When subjected to the influence of a magnet or a needle, the field is modified and the whole pattern changes. The same also holds true for bones, which consist of vibrating patterns and changing energy fields—dissolving into the nothingness of pure oscillation when observed closely under the microscope.

The mind, too, is essentially the same as the body. There is no separation of consciousness from physical existence. Both are energy fields; they just vibrate at different speeds: 10^{22} Hz for the atomic nucleus, 10^{15} for the atom itself, 10^{9} for molecules, and 10^{3} for cells. Sensations in the body accordingly do not come from specific sense organs but arise through the fluctuation of different vibratory fields—all of which are immediately linked with consciousness in a nonlocal way and, in fact, *are* consciousness.[14]

Mental and emotional states thus form part of the larger picture of the body, so that intention becomes a kind of directed vibration that can have a disturbing or enhancing effect on health. Mental attitudes give rise to specific patterns of energy so that magnetic activity in the nervous system of the individual can spread through his or her body into the energy fields and bodies of others. This understanding can account for the efficacy of therapeutic touch and distant energy healing, during which the practitioner goes into a meditative state of mind and directs healing thoughts toward the patient. Measuring experiments have shown that we all emit energies through our bodies and into our auras; the field emanating from the hands of a skilled practitioner, moreover, is very strong, sometimes reaching a million times the strength of the normal brain field. It can, moreover, contain infrared radiation, creating heat and spreading light as part of the healing effort.

The vision of the body as an energetic network and of the mind as a key factor in body energetics, a key concept in Chinese medicine and at the root of all Daoyin practices, is not as alien to Westerners as one might think at first. Without specifi-

---

14. On quantum physics and its take on the mind, see Zohar and Marshall 1994, Nadeau and Kafatos 1999, Targ and Katra 1999, Varela, Thompson, and Rosch 1991.

cally speaking of yin and yang, the five phases, and a network of acupuncture channels, modern science is yet adapting an understanding of body and self that has
been at the root of Chinese traditional practices for millennia. As science verifies
energetic patterns with modern technology and precise measurements, it helps
translate the ancient systems into a contemporary understanding.

Energy Psychology

A different modern development along the same lines that makes more conscious and active use of Chinese energy patterns is the evolving field of energy
psychology. It sees the body as consisting of "various interrelated energy systems
(such as the aura, chakras, and meridians), which each serve specific functions"
(Feinstein, Eden, and Craig 2005, 197). According to this understanding, the visible and measurable material body is supported by an underlying network or
skeleton of living energy that forms the foundation of all bodily systems.[15]

Supported increasingly by electromagnetic measurements, followers of this
new method distinguish eight major aspects of this energy network:

1.   the meridian system, defined as the energy bloodstream, which "brings vitality,
     removes blockages, adjusts metabolism, and even determines the speed and
     form of cellular change" (Feinstein, Eden, and Craig 2005, 198)
2.   the chakras, energetic vortexes adapted from Indian body geography, which are
     concentrated centers of energy that supply power to specific organs and resonate
     with universal principles, such as creativity, love, survival, and transcendence (200)
3.   the aura, a fundamental energy shield surrounding people that was studied ex-
     tensively in the seventies [e.g., Krippner and Rubin 1974] [and] that is now seen as
     a protective energetic atmosphere that surrounds the person "like a space suit"
     and serves to filter outside energies (Feinstein, Eden, and Craig, 2005, 200)
4.   the basic grid, a sturdy fundamental energy net that can be compared to the
     chassis of a car (201)
5.   the celtic weave, a spinning, spiraling, twisting, and curving pattern of energies
     that creates a "kaleidoscope of colors and shapes" and functions as an "invisible
     thread that keeps all the energy systems functioning as a single unit" (201)
6.   the five rhythms, matching the five phases and their related organs, senses,
     muscles, and so on, which establish a person's primary rhythm and provide the
     basic blueprint of personal and interactive functioning (202)
7.   the triple warmer, adapted from Chinese medicine and reinterpreted as an en-

15. Other, earlier works on energy psychology include Pert 1997, Gallo 2004, and Gach and Henning
2004.

ergy line that "networks the energies of the immune system to attack an invader and mobilizes the body's energies in emergencies," which is the key factor in the stress response according to this energetic vision (202)

8. the radiant circuits, an adaptation of the eight extraordinary vessels, now described as primary to the body's system in terms of evolution, "operating like fluid fields and embodying a distinct spontaneous intelligence" (203)

On the basis of this vision of the human body, practitioners of energy psychology propose that people should enhance their "energy aptitude," perform daily exercises to harmonize the energies, and use specific tapping techniques to release tensions, emotional trauma, and even physical ailments.

Energy aptitude means the ability to work effectively with one's internal energies. It has four components: a fundamental, careful awareness of one's energetic patterns, the ability to influence these patterns in a beneficial way, the faculty to perceive energies in other people and outside objects, and the ability to join or transform these outside energies in a beneficial way (Feinstein, Eden, and Craig 2005, 204–205).

Daily exercises include many moves familiar from qigong and already used in Daoyin; they involve pressing key acupuncture points while breathing deeply and visualizing energies flowing through the body. Like Daoyin exercises, they make use of various bodily postures and involve self-massages of key areas, such as the face, the scalp, and the abdomen. In some cases, meridian lines are opened through placing the hands at either end and allowing the energies to flow; in others cases, simple bends or stretches in conjunction with conscious breathing and mental release serve the purpose. While these are all similar to practices already advocated in Daoyin, the closest exercise is the Auric Weave, a passing of the hands over the energy lines of the body, which is known as Dry Wash in traditional Daoyin and practiced as Marrow Washing in modern qigong (Feinstein, Eden, and Craig 2005, 233–235). From this perspective of energy psychology, it becomes clear just to what degree Chinese healing exercises work with the underlying energy patterns of the body, above and beyond limbering up muscles and opening joints.

The third and most important clinical application of energy psychology lies in tapping techniques that ease stress, release trauma, and heal ailments. Also known as EFT or emotional freedom technique, the method has patients measure a problem on a scale from 1 to 10, then imagine the feeling associated with the issue, create a positive affirmation ("Even though I have ——, I deeply and completely accept myself"), and repeat the affirmation while tapping a set of eight acupuncture points. The points range from the center of the forehead through the face, neck, and upper torso to the sides of the hands. After completion, patients remeasure the feeling, then repeat the technique—often with a slightly modified affirmation ("Even though I still have a remnant of ——")—until it goes down to zero. Not only are urgent issues immediately relieved with this method, but even long-standing issues are resolved with persistent tapping.

The technique in this form is not obviously documented in traditional Chinese texts, but there is a Daoist method practiced today that involves tapping the three cinnabar fields and the third eye while chanting an incantation to the powers of chaos underlying all creation.[16] There are also multiple qigong tapping routines that help recover health and stabilize energy (Johnson 2000, 703–707). Within Daoyin, moreover, time and again practitioners are asked to "drum" (*gu* 鼓) certain areas of the body, most commonly the chest or abdomen, while holding the breath, thereby releasing stale or wayward *qi*, the traditional way of referring to past trauma, unwanted emotional baggage, and physical obstructions. Self-massages that involve tapping energy channels on arms and legs as well as around eyes and ears, moreover, are very common and considered essential to healing, long life, and the development of the subtle energy body necessary for transcendence.

Daoyin, therefore, while ancient in its origins and deeply embedded in a traditional Chinese culture, in both concepts and practice has relevant counterparts in modern Western science and psychology, has much to offer in terms of stress reduction, and can be best understood in comparison with yoga and contemporary movement therapies. Its full power, however, can be appreciated only by understanding just how it has changed and unfolded over the centuries.

---

16. I received this method through personal transmission from J. Michael Wood, who obtained it from Robert Peng, a high-ranking Daoist qigong master, at the National Qigong Association meeting in 2005.

Chapter One

Early Medical Manuscripts

The earliest systematic and detailed information on Chinese healing exercises comes from ancient medical manuscripts that were excavated over the last twenty years and date for the most part from the early Han dynasty (late second century B.C.E.). The manuscripts include both technical medical texts and materials on longevity techniques. Medical texts deal mainly with the structure of the channels and the healing of diseases with herbal and magical recipes. Works on longevity techniques discuss ways of preventing disease and attaining long life through *qi*-cultivation. They present breathing techniques, dietary recommendations, sexual practices, and healing exercises as well as advice on the execution of daily activities such as sleep, hygiene, and grooming (Engelhardt 2000, 85).

All these texts are essentially part of the medical tradition. They were not in any major way related to Daoist philosophical speculation or the cult of immortality. As Donald Harper points out, "[The manuscript] texts describe a kind of baseline macrobiotic hygiene for the elite that focuses on care of the body, not on the more philosophical and mystical programs of the 'Neiye' 內業 (Inner Cultivation) chapter of the *Guanzi* 管子, *Zhuangzi* 莊子, or *Laozi* 老子 *[Daode jing].* The texts' goal of long life is not identical to the *xian* 仙-cult goal of immortality and transcendence" (1998, 114). Exercises in this context are, therefore, very much a health practice that is not meant to lead to higher states or religious cultivation.

What, then, are the major medical manuscripts? Where were they found? What was their overall social context? What do they tell us about the social situation of healing exercises in Han China? What kinds of ailments do they discuss? What postures of the body do they describe? And how can the exercises in the manuscript be understood? To answer these questions, let us first look at the texts themselves.

The Manuscripts

The most important and best-documented find of medical manuscripts, written on silk, bamboo, and strips of wood, was discovered in December 1973 in tomb 3 at Mawangdui 馬王堆 near Changsha 長沙 in the province of Hunan 湖南 in south-central China (figure 1).

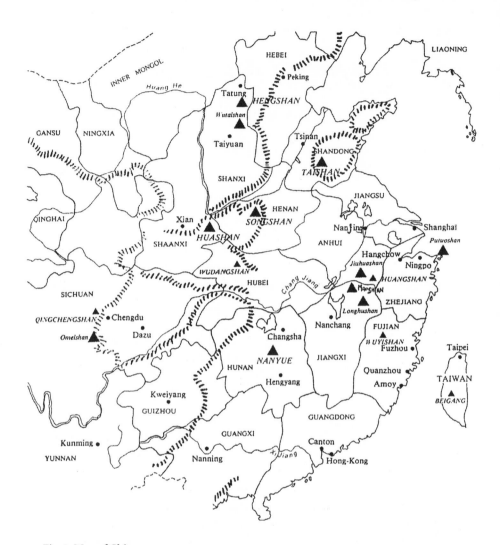

Fig. 1: Map of China

In the Han dynasty, this region was part of the ancient southern kingdom of Chu 楚, where feudal lords still ruled over their own small enclaves in semi-independence. The tombs at Mawangdui accordingly belonged to members of a local feudal family—the Marquis of Dai, his wife, and his son.

All three tombs consisted of a vertical pit about 17 meters (55 ft.) deep, with a wooden burial chamber at the bottom. The burial chamber had a central area to hold three internested coffins plus four surrounding storage areas for burial goods (Harper 1998, 14). Undisturbed, the three tombs contained a veritable treasure trove, which included not only foodstuffs, garments, and miniature servants and companions, but also the famous Mawangdui banner from tomb 1. A T-shaped, rectangular piece of colorfully illustrated silk, it covered the inner coffin and showed the move of the tomb's inhabitant toward the celestial realm, presided over by the Sun and the Moon together with various deities (Loewe 1979, 10).

This tomb held the body of the local ruler's wife, the Marchioness of Dai, a lady of about fifty years of age. Although her tomb was excavated first, she was in fact the last of the three to die—in 168 B.C.E. Tomb 2 was the last resting place of the marquis himself, a man by the name of Li Cang 利蒼, who served as chancellor of the Chu kingdom in Changsha. He was installed as marquis in 193 and died in 186, his tomb therefore being the oldest. Tomb 3 housed the son, a younger man of about thirty who, like his mother, was buried in 168. It is not clear which of the marquis's children he was. Some think he was the oldest, Li Xi 利豨, who succeeded him as lord; others think he was a younger son who pursued a military career, as possibly indicated by the various weapons and other military insignia found in the tomb (Harper 1998, 14).

His tomb contained the manuscripts in a rectangular lacquer box with a roof-shaped lid, 60 centimeters long, 30 centimeters wide, and 20 centimeters high (2 ft. by 1 ft. by 8 in.), found in a storage area east of the coffin. Most manuscripts appeared on silk sheets, but some were also written on slips of bamboo or flat sticks of wood. In general, bamboo and wood were less expensive and easier to work with, since scribes could erase any errors with a sharp carving knife. Silk was more precious and demanded higher skill, as technicians had to blot out any mistakes they made. On the other hand, silk was much easier to handle, fold, and store. Also, it preserved the contents better, because wood or bamboo slips would over time come out of their fastenings and be mixed up (Harper 1998, 18).[1]

The total number of manuscripts found at Mawangdui is thirty, covering forty-five separate texts (Harper 1998, 17). This means that some pieces of silk or bundles of bamboo slips contained more than one text. This grouping in some cases gives an indication of how certain techniques or ideas were possibly related. Many of the texts are nonmedical, and discuss various aspects of traditional Chinese thought. The best-known among them are two versions of Laozi's *Daode jing* 道德經 (Book of the Dao and Its Virtue), which closely resemble the standard, transmitted version we are familiar with and thus establish the presence of this classic in the early second century B.C.E. (trl. Henricks 1989). The texts are written in both Han clerical and traditional seal script, the latter—according to tradi-

1. A classic example of mixed-up bamboo tablets found in tombs is the so-called *Bamboo Laozi*, an early version of the *Daode jing* discovered in combination with various other works at Guodian, also in Hunan. For a study and translation, see Allan and Williams 2000, Henricks 2000.

tional historiography—being the dominant form of Chinese writing before the script reform under the first emperor of Qin in 214. Using the scripts as a basis, Donald Harper dates some of the manuscripts to the third century B.C.E. and others a bit later (Harper 1982, 2:15; 1998, 4). Recent research, as for example the study on the development of Chinese writing by Imre Galambos (2006), suggests, however, that all kinds of different scripts were still being used well into the Han dynasty, so we cannot be certain of the texts' date on this basis.

Fifteen texts are specifically medical manuscripts on *qi*-channels and ways of preserving health. For the most part, they deal with technical questions, such as the diagnosis of disorders and the use of moxibustion or cautery—the burning of dried mugwort or *Artemisia vulgaris*—on points of the major channels (Lo 2001a, 65). Five texts among them, one included in two editions, clearly represent an early stage of the channel and diagnostic system as it became dominant later and was standardized in the central medical classic, *Huangdi neijing.* Three contain herbal and magical recipes; one specializes in childbirth (Engelhardt 1998; Harper 1998, 22–30).

Longevity practice is the key subject in six texts. Two deal almost solely with sexual cultivation, discussing the best times for and frequency of sexual intercourse as well as herbal remedies for impotence and weakness. They are the *He yinyang* 和陰陽 (Harmonizing Yin and Yang; trl. Harper 1998, 412–422) and the *Tianxia zhidao tan* 天下至道談 (Discussion of the Perfect Way in All under Heaven; trl. Harper 1998, 425–438). Two others touch on sexual techniques but for the most part provide information on how to improve health through breathing techniques, dietetics, and drugs (Stein 1999, 50–65). They are the *Yangsheng fang* 養生方 (Recipes for Nourishing Life; trl. Harper 1998, 328–362) and the *Shiwen* 十問 (Ten Questions; trl. Harper 1998, 385–411).

The last two focus on breathing and exercises. The *Quegu shiqi* 卻穀食氣 (Eliminating Grains and Absorbing *Qi;* trl. Harper 1998, 305–309) covers ways of fasting by means of breathing exercises. The text repeatedly contrasts "those who eat *qi*" with "those who eat grain" and explains this in cosmological terms. Essential among them for the study of healing exercises, finally, is the *Daoyin tu* 導引圖 (Exercise Chart; trl. Harper 1998, 310–327). It contains forty-four color illustrations of human figures performing therapeutic exercises together with brief captions that in some cases resemble names known from earlier literature, such as the Bear Amble and Bird Stretch.

Texts and Tombs

How would the son of a local ruler come to possess a treasure trove of philosophical and medical texts? How did texts circulate and come to be copied in ancient

China? In general, texts were not common at the time, and illiteracy was the norm. Only institutions or people of means—governments, aristocrats, local rulers—could afford the luxury of having materials committed to writing, hiring a professional scribe and procuring the expensive necessary materials. Written texts, moreover, were regarded with awe, since they could transmit knowledge without personal contact and were in themselves carriers of power. They could also potentially fall into the wrong hands, and their owners protected them accordingly, either stashing them away safely in a treasury or transmitting them only in conjunction with various reliability tests, pledges of valuables, and serious vows of trust—not unlike the blood covenants of antiquity, sworn to establish fighting alliances (Harper 1998, 63; Lewis 1990, 44).

Aristocrats with an interest in medicine and philosophy thus collected relevant materials. Some searched out already written works and had them transcribed; others invited knowledgeable people to their estate and had them dictate their philosophical sayings and medical recipes to an experienced scribe. Even the *Daode jing* supposedly came into being this way. The story goes that Laozi was on his way west when he encountered the border guard Yin Xi 尹喜, who had him dictate his precious teachings to a scribe (Kohn 1998, 264–267). Similarly, the *Huainanzi* 淮南子 (Book of the Master of Huainan, *DZ* 1184[2]), another important Daoist collection of the mid–second century B.C.E., was created on the basis of the collected knowledge of various masters, assembled at his estate by Liu An 劉安 (197–122), the Prince of Huainan.

The medical manuscripts may well have come into being in a similar fashion. Guided by a strong interest in Daoist thought, medical recipes, and ways of nourishing life, the Marquis of Dai and his family probably searched out already existing texts or invited competent masters to learn from. These masters served the people as physicians and—as clarified in their biographies in the dynastic histories—commonly transmitted their knowledge orally in a three-year apprenticeship either from father to son or from master to disciple among itinerant practitioners (Harper 1998, 61). When invited to work with an aristocratic family, they would generously impart their knowledge.

Medical specialists were one subgroup among the so-called *fangshi* 方士 or "recipe masters." Highly skilled and professionally trained people, *fangshi* predicted fortunes and performed astrological divinations, analyzed weather patterns and made rain, healed diseases and exorcised demons, communicated with the dead and conjured up spirits, advised on military strategy and provided magical weaponry

2. "DZ" stands for *Daozang* 道藏 (Daoist Canon). Texts in this collection are referred to according to numbers in Schipper 1975b, Komjathy 2002.

(DeWoskin 1983, 23–35; see also Ngo 1976). Not unlike the shamans of old, they were socially marginal figures with spiritual clout who had a direct link to the divine and the greater workings of the cosmos. There were accordingly shaman-physicians (*wuyi* 巫醫) among the early medical men, people who used many different methods for healing, thinking of disease alternatively as the attack of demonic forces or as caused by an energetic irregularity or invasion of wayward *qi* (Harper 1998, 41).[3] Early physicians applied magical, exorcistic, herbal, and other treatments and commonly used stylized movements and formal incantations (Harper 1998, 56). Valued for their expertise and techniques, they tended to ascribe their knowledge to the masters of high antiquity and often used the Yellow Emperor (Huangdi 黃帝) as main interlocutor in their transmitted recipes. However, they made little effort to connect directly to the sages of the past and were not much concerned with establishing hierarchies and lineages or with keeping their knowledge secret.

Some early doctors also belonged to the elite. They practiced out of personal interest and had no need to charge for their services. They studied with a variety of masters and, moving among literati circles, left some information on their craft behind (Harper 1998, 46). For example, Sima Qian's 司馬遷 *Shiji* 史記 (Record of the Historian, ch. 105) records the medical case histories of the leading physician, Chunyu Yi 淳于意 (216–ca. 150 B.C.E.), and of his disciple Yang Qing 陽慶, showing their skills and wide social connections (Harper 1998, 7). However, despite their master-disciple relationship, there is no family connection between them nor—unlike later masters and religious organizations—did they make an effort to create a lineage. On the contrary, Chunyu Yi never revealed where his knowledge came from and made no major claims on famous predecessors or divine inspiration (Harper 1998, 58–59).

Medical knowledge not being tightly guarded as part of established formal lineages, a local ruler such as the Marquis of Dai could thus reasonably be expected to own a number of relevant documents. Still, why bury the texts? Why place materials on nourishing and extending life in tombs of all places? Why should there be not only texts but also images of feathery immortals, murals of the Queen Mother of the West (Xiwangmu 西王母), mirrors with cosmic designs and inscriptions that contain wishes for long life? Somehow this seems to contradict the whole idea of living for a long time and attaining a transcendent state that bypasses death. Scholars including Michael Loewe (1979) and Anna Seidel (1982) have argued variously about this question, and a satisfactory solution has yet to be found.

---

3. Both models of disease interpretation were common in traditional China, and Western scholars have argued for years which was dominant (see Porkert 1974, Unschuld 1985). More recent research suggests the gradual change from demon to energetic medicine in the Han period and under the influence of *yangsheng* practices (see Lo 2000, 29–30).

What we know so far is that the ancient Chinese understood death as the separation of two essential spirit aspects or "souls" that form the nucleus of primordial *qi* (*yuanqi* 元氣) and make up the living person: the *hun* 魂 or spirit soul of celestial origin and the *po* 魄 or material soul that belongs to Earth. As the embryo forms in the womb, the two souls join together to give it life and consciousness. When the person dies, the souls separate: the *hun* returns to Heaven in the form of an ancestral spirit (*shen* 神); the *po* returns to Earth as the decaying body and its ghost (*gui* 鬼). Gradually, over five to seven generations, both merge back into their original element. But especially during the first several years, the deceased spirits remain close to the living, require human-style sustenance, and are potentially dangerous. Essentially uninterested in the affairs of the living, both spirit components after death have to be mollified and controlled. With a series of complex rituals and the creation of often artificial lineages, they are enticed to support the living (Puett 2002, 52). Corpses *(po)* are accordingly buried with extensive grave goods—the real thing in high antiquity, clay images in the Han and middle ages, paper replicas today. The ancestral spirits *(hun)* receive regular offerings of food, drink, and incense at specially erected altars in the home.

In Han understanding—as also in later Daoist views—the newly buried person was thus still thought to be present. At this stage, with the two souls just starting to separate, the *qi* would still be active in the body, and it might be possible that in this new state, removed from the sensory involvements and passions of the world, the person could still undertake the refinement of *qi* and transformation necessary to enhance life and attain a heavenly state.

This is also borne out by various other death practices of traditional China. First, there is the practice of calling back the soul (*zhaohun* 招魂) at the time of death, a formal ritual chanting to entice the soul to desist from its wanderings and come home (Hawkes 1959, 101). Then there is the equipment of the grave as the new home of the dead, formally deeded to the deceased in a legally phrased tomb contract. Then, of course, there is the enormous range of grave goods, both to make the dead comfortable and to bribe otherworldly bureaucrats. And finally there is the option to continue worldly activities from the grave, such as, for example, Moneylender Zuo's vigorous suing of his clients, documented in sixteen contracts buried with him.[4]

The fact that medical and philosophical manuscripts are buried in the tomb of a local aristocrat's son may, therefore, show a strong family dedication to related ideas and practices during life. It may also indicate the hope that the young man,

---

4. For studies of tomb contracts and otherworld bureaucrats, see Seidel 1985, Dien 1995, Hansen 1995.

taken from his activities earlier than expected, might continue to pursue life-enhancing and healing practices in his more spiritual state.

The Exercise Chart

The medical manuscripts from Mawangdui provide the oldest extant Chinese instructions of how to regulate life to one's best advantage and how exactly to ensure health and vitality. They also contain the oldest illustrations of healing exercises, discovered on a silk manuscript that was placed together with a map of the burial ground in the lacquer box in tomb 3 (see cover illustration). Partly soaked in water and already broken into fragments, the manuscript was restored to its original size of 53 centimeters high and 110 centimeters wide (1 ft. 9 in. by 3 ft. 8 in.). It held three texts that were untitled and later named by the excavators. One was a technical manual on moxibustion of the eleven meridians, the *Yinyang shiyi maijiu jing* 陰陽十一脈灸經 (Yinyang Eleven Channels Moxibustion Classic); another was the above-mentioned *Quegu shiqi,* which focuses on breathing (Engelhardt 2001, 214).

The third consists of forty-four figures showing specific exercise poses. They are arranged in four horizontal rows with eleven figures each and are commonly counted from top right to bottom left. The figures average 9–12 centimeters (3.5–5 in.) in height, and each was originally accompanied by a caption naming or explaining the move. Both the images and the captions are fragmentary and have been partly restored—in some cases with arms, feet, and facial expressions added. As Donald Harper says, "The drawings are skillful, yet few of the captions remain and the original exercises are often difficult to reconstruct from the static poses of the figures" (1998, 132).

A key representation of the early exercise tradition, the chart shows figures of both sexes and different ages, variously clothed or bare-chested, in different postures and from a variety of angles. The majority are fully dressed in knee-length kimono-style robes over bulging pants and pointy shoes, some with belts, some without, but a few also wear a mere hip wrap or loincloth. The garments closely resemble the dress shown in Han-dynasty brick figures and funerary art and are similar to the uniforms of the terra-cotta soldiers. The same holds true for their hairstyles. Most have their hair either tied up in various kinds of knots or wear a cap, again representing Han standard.

The majority of figures appear in standing poses, but four are kneeling or sitting—and all of these have surviving captions. One is sitting on the floor while hugging his knees into the chest "to alleviate ham pain" (#39); another is kneeling "to relieve knee discomfort" (#23). Two others are in awkward-looking positions with knees slightly bent and arms extended—one "to stretch the neck" (#29), the other "to enhance *qi*-flow in the eight extraordinary channels" (#37). Beyond these, all figures are depicted on their two feet, bending and stretching their torsos, arms, or legs, and showing various forms of mild exercise. None seem to be engaged in vigorous movements, wide stances, or athletic poses.

Some are standing upright in what yoga practitioners know as Mountain Pose (*tadāsana;* Iyengar 1976, 61): properly aligned and straight, with arms close to the sides, extended loosely, spread at shoulder level, or raised overhead. In many cases, one arm reaches up while the other stretches down or one arm moves forward while the other extends back, indicating rhythmical movement. Two figures are in a forward bend, one with head lowered, the other with head raised (#28, 32). Another is bending slightly forward with a rounded back and hands dangling down toward the knees (#43). Yet another has one arm on the ground and the other extended upward in a windmill-like pose (#21). One clearly demonstrates a standing back bend (#8), while another seems to be in a standing side stretch, with one arm raised and the torso stretched in a slant (#10), not unlike the yoga pose known as Half Moon *(ardha chandrāsana).* The very last figure, called Merlin, shows something akin to the yoga pose Warrior II (*vīrabhadrāsana;* Iyengar 1976, 72), with legs in lunge position and arms extended forward and back (#44).

Most figures work with their limbs only, but some also have utensils. Two hold a long pole. One, titled Penetrating Yin and Yang with Pole, stretches the arms in a quasi windmill away from each other while bending forward and twisting (#30). The other, with no caption, seems to do calf stretches while standing upright and holding onto a pole (#17). In addition, there is a figure standing with arms straight by the sides facing a kind of flat disc (#19) and another in forward bend who may be working with a ball of sorts (#32).

The figure in #24, moreover, with the caption Relieving Upper Side Blockages, is shown with one foot forward and head bent (Harper 1998, 313, 318). He appears to be holding a sacklike object on which small rings are painted. As Patricia Leong points out, some Chinese scholars think that this may be an early representation of an ingeniously constructed massage device still used in folk practice (2001). It consists of one or several beads set in a closed frame, with an opening at the back to inject ointment. Instead of massaging with the hands, one could roll the beads against the skin for an ointment massage. Without ointment or such, the device could also be rubbed over clothing. Seen differently, the object might also be a massage bag filled with smooth pebbles, such as later applied in the Brahmanic Massage Method to relieve congestion and stimulate the *qi*-flow (Berk 1986, 155).

Both the variety of the figures and the mix of poses preclude the possibility that the *Daoyin tu* shows an integrated sequence. It is much more likely that the chart presents different modes of body movements for specific conditions or ail-

Fig. 2: "Look up and shout." Source:
Daoyin tu.

ments. This is also borne out by the remaining captions, many of which name specific disorders or areas of the body to be treated. These captions often include the character *yin* 引, "to pull [out diseases]" or "to relieve." Conditions mentioned include pain in the ribs, hams, neck, and knees as well as inguinal swelling, abdominal problems, deafness, fever, upper side blockages, internal heat, warm ailments, and muscle tension—reflecting the areas for which the exercises are most often used: locomotive and gastrointestinal problems (Despeux 1989, 242; Lo 2001a, 94).

Beyond these there are several plain, descriptive captions. For example, Limbs Dropping indicates that one should raise one arm up while dropping the other (#10); Arms Swinging means that one should swing both arms out horizontally to the side (#31); Snapping Yin is depicted as standing while raising the arms forward and up (#6); Bending Down with Head Back is shown as a forward bend with both hands on the floor (#28); and Look Up and Shout means to stand with head raised, arms pulled up and back, then open the mouth for a strong exhalation with sound (#34; fig. 2).

A few postures in the *Daoyin tu* are also named after animals, typically creatures of the air and of water, as well as those closest to humanity. The best known animal-based exercises are Bear Amble (#41) and Bird Stretch (#32), showing a figure walking in a stately fashion with arms swinging (fig. 3) and one bending forward with hands on the floor and head raised.

Two monkey poses are Gibbon Jump (#40) and Monkey Bawl (#35). Gibbon Jump is done by standing with arms extended diagonally up and down. Monkey Bawl, geared to relieve internal heat, requires standing with fisted hands near the belly. Two bird poses are the Merlin (#44), shown as a lunging figure with arms extended, and Crane Call (#25), a figure represented in half profile that stands with the left foot slightly behind and arms stretched horizontally to the front and back (Harper 1998, 313). Another animal pose is Dragon Rise (#27), shown as a wide stance with arms raised diagonally upward in a V shape. Last, but not least, there is also a Turtle move (#42), with partial caption, depicted as a standing figure with both arms raised forward at shoulder height.

Animal names are, of course, among the earliest ways of referring to healing

Fig. 3: The Bear Amble. Source: *Daoyin tu.*

exercises and still some of the most popular today, linking exercise practice with shamanism and traditional understandings of nature (Sterckx 2002, 188–190). It is interesting to see that three of the famous five animals in the Five Animals' Frolic, the bird, the bear, and the monkey, are already present in the manuscripts, indicating that the third-century physician Hua Tuo 華佗 did not create the forms but just developed a coherent system from already existing patterns. The animals also link exercise practices back to shaman medicine, which involved trance healing often aided by animals or effected by the shaman's turning into an animal through an ecstatic dance. Most popular here was the bird—an intermediary between Heaven and Earth, a symbol of freedom and lightness, and, in the case of the crane, a sign of longevity and immortality (Despeux 1989, 39). Ancient Chinese shamans practiced various animal-inspired dances, best known among them the twelve animals practiced to drive away the demons of pestilence (Granet 1926, 1:216).

Another aspect of healing exercises that has remained important over the ages is the central role of breathing, mentioned in a few of the captions (Monkey Bawl and Look Up and Shout), for the best alignment of limbs and the optimal flow of *qi*. One manuscript explains how the different practices were viewed at the time, noting that "when a person is born, there are two things that do not need to be learned: the first is to breathe and the second is to eat. Except for these two, there is nothing that is not the result of learning and habit" (*Tianxia zhidao tan;* Harper 1998, 432). This makes clear that breathing and eating were seen as natural processes that served to replenish and maintain the vital forces. People did them naturally but could supplement them with specific techniques to aid in the extension and greater enjoyment of life (Engelhardt 2000, 87).

Breathing, moreover, as the *Shiwen* notes, "must be deep and long, so that pure *qi* is easily held" and stale *qi* can be thoroughly cleansed. "Stale *qi* is that of old age; pure *qi* is that of longevity. He who is skilled at cultivating *qi* lets the stale *qi* disperse at night and the new, pure *qi* gather at dawn, thereby allowing it to penetrate all nine orifices and six viscera of the body" (Harper 1998, 395).[5] Having gained *qi* through breathing deeply, at the right times, and in the right manner, practitioners circulate it through the body, hold it for some time, move it mentally to certain regions, and guide it purposely to relieve ailments and open blockages. They can also use it to stimulate or calm the body, depending on the need. For example, before going to sleep, one might practice "dusk breathing by breathing deeply, long and slow, causing the ears to not hear; thus becoming tranquil, go to bed" (Harper 1998, 396). In-

---

5. As Donald Harper notes, the nine orifices are the ears, eyes, nostrils, mouth, genitals, and anus; the six viscera are the transformative or yang organs—large and small intestine, bladder and gall-bladder, stomach, and Triple Heater (1998, 395n2).

tegrating healing exercises and breathing into daily life, people could hope to maintain health and vigor well into old age.

The Stretch Book

Another important manuscript on healing practices was found in 1983 in tomb M247 at Zhangjiashan 張家山 in Jiangling 江陵 district of Hubei 湖北 province. About two hundred kilometers north of Mawangdui, this was also part of the old country of Chu (Wenwu 1989). Closed in 186 B.C.E., the tomb contained two medical manuscripts written on bamboo slips, about 27 centimeters long and 4 centimeters wide (11 in. by 2 in.) (Ikai 2002, 30–31). One of them is the *Maishu* 脈書 (Channel Book). It consists of several texts containing lists of ailments and descriptions of eleven *qi*-conduits. Closely related to the Mawangdui medical texts, it similarly includes a short statement on practices of nourishing life (Harper 1998, 31–33; Ikai 1995, 29).

The other manuscript bears the title *Yinshu* 引書 (Stretch Book).[6] It is divided into three parts: a general introduction on seasonal health regimens, a series of about a hundred exercises in three sections, and a conclusion on the etiology of disease and ways of prevention (fig. 4).

The first part begins with the description of a daily and seasonal health regimen, including hygiene, dietetics, regulation of sleep and movement, and times for sexual intercourse. It is ascribed to Pengzu, a famous immortal of antiquity who allegedly lived for more than eight hundred years:

Spring: generate; summer: grow; fall: collect; winter: store—such is the way of Pengzu.

Spring days. After rising in the morning, pass water, wash and rinse, clean and click the teeth. Loosen the hair, stroll to the lower end of the hall to meet the purest of dew and receive the essence of Heaven, and drink one cup of water. These are the means to increase long life. Enter the chamber [for sex] between evening and late midnight [1 a.m.]. More would harm the *qi*.

Summer days. Wash the hair frequently, but bathe rarely. Do not rise late and eat many greens. After rising in the morning and passing water, wash and rinse the mouth, then clean the teeth. Loosen the hair, walk to the lower end of the hall and after a while drink a cup of water. Enter the chamber between evening and midnight. More would harm the *qi*.

---

6. The text is reprinted with modern character equivalents in Wenwu 1990 and Ikai 2004. A complete listing of topics and partial reprint that also includes a numbering of exercises is found in Li 1993, 337–343. For a complete translation and study of this important document as well as of the accompanying *Maishu*, see Lo forthcoming. Partial translations can be found in Lo 2001b. I am very grateful to Vivienne Lo for sharing her translation draft and helping with the stickier passages in the text.

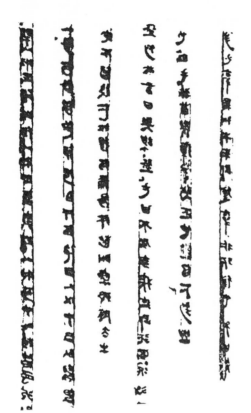

Fig. 4: The bamboo slips of the *Stretch Book*. Source: *Yinshu*.

Fall days. Bathe and wash the hair frequently. As regards food and drink, let hunger or satiation be whatever the body desires. Enter the chamber however often the body finds it beneficial and comfortable—this is the way to greatest benefit.

Winter days. Bathe and wash the hair frequently. The hands should be cold and the feet warm; the face cold and the body warm. Rise from sleep late; while lying down, stretch out straight. Enter the chamber between evening and early midnight [11 p.m.]. More would harm the *qi*. (Harper 1998, 110–111)

Obviously directed at an elite, male audience, this addresses people with enough free time to rise at ease, stroll along their estate, eat and drink in leisure, take regular baths, and pick the best time for sexual activities. The routine stays fairly constant over the year, but small adjustments accommodate changes in temperature and light. Thus, in the summer one should rise earlier and take fewer cold baths to prevent overly cooling the body.[7]

---

7. The same recommendation is still part of modern longevity practice. See Liu 1990, 5–10.

In its second part, the text lists more than a hundred different exercises in three separate sections, some preventive, others more curative. It begins with naming a series of mainly standing practices and describes briefly how to do them (Wenwu 1990, 82–83; Ikai 2004, 3–12). Its forty-one routines address different aspects of the body, in all cases encouraging a variety of motion, thereby enhancing flexibility and an open flow of *qi*.

Following this, the text changes gear and focuses on healing modalities, emphasizing what methods to undertake to relieve or "pull" pain from various parts of the body as well as describing ways to increase or lessen *qi* in the yin (front) or yang (back) parts of the body—those for yang involving upward gazes, back bends, and fingers interlaced in front while yin exercises require that one look down, bend forward, and interlace the fingers at the back (Li 1993, 344). The forty-five procedures in this section begin with remedies for general fatigue and symptoms at the onset of disease, then focus on isolated body parts, moving from the feet up and ending with the various sense organs.

The exercises are undertaken in various postures: standing, sitting, and lying down. In some cases, they consist of an integrated sequence of practices outlined earlier, but for the most part they are quite different, geared specifically toward relieving certain symptoms. The text usually gives a set number of repetitions and emphasizes the right or left side of the body. Following this, the *Yinshu* notes in short, rhythmical sentences which technique is good for what ailment, as for example, "Tiger Turn is good for the neck; Limbs Dropping is good for the armpits"; and "Turn and Shake is good for abdomen and belly" (Wenwu 1990, 84–85; Ikai 2004, 12–27; Harper 1998, 133).

After concluding this main part of the text, the *Yinshu* in its third and final main part deals with etiology and the prevention of diseases, focusing particularly on climatic changes in combination with an unstable diet, excessive emotions, and a lifestyle inappropriate to the season. The text recommends various therapies, such as breathing exercises, bodily stretches, and the careful treatment of the interior *qi*, concluding with an analogy of physical cultivation and the functioning of a bellows.

Exercise Routines

About a quarter of the *Yinshu* is dedicated to naming and describing basic exercise routines (Wenwu 1990, 82–83; Ikai 2004, 3–12). The text first presents forty practices, which can be divided into five groups according to body parts and types of movements: legs and feet, chest and neck, lunges, forward bends, and shoulder openers.[8]

LEGS AND FEET

The grammatical structure changes after this first group, which comprises nine exercises. It reads as follows:

1. Lifting one shin across the opposite thigh and moving it up and down thirty times is called Crossing Thighs.
2. Extending the shin, then pointing and flexing the toes thirty times is called Measuring Worm.[9]
3. Placing the feet parallel, then rocking back and forth thirty times is called Shifting Toes.
4. Extending the shin, straightening the heel, and rocking thirty times is called The Parapet.
5. Stretching the toes, then raising and rocking them thirty times is called Stretch Move.
6. Bending the shins, alternating right and left, forward and back thirty times is called Forward Push.
7. Rubbing the shin with the opposite foot, moving along its front and back thirty times is called [unnamed].
8. Extending the feet straight forward thirty times is called Stretching Yang.
9. Rubbing the backs of the feet thirty times on each side is called [unnamed].

Unlike the exercises in the *Daoyin tu,* which clearly stood in isolation, these nine practices, each undertaken thirty times in rhythmical movement, may well form a standing sequence. The set focuses on legs and lower joints, such as hips, knees, ankles, and toes, activating the synovial fluid and working the sartorius muscles to enhance flexibility and prevent stiffness. Working with both the inner and outer legs, they also stimulate the channels that run through them: the spleen, liver, and kidney meridians on the inner legs; the stomach, gallbladder, and bladder channels on the outer legs. Moving the toes similarly not only enhances flexibility and prevents arthritis, but also engages the numerous points on channels ending there. In addition, some exercises enhance balance as, for example, when one mas-

---

8. Li Ling divides the forty exercises into three groups: lower-body movements (#1–9), head and neck (#10–16), and hips, back, and upper limbs (#17–40) (1993, 337–339).

9. "Measuring Worm," as Donald Harper points out, is also the name of a sexual position in the Mawangdui text *He yinyang* (1998, 132).

sages one shin with the sole of the opposite foot—a practice that also stimulates the
root point of the kidney meridian and the yang channels on the shin.

BACK AND NECK
The next seven exercises, plus one listed a bit further down, focus on the neck
and back. They all begin with the same instruction ("interlace the fingers at the
back") and detail a variety of bends, forward and back, right and left. From here
onward, the grammar changes. Instructions now begin with the name of the practice, then describe the routine, but they no longer give the number of repetitions:[10]

1. Hamstring Stretch: interlace the fingers [lit. "join the hands"] at the back and
    bend forward (#10).
2. Upward Gaze: interlace the fingers at the back, then look up and turn the head
    (#11).
3. Bend and Gaze: interlace the fingers at the back and bend forward, then turn
    the head to look at your heels (#12).
4. Side and Back: interlace the fingers at the back, then lean sideways and turn [the
    head] toward the [opposite] shoulder (#13).
5. Duck in Water: interlace the fingers at the back and move the head back and
    forth (#14).
6. Rotating Stretch: interlace the fingers, raise the arms, and twist backward (#15).
7. Upright Swivel: interlace the fingers at the back, contract the neck, and turn the
    head (#16).
8. Snake Wriggle: interlace the fingers at the back, click the teeth, and swivel the
    head around (#21).

As in the preceding set, the exercises have largely descriptive appellations rather
than animal names or colorful metaphors. They encourage a wide range of motion
in the torso and stretch the chest muscles as the arms are bent backward and the
fingers interlaced, often with palms facing out. They strengthen the erector muscles
in the back, aid the vertebral alignment of the neck, reverse gravity on the neck and
spine, release vertebrae that have moved forward back into their proper place, and
create a stretch with rotational pressure. All these have the effect of a self-induced
chiropractic session, helping the bones and muscles into proper alignment.

Besides opening and aligning the neck and back, the exercises also stretch the
arms and thereby open the chest and shoulders. Doing so, they stimulate various

---

10. Numbers in parentheses refer to the order in which the exercises occur in the text. I added the
numbers at the beginning of each entry for easier reference.

channels running through the chest, shoulders, and arms, such as the lungs and heart meridians on the inside of the arms and the large and small intestine channels on their outside. As Michael Wood points out, moreover, "stretching the shoulders downward is important to fostering a posture that promotes a parasympathetic response (relaxation). This is the opposite of the sympathetic (fight-or-flight) posture of the 'turtle neck,' where the shoulders and the neck contract and tighten."[11] The work with the hands clasped behind the back, moreover, is also reminiscent of the pose Yoga Mudra in yogic practice, a standing or kneeling forward bend with hands interlaced behind the back and reaching up toward the ceiling. This pose is explicitly associated with surrender and a psychological release of tension, allowing practitioners to "let go in all aspects of their being" (Lee 1997, 79).

Lunges

To balance this emphasis on the upper body, the next set of procedures focuses again more strongly on the legs, encouraging practitioners to hold a lunge position while bending or stretching:

1. Snapping Yin: place one foot forward [with bent knee], interlace the fingers, bend forward, and hook them around [the knee] (#17).
2. Dragon Flourish: step one leg forward with bent knee while stretching the other leg back, then interlace the fingers, place them on the knee, and look up (#19).
3. Lower Back Stretch: step one leg forward with bent knee while stretching the other leg back, then interlace the fingers, twist, and revolve backwards (#20).
4. [Reaching] Below: step one leg forward with bent knee while stretching the other leg back, then lift one arm and stretch it with vigor (#31).

Again, the phrasing is formulaic, repeating the same basic instructions in three out of four exercises. Two involve forward bends, and two encourage upward stretches, thus providing a good basic menu of moves from a lunge position. Lunges in general, as also the various Warrior poses in yoga, strengthen the quadriceps muscles, engage the abdominals, open the hips, and stretch the front of the torso, engaging the lower back and opening the chest. Besides the iliapsoa and ischia muscles, they also exert a rotational pressure on the low back in a self-chiropractic fashion. In terms of Chinese medicine, they activate the channels that run through the hip area (liver, kidney, and spleen) as well as those running along the back (gallbladder, bladder). As the hips are stretched, furthermore, the lower pelvic floor is opened, increasing awareness of the perineum, the small muscle juncture between the anus and the genitals,

---

11. Personal communication, October 2005.

which in yoga is the seat of the Root Lock (*mūlabhanda;* Iyengar 1976, 344–346) and in Chinese medicine the location of the first point of the Conception Vessel (*renmai* 任脈), known as Meeting Yin (*huiyin* 會陰). Both are considered essential in keeping energy in the body and in an upward-flowing motion (Kohn 2005, 59).

FORWARD BENDS

The next set is all about forward bends. Some are executed standing upright with legs hip-width apart and parallel, as shown in some *Daoyin tu* illustrations; others involve a wider stance and the twisting of the upper body as the arms reach for the legs or the floor. Here we have the following:

1. Twisting the Tail Bone: with both hands [text missing] (#22).
2. Great Spread: place both hands on the floor with vigor, then step the feet back and forth between them (#23).
3. *[Characters missing]*[12]: spread the legs wide and bend to hold the left foot with the right hand; alternate right and left (#24).
4. Limbs Dropping: place the hands on the hips, then twist one arm forward toward the feet and bend (#25).
5. Gibbon Hold: hold the left foot with the right hand and twist the left hand back as you bend to the right and left (#26).
6. Triple [Stretch]: raise both arms high and [while bending] extend them forward, then out to the sides (#27).
7. Hanging Forward: bend forward, raise both hands and look up as if looking for something (#28).
8. Yin Stretch: interlace the fingers with palms facing out and lift them, then bend forward as far as you can (#33)

These exercises include classic variations of the forward bend that are executed in both narrow and wide stance and by bringing either both hands or only one hand down. They enhance flexibility in the torso, open the hips, and strengthen the legs. Lengthening the back, they work on the yang aspect of the body and help ease tension in the lower back. Encouraging the abdominals to contract vigorously, moreover, in combination with deep breathing and focusing the attention, they also allow the release of the fear or "red light" reflex (Hanna 1988, 49).

Yoga, too, has both narrow and wide-angled forward bends. The classic narrow bend is called *uttānāsana* and is said to

---

12. From a later prescription of a similar pose used against back pain this may well be called Forward Hold.

cure stomach pains and tone the liver, the spleen, and the kidneys.... The heartbeats are slowed down and the spinal nerves rejuvenated. Any depression felt in the mind is removed if one holds the pose for two minutes or more. The posture is a boon to people who get excited quickly as it soothes the brain cells. (Iyengar 1976, 93)

The wide-angled forward bend is called *pādōttānāsana*. It strengthens the legs and increases blood flow to the brain (Iyengar 1976, 85). In addition, the twisting motions prescribed in the *Yinshu* list also strengthen the rotator cuff muscles and encourage a lengthening of the side muscles of the body. They thereby provide rotational pressure on the lower back as well as along the middle spine and help relieve scoliosis, often caused by trauma and a potential cause of major discomforts (Hanna 1988, 80).

SHOULDER OPENERS

The last group of *Yinshu* practices deals again with the upper body and focuses on movements of the arms and shoulders, enhancing motion in the upper body and increasing strength and flexibility:

1. Reverse Rotation: interlace the fingers, bend forward, and look up, moving the arms from side to side (#18).
2. Arm Punch: propel both arms forward as if hitting someone (#29).
3. Pointing Back: interlace the fingers, raise them overhead, and bend back as far as possible (#30).
4. Tiger Stretch: place one foot forward, raise one arm, and bend (#32).
5. Yang Stretch: interlace the fingers, stretch the arms forward, and look up as far as you can (#34).
6. Double Deer: raise both arms, push up, then bend forward as far as you can (#35).
7. Tiger Crouch: with arms parallel, rotate the shoulders up and back, alternating on the right and left (#36).
8. Leaping Toad: with arms parallel, swing them to the right and left, up and down (#37).
9. Cart Cover: with arms parallel, swing them outward to the right and left, then lower them straight down and swing them back and forth (#38).
10. Nose to Belly: bend forward and lift both arms to the right and left (#39).
11. Calculating Wolf: place the hands beneath their respective armpits and rotate the chest (#40).
12. Warrior Pointing: with the left foot forward, use the left hand to point the fingers forward, stretching the arm (#41).

Emphasizing movement in the shoulder and arm joints, these exercises enhance the flow of synovial fluid and open the joints in the upper body. They strengthen the fascia muscles along the upper spine; release tensions from the iliapsoa muscles, which tend to hold emotional trauma; and work the levitator muscles, which reach from the shoulder blades to the top of the neck. At the same time, they stimulate the *qi*-flow through the upper chest, shoulders, and arms and encourage a sense of freedom and ease. They help extend people's reach and warm up the body through rhythmical swinging and back-and-forth movements.

Taken together, the forty *Yinshu* exercises provide an integrated and complete workout for the body, bending, stretching, and twisting its various parts and activating all the different joints and muscles. They are easy to learn and can be done in very little space. Like most practices depicted in the *Daoyin tu,* they are undertaken while standing, although some could also be executed while kneeling or sitting. Supplementing the visual information of the *Daoyin tu* in various ways, they present a well-structured and clearly integrated system that enhances overall mobility and thus contributes to greater health and well-being.

Healing Modalities

Following its presentation of these forty exercises, the text moves on to focus on the medical use of the practices. Beginning with the condition to be remedied, it contains a total of forty-five items (#42–86; Wenwu 1990, 83–85; Ikai 2004, 12–27), some of which include more than one possible treatment. The practices can be divided according to types of ailments, body postures, utensils, and various other characteristics. Several instructions closely resemble practices already outlined in the previous section or prescribe a combination of them:

For example, a variation of lunges is the following walking lunge:

> To relieve tense muscles: Stand with legs hip-width apart and hold both thighs. Then bend the left leg while stretching the right thigh back, reaching the knee to the floor. Once done, [change legs and] bend the right leg while stretching the left leg back and reaching that knee to the floor. Repeat three times. (#47).

Just like the yoga pose Warrior I *(vīrabhadrāsana),* which is said to make "the legs sharper and stronger, relieve cramp in the calf and thigh muscles, and bring elasticity to the leg and back muscles" (Iyengar 1976, 73), this practice is good for the muscles of the back and lower body. It opens the hips and tones and stretches the various aspects of the legs.

Another variant on lunges is recommended to relieve *qi*-disruptions or cramps in the muscles and intestines. Lunging with the left foot forward and the right leg back, one goes into a twist by bending the right hand at the elbow and looking back over the left shoulder. After three repetitions on both sides, one is to maintain the lunge position while raising one arm at a time and then both arms up as far as one can (each three times), bending the back and opening the torso (#69).[13] The idea seems to be that the stretching of the legs and arms opens blockages in the extremities while the twisting and opening of the abdominal area aids the intestines. Similarly, the lunging twist Reversed Triangle *(parivrtta trikonāsana)* in yoga not only "tones the thigh, calf, and hamstring muscles," but also "increases the blood supply to the lower part of the spinal region" (Iyengar 1976, 66). Again, the stretch in the legs enhances muscle power while the twist opens the side and waist muscles, allowing greater flexibility and better circulation.

A variation of the shin stretches described above is the following:

> To relieve ankle pain: Put your weight on [lit. "stand on"] the inner ankle of the right foot and stretch the right inner calf. Then put your weight on the outer ankle and stretch the right outer calf. After this, put your weight on the inner ankle of the left foot and stretch the left inner calf. Then put your weight on the outer ankle and stretch the left outer calf. Repeat this three times on each side. (#49)

Here the connection between exercise and ailment seems obvious and a natural way of finding relief.

Unlike the earlier instructions, which implied the alternation on both sides, the medical exercises spell out in detail how to do each practice. They also have a tendency to be more specific about the number of repetitions and the exact location of pain and practice. For example,

> to relieve shoulder pain: If the pain is in the upper shoulders, roll them carefully 300 times; if it is in the back of the shoulders, pull them forward 300 times; if the pain is in the front of the shoulders, pull them back 300 times; and if it is under the armpits, drop the arms easily 300 times (#73; Harper 1998, 133)

Again, the remedy matches the ailment closely, and movement in the shoulders seems appropriate for relieving tension and discomfort in the area specified. It encourages a great deal of awareness of where the pain is and how the shoulder joint and its numerous surrounding muscles can be moved to best have an effect. Isolat-

---

13. A similar lunge exercise, with the forward foot and hand against a wall and the back hand on the buttocks, is said to relieve spasms, especially in children (#74).

ing specific parts and controlling reflexes through differentiated movements has been found very effective in raising awareness of the stress response, thus curing muscle tension and various kinds of related ailments (Feldenkrais 1972, 163–164).

Other exercises that reflect practices listed earlier in the text include a method to relieve hip pain—it involves placing the hands on the lower back and pressing them in while looking up as far as one can, then placing the hands on the buttocks, raising the head, and bending forward from the hip, all for three repetitions (#55)—and a triple move to relieve chest pain—it involves lifting the chest while moving the arms back ten times, stretching them forward ten times, and alternating backward and forward ten times (#65).

In addition, the medical application of the practices also prescribes integrated sequences of practices listed earlier. Thus, to ease back pain, one is to practice Bear Amble and Forward Hold ten times each, after which one should stand with legs wide and bend forward and backward ten times, each time allowing one's hands to touch the ground (#54). Another prescription, whose benefits are missing in the manuscript but probably involve the relief of neck pain or stiffness, is to repeat Duck in Water and Tiger Turn thirty, forty, and fifty times, lying down and resting between each set (#64). To relieve blockages of *qi* in the head, moreover, one should hold the head with the right hand, bend the neck toward the right shoulder, and stretch the left arm away. Change sides and repeat three times, then follow this up with ten repetitions each of Side and Back, Upward Gaze, and Duck in Water (#75).

In addition to these standing practices, the medical section of the *Yinshu* also has a number of exercises in different positions of the body. Some involve lying down flat. For example,

> to relieve neck pain and difficulties in turning the neck: Lie down flat, stretch the hands and feet *[next five characters illegible]*. Then lift the head from front to back as far as you can. Very slowly come back to a straight position and rest. Repeat ten times. Afterwards cover the mouth and hold the breath. Wait until you sweat and you will feel better. (#43)

It is possible that the intended placement of the arms and legs here is to stretch them away from the torso on a diagonal line, so that the body looks like an X when seen from above. This allows a maximum stretch in the front and back and causes a greater impact of small movements, such as the lifting of the head. When one lifts the head and moves it forward, the spinal column is straightened and the muscles of the neck are tightened, then released. The holding of the thumb at the end may have to do with the presence of the acu-point Meeting Valley (Hegu 合谷) in the bone cradle between thumb and index finger. Also known as the endorphin point, it is said to activate positive brain chemicals and allow a feeling of euphoria and well-being, thus again releasing tensions from the body.

Similarly, to relieve intestinal obstruction, one should lie flat on one's belly, with the chin supported on a low pillow and the fingers interlaced behind the neck. While the patient is holding his or her breath, someone else presses down on the hip and lower back area. Next, the patient vigorously lifts the buttocks to bend the back in the opposite direction. This is repeated three times, with further assistance should the patient be too weak to lift the buttocks alone (#53). This practice provides strong pressure on the intestines combined with a vigorous and sudden contraction, bound to release pressures in the body.

Another lying-down exercise is for lower back pain. Lying on one's back, one should rock the painful area back and forth three hundred times—possibly with knees bent into the chest. After this, lift the legs up straight to ninety degrees, point the toes, and—with hands holding onto the mat—vigorously lift the buttocks and lower back up three times (#56). Similarly, a remedy for fatigue has the patient lie down with knees bent into the chest and do thirty rounds of spinal rocking, then stretch out with vigor (#63). Either practice opens the qi-channels in the torso through vigorous contraction and expansion of the muscular and intestinal systems. They both also involve spinal rocking, which stimulates the tissues and nerves along the back while softly engaging the erector spinae muscles, which hold up and move the spinal column. By strongly engaging the abdominal muscles, the practices help to relieve back pain, since the transverse aspect of the muscles forms a girdle around the belly and thus intimately connects to the lower back. And the practices also ease fatigue by opening blood flow to the intestines and major muscle groups of the torso.

The other major position of the body is to sit, kneel, or squat on the floor. Among kneeling exercises, one involves a stretch of the hamstrings and thighs:

> To relieve thigh pain: Sit upright, stretch the left leg forward while rotating the right arm down to bring them together with some vigor. Then stretch the right leg forward while rotating the left arm down to bring them together. Repeat ten times. (#51)

Other seated exercises involve the "dignified kneel" (weizuo 危坐), in which one knee touches the floor with buttocks resting on the calf while the other knee is upright, the hips are open, and the back is straight. For example, for lower back pain, one should maintain one leg kneeling while pressing that hand on the floor to support oneself, then stretch the other leg away holding its toes with the hand on that side (#59). This practice, not unlike a yoga exercise called Heron Pose (krounchāsana;

Iyengar 1976, 158–159), stretches the hamstrings on one side while lengthening the quadriceps on the other, all the while contracting the abdominal muscles and thus exerting a certain tension on the intestines. A variation of this pose in the *Yinshu*, for weakness in the legs, is to stretch one leg away while the opposite hand pushes down on the thigh (#60). These are among the more acrobatic moves listed in the text, requiring a good sense of balance, flexibility in the hips, and loose hamstrings.

Another exercise executed in dignified kneel is for chest pain. Kneeling on the floor, one is to hold the left wrist with the right hand, then lift with vigor and stretch the arm as far as one can. After repeating this on the other side, lower the arms and massage the face with both hands, then place the hands on the thighs and bend forward as far as possible (#66). This opens the sides of the torso, encourages blood flow to the face, and extends the back, relieving pressure on the chest from different directions. An alternative to this treatment, listed in the same item, is a forward bend with legs straddled while holding onto a pole. A third involves the use of a swing:

> Take a rope about forty feet long, tie it in the middle, and loop it around a beam about ten feet off the floor. Then put a board in the middle and stand on the board with both feet, the hands holding the rope. In this position, lean back with vigor as far as you can. Repeat three times. (#67)

This, too, engages the legs and back, while allowing the abdominal muscles to contract, thus releasing tensions from the chest area. It is also an enjoyable move, swinging back and forth like a small child.

The childlike use of the swing, this time in seated mode, will also relieve difficulty in flexing the feet when walking, knee pain, and cold shins. The instructions are as follows:

> Get a piece of wood that can be easily carved, about a fist in circumference and four feet long. Cover its ends [with cloth] and hang it about four feet above the floor with a new rope. Sit on the piece of wood, hold the rope with both hands and kick out with your feet. Do one thousand repetitions each in the morning, at noon, in the evening, and at midnight, and within ten days you will be fine. (#48)

Another way to help with knee pain is to hold on to a staff with the hand while turning the foot in and out one thousand times:

> If the right knee hurts, hold onto a staff with the left hand, then turn the right foot in and out one thousand times. If the left knee hurts, hold onto a staff with the right hand, then turn the left foot in and out one thousand times.

Next, grab the left toes with the left hand and pull them backwards ten times, while the right hand still holds the staff. Then grab the right toes with the right hand and pull them back ten times while holding the staff with the left hand. (#50)

This is an easy, gentle, and fairly obvious exercise for the condition in question. First, it makes use of the muscles around the ankle, thus releasing tension from the lower leg and easing pressure on the knees. Next, it has the patient hold onto his or her toes, pulling them back and forth, thereby not only engaging the numerous nerve endings at the end of the toes but also loosening up the muscles in the front of the foot. The practice shows the awareness that knee pain, more often than not, originates with problems in walking: placing the toes and moving the ankles.

Another exercise that involves the help of a pillar relieves weakness. The patient is to stand upright while holding onto a pillar with both hands, then—with someone else grasping his or her hip—hold the breath and stretch up with vigor (#61). This lengthens the entire body, pulling down toward the earth, engaging the hip, and opening up along the pillar. It encourages more active qi-flow through all the channels, thus relieving weakness and obstructions.

The pillar is also used in a practice to relieve a feeling of sickness or injury. The *Yinshu* says,

> Grasp a pole with the right hand, face the wall, hold the breath, and place the left foot forward and up against the wall. Rest when you get tired. Similarly, take the pole in the left hand and step forward with the right foot against the wall. Again stop when tired. This makes the qi flow down from the head. (#46; Lo 2001b, 30)

Engaging the lower body vigorously opens the hips and stretches the leg muscles. It pulls the energetic flow downward and thus gives relief to a feeling of sickness.

A wall is also prominent in an exercise to relieve chest congestion and cough. It involves standing up straight with one's back against the wall and lifting the chin with the hands, then coming away from the wall as far as one can, opening the chest and throat area (#72). This can be described as a standing back bend, clearly useful for widening the chest and stimulating deeper breathing, not unlike the standing modification used in yoga for Camel Pose (*ustrāsana;* Iyengar 1976, 87; Farhi 2000, cover).

Similarly, to open throat blockages, one should place the hands on the chest, lift the chin, and push the jaw forward so that the lower teeth are on the outside of the upper teeth. From here one should look up three times with vigor, opening the throat area. Should the congestion be debilitating, someone else can stand behind the patient and hold his or her chin (#76). In either case, the emphasis is on opening the constricted area and releasing tension in the chest and throat muscles.

In contrast to these straightforward and simple exercises, others seem complex and maybe even a bit dubious. To ease stomachache, for example, hang a rope over a beam, then get someone else to lift you a few inches off the floor, so that you hang from the rope. In this position, swing the legs back and stretch vigorously three times. Next, lie down on the belly with your feet against a wall, making sure that belly, thighs, and knees are all on the mat. Interlacing the fingers under the chest, push up from the floor and slowly lift the head into a position not unlike the yoga pose called Cobra (*bhujangāsana;* Iyengar 1976, 107). Releasing this, go into an upper back stretch by lifting the buttocks with vigor while pushing the chest toward the ground, a move reminisicent of Puppy Stretch in yoga (#70). Again, this is to be repeated three times, encouraging flexibility in the muscles of the upper body and opening the torso in vigorous back and forth movement. On the other hand, it seems a bit vigorous for someone already suffering from stomachache and indigestion. The exercise is one of those instances where the cure may be worse than the sickness.

Another rather unusual practice involves the inhalation of grain vapors to increase yin-*qi,* the inherent vitality of the person that determines sexual prowess, procreative power, and overall health—a feeling of being cool, calm, bright, and resourceful (Lo 2000, 57). The instructions are as follows:

> Squat low with thighs straddled. Ease your mind off food, then, with the left hand pressing on the ground, take a bowl of cooked grain in the right hand and move it in front of your mouth. Inhale the *qi* of the cooked grain as much as you can, then eat it. Next, lower your thighs to the ground, bend forward from the waist, and extend the lower abdomen as much as you can. Hold the saliva and do not swallow. Repeat again, stopping after the third time. (#57; Harper 1998, 133)

This integrates an exercise called Releasing Yin, which involves a seated forward bend and abdominal extension (#68), with *qi*-inhalation. Physically, the practitioner is in two basic postures, a low squat (*kua* 跨) with the thighs spread away from the body and a seated pose with the thighs pressed to the ground and the soles of the feet touching. The practice also involves dietetics and breath cultivation, based on the idea that *qi* is present both in the grain and in the body and that it can be transferred from one to the other by first inhaling the steaming vapors and then by partaking of the grain itself—activating various forms and definitions of *qi* (Ikai 2002, 31).

Taken together, the medical exercises of the *Yinshu* present a comprehensive catalog of practices that are generally easy to learn and execute and that match the condition in question. Most of them require some vigorous activity, and sweat is usually seen as a good sign. They tend to focus on clearly discernible pains, mostly in the locomotive and gastrointestinal systems, and see the body largely from the outside—as is typical for materials of this period (Lo 2000, 26). Unlike later practices, which show an internalization of awareness and often use only minimal movement with conscious guiding of *qi,* the prescriptions here use the breath mainly as a supplementary aid to physical work, making it clear that healing means the recovery of harmonious body functions, clearly visible and tangible from without.

Breathing and Sensory Cleansing

Still, breath is an important factor in the exercises, usually applied in a particular way of exhalation. For example, the *chui* 吹 breath is a sharp expulsion of air, with the lips almost closed and the mouth barely open. It is said to have a warming and relaxing effect on the body (Despeux 1995, 131). The *Yinshu* prescribes it as follows:

> If you have angina and are lying down, either day or night, and feel discomfort in your heart, chest, or belly area, massage it with your hands while focusing on exhaling with *chui*. Repeat twenty times. (#66)
>
> To relieve the onset of an intestinal ailment: The first sign is swelling. When you notice the swelling, place your mind on the lower abdomen and exhale with *chui*. Repeat one hundred times. (#45)

Another way of exhaling is known as *xu* 嘘. Completely different from *chui,* it indicates a gentle expulsion of breath. The mouth is wide open and the air is released from the bottom of the lungs. When placing a hand in front of the mouth, one gets a feeling of lukewarm air. Also described as a cooling breath, it may serve to expel burning, heat, or tension—for which it is used in the *Yinshu:*

> To relieve inner tension: Sit in dignified kneel with the tailbone supported. With the left hand stroke the neck and with the right hand stroke the left hand. Now, bend forward as far as you can, then very slowly let go as you exhale with *xu*. Sit up straight and look up. Repeat five times, then change sides in the handhold, for a total of ten repetitions (#42).

The mildest of the exhalations mentioned in the text is *hu* 呼, the standard term for "exhale," which indicates a blowing out of breath with rounded lips and is also depicted among the figures of the *Daoyin tu*. *Hu*, being rather unobtrusive, is rarely used by itself but comes in combination with the other breaths. For example,

> to relieve fatigue at the onset of a disease, when you note that your mind wanders
> restlessly and your body aches all over, practice Eight Meridians Stretch and quickly
> exhale with *hu* and *xu,* thereby releasing yang. Also, soak the face with cold water for
> the time it takes to eat a bowl of rice, then discard the water. Take a bamboo cloth in
> both hands and rub it over your face, moving it up and down. All the while continue
> to exhale *hu, hu*. Repeat ten times. (#44)

The third and last part of the *Yinshu* has some additional information on the Eight Meridians Stretch and the use of breathing in the prevention and cure of diseases. To do the stretch, one should exhale with *chui, xu,* and *hu,* then inhale the essential *qi* of Heaven and Earth for a general strengthening of the body and harmonizing of *qi*-flow. This is to be supported by an abdominal stretch, a forward bend from the waist, and a vigorous stretch of both arms and legs, and some time resting supine (Wenwu 1990, 86; Ikai 2004, 27–28).

The text further specifies seasonal variations on the use of the breaths.

> Lie down on your back and exhale with *chui* and *xu* in order to pull in yin-*[qi]*. In spring,
> exhale several times with *xu* plus once each with *hu* and *chui*. In summer, exhale several
> times with *hu* plus once each with *xu* and *chui*. In [fall and] winter, exhale several times
> with *chui* plus once each with *xu* and *hu*. (Engelhardt 2001, 220; Ikai 2002, 34)

The effect of regular breathing practice includes the control of excessive emotions as well the expulsion of harmful influences from the body, such as dryness *(hu)*, dampness *(chui)*, and heat *(xu)*. These three breaths become also the mainstays of breathing practice in later literature, representing three of the famous Six Healing Breaths (*liuzi jue* 六子訣), which also include *si* 四, a gentle, relaxed exhalation that lets the breath escape between slightly opened lips; *he* 呵, a strong breath with open mouth that is accompanied by a guttural rasping through tightening of the throat at the base of the tongue, not unlike the *ujjayi* breath in yoga; and *xi* 嘻, the sound of sighing, which describes a soft exhalation with the mouth slightly open that comes from deep within the body (Despeux 2006, 40).

To be able to breathe properly, one needs to remove blockages from the breathing organs and keep them in good conditions. Several exercises serve this goal. In addition to the exercise mentioned earlier to relieve throat blockages, (#76) there is one, to open up a stuffy nose: One kneels and with both hands vigorously rubs the nose while bending the head back as far as possible. One then massages the heart area and stretches the chest. After repeating this three times, one stands up with legs in a wide straddle and, again three times, bends from the waist to place the hands on the floor (#77).

Pain in the mouth is eased with a strong stretch that involves placing fingers into the mouth and opening the jaws, then blowing first one, then the other cheek up as much as possible, expanding the muscles and relieving tension (#78). For lockjaw, one supports the chin with both hands, places the thumbs into the sides of the mouth, uses the other fingers to press against the ears, then lifts the chin with some force (#79). All these will help the smooth functioning of the respiratory organs and aid in proper breathing.

In addition, the text presents some practices to enhance eyesight and hearing. To relieve eyestrain, it offers three methods. First, one can place the fingers of the opposite hand into the inner corner of the eyes and press firmly, while the other hand holds onto the head and pulls it sideways. Second, one can place the fingers of both hands into the inner corners of the eyes, then rub upward toward the forehead for ten repetitions. Third, one can sit in dignified kneel, rub the hands together to create heat, then massage both eyes ten times (#81).

For the ears, the text has two offerings. The first, against deafness, involves kneeling with a straight back while raising the arm on the side of the deafness and stretching it up vigorously with fingers spread wide, then stretching the neck on the side of the same ear (#82). The other, against earache, has the patient place a finger in the ailing ear with some pressure, then move it up and down, back and forth. After this he or she is to place one hand on the opposite shoulder and stretch to open the side of the face and neck, alternating for three repetitions on each side (#84).

These, as most of the other exercises presented in the text, are simple and clear and seem to match the intended ailment—although there also are some that require a bit of assistance and others that seem a bit on the acrobatic side. Overall, the *Yinshu* focuses on improving and increasing the *qi* in the body, reflecting practices and concerns in various other manuscripts, such as the *Yangsheng fang, Shiwen,* and *Tianxia zhidao tan* from Mawangdui. The *qi,* internal and precious like an embryo in the womb, needs to be nurtured and taken care of with special methods—regular practice of morning and evening routines, an awareness of good posture (relaxed shoulders, straight back, engaged legs, open hips, and tight abdomen), as well as a conscious effort to keep the *qi* moving in accordance with the rhythm of the days and seasons by practicing breathing exercises, swallowing saliva, and visualizing it flowing smoothly in the body and nourishing the brain (Li 1993, 345).

Concluding Observations

To conclude its presentation of the healing exercises, the *Yinshu* presents a collection of twenty-four short phrases, mnemonic verses that summarize the most
pertinent information in terse and precise statements:

> Holding the Breath is good for stretching the muscles.
> Hall Dropping is good for balancing the channels.
> Snake Wriggle is good for enhancing the brain.
> Duck in Water is good for opening the neck.
> Flushing Flesh and Bones along the channels is good for all from heel to head.
> Side and Back is good for the ears.
> Upward Gaze is good for the eyes.
> Opening the Mouth and looking up is good for the nose.
> Spitting without Emitting is good for the mouth.
> Rubbing the Heart and lifting the head is good for the throat.
> Upright Swivel is good for the base of the neck.
> Tiger Turn is good for the neck.
> Triple Stretch is good for the shoulder muscles.
> Limbs Dropping is good for the armpits.
> Bird Stretch is good for the shoulder joints.
> Turn and Shake is good for abdomen and belly.
> Turn and Twist is good for the sides.
> Bear Amble is good for the lower back.
> Repeated Hold is good for the hips.
> Step of Yu is good for the thighs.
> Forward Loosening is good for the knees.
> Turn and Push is good for feet and heels.
> Shifting Toes is good for the *qi* of the feet.
> Stomping Heels is good for the chest.
> All these should be done with three repetitions. (Wenwu 1990, 84–85; Li 1993, 340;
> Ikai 2004, 27–28)

These twenty-four statements explain briefly which exercise should be used
for what condition and to enhance which part of the body. About half of them
match exercises described in the first section; others supply shorthand names to
information contained in the medical section. Most are descriptive enough to be
clear just by reading them, but some also have special names, again including
various animals, such as snake, duck, tiger, bird, and bear. Not mentioned previ-

ously is the Step of Yu (Yubu 禹步), a formal set of steps still used in Daoist ritual today (Lagerwey 1987, 100–102) that may go back to shamanic and thence healing moves. Unfortunately, the text only notes that it benefits the thighs and does not explain how it is performed.

The exercises in the *Yinshu* are to a large extent also reflected in the illustrations of the *Daoyin tu*. Both have in common that they present mainly standing poses. However, the remaining captions are quite different, and only two poses, Limbs Dropping and Snapping Yin, bear identical names. Many movements, on the other hand, seem very close, although more subtle moves of the legs and neck are impossible to identify from the *Daoyin tu* pictures. Forward bends, on the other hand, are more obvious. The *Daoyin tu* shows one with head lowered, one with head raised, one involving a pole, and one with one arm on the ground and the other arm stretched upward. Matching this, the *Yinshu* has a complete sequence of forward bends.

Similarly, the back bend called Pointing Backward (#30), the calf stretch known as the Parapet (#4), the runner's stretch described as Tiger Stretch (#32), and the swinging of the arms called Cart Cover (#38) all appear in *Daoyin tu* illustrations (#8, 17, 24, 31). Side and Back (#13), moreover, is shown in the *Daoyin tu* as a figure stretching one arm up (#10). Warrior Pointing (#41), a lunge with arms pointed straight forward and back, is essentially the same as the Merlin of the *Daoyin tu* (#44). A few poses, furthermore, are mentioned but not described in the *Yinshu* yet appear in the *Daoyin tu*. Bear Amble and Bird Stretch are obvious examples.

Overall, the *Daoyin tu* seems to follow the same tradition and present the same knowledge as the *Yinshu*, with some variation in the appellation of practices. Like the twenty-four mnemonic statements in the *Yinshu*, the illustrations in the *Daoyin tu* help physicians, patients, and practitioners to remember the repertoire and pick the correct move for the condition in question. They are supplemented and explained by the more detailed presentation in the second part of the *Yinshu*, which clarifies how to execute the moves and what ailments to use them for. The *Yinshu*, moreover, also places the practice into a larger social and cultural context, noting in its third part how to prevent the arising of diseases. The most important factors that cause diseases, it says, are climatic and dietary excesses:

> People get sick because of heat, dampness, wind, cold, rain, or dew as well as because of [a dysfunction] in opening and closing the pores, a disharmony in eating and drinking, and the inability to adapt their rising and resting to the changes in cold and heat. (Wenwu 1990, 86; Engelhardt 2001, 216)

The same six causes for ailments are also found in the medical classic *Huangdi neijing lingshu* 黃帝內徑靈樞 (The Yellow Emperor's Internal Classic:

Numinous Pivot, ch. 44), where they are supplemented by imbalances of yin and yang, joy and anger, eating and drinking, as well as living conditions and housing issues (Engelhardt 1996, 17). The *Yinshu* similarly adds unstable diet, excessive emotions, and a lifestyle inappropriate to the season as possible causes of *qi*-imbalance. The text recommends various general therapies, such as breathing exercises, bodily stretches, and the careful treatment of inner *qi*. It says, "If you can pattern your *qi* properly and maintain your yin-energy in fullness, your whole person will benefit" (Wenwu 1990, 86; Ikai 2004, 29).

It is also interesting to note that in its concluding section the *Yinshu* makes a distinction between "noble people" of the upper classes, who fall ill because of uncontrolled emotions such as anger and joy (which overload yin and yang *qi*), and "base people," whose conditions tend to be caused by excessive labor, hunger, and thirst. It further notes that poor people have no opportunity to learn the necessary breathing exercises and therefore contract numerous diseases and die an early death. Again, as it did in the first part on seasonal regimens, the text makes it clear that longevity techniques were very much the domain of the aristocracy and the upper classes (Engelhardt 2000, 88; 2001, 217; also Harper 1985a, 381).

The text ends with an analogy of physical cultivation and the functioning of a bellows (for more detailed discussion of bellows as metaphor, see Harper 1995). As the bellows takes in and expels air, so the human body breathes deeply and regularly if healthy. The text says, "The reason why people are prone to collapse and suffer early degeneration of yin [vital potency] is because they are unable to regulate their *qi*. Those who can regulate their *qi* well and solidify yin will benefit their body" (Harper 1998, 122).

By regulating the *qi* through exercises and breathing—and the conscientious avoidance of strenuous labor, hunger, and thirst—the perfectly adjusted human being, the "person of the Dao," prevents all kinds of health problems, instead maintaining the proper balance of *qi*. Familiar with all the major ways of the body, such a one knows the routines and medical methods to be applied as various situations arise and uses them conscientiously and with moderation to attain youthful vigor and personal satisfaction in the fullness of life.

Chapter Two

Officials, Hermits, and Ecstatics

Moderation and elementary healing are also at the core of the next sources on healing exercises, from the fourth century C.E., written by literati aristocrats of southern China. Engaged in different social contexts and cultural pursuits, they include imperial officials striving to attain a more balanced and longer life, hermits withdrawing to the mountains to find longevity and prepare the concoction of an alchemical elixir, and Highest Clarity Daoists pursuing contact with the gods and ascension to the heavens of the immortals.

All three had in common that they had the means and the leisure to be concerned with their physical health and spiritual well-being. They all practiced exercises in continuation of the medical tradition as established in the early manuscripts: applying seasonal awareness and moderation in food, sex, and activities and working with the classical combination of physical exercises, breathing, and the sensory refinement of eyes and ears. In addition, they developed the earlier tradition through the creation of short, organized sequences; the use of specific dates and times of day; an emphasis on early morning practice; the integration of several other practices, notably swallowing the saliva, clicking the teeth, and various forms of self-massages; and the connection to divine forces, be they demons to be kept at bay or divinities to be attracted or activated.

While the three aristocratic groups of the fourth century have all this in common and provide a clear picture of how the exercise tradition developed in the early middle ages, they are yet different in accordance with their varied goals. Imperial officials were interested in a harmonious life within society that would allow them to enjoy mundane pleasures and a long life. Hermits lived on the fringes of society. Like officials, they encouraged moderation but less to enjoy life than to become physically strong enough for higher attainments. Also, they proposed breathing and other techniques for exorcism rather than self-enhancement and strongly emphasized that control of *qi* was very useful but would not in itself lead to immortality or transcendence, which ultimately required the concoction of the cinnabar elixir. Followers of Highest Clarity, finally, had largely given up on this world; they were interested primarily in interacting with the deities and ascending to the otherworld. Their texts accordingly speak less about moderation and healing, focusing instead on interior palaces of body gods and various methods to activate divine connections. The latter two groups, moreover, provide the first documents that show how healing exercises expanded into religious dimensions.

Why all this attention to long life and religious activity among southern aristocrats of the fourth century? What was their social and political situation at the time? What kinds of texts did they leave behind? What audience were they addressing? And how did they adapt the exercises in accordance with their social position and overall goals?

Aristocratic Endeavors

The main event that predicates the new unfolding of the Daoyin tradition is the move of the imperial capital from the northern city of Chang'an 長安 (modern Xi'an 西安) to Jiankang 建康 in the south, the city on the southern bank of the Yangzi now known as Nanjing 南京. This move was caused by the invasion of Huns (Xiongnu 匈奴), who had come under economic and geographical pressure and were seeking additional space. Instead of peacefully tending their herds on the steppe, they came to ransack wide stretches of northern China with strong military power. Led by a group called Toba, the Huns consisted of a considerable federation of tribes who, in the course of the fourth century, extended their dominion over all of northern China. Ruling under the dynastic name of Wei 魏, they were gradually sinicized and came to spread their newly adopted creed of Buddhism in China, thus greatly contributing to the East Asian adaptation of the Indian religion. Far from stable and peaceful, however, the Toba rule was frequently shaken from within, both by rival chieftains rising in rebellion and by messianic Chinese cults spreading discontent and apocalyptic revolts.[1]

In 317, the Toba conquered the capital of the then-ruling Jin dynasty. The imperial court together with the army and large contingents of retainers as well as masses of ordinary people fled southeast, thereby transforming the dynasty from the Western to the Eastern Jin. Within a few years, they had settled in Jiankang, where they displaced the local administration of the province and filled all major positions with émigré northerners. Resident southern aristocrats could do nothing but return home to their landed estates, where they engaged in various cultured activities, some letting themselves go into gluttony and excess, others turning to long-life and religious practices.

Newly installed northerners and those southerners who still hoped for official employment were eager to stay healthy and keep active so they could enjoy

---

1. For more on Toba history, see Eberhard 1949, Warshaw 1987.

their power. They pursued personal health and well-being and on occasion discovered new, interesting ways of living it up without getting too seedy and debauched. Disenfranchised and disappointed southern aristocrats, on the other hand, turned their backs on society. Some began to learn longevity and alchemical techniques that might lead to otherworldly dimensions, enhanced personal powers, and eventual ascent to the higher spheres. Others sought official rank and appointments in newly discovered heavens of high quality, creating status well beyond the petty positions to be had in the northern-infested capital. The sources we have on healing exercises echo these three main tendencies.

Officials

The health practices of officials in service or in waiting are mainly documented in the *Yangsheng yaoji* 養生要集 (Long Life Compendium) by the aristocrat and official Zhang Zhan 張湛. He is best known as the first and most important commentator to the Daoist philosophical text *Liezi* 列子 (Book of Master Lie; trl. Graham 1960), which supports a similar view of the body as the *Yangsheng yaoji* (see Sakade 1986a, 10; Kohn forthcoming).[2] Zhang Zhan, also called Chudu 處度, does not have a biography in the dynastic histories despite the fact that he wrote several philosophical commentaries in the Profound Learning (Xuanxue 玄學) tradition of Daoism, authored two compendia on longevity practices, served as imperial secretary under the Eastern Jin, and was born into a family of senior officials under the Western Jin (Despeux 1989, 228). Rather, information about him is anecdotal, some found in the story collection *Shishuo xinyu* 世說新語 (A New Account of Tales of the World; trl. Mather 1976), some in the biographies of contemporary officials and later descendants.

According to these sources, Zhang Zhan was philosophically minded and a follower of Dark Learning thinkers such as the *Zhuangzi* commentator Guo Xiang 郭象, whom he frequently cites in his *Liezi* commentary. He also had medical knowledge and was eager to improve the *qi* in his residence by planting various kinds of pine trees. The *Jinshu* 晉書 (History of the Jin Dynasty) biography of Fan Ning 范寧 further mentions that he was susceptible to eyestrain, for which he took a longevity recipe consisting of six ingredients: read less, think less, focus inward, scan outward, sleep late, and go to bed early. He was to mix these ingredients with *qi* and take them to heart for seven days. This would enhance his vision and extend his life (Stein 1999, 101).

---

2. The first mention of authorship of the commentary is in the bibliographic section of the *Suishu* 隨書 (History of the Sui Dynasty) of the seventh century (Despeux 1989, 228). Zhang Zhan is a common name, and it is also remotely possible that the author was an official in northern China known as Zhang Ziran 張自然 (Zhu 1986, 102).

An imperial official and well-educated thinker with time on his hands, Zhang Zhan engaged in wide reading and practiced long-life techniques. He had the material cushion necessary to indulge his interest in medical learning and was well connected to officials and literati. The practices he mentions were probably well known and widely used at the time, and he may well have put together the *Yangsheng yaoji* to help his fellow aristocrats stay healthy and live moderately despite their riches and newly found leisure, thus using long-life practices predominantly for this-worldly advancement.

The *Yangsheng yaoji* has not survived as an independent text but was reconstituted on the basis of fragments.[3] It consists of ten sections:

1. Harboring Spirit
2. Loving *Qi*
3. Maintaining the Body
4. Practicing Exercises
5. Proper Language
6. Food and Drink
7. Bedchamber Arts
8. Rejecting Common Habits
9. Herbal Medicines
10. Taboos and Prohibitions

The section on Daoyin exercises is conspicuously short and focuses dominantly on maintaining a harmonious *qi*-flow. In contrast to this, the sections on food and sexual activities are extensive and very detailed (Stein 1999, 187–222). The one on food and drink notes the best way to eat in the different seasons, provides remedies for overeating and intoxication, outlines the optimal diet during pregnancy, and suggests the healthiest way to eat various delicacies, such as game, pheasant, pork, scallops, and exotic fruits and vegetables. The section on bed-

3. The text appears to have been lost after the rebellion of An Lushan 安錄山 in 755 (Barrett 1980, 172). Fragments and citations appear mainly in three sources: the *Zhubing yuanhou lun* 諸病源候論 (Origins and Symptoms of Medical Disorders), a medical compendium in 50 *juan* put together by a committee headed by the court physician Chao Yuanfang and presented to Emperor Yang of the Sui in 610 (trl. Despeux and Obringer 1997); the *Yangxing yanming lu* 養性延命錄 (Record on Nourishing Inner Nature and Extending Life, DZ 838), a Daoist collection of meditative, breathing, and physical practices in two *juan*, ascribed to Sun Simiao 孫思邈 and probably of the mid-seventh century (trl. Switkin 1987), which also lists the titles of the ten sections; and the *Ishinpō* 醫心方 (Essential Medical Methods), an extensive Japanese medical collection by the court physician Tamba no Yasuyori 丹波瀬康 (912–995), which was presented to the emperor in 984 (Sakade 1989, 3–9). The fragments are collected, translated, and analyzed in Stein 1999.

chamber arts similarly gives seasonal advice and suggests that one should abstain after overeating or getting drunk. The text clearly addresses members of the upper classes with the leisure and material means to indulge their preferences and a correspondingly great need to stay healthy despite their indulgence.

Hermits

In contrast to this, aristocrats who opted out of the dominant society and pursued otherworldly goals through Daoist cultivation and alchemy used healing exercises for enhancing control over their *qi*—thereby lessening the need for food and developing magical powers. Their goal was to guide the *qi* in such a way that the body would be completely satisfied without food and drink and to attain

Fig. 5: A Daoist with magical powers subduing a tiger. Source: *Liexian quanzhuan.*

powers of control over people, objects, and energetic constellations (fig. 5). This state of physical independence and empowerment then served as the basis for alchemical experiments.

The best-known representative of this group is the would-be alchemist and scholar Ge Hong 葛洪 (283–343), who called himself Baopuzi (Master Who Embraces Simplicity 抱朴子). Unlike the northern émigré Zhang Zhan, Ge Hong was born into the southern aristocracy and grew up in a small town near Jiankang. Inspired by a family interest for otherworldly pursuits, he became a disciple of the hermit and alchemist Zheng Yin 鄭隱 at the age of fourteen and studied with him for five years. After serving in the imperial administration in various minor capacities, he resigned his position to study longevity and immortality full-time (Pregadio 2000, 167). He wandered around the country in search of ancient manuscripts and learned masters, then came home to write down his findings.

In his autobiography—the first of its kind in Chinese literature—he describes how he eschewed official positions and even avoided social interaction with his peers because his one aim in life was to become immortal, that is, reach a state of perfect health and extended longevity that would allow the concoction of an alchemical elixir and ascension to the heavens (Schipper and Verellen 2004, 70–71). For Ge Hong, immortality was not reached primarily through religious observances, such as prayers and rituals, although he certainly believed in the magical efficacy of talismans and incantations. Rather, for him the desired state could be attained by laying a groundwork of long life through longevity techniques—exercises, breathing, dietetics, and meditations—followed by the great alchemical endeavor, which alone could lead to ultimate immortality (Pregadio 2006b, 125). All alchemical work, moreover, had to be undertaken in secrecy in the seclusion of the mountains and required numerous costly ingredients and holy scriptures, revealed either by the gods in séances or by hermit masters after the passing of strict tests (Kohn 1991, 85–86). Although he had never compounded any elixir by the time he compiled his writings, hagiographic accounts suggest that he later retired to Mount Luofu 羅浮山 late in life to devote himself fully to the great work (Ware 1966, 6–21).

His most important work is the *Baopuzi neipian* 抱朴子內篇 (Inner Chapters of the Master Who Embraces Simplicity, *DZ* 1185; trl. Ware 1966), which was first completed in 317, that is, "before the influx of refugees from the north was to profoundly change the culture and religion of the Jiangnan region" (Schipper and Verellen 2004, 71). A twenty-chapter compendium on the techniques and practices of the immortals, it provides an overview of the religious, medical, exorcistic, and esoteric practices prevalent at the time, partly based on passages copied or summarized from scriptures that Ge Hong had received from Zheng Yin (Robinet 1997, 78–113). The text describes how to use protective measures that will keep demons and evil spirits at bay; how to reach alignment with the yin and yang energies of the universe; how to absorb the *qi* of the Sun and the Moon; how to use various herbs and minerals to improve health and extend life; how to attain magical qualities such as being in several places at once, becoming invisible, flying in the air, knowing the future, and reading other people's thoughts; and how to prepare various kinds of cinnabar elixirs that would transform one into an immortal or bestow very long life on earth and power over life and death (Needham et al. 1976, 81–113).

The book discusses long-life methods as preliminary to alchemy and emphasizes the antisocial nature of this endeavor. As Ge Hong says,

> Those who wish to nourish life settle far away, stay in hiding, conceal their shining radiance, and veil their elegance. They repress the eye's desire to see and banish the beauties that weaken their vision. They plug the ear's very thought of sound and put afar the music which only confuses hearing. They cleanse the dark mirror of the mind, maintain a feminine approach, and embrace oneness. Concentrating on their *qi* to produce softness, they fortify themselves with calm and impartiality. They dismiss the evils of joy and sadness; they are alien to the glory and disgrace associated with success and failure; and they lop away rich living that later turns to poison. (ch. 5; Ware 1966, 99)

In contrast to this rejection of social involvement, the text also has several short spin-offs that, like Zhang Zhan's work, address a wider aristocratic audience, hoping to help them with health issues and to guide them away from gluttony and indulgence. Ge Hong, therefore, without giving up on the basic principles of the health regimens, replaces the pursuit of official fame and wholesome indulgence with the search for alchemical recipes that would grant an extensive long life, magical powers over self and others, and the eventual ascension to the immortals.

Ecstatics

The same goals are also apparent in the third set of texts on healing exercises in this period, which go back to a group of southern aristocrats who channeled their officially unwanted energies into interaction with the gods and ecstatic journeys to the otherworld (see Strickmann 1978). Confronted with the religious beliefs of the northern émigrés, some of whom had become followers of the early Daoist movement of the Celestial Masters (Tianshi dao 天師道), they were initially uneasy because the newcomers introduced new ways that were neither wanted nor comfortable. Gradually, however, they came to a compromise, which in due course gave way to a degree of integration and merging and eventually led to the growth of an entirely new religious movement, the Dao of Highest Clarity (Shangqing 上清).

It began with the popular practice to establish communication with one's ancestors with the help of a spirit-medium, mainly to find causes for unexplained illness and misfortune, but also to learn of their fate in the otherworld and to obtain advice on current affairs. In the 360s, Xu Mai 許邁 (301–?) and Xu Mi 許謐 (303–373), two brothers of the aristocratic Xu family who lived in the same village as Ge Hong's clan, hired the medium Yang Xi 楊羲 (330–386?) to establish contact with Xu Mi's wife Tao Kedou 陶可斗, who had died in 362. She appeared and told them about her status in the otherworld, explained the overall organization of the heavens, and introduced the medium to various other spirit figures.

Among them were underworld rulers, divine officers of the dead, spirit masters of moral rules, denizens of the Huayang grotto 華陽洞 on nearby Mount Mao 茅山, as well as some deceased leaders of the Celestial Masters, notably the former libationer Lady Wei Huacun 魏華存 (251–334). Together they provided the medium with a detailed description of the organization and population of the otherworld, and especially of the top heaven of Highest Clarity (Robinet 1993, 3–4; Strickmann 1979, 126). They also revealed specific methods of personal transformation, meditations, visualizations, and alchemical concoctions; gave thorough instructions on how to transmit the texts and their methods; and provided prophecies about the golden age to come.

The Xu brothers recorded everything Yang Xi transmitted from the otherworld, however disparate it may have seemed, and created a basic collection of sacred texts. They shared their new revelations with their immediate neighbors and relatives, who included the Ge family of Ge Hong, the Taos of Tao Kedou, and the Wangs of the famous calligrapher Wang Xizhi 王羲之 (Robinet 1984, 1:108). These aristocrats welcomed these visions heartily, finding in the newly discovered heavens a rank and nobility they had lost on this earth. They learned all about the organization of the thirty-six heavens above and practiced visualizations and ecstatic meditations to experience the higher planes. They integrated the exercise tradition as part of their practice in a daily routine of stretches, breathing, and self-massages. In combination with the use of talismans and incantations, the exercises served to purify their bodies and maintain their vigor for the great endeavor of becoming immortal.

Like socially active aristocrats, they emphasized moderation; like mountain hermits, they were interested in controlling their *qi*. However, their main mode of transformation was less by longevity exercises and alchemical elixirs—although cinnabars also formed an active part of Highest Clarity practice (Strickmann 1979, 130–133)—than through their strong connection to the divine, established with the help of talismans, incantations, and visualizations of gods in the body and the otherworld. Their major contribution to the Daoyin tradition was that they added these religious and devotional elements to the practice of healing exercises. Their regimens and sequences are documented best in a record of revelations associated with the Queen Mother of the West and various other deities, as well as in various other Highest Clarity works.

Moderation

All of these texts, despite their different origins and varied social settings, agree that the base of health and long life is moderation. They warn against excesses and provide remedies to improve bodily functions through diet and herbal decoctions, supported by prescriptions for proper sleep, hygiene, sexual activity, and exercise.

For example, the *Yangsheng yaoji* recommends that practitioners avoid specific combinations of food, such as anything hot and cold, sweet and raw, or more specifically, wheat and oats, onions and honey, celery and pig's liver, dried ginger and rabbit (Stein 1999, 200–204). They should use alcohol sparingly, boil water before drinking, and take care not to get cold when sweaty. The text also has specific recipes for beneficial food combinations, descriptions of the qualities and healing properties of herbs and foodstuffs, as well as a series of instructions for pregnancy (208–210). In many cases, it provides specific remedies for certain conditions, notably stomach and digestive problems, including cramps, flatulence, constipation, and diarrhea (226–228).

The overall goal of the presentation is to encourage people to live as healthily as possible, working closely in harmony with nature and the four seasons. Citing the ancient immortal Pengzu 彭祖, the text says,

> The method of nourishing longevity consists mainly in not doing harm to oneself. Keep warm in winter and cool in summer, and never lose your harmony with the four seasons—that is how you can align yourself with the body. Do not allow sensuous beauty, provocative postures, easy leisure, and enticing entertainments to incite yearnings and desires—that is how you come to pervade the spirit. (*Ishinpō* 23.3a; Stein 1999, 169)

The most important advice is to remain moderate in everything, since any excess will harm the lungs and kidneys: to eat and drink with control, to stay away from various luxuries that lead to a weakness of *qi,* and to keep speech and laughter within limits (Stein 1999, 179, 186). Citing Pengzu once more, the text points out that heavy clothing and thick comforters, spicy foods and heavy meats, sexual attraction and beautiful women, melodious voices and enticing sounds, wild hunting and exciting outings, as well as ambition and striving for success will inevitably lead to a weakening of the body and thus a reduction in life expectancy (178). In the same vein, various mental activities will harm key psychological forces and thus bring about a diminishing of *qi,* which takes one further away from the Dao and reduces life. The text formulates this in a set of twelve things to do only in "little" increments. It says,

> Those who wish to preserve harmony and complete their perfection should: think little, reflect little, laugh little, speak little, enjoy little, anger little, delight little, mourn little, like little, dislike little, engage little, deal little.
>
> If you think much, the spirit will disperse.
>
> If you reflect much, the heart will be labored.
>
> If you laugh much, the organs and viscera will soar up.
>
> If you speak much, the Ocean of *Qi* will be empty and vacant.
>
> If you enjoy much, the gallbladder and bladder will take in outside wind.
>
> If you get angry much, the fascia will push the blood around.
>
> If you delight much, the spirit and heart will be deviant and unsettled.
>
> If you mourn much, the hair and whiskers will dry and wither.
>
> If you like much, the will and *qi* will be one-sided and overloaded.
>
> If you dislike much, the essence and power will race off and soar away.
>
> If you engage yourself much, the muscles and meridians will be tense and nervous.
>
> If you deal much, wisdom and worry will all be confused.
>
> All these attack people's lives worse than axes and spears; they diminish people's destiny worse than wolves and wolverines. (Stein 1999, 170–171)

In other words, harmony with the Dao manifests itself in mental stability and physical wellness, and any form of agitation or sickness indicates a decline in one's alignment with the forces of nature. Thus "going along with Heaven and Earth brings good fortune; going against Heaven and Earth brings misfortune" (*Ishinpō* 23.29b; Stein 1999, 182), the text says, and notes, "The Dao is *qi.* By preserving *qi* you can attain the Dao, and through attaining the Dao you can live long. Spirit is essence. By preserving essence you can reach spirit brightness, and once you have spirit brightness, you can live long" (23.17ab; Stein 1999, 172).

The major points on moderation made in the aristocratic *Yangsheng yaoji* during the same period also appear in more religiously inspired texts that can be linked with the hermit tradition. Most important among them are two short synopses of the *Baopuzi* contained in the Daoist canon: the *Pengzu shesheng yangxing lun* 彭祖攝生養性論 (Preserving Life and Nourishing Inner Nature As Practiced by Pengzu, DZ 840; hereafter abbreviated *Pengzu lun*) and the *Baopuzi yangsheng lun* 抱朴子養生論 (Nourishing Life According to the Master Who

Embraces Simplicity, *DZ* 842; abbr. *Yangsheng lun*). Although in title and edition linked with the hermit tradition and probably compiled on the basis of eremitic documents (see Schipper and Verellen 2004, 362, 357), they closely match Zhang Zhan's attitude and recommendations. Like the *Yangsheng yaoji*, they do not speak of mountain isolation, alchemy, or specific recipes, but emphasize the need for moderation in daily life. Thus, the *Pengzu lun* says,

> The method of nourishing life involves not spitting far and not walking hastily. Let the ears not listen to excess; let the eyes not look around extensively. Do not sit until tired; do not sleep beyond your needs. Wait until it is cold before you put on more clothes; wait until it is hot before you take them off. Do not get too hungry, because hunger harms the *qi*, and when you eat beware of overindulging. Do not get too thirsty before you drink and do not drink too deeply at a time. If you overeat, your bowels will be blocked and obstructed to the point of illness; if you drink too deeply, phlegm will accumulate into lumps. (2a; also in *Yangsheng lun* 2a; *Baopuzi* 13; Ware 1966, 223)

The *Yangsheng lun* proposes similar guidelines, which it supplements with a set of six exhortations to release mental strain and sensory involvement:

1. Let go of fame and profit.
2. Limit sights and sounds.
3. Moderate material goods and wealth.
4. Lessen smells and tastes.
5. Eliminate lies and falsehood.
6. Avoid jealousy and envy. (1b)

It then repeats the set of twelve "little" activities (1b–2a) as found in the *Yangsheng yaoji* and moves on to echo Pengzu's warning against wearing "heavy clothes and thick sleeves," against eating "meats, fatty foods, and sweets and getting intoxicated," and against enjoying "sexual infatuation, engagements with the opposite sex, and overindulgence in the bedroom," similarly found in the mainstream work.

Both the list of twelve "little" activities and the various concrete warnings appear also in the more technical Daoist work *Shenxian shiqi jin'gui miaolu* 神仙食氣金櫃妙錄 (Wondrous Record of the Golden Casket on the Spirit Immortals' Practice of Eating *Qi*, *DZ* 836, 16a; abbr. *Jin'gui lu*).[4] As discussed in more detail

---

4. The *Jin'gui lu* is ascribed to Master Jingli 京里 or Jinghei 京黑 who supposedly lived in the fourth century. The text may be a Tang compilation but in contents predates the Sui. See Loon 1984, 130; Schipper and Verellen 2004, 355. A modern Chinese presentation of its practices is found in Ma 1999.

below, like the other texts it provides general prescriptions for moderation, but it is also more religious in nature in that it includes a number of specific exercises and recipes for spiritual attainments.

The fact that general admonitions for moderation—physical, mental, and social—are equally found in the *Yangsheng yaoji*, in offshoots of the *Baopuzi*, and in more technical Daoist texts shows that they formed part of an aristocratic culture of simplicity and self-control that favored working toward long life and well-being, but did not necessarily involve seclusion, devotion, or alchemical experiments. The two short synopsis texts, although contained in the Daoist canon today, like the *Yangsheng yaoji* probably addressed a general audience among literati and did not necessarily form part of the hermit tradition. Still, both officials and hermits being literati, they participated in the same general culture of nourishing life and accordingly integrated aristocratic recommendations even into their more technical texts. The close connection among these various works is a formidable example of how aristocratic and hermit culture interlinked and interacted in medieval China. It contradicts the view that tends to see Daoist activities as the domain of outsiders and eccentrics, completely separate from the dominant aristocratic culture.

Techniques for Healing

In accordance with the understanding that moderation is key to a harmonious and healthy life, the texts describe medical conditions as the result of excesses and uncontrolled behavior. For example, as the *Pengzu lun* points out, the different flavors associated with the five phases not only affect the organ immediately associated with it but, when taken in excess, can also harm the organ associated with the phase that follows it in accordance with the controlling cycle. The text says,

> Make sure to eat selectively of the five flavors. Too much sour food [wood] harms the spleen [earth]; too much bitter [earth] harms the lungs [metal]; too much pungent [metal] harms the liver [wood]; too much sweet [earth] harms the kidneys [water]; and too much salty [water] harms the heart [fire]. All these follow the system of the five phases as they invisibly underlie the four limbs. Following this, you can understand and penetrate the patterns. (2b)

The text further notes that extreme emotions—such as joy and anger, love and hate, desire and anxiety, urgency and worry—trouble the spirit and that too much speaking and laughing harm the inner organs, while long periods of either sitting or standing burden muscles and bones, and excesses in sexual activities create ulcers and exhaustion. More specifically,

> Sleeping and resting without limit harms the liver.
> Moving and panting to fatigue and exhaustion harms the spleen.
> Holding the bow and pulling the string harms the muscles.
> Floating high and wading low harms the kidneys.
> Getting drunk and throwing up harms the lungs.
> Eating to fullness and sleeping on the side harms the *qi*.
> Galloping like a horse and running around wildly harms the stomach.
> Shouting and cursing with vile language harms the gallbladder.
> Failing to keep yin and yang in proper exchange causes ulcers.
> Lacking balance in bedchamber activities creates fatigue and exhaustion. (1b)

These effects, moreover, are not visible immediately but build up over time. Moving gradually from the outer to the inner body (Lo 2000, 28), the various excesses accumulate to diminish *qi,* which controls the bones, marrow, and brain, and at the same time cause confusion in the spirit, the psychological force associated with the heart and the "ultimate master of the five organs" (2b). To prevent this, according to the *Jin'gui lu,* it is essential for long-life followers to nurture the spirit by maintaining an attitude of awe and care.[5] Awe and care, it says, "are the gateway of life and death, the key to rites and good teaching, the cause of existing and perishing, the root of good and bad fortune, as well as the prime source of all auspicious and inauspicious conditions" (14b). If lost, moreover, "the mind will be confused and not cultivated, the body will be hectic and not at peace, the spirit will be scattered, the *qi* will go beyond all bounds, and will and intention will be deluded" (14b). This condition, which we would today describe as stress, is accordingly the ultimate antithesis to long life and the preservation of health.

To remedy or prevent these problems, the *Pengzu lun* and *Yangsheng lun* both recommend regular exercise of the body, moderation in food and drink, and the cultivation of a serene mind. Beyond this, the *Jin'gui lu* also provides specific exercises that create a sense of balance and help alleviate any problems that may have appeared. The most basic among them is a breathing practice called "guiding the *qi*" (*xingqi* 行氣), which serves to balance the overall energies in the body. The text says,

> Lie down flat on your back, make your hands into fists, keep your feet about 4–5 inches apart and your shoulders about 4–5 inches from the pillow. Breathe softly for

---

5. The same discussion of awe and care appears later in the biography of Sun Simiao (see ch. 4).

four sets of 90 repetitions, i.e., 360 times. Like a soft robe, all your bones and joints begin to dissolve, and you feel the *qi* like a cloudy vapor flowing through the body, pervading the meridians and arteries, moving all around, rich and moist, lubricating and enhancing skin, organs, and intestines. (4b; *Baopuzi* 8; Ware 1966, 139)

In this relaxed, meditative state of deep breathing, the text continues, the *qi* flows smoothly, the body is calm, and the various emotions are dissolved (fig. 6). In deep harmony the Dao can manifest itself. The breath, moreover, should be subtle and long, thereby creating peace among the inner organs and sending all diseases

Fig. 6: A practitioner working with the *qi* while lying on the back. Source: *Chifeng sui*.

into retreat. "The *qi* in perfect alignment, the body light and strong, you reach high old age and can live forever" (5a).

On the other hand, if there is some imbalance in the body, the breathing technique can be modified according to different kinds of exhalations, which include those already mentioned in the medical manuscripts: *chui, xu,* and *hu* (respectively, the sharp, gentle, and open-mouthed expulsion of air). Unlike the manuscripts, though, which prescribe *chui* for ailments in chest or abdomen, *xu* to provide cooling, and *hu* as a supplement to the other breaths, the *Jin'gui lu* defines *chui* as a warming breath to be used for cold conditions, *hu* as a cooling breath to expel heat, and *xu* as a solvent to disperse blockages (6a). In addition, it also lists three further breaths, *xi, he,* and *si,* thus completing the classic list of the Six Breaths (Despeux 2006, 40). It notes that *xi* helps to dispel wind or pain, *he* removes anger and calms the *qi,* and *si* dissolves all sorts of extremes. Knowing how to recognize the various states of the energetic body and to apply the correct breath for each situation thus allows the establishment of perfect balance and harmony, the foundation of health and long life.

As this first exercise indicates, the *Jin'gui lu* addresses people who are interested not only in basic healing but also in extended longevity and even immortality. Its practices represent an advanced and more meditative level of health restoration that can either complement and enhance healing or support the pursuit of higher attainments, such as extending life beyond its natural span, acquiring magical powers, and ascending to the otherworld. In this respect, the exercises in the *Jin'gui lu* perform a function not unlike longevity techniques in later Daoist systems, which too are at the borderline between medical practice and spiritual attainments. In fact, the text represents the first documentation of the more spiritual use of originally medical practices.

This is further borne out in thirty-three exercises listed next in the *Jin'gui lu* that combine deep breathing with various physical moves and positions, each geared to remedy suffering from a certain condition and focusing on a particular group of joints or muscles. Before specifying the practices, the text presents some general guidelines:

> If the disease is in the throat or chest area, use a pillow seven inches high.
>
> If it is below the heart area, use a pillow four inches high.
>
> If it is below the navel, remove the pillow.
>
> To disperse *qi,* breathe in through the nose and out through the mouth.
>
> To tonify *qi,* close the mouth to warm the *qi,* then swallow it.
>
> To relieve diseases of the head, lift the head.
>
> To relieve diseases of the hips or legs, lift the toes.
>
> To relieve diseases of the chest, bend the toes.

To relieve cold, heat, or other imbalances in the stomach, hold the breath in the
belly. (9a)

Then it lists thirty-three healing exercises (9a–13b), in each case specifying the
posture but not providing an obvious order or systematic sequence. However, if
grouped according to posture (as presented below with the original number of
each exercise in parentheses), the practices move systematically through the body
from top to bottom, in each case alleviating tension, reducing obstruction, and
increasing *qi*-flow. They can easily form an integrated routine.

The first group is done while kneeling or sitting upright with pelvis engaged.
It is not entirely clear whether a kneeling or sitting posture is preferred, and all
exercises can be done either way. Since the ancient Chinese, like the modern Japanese, did a lot of kneeling, it may have been more comfortable for them to begin
in this pose. However, the practice should also be efficacious when undertaken in
a cross-legged or other seated posture, as long as the back is straight and the hip
and pelvis are engaged. There are eleven exercises in this group:

KNEEL OR SIT UPRIGHT WITH PELVIS ENGAGED
(*duanzuo shengyao* 端坐生腰):

1. Inhale through the nose and hold the breath. Rock the head back and forth
    slowly thirty times. This will remove all emptiness, confusion, and dizziness
    from the head. Close the eyes while rocking the head (#2).
2. Slowly inhale through the nose while holding the nose with your right hand.
    This removes dizziness from the eyes. Should tears emerge, let go of the breath
    through the nose. It also helps with deafness and with headaches due to
    obstruction. In each case, the appearance of sweat is a good sign (#4).
3. Extend both arms straight up, raising the palms to the ceiling. Inhale through
    the nose and hold the breath for as long as possible. Repeat for seven breaths.
    This is called the King of Shu's Terrace. It removes ailments due to accumula-
    tions of *qi* beneath the waist (#7).
4. Lift the left hand with palm facing up, then do the same with the right.
    Alternate the arms. This removes ailments associated with pain in shoulders
    and back as well as diseases caused by *qi*-obstructions (#9).
5. Stretch the right and left sides. Close the eyes and inhale through the nose.
    This removes head wind. Do this as deeply as you can. Repeat for seven
    breaths, then stop (#11).
6. Inhale through the nose to the count of ten. This removes hunger and thirst
    from the belly and makes you feel full. Once satisfied, stop. If you are not yet
    satisfied, do it again. It also helps to relieve cold in the belly (#12).

7. Raise the right hand with palm up, then take the left hand and hold the left hip. Inhale through the nose. Work as deeply as you can and repeat for seven breaths. This removes cold from the stomach and helps with indigestion (#14). Change sides. This helps with blood contusions (#15).
8. With both hands pushing against the floor, raise the head. Inhale through the nose and swallow the *qi* ten times. This removes fever and helps with injured muscles and removes old skin (#16).
9. If you have a disease on the left, look to the right. Inhale through the nose, then exhale while counting to ten. Close your eyes while you do this (#31).
10. If you have a disease on the right, look to the left. Inhale through the nose, then exhale while counting to ten (#33).
11. If you have a disease beneath the heart, lift the head and look up toward the Sun. Inhale slowly through the nose, then swallow the saliva. Repeat thirty times. Keep your eyes open while you do this (#32).

This set of practices focuses entirely on the upper body—head and neck, eyes and nose, shoulders, arms, and sides—working the various muscles and joints systematically to relieve strain and tension. It targets headaches, dizziness, *qi*-obstructions, and other problems in the torso. The implication is that while doing the exercises, often with eyes closed and breath held, practitioners use their intention to consciously guide the *qi* to the affected area, thus opening the body for healing. Unlike the body movements in the exercises found in the medical manuscripts, body movements here are kept to a minimum, with just the head being turned and the arms being raised. The key emphasis is on breathing correctly, slowly, to the proper count, and for the correct number of repetitions. There is a clear increase in the internal experience of the body as *qi*, a more conscious focus on the energetic substructure of material existence.

More specifically, the first and second practices create a deep calm and sense of balance in the body, while the third exercise, where practitioners raise the arms, activates the lung and large-intestine channels. The fourth is a side stretch, which helps with shoulder tension and also increases lymphatic flow in the body, while the fifth is a side bend, which can be modified with different arm positions, increasing the intensity as the arms are raised higher. The sixth exercise, the very slow inhalation, triggers a parasympathetic response, creating more calmness and internal stability. After that, number seven activates channels running through the torso by placing hands at different energy points, while number eight stretches the neck and opens the chest. The ninth and tenth practices, with their slow exhalation, represent a purging technique; they also serve to dilate the channels on the sides of the neck. The last one opens the Conception Vessel and stomach meridian in the front of the torso and allows the *qi* to flow into the Triple Heater.[6]

The next group aims at conditions in the chest and belly. The exercises are done while sitting. The word for "sit" is still *zuo* as above in "kneel or sit"; however, instead of "upright" the text uses "level," which in most cases seems to indicate sitting with straight back and legs stretched out on the floor.

SIT UP LEVEL (*pingzuo* 平坐):

1. Engage the legs and pelvis, then extend the arms downward to spread the fingers of both hands, pressing them hard against the floor [next to your hips]. Slowly exhale from the mouth and inhale through the nose. This removes pain from chest and lungs. To swallow the *qi,* let it get warm, then close the eyes (#1).
2. Interlace the fingers and wrap them around the knees. Hold the breath and drum the belly for two or three sets of seven. When the *qi* is full, exhale. Measure the practice according to the degree in which the *qi* penetrates the intestines. Do this over ten years and you will look young even in old age (#10).
3. Hold the hands as if shooting a bow, pulling them as far apart as you can. This cures ailments in the four limbs, anxiety, and depression, as well as back problems. It is best when done daily at a set hour (#13).
4. With both hands hold the head, then turn and twist the torso, moving it up and down. This is called Opening the Waist. It removes dullness and heaviness from the body and cures all diseases due to lack of pervasion (#19).

The basic position here is what yoga practitioners call Staff Pose (*dandāsana;* seated with back straight and legs extended forward). The position, especially when supported with the hands pressing into the floor, as described in the first exercise, has the effect of pulling the shoulder blades together, opening the chest, and lengthening the back while releasing the hips and legs. It also dilates the channels running through the hands and purges the breath as it is exhaled through the mouth.

In accordance with this effect, most exercises in this sequence affect the chest and stomach, removing constrictions from the lungs, smoothing the workings of the intestines, and helping to alleviate depression. This choice of ailments also reflects the system of traditional Chinese medicine, according to which the lungs are the yin organ that matches the large intestine and the seat of the excessive emotion of sadness or melancholy. Obstructions in the lungs, intestinal problems, and depression are thus closely related in Chinese medical thinking, and doing this series of seated exercises alleviates the entire complex.

---

6. I am indebted to J. Michael Wood for information on the specific effects of the exercises in this set.

A special aspect is the use of "drumming" in the second practice, the stimulation of the belly with slight taps or hits, which is not only a form of abdominal massage but also activates the energy structure underlying the organs. Still undertaken today, this exercise is now known as Spin the Ball and involves inhaling fully, then rolling *qi* up and down all through the belly and into the kidney area to the accompaniment of gentle taps (Johnson 2000, 686). Thomas Hanna has a very similar practice in lesson 7 of his series The Myth of Aging: lying on their backs, stomachs, or sides, practitioners inhale deeply into either the belly or the chest, then shoot the condensed ball of breath from one into the other, moving up and down or diagonally across. The practice serves to free the central muscles of the torso from tensions and obstructions, creating more freedom in the center of the body and thus in life in general (Hanna 1988, 137–144). A yogic variant that also serves to enhance and move energy around the body is called stomach lock *(uddīyāna bandha)*, practiced while standing and activating the stomach muscles after complete exhalation (Iyengar 1976, 425). In all cases, it is a strengthening, purging, and channel-opening practice.

The same holds true for the third practice in this set: opening the hands into a position of shooting a bow, with one hand bent at the elbow and pulled back while the other stretches horizontally across. Centered on the central cinnabar field at the sternum, the exercise engages the chest muscles and again opens the area of the lungs, thus releasing potential sadness and depression. The rather mechanical pattern breaks through physical barriers into the energetic body and thus serves to balance and harmonize emotional tendencies.

The last item here is a twist of the torso, turning in different directions while holding the head with both hands. Lengthening the spine, this is a chiropractic stretch that also opens the sides of the body, thus releasing any tensions caused by the trauma reflex. As the text says, it removes heaviness from the body, allowing practitioners to let go of stored tensions.

The next series is executed while squatting, a position that spreads the hips and enhances hip openness and flexibility. It requires a bit more exertion than the others, although for people used to squatting the practice may be easy:

SQUAT (*juzuo* 踞坐):

1. Stretch out the right leg while holding the left knee with both hands. Engage the pelvis. Inhale through the nose. Work as deeply as you can and repeat for seven breaths. This removes difficulties in bending and stretching and helps with pain in the calves as well as with rheumatism (#20).

2. Repeat on the other side, then spread the left leg to rest wide on the outside. This removes difficulties in bending and stretching and helps with pain in the

calves. According to one source, it also removes wind and helps with blurry vision and deafness (#21).

3. With both hands embrace the kneecaps. Inhale through the nose. Work as deeply as you can and repeat for seven breaths. This removes rheumatism from the hips and pain from the back (#24).
4. Engage the pelvis and use both hands to pull at the heels. Inhale through the nose. Work as deeply as you can and repeat for seven breaths, always facing the kneecaps. This removes rheumatism and internal spasms (#27).

The effect of these practices, matching the nature of the basic pose as a hip opener, focuses on the hips, lower back, and legs. Activating the hip joint, which is central to numerous body movements, they remove difficulties in bending and stretching and increase overall flexibility. They also help with strain and tension in the back and legs, alleviating the tendency to spasm or toward rheumatism. Energetically they work on the channels that run through the legs, the first two focusing on the bladder and kidney meridians, thus also cleansing anxiety and fear. The third with its hugging of the knees into the chest and the fourth with the strong pull on the heels both open the back of the torso, expand the chest, and—since they also compress the belly—force the breath into the back and sides of the lungs. As practitioners learn to open the back to the breath, they can push it down to alleviate pain in the lower back and hips. Breathing in this manner is also a form of reversed breathing. This not only creates a sympathetic nervous response with increased enthusiasm and will toward activity, but sets the stage for immortality practice where breathing tends to be reversed.

All remaining exercises in the *Jin'gui lu* are done while lying down, either on the back, the belly, or one side. The first group centers on calming the nervous system and strengthening the abdominal muscles. It includes eight exercises.

LIE FLAT ON YOUR BACK (*zhengyan wo* 正偃臥):

1. Slowly exhale through the mouth and inhale through the nose. This removes pressure from having eaten too fast. Afterward, swallow the *qi* in small gulps. After ten swallows, let its warmth be your measure. If the *qi* is cold, it will make people retch and cause stomach pain. Inhale through the nose, counting to seven, ten, and up to a hundred, until you hear a big rumbling in your stomach. This will remove wayward *qi* and tonify proper *qi* (#5).
2. Raise both legs and arms straight up. Inhale through the nose. Work as deeply as you can and repeat for seven breaths. Then shake and rock the legs thirty times. This removes cold from the chest and legs, helps with rheumatism in the body, and relieves coughs (#17).

3. Bend the knees and bring them in toward the head. With both hands hold the knees and engage the pelvis. Inhale through the nose. Work as deeply as you can and repeat for seven breaths. This removes fatigue, fevers, and pain in the thighs (#18).

4. Extend both hands [with shoulders off the floor] and let them intertwine each other as if they were kneading cinnabar sand in a bag. This will reduce dampness in the body and relieve difficulty in urination and heaviness in the lower abdomen. If there is heat in the belly, exhale through the mouth and inhale through the nose. Repeat ten times, then stop. There is no need to swallow in small gulps. If there is no heat in the belly, practice for seven breaths, then swallow the warm *qi* ten times and stop (#22).

5. Stretch both calves and both hands, allowing the heels to face each other. Inhale through the nose. Work as deeply as you can and repeat for seven breaths. This removes dead skin, as well as cold and pain in the legs and calves (#25).

6. Twist both hands and both calves to the left, allowing the heels to meet. Inhale through the nose. Work as deeply as you can and repeat for seven breaths. This removes stomach ailments from undigested food (#26).

7. Stretch out the arms and legs, with palms and soles facing upward. Inhale through the nose. Work as deeply as you can and repeat for seven breaths. This removes tension and urgency from the belly (#28).

8. Hook the heel of your left foot over the first two toes of your right foot. Inhale through the nose. Work as deeply as you can and repeat for seven breaths. This removes cramps (#29). Repeat on the other side. This removes rheumatism (#30). If the heel is off and you cannot reach the toes of the opposite foot, use a stick to complete the pose.

Working the abdominal muscles systematically to include their lower, central, and upper sections as well as the sides of the body, this sequence provides a general core strengthening while individual practices serve to release various tensions and ailments from the stomach area. The exercises aid digestion and relieve heartburn, ease difficulty in urination, and alleviate fatigue. Since they also involve leg movements, they can in addition help relieve pain in the thighs, rheumatic pain, and cramps.

A different kind of release is found in the next group of two practices, which are performed face-down.

LIE DOWN ON YOUR BELLY (*fuwo* 腹臥):

1. Remove the pillow and lift the feet [legs bent at knees]. Inhale through the nose for four, then exhale through the nose for four. At the end of each exhalation, let the *qi* come back to the nose very subtly, so softly in fact that the nose cannot feel it. This removes heat from the body and cures ailments associated with back pain (#8).

2. Turn your face to one side and press both heels against your hips. Inhale through the nose. Work as deeply as you can and repeat for seven breaths. This removes tension and pain in the legs, muscle knots, and leg acidity (#23).

Unlike many other exercises, these two provide general relief of tension in the body and a relaxing opening of the spine, the body's central axis. The first, especially, is reminiscent of a preparatory and restorative practice recommended by yoga teacher Donna Farhi, called Spinal Elongation and Riding the Breath. Lying face-down, practitioners are encouraged to feel how "the spine elongates and condenses in unison with the breath," creating a central mobility that allows them to move from the core of the body, whether standing, sitting, or in a yoga posture (2000, 45). Farhi also notes that "the release and elongation of the spine comes through relaxation rather than effort," echoing the Chinese contention that the ideal state is one in which the *qi* flows smoothly and freely without conscious pushing or pulling. She describes its release as being "like opening up the gate to a dam: As you open the gate the current of breath surges through the spine. All that is left to do is to ride the wave and let the breath move the spine" (Farhi 2000, 45). When practiced regularly, the exercise will release physical and mental tension, improve the immune system, and allow the body to heal itself (240).

The last two exercises listed in the *Jin'gui lu* are executed while lying on the right and left sides of the body. Breathing in these positions provides general relief for certain areas. As the text says,

LIE DOWN ON YOUR SIDE (*xiewo* 脅臥):
1. On your left: Exhale from the mouth and inhale through the nose. This removes all signs of unresolved blockages that have accumulated beneath the heart (#3).
2. On your right: Inhale through the nose and exhale through the mouth in small puffs, counting to ten. Then rub both hands together to generate heat and massage the stomach with them. This will make the *qi* descend and leave. It also removes pain from the hips and the skin, and helps with depression (#6).

The complete set of thirty-three exercises thus works all different parts of the body, whether listed in sequence according to basic position or taken individually to remedy various ailments. The dominant emphasis is on the flow of energy through the body—guided and controlled through the breath, activated and enhanced through specific postures, and consciously worked through directional intention. All three major factors in healing and exercise—body, mind, and breath—are strongly present in medieval healing exercises, allowing practitioners to balance their *qi* and increase their health as suitable for their specific situations.

Empowerment through *Qi*

Having gained a healthy and vigorous constitution through healing exercises and *qi*-circulation, fourth-century practitioners of Daoyin who wished to develop further could embark on various regimens of *qi*-management that would eventually lead to a strong personal empowerment, expressed in control over the body, which would cease aging and not need food and drink, and in control over the outside world, which could be manipulated at will through a variety of magical powers. The practices listed for these advanced goals demand a great deal more dedication than the occasional healing and represent a step away from ordinary society and the pleasures of the senses. It is thus not surprising that the *Yangsheng yaoji* offers only tiny glimpses of this level of practice and that most detailed information comes from the more technical texts, the *Baopuzi* and the *Jin'gui lu*.

To begin, practitioners have to arrange their schedule to fit their regimen. They have to get up early in accordance with the general rule, expressed in practically all Daoist and longevity texts since antiquity, that the universe like the human body is a living and breathing entity (Maspero 1981, 500). Creating the patterns of the circadian rhythm that govern human wake and sleep cycles, the cosmos has an inhalation or living breath (*shengqi* 生氣), which is dominant from midnight to noon, and an exhalation or dead breath (*siqi* 死氣), which controls the period between noon and midnight. For example, the *Baopuzi* says, "The circulating of *qi* should be undertaken at an hour when the *qi* is alive and not when it is dead" (Ware 1966, 139). Similarly, the *Jin'gui lu* notes that one should "always practice after midnight [and before noon] in the period of living *qi*.... In this *qi*-practice, the time after noon and before midnight is called the period of dead *qi*. Do not practice then" (8a). Most exercises are accordingly scheduled to occur in the hours after midnight and around dawn, enhancing the quality of *qi* in the body through the rising energies of nature—a tendency that has continued to the present day, when most practitioners of qigong and taiji quan go to the parks to exercise in the early morning.

Beyond the hours of midnight and dawn, noon and dusk are also auspicious. Thus the *Yangsheng yaoji* notes that healing exercises and *qi*-cultivation should be undertaken several times a day for best results, preferably at the four hours *zi*, *mao*, *wu*, and *you* (midnight, dawn, noon, and dusk) (Stein 1999, 183). The *Jin'gui lu* echoes this and adds some subtle modifications based on the seasons and specific physical conditions. It says,

> For all absorption of *qi*, use the hours *zi*, *wu*, *mao*, and *you*—with certain exceptions:
> in the third month of winter, the *zi* hour [midnight] is not good because it is too cold;

in the third month of summer, the *wu* hour [noon] is not good because it is too hot. In all cases, adjust your intention to slow breathing.

Also, if there is great cold in your belly, take in *qi* in the morning and at noon. If there is great heat, take it in at midnight and dawn. To practice in the third month when it is very cold, place a brazier in the room to warm it to get a sense of balance and harmony in your belly. When there is extreme heat in the summer, take in the *qi* of the moonlight so you feel fresh and cool. (8ab)

Another version of practice, also found in the *Jin'gui lu* and the *Baopuzi,* and later taken up in the *Taixi qijing* 胎息氣經 (Qi Scripture on Embryo Respiration, *DZ* 819) of the Tang dynasty, is to practice throughout the day but to adjust the number of repetitions in accordance with the dominant hour:

first light: 7 x 7	sunrise: 6 x 6	daybreak: 5 x 5
midmorning: 4 x 4	noon: 9 x 9	midafternoon: 8 x 8
last light: 7 x 7	sunset: 6 x 6	dusk: 5 x 5
midevening: 4 x 4	midnight: 9 x 9	cock crow: 8 x 8
(2a; *Baopuzi* 15; Ware 1966, 245)[7]		

This subtler use of *qi* in accordance with the cosmic patterns occurs mainly in the advanced stages of Daoyin, where practices serve to make the body increasingly independent of food and drink, allowing practitioners to completely "avoid grain" (*bigu* 辟穀), that is, live without outside nourishment for prolonged periods (Arthur 2006, 91). For this, in addition to guiding the *qi* as described earlier, they hold the breath for extended periods—technically known as "enclosing the *qi*" (*biqi* 閉氣)—stimulate *qi* through various modes of self-massage, and swallow it as saliva.

The *Jin'gui lu* provides a basic description of *qi*-circulation with holding the breath:

Set yourself up in a secluded chamber, with doors closed and curtains drawn, and with a restful bed, warm and secure. The pillow should be two and a half inches high and support your neck so your head is level with your body. Lie down flat on your back, close your eyes, make your hands into fists, and hold your breath. Allow the breath to

---

7. The adjustment of practice to the twelve double-hours of the day also echoes the contention in Chinese medicine that each of the twelve meridians has a time of day when it is dominant and when it can either be treated most effectively or is most vulnerable. See Kohn 2005, 57. For various other hour systems used in *qi*-cultivation, see Maspero 1981, 501. On the *Taixi qijing*, see Schipper and Verellen 2004, 368.

stop in your chest and keep it so quiet that a down feather held before your nostrils will not move. Count to three hundred. Your ears will no longer hear, your eyes will no longer see, there will be no thoughts in your mind. Then exhale very slowly. (7b)

The text clearly states that the required prerequisite is a moderate and even eremitic lifestyle. It notes that if one eats "raw and cold food, the five strong vegetables, meat and fish, and tends to be given to joy and anger, sadness and rage," the practice will not work and it will be next to impossible to hold the breath for anywhere near the required period. On the contrary, the technique might actually do harm, increasing the "ailments of *qi* as it battles and goes against the highest course." To do the *qi*-guiding properly, it is best to practice holding gradually, beginning with "counting to three, five, seven, and nine," and eventually going on to 120 or more, in all cases counting silently and without moving the lips (8a).

The *Baopuzi* has a similar description, noting that what is counted during the holding period is the number of heartbeats and that it is optimal to go on to much higher numbers, even into the thousands. It says,

> Those who begin to study *qi*-circulation must inhale through the nose and hold the breath. While it is held fast, the number of heartbeats is counted to 120. Then it is expelled gently through the mouth. Neither when expelling nor while inhaling the breath should you with your own ears hear it enter or leave. Much of it must always enter, and little should leave. Set a feather on the nose and mouth and exhale without making it move. Then increase the time of retention in proportion to your practice. The number of heartbeats should gradually go up to 1,000. When it reaches that, from being an old man you will become young again. (ch. 8; Ware 1966, 138)

As Maspero points out, this is only one method of counting the time of holding. Others include marking dots as big as grains of rice or dropping a set number of sticks. Some texts even suggest that it is best to have someone else there to keep track of the count (1981, 464n17). In Western terms, about 80 heartbeats make one minute, so a count of 120 would mean holding the breath for about ninety seconds and a count of 300 about three or four minutes, which seems not unreasonable. Moving into the thousands, however, practitioners may well enter states of asphyxiation and oxygen deprivation, leading to a state of "ears no longer hearing and eyes no longer seeing," as indicated in the *Jin'gui jing*. More generally, holding the breath for limited periods is also practiced in yogic *pranayāma* and other forms of self-cultivation. A key method to establishing control over the breathing patterns of the body and thus the autonomic nervous system, it increases diaphragmatic flexibility and enhances breath capacity. It also increases tranquility and calmness of mind, since for the time of holding, the vibrational frequencies in the body stabilize and no mental input takes place. It is important, however, to increase the holding times slowly and carefully, since overlong holding will trigger a sympathetic nervous response and can lead to renewed stress.[8]

Not only concentrating and holding the *qi* on the inside, practitioners also follow regimens that involve stimulating and enhancing it on the outside and in less subtle form. One such method, as already noted in the *Yangsheng yaoji,* is the practice of self-massage, again usually undertaken in the early morning. Practitioners sit facing east, rub the hands together to generate heat, then press them over the eyes for two sets of seven repetitions. Next they massage the face from top to bottom to eliminate pathogenic *qi* and increase facial glow. They also rub from the forehead to the top of the head for two sets of nine repetitions in an exercise called Preserving the Niwan 泥丸 (palace at the center of the head). They may also cross the hands over the head to take hold of the opposite ear to pull the ears up and down for two sets of seven in a practice that will prevent deafness. Or they may rub the entire body from top to bottom to do a so-called Dry Wash (*ganxi* 乾洗), which eliminates obstructions, wind invasions, and headaches (*Ishinpō* 23.23ab; Stein 1999, 184–185).

Yet another method that helps to establish control over the *qi* is swallowing the saliva. According to the *Yangsheng yaoji,* in a room that is neither too cold nor too hot practitioners should begin by accumulating saliva in the mouth while breathing in, then rinse the mouth with a breath-saliva mixture called Jade Spring and swallow it consciously. Repeating this three times, one should click one's teeth for two sets of seven, thereby refining one's essence and enhancing *qi* (*Ishinpō* 23.22b–23a; Stein 1999, 183–184).

Beyond general *qi*-enhancement, a more potent reason to swallow the saliva is that it will replace the need for food and drink. As the *Baopuzi* points out, this can be very effective. Once, when the daughter of a local official was four years old, a major disaster struck her hometown, and her parents had to abandon her in an old tomb. Three years later the family returned to collect her bones for proper burial. But they were in for a surprise:

> When they went and looked into the tomb, they found the girl still sitting there. On seeing her parents, she recognized them and was very happy, but they first thought she was a ghost. Only when they entered the tomb did they discover that she was in-

deed not dead. When asked how she had survived, she replied that when her initial food supplies were exhausted she first became very hungry. On noticing a creature in the corner that stretched its neck and swallowed its breath, she tried doing the same thing and became less and less hungry. (ch. 3; Ware 1966, 57; Reid 1989, 174)

The creature turned out to be a large tortoise, an animal known for its exceptional longevity. By imitating its breathing and swallowing techniques, the little girl survived—in a manner also followed by many would-be immortals.

The *Jin'gui jing* similarly emphasizes that swallowing saliva is a way of "eating and drinking spontaneously." As adepts breathe softly and deeply and swallow the breath mixed with saliva, they "will never be hungry again" and can avoid grains for three to seven days. If they do not get dizzy during this time, they can extend the period for as long as three weeks, finding all the while that "*qi* and vigor increase daily." After reaching this level, "if you want to eat, you can eat, and if you don't want to eat, you can just breathe" (3b). The text describes the practice as follows:

> Close the mouth and inhale. After taking in *qi,* swallow it. Do this 360 times and you won't lose the method again. The more you do this, the better. If you can do it 1,000 times in one day, you can start to reduce your food intake, and after ten days you can give up food completely. After that, *qi* will always come in and not leave again. And if you maintain the intention that the *qi* be always full, you will find no need to eat for three days and yet feel satisfied in your stomach.
>
> Should you be hungry or need to urinate or have sex, pick nine ripe dates and take them one at a time in the morning and evening to satisfy your need for sustenance. However, if you don't think of eating, you will have no such need. Should you use the dates, on the other hand, always keep the pit in your mouth for a while to accumulate more *qi*. This will also improve the saliva and other bodily fluids. (3b–4a)[9]

With the help of guiding, holding, and swallowing the *qi*, practitioners can thus gain a great deal of control over their bodies, becoming independent of outer nourishment and being able to live on pure *qi* for extended periods of time. They also gain the ability to project their *qi* outward and control natural elements and animals through their exhalation. The *Baopuzi* says, "Exhale *xu* at water, and it will flow backwards for several yards; *xu* at fire, and it will go out; *xu* at tigers or wolves, and they will crouch down motionless; *xu* at snakes, and they will coil up in awe" (ch. 8; Ware 1966, 139).

---

9. A number of later texts echo these early practices. For a collection and translation, see Huang and Wurmbrand 1987.

In addition, this potent exhalation can be used for healing. It can stop bleeding if someone has been wounded by a weapon and eliminate the poison from a snake or scorpion bite. More than that, the method can be applied over a distance, so that just the healing intention of the mind, coupled with a concentrated *qi*-exhalation and a pointing gesture with the hand—left hand for a male subject, right hand for a female—is sufficient to effect a cure. "People will get better immediately even if they are hundreds of miles away" (Ware 1966, 139).

The power of *qi*, moreover, also extends to supernatural entities and demons. The *Yangsheng yaoji* points out that curling the hands into fists and enclosing the *qi* can create an inner power that will keep demons at bay (Stein 1999, 184). The *Baopuzi* notes,

> By avoiding grain one can become immune to weapons, exorcize demons, neutralize poisons, and cure illnesses. On entering a mountain, one can render savage beasts harmless; when crossing a stream, one will not be attacked by dragons. There will be no fear when plague strikes; and should a crisis or difficulty suddenly arise, one will know how to cope. (ch. 6; Ware 1966, 114)
>
> Sometimes evil demons or mountain sprites attack. They throw tiles or stones or burn our homes. At times they can be seen going to and fro, while at other times only their sounds or voices can be heard. However, when practitioners use their *qi*-powers against them, all their activity ceases. (ch. 5; Ware 1966, 107)

The magical or supernatural powers acquired by successful practitioners of *qi* in many ways are similar to the abilities of shamans. They can heal the sick, exorcise demons or beasts, make rain or stop it, foretell the future, prevent disasters, call upon wild animals as helpers, and remain unharmed by water and fire, heat and cold. Control over the body, a subtle harmony with the forces of nature, and an easy relationship with gods and spirits, ghosts and demons are important characteristics of successful followers of longevity and immortality practice.

In addition, the *qi*-powers may also involve feats that are more reminiscent of the powers of sorcerers and wizards. As pointed out in biographical notes in the *Baopuzi* as well as in Ge Hong's collection of biographies of immortals (*Shenxian zhuan* 神仙傳; see Güntsch 1988; Campany 2002), masters of *qi* can be shape changers who can appear in any form they please. They can multiply themselves into many different people, be present in more than one place at the same time. They can become visible and invisible at will and travel thousands of miles in an instant. They can make rivers flow backward and mountains tumble. Plants, animals, and people die at their command and come back to life if they tell them to do so. They transport buildings to far-off places, open up mountains and reveal grottoes. In all these arts, successful practitioners take their control of *qi* to the utmost, becoming one with the core power of the universe and essentially divine in nature. They go beyond humanity not just by separating themselves from ordinary society and attaining superb health and extended longevity, but even more so by perfecting their control over the energetic constellations of the universe.

The Divine Connection

The goal of becoming divine and perfecting control over self and the outside world was also central to the healing practices of Highest Clarity followers, but with some important differences. Unlike other adepts of the fourth century, their main focus was not so much on transforming the body but on their relation with various deities, both outside in the greater universe and deep within the body. To activate this divine connection, they used physical moves and various forms of *qi*-manipulation as part of their daily routine, especially after getting up in the morning. In addition, they integrated religious and ritual activities, such as specific guided visualizations of divine manifestations as well as the use of talismans and incantations—sacred strips of paper covered with celestial script in red ink that tallied with the divine powers of the otherworld (fig. 7) and lengthy prayers that invoked specific deities and expressed the seeker's aspirations to immortality.

Rather than healing or acquiring magical powers, their main reason for doing these practices was the prevention of aging in conjunction with the improvement of vision and hearing to allow a subtler perception of messages from, and visions of, the otherworld. Then again, Highest Clarity was different in that all its practices, including exercises and self-massages, were obtained through revelation from the gods. As a result, and reflecting a feature that is common to channeled literature worldwide, the same or similar methods are often recorded in numerous different formulations and represented as originating from different deities.

Thankfully, Highest Clarity practitioners were not only dedicated seekers but also well-organized recorders, so that their exercise methods are today collected in one key text, the *Xiwangmu baoshen qiju jing* 西王母寶神起居經 (The Queen Mother's Scripture on Treasuring the Spirit Whether Rising or Resting, *DZ* 1319; abbr. *Qiju jing*), supplemented by similar texts, such as the *Shangqing wozhong jue* 上清握中訣 (Highest Clarity Instructions to Be Kept in Hand, *DZ* 140) and the *Yanshou chishu* 延壽赤書 (Red Book of Master Yanshou, *DZ* 877; Robinet 1984, 2:359–362; Schipper and Verellen 2004, 620, 628). Presenting practices revealed by a number of deities, including the Queen Mother of the West, Wei Huacun, and Lady Wang, as well as the Green Lad, the God of Ninefold Flo-

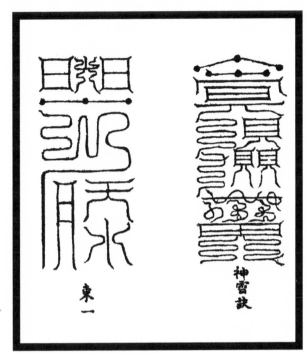

Fig. 7: Purifying
talismans of Highest
Clarity. Source:
Shangqing lingbao dafa.

rescence, and Lord Pei, they cite various major Highest Clarity scriptures. Although their compilation may date from as late as the Tang dynasty, the works contain information on practices that formed part of the original revelations. This is documented by the inclusion of highly similar instructions in chapters 9 and 10 of the *Zhen'gao* 真誥 (Declarations of the Perfected, *DZ* 1016), a well-documented and systematic collection of original Highest Clarity materials by Tao Hongjing 陶弘景 (456–536), the first official patriarch of the school.

Revelations of practices took place in a trance setting, with a medium—such as the oft-praised Yang Xi—acting as interlocutor for the deities and providing descriptions of their looks, actions, and words that were then collected into integrated scriptures. The *Qiju jing* gives one example of such a revelation, telling how the Ruler of Fates (Siming 司命) descended to bring practical advice:

> In the third year of the reign period Flourishing Peace [375 C.E.], in the night of the 4th day of the 7th month, the Ruler of Fates, Lord of the Eastern Minister, descended with seven retainers. As they entered the house, they were seen to hold flowery banners, called Numinous Banners of Tenfold Elimination. One of them carried a bag ornamented with metal rings. Three others were holding white ivory caskets that

contained sacred writings. Yet another came with a fire bell made of flaming gold. All retainers were clad in vermilion robes.

The Ruler of Fates was very impressive, but only a little more so than his retainers. He wore an embroidered skirt of green brocade under a purple feather cape, and his head was covered with a hibiscus headdress. As he entered, his retainers stepped forward and set up a Throne of Fates for him. He sat down and we talked for a long time. (14b)

A typical exercise that would evolve from such a revelation is the following:

When you get up in the morning, always calm your breath and sit up straight, then interlace your fingers and massage the nape of your neck. Next, lift the face and look up, press the hands against the neck while moving the head back. Do this three or four times, then stop.

This harmonizes essence, increases blood flow, and prevents wind and bad *qi* from entering. Practiced over a long time it will keep you free from disease and death.

Next bend and straighten the body; extend the hands in the four directions [up, sideways, forward, back]; bend back and stretch out the sides; and shake out the hundred joints. Do each of these three times. (*Qiju jing* 6a)

Characterized by even less body movement and an even higher internal awareness and attention to *qi,* this provides a general outline of basic upper-body motions. It is, moreover, the only exercise sequence in the text, all other practices focusing either on self-massages for strengthening eyes and ears or on the visualization of cosmic energies to create a deeper connection to the universe. Yet its presence shows that Highest Clarity followers were aware of the Daoyin tradition and used physical exercises in preparation for spiritual exploits.

Eyes and ears are key elements in the pursuit of perfection. "The gateway to pervasive numen, they are essential for all success and failure, life and death" (3b). For daily improvement of eyesight and the eventual ability to see in the dark, the text recommends that one "rub the small hollow outside the eyebrows three times, massage underneath the eyes and above the cheekbones as well as around the ears thirty times, and push all the way up to the forehead nine times" (4a). These exercises, which stimulate key pressure points around the eyes, are similar to practices still undertaken in contemporary China and prescribed for elementary- and middle-school children.

Another form of eye massage is accompanied by the visualization of divine *qi* and the invocation of the deities of the eyes. As the *Qiju jing* says,

Every day, in the morning and evening, close your eyes, face your birth direction, then rub the hands to generate heat and rub the eyes to the right and left all the way to below the ears, allowing the palms to meet time and again in the middle of the forehead. Repeat nine times.

Next, visualize a cloudy vapor in the eyes in three colors: purple, red, and yellow. Each sinks down and enters the ears. Observing this for a long time, recite the following incantation:

> Oh, Eye Lads of the Three Clouds,
> Perfected Lords of Both Eyes:
> Be radiant and light in bringing forth essence,
> Open and pervasive as imperial gods.
>
> Oh, Great Mystery of Cloudy Righteousness,
> Jade Numen of the Expanded Chapters:
> Preserve and enhance my two towers [ears],
> Open and spread my nine gates [orifices].
>
> Let my hundred joints respond and echo
> And my various fluids return to the Niwan Palace.
> Allow my body to ascend to the jade palaces above
> And let me rank among the highest perfected. (7a)

This is a good example of a Highest Clarity incantation. It begins by addressing the deities most immediately involved with the current practice, praising them and imploring them to bring their good energies to the practitioner. It then expands the prayer to gods of related organs and wider areas of the body, to eventually come to the nub of the matter, the wish for ascension to the otherworld and a proper ranking among the celestial perfected (fig. 8).

The exercise is also typical in that it involves a visualization, the key meditative practice of Highest Clarity (Robinet 1993, 125). In another variation of this, practitioners exhale various negative energies by visualizing them in different colors, then inhale positive powers by seeing them located in the body in bright radiance. They begin by "seeing the sun like a chicken egg in the Niwan Palace," then exhale "corpse qi," visualized as black; "old qi," seen as white; and "death qi," seen as azure (*Qiju jing* 13b). After doing this over a period of time to make sure all these negative energies are gone, they "inhale very slowly, taking in yellow qi four times," visualizing it as arising from a bright sun in the Niwan center. Following this, they bring the sun deeper into the body:

Fig. 8: A Highest Clarity practitioner visualizing and invoking the gods.
Source: *Yuyi jielin*.

> Visualize the Sun-*qi* again in the Niwan center. Let it reach down to the ears and emerge
> through them. See how it assembles before your mouth, about nine inches in front of
> your face. Make it subtly clearer to the eyes, so you can see it well. Then, using the sun,
> take in red *qi* seven times. Pause. Swallow the saliva three times. Get up and shake your
> four limbs, bending and stretching the body. This will make the joints and arteries
> harmonious. To conclude, visualize the saliva to be swallowed as green *qi*. (13b)

The text adds that the same exercise can also be done at night by visualizing the
Moon in the Niwan center, but that moon work should be done only during its wax-
ing and not during its waning period, that is, only in the first two weeks of the lunar
month (14a). The practice serves to enhance the cosmic energy in the body, allowing
practitioners to join the divinities in their very own energetic constellation.

Over a period of extended practice, Highest Clarity practitioners gradually
transform their bodies into a divine replica of the universe, complete with palaces,

towers, passages, grottoes, and numerous divinities. These divinities can be quite simple and mundane, such as the gods of the eyes or the lords of the head and hair. For example, the *Qiju jing* says that every morning when practitioners comb their hair, they should face the direction associated with the cyclical sign of their birth and chant an incantation addressed to the gods Niwan and Xuanhua 玄華, resident deities in the head, to "preserve my essence and let me live long" (7b). Beyond this, deities can also be more potent and complex, such as the Perfected of the Yellow Court (Huangting zhenren 黃庭真人) or the Three Ones (Sanyi 三一), cosmic potencies that have to be carefully cultivated so they can exude their beneficial presence.

As described in the *Jin'gui lu*, the God of Central Yellow is activated in a *qi*-exercise that helps the avoidance of grain. The text says,

> Be aware of a yellow *qi* in your belly, rich and abundant. Then find that there is a spirit being present, three inches tall in a yellow robe and standing tall like a statue. With each hand he leads yet another figure, also clad in yellow.
>
> When you see them clearly, call silently out to the central figure: "Perfected of the Yellow Court, having arisen in me, become myself!" Then use the sweet spring and pure liquor [of saliva] to tonify your inner elixir. Imagine all you might want to eat and drink and have it come before you. Practice this swallowing always at cock crow and dusk. Also, if you ever get hungry, face the Sun and do this, and the hunger will go away. (4ab)

Similarly, the Three Ones are made present by visualizing them in the three cinnabar or elixir fields:

> The three cinnabar fields are the upper, called Niwan Palace 泥丸宮, in the center of the head between the eyebrows; the middle, called Scarlet Palace 絳宮, in the heart; and the lower [Ocean of *Qi*], beneath the navel. Always think of the divinity Red Child 赤子 in the three Cinnabar Fields. If you keep them there, the perfected infant and thus the Dao will remain always present. Like this, if you guard the One, the myriad affairs are done. (6ab)[10]

---

10. The Three Ones are central to Highest Clarity practice. For a detailed description of their nature and activation, see Andersen 1980; Kohn 1993, 204–214. Other texts on Highest Clarity body gods include the *Huangting jing* 黃庭經 (Yellow Court Scripture, *DZ* 332) and the *Laozi zhongjing* 老子中經 (Central Scripture of Laozi, *DZ* 1168), both of the fourth century. On the nature and date of the *Huangting jing,* see Robinet 1993, 55–56; Mugitani 1982; Schipper 1975a; Schipper and Verellen 2004, 96–97. For partial translations and studies, see Kohn 1993, 181–188; Kroll 1996; Saso 1995. On the *Laozi zhongjing,* see Schipper 1979; Schipper and Verellen 2004, 92–94.

Following the early example of sexual manuals, which were the first to couch physical phenomena in lyrical terms (Lo 2000, 35), the text calls for maintaining a cosmic awareness of the body in Highest Clarity practice; this awareness is aided by a specified nomenclature for the various body parts, which cease to be just ordinary eyebrows, foreheads, and noses, and instead become numinous entities and wondrous caverns. A set of instructions for facial massage accordingly reads,

> With your hands spread over the sides of the Flowery Court, roll [the fingers] and extend harmony to Heavenly Perfection. Moving upward, enter with spirit into the Luscious Chamber, where the Jade Valley meets the Heavenly Mountains. Further inward, the Mountain Spring is mysterious and numinous to behold. Practicing thus, the myriad demons naturally find destruction, and you can live forever without dying. (*Qiju jing* 2a)

Thankfully, the text provides an explanation for all these technical terms, noting that "Flowery Court" indicates the upper eyelids, "Heavenly Perfection" refers to the inner end of the eyebrows, and "Luscious Chamber" is the third eye at the base of the forehead. The "Jade Valley" is the nose, the "Heavenly Mountains" indicate the forehead, and the "Mountain Spring" is the area beneath the nostrils, the point in the body where pathogenic *qi* can most easily enter (9b).[11] In other words, practitioners are to place their fingers over their eyebrows, rub the inner corners of the eyes, push toward the third eye and the area where the nose meets the forehead while envisioning the opening of the nostrils below as an entrance into the caverns of the sacred Mount Kunlun in the head. All this serves to create a cosmic landscape in the most personal and intimate sphere of the practitioner, transforming the body—the very root of mundane, earthly existence—into a divine realm that participates actively in the transformations and the eternity of the Dao.

By the early middle ages, therefore, the practice of healing exercises has expanded widely and taken on various new forms and dimensions. Far from being merely a series of exercises that bend and stretch the body to relieve ailments and release tensions, it has become part of the official culture of moderation, the preferred method of hermits to eliminate hunger and thirst and defend themselves against demons, and among Daoist practitioners—in combination with various devotional activities—a preparatory technique for the attainment of otherworldly visions and the ascension into heaven. In this process, healing exercises also came

---

11. Other technical terms mentioned in the *Qiju jing* include Upper Prime for the small hollow outside the eyebrows, Open Brightness for the area underneath the eyes and above the cheeks (4b), Human Center for the nose, and Spirit Pond or Spirit Soul Terrace for the area inside the nostrils (9a).

to include a greater and subtler awareness of the breath, meditative techniques of guiding and holding the *qi,* self-massages of the face and various other body parts, as well as the recognition of *qi*-fluctuations in time and space, the harnessing of *qi*-power in influencing self and others (including animals and demons), and the activation of *qi* in the form of body gods and interior pathways and palaces. What began as a medical routine to prevent aging and cure diseases, in the varied setting of fourth-century southern aristocracy, has thus grown into a complex and multi-layered phenomenon, its different parts at variance with one another yet already showing the potential for the integration and systematization that would soon come to the fore.

Chapter Three

The Exercise Classic

The first such systematization of healing exercises and routines appears in the *Daoyin jing,* the only text in the Daoist canon that deals exclusively with physical practices. Its full title is *Taiqing daoyin yangsheng jing* (Great Clarity Scripture on Healing Exercises and Nourishing Life, *DZ* 818; see Despeux 1989). Like the *Jin'gui lu* ascribed to Master Jingli or Jinghei of the fourth century (see Loon 1984, 130), the text is recouped in two shorter versions in the Daoist canon, one contained in the eleventh-century encyclopedia *Yunji qiqian* 雲笈七籤 (Seven Tablets in a Cloudy Satchel, *DZ* 1032; ch. 34) and another found in the compendium *Daoshu* 道樞 (Pivot of the Dao, *DZ* 1017; ch. 28; trl. Huang and Wurmbrand 1987, 2:134–143) by the Daoist master and inner alchemist Zeng Zao 曾造 (d. 1155).[1]

How does this classic advance the practice of healing exercises? What does it add to the tradition? How does it join its various elements? And how does it provide a stepping-stone toward the fully integrated exercise, longevity, and immortality system that emerges fully in the Tang? Let us begin by looking more closely at the text.

The Text

The *Daoyin jing* stands out from previous medical practices and animal forms in that it presents exercise sequences associated with four major ancient immortals, all with first biographies in the Han-dynasty *Liexian zhuan* 列仙傳 (Immortals' Biographies, *DZ* 294; trl. Kaltenmark 1953). Important legendary figures of the Daoist tradition, they are Pengzu 彭祖, who allegedly ate only cinnamon and lived for hundreds of years through the Xia and Shang dynasties; Chisongzi 赤松子 or Master Redpine, the Lord of Rain under the mythical Divine Farmer (Shennong 神農), best known for his magical powers of riding the wind (fig. 9); Ningfengzi 寧封子 or Master Ning (the Lord of Fire under the Yellow Emperor), who was immune to heat and burning; and Wangzi Qiao 王子蹻 who could travel through the universe at will. As

---

1. A full translation of this important text will be included in a future project (working title: "A Sourcebook in Chinese Longevity").

different methods and sequences are ascribed to them, it is quite possible that these four ancient masters were representatives of different schools (Despeux 1989, 230).

The first mention of the *Daoyin jing* occurs in chapter 19 of the *Baopuzi*, the bibliographic list of Ge Hong's library, but it is doubtful whether this early scripture is identical with the text surviving today. An indication that at least parts are indeed of the fourth century is found in the fact that the *Daoyin jing* contains the same list of thirty-three exercises as the *Jin'gui lu* (9a–13a), combining deep breathing with various moves and positions. Most of the *Daoyin jing* materials, however, surface only from the seventh century onward. They closely match a

Fig. 9: A portrait of Master Redpine dressed in leaves. Source: *Zengxiang liexian zhuan*.

section of the *Zhubing yuanhou lun* of the early seventh century (Despeux 1989, 229);[2] the Exercise part of the *Yangxing yanming lu*, which probably dates from the mid-seventh century (Stein 1999, 185; Maspero 1981, 542–552); the *Shesheng zuanlu* 攝生纂錄 (Comprehensive Record on Preserving Life, *DZ* 578; trl. Huang and Wurmbrand 1987, 2:75–90) by Wang Zhongqiu 王仲丘 of the mid-Tang, which lists six seated exercises ascribed to Master Redpine (Schipper and Verellen 2004, 356); the *Huanzhen neiqi fa* 幻真內氣法 (Master Huanzhen's Method of Internal *Qi*, *DZ* 828, *Yunji qiqian* 60.14a–25b), also from the mid-Tang, which has two methods of *qi*-control (Maspero 1981, 461n3);[3] and various fragments of the *Yangsheng yaoji* as found in the ninth-century *Ishinpō*. Here the *Daoyin jing* is associated especially with the name of Master Ning, again casting some doubt on whether it is the same text that we have today (Stein 1999, 141).

From these citations and cross-listings of practices it becomes clear that most of the exercises listed in the *Daoyin jing* were present and accounted for in the Tang dynasty and probably existed before it. However, since there is no *Daoyin jing* listed in extant bibliographies before 1145, it may well be that the work we have today is a Tang-dynasty compilation that summarizes and organizes various earlier materials (Despeux 1989, 231; Schipper and Verellen 2004, 95). At the same time, it may also be that the text existed earlier and was simply not mentioned, or again that it formed part of a more extensive version of the *Yangsheng yaoji* and with it was lost in the eighth century.

Whatever the case may be, since the methods described in the text are recouped in various early sources, the *Daoyin jing* represents a medieval development of the tradition. It continues classical practices and is firmly based in the medical tradition. Like earlier sources, it has healing as its primary focus and sees the body as the interactive functioning of various organ complexes and channels. Thus, Master Ning says,

The practice of healing exercises eliminates all wayward *qi* from the limbs, skeleton, bones, and joints. Thus only proper *qi* remains in residence, becoming ever purer and more essential.

Practice the exercises diligently and with care whenever you have time. If you

2. The *Zhubing yuanhou lun* repeats thirty of the fifty-five movements associated with Master Ning together with eight of the ten practices of Pengzu, five of twenty-nine other exercises of Master Ning, nine of nineteen miscellaneous practices, as well as thirteen of the thirty-four movements associated with Wang Qiao (Despeux 1989, 230).
3. The same essential text appears also in the *Taiwu xiansheng fuqi fa* 太無先生服氣法 (Master Great Nonbeing's Method of *Qi*-Absorption, *DZ* 824) from the late eighth century with a preface that mentions the Dali reign period (766–779). See Maspero 1981, 469; Schipper and Verellen 2004, 370–371. It is later reprinted in the Ming-dynasty *Chifeng sui* (Despeux 1988, 65–84).

do them both in the morning and at night, gradually your bones and joints will become firm and strong, causing the hundred diseases to be cured. (6ab)

He then lists various kinds of diseases that will greatly benefit from the practice, including exhaustion and fatigue, chest chills, hip pain, deafness, dizziness, mental confusion, and hyperactivity, as well as other forms of "*qi* moving against its proper current and rising up violently." In all cases, he emphasizes, it is beneficial to practice appropriate healing exercises and guide the *qi* to the ailing area. More specifically, he says,

> By guiding the *qi* you can supplement the inner *qi* of the organs; by practicing exercises you can heal the four limbs. Thus following the Dao of natural spontaneity as diligently as you can, you attain a state of mutual protection with Heaven and Earth. (6b)

Integrating various forms of exercises and modes of guiding the *qi*, the *Daoyin jing* brings the tradition to a new level of development, characterized by certain key features. They are the refinement and variation of medical exercises and animal forms, the organization of healing practices into integrated sequences and their ascription to legendary Daoist immortals, and the use of meditation techniques that integrate the guiding of *qi* with various body imaginings and Daoist visualizations. The text accordingly has three major kinds of instructions: methods for medical relief that constitute a development of those first found in the manuscripts, integrated sequences of practice that can be used to create healing but are more dominantly marked as methods of long life and immortality, and meditative ways of guiding the *qi* and visualizing the body that put the practitioner into a more divine and spiritual context. Within these three areas, the *Daoyin jing* first shows the systematic progress from healing through longevity to immortality, which becomes central in all later Daoyin forms and systems.

Medical Relief

Breathing
The *Daoyin jing* continues the ancient medical tradition by paying much attention to breathing. It not only lists all six healing breaths like the *Jin'gui lu*, but associates each of them with a particular organ and set of ailments, thus representing the system that has remained standard to the present day (Despeux 2006, 49; Chiu and Chia 1993, 106–108).

For example, the first breath is *he:*

He is the breath associated with the heart, and the heart governs the tongue. If the mouth is dry, even well-assembled *qi* cannot pervade the body, thus allowing various forms of wayward *qi* to enter. Heaven will take care of that. If there is great heat, open the mouth wide. If there is little heat, keep the mouth lightly closed. Also, use your intention to measure it suitably. If you do it beyond being cured, however, the practice will caused renewed diminishing. (16a)

Similarly, *hu* is related to the spleen and helps with conditions of low fever and discomfort; a feeling of fullness in belly, stomach, and intestines; bad circulation; and energetic compression. Third, *xu* belongs to the liver, which governs the eyes; it is effective in cases of inflamed and congested eyes and other vision troubles. The next breath is *chui*, which corresponds to the kidneys and the ears and helps in cases of abdominal cold, infertility, and hearing afflictions. Fifth comes *si*, the breath of the lungs and the nose, effective in cases of temperature imbalances and skin troubles. Sixth and finally, the *xi* breath activates the Triple Heater and alleviates all maladies associated with this digestive and energy-processing organ (16ab). The text concludes by saying, "Each of the six breaths—*he, si, hu, xu, chui,* and *xi*—is ruled by one of the five organs. In case of extreme fatigue, one can use them easily to regulate the *qi* and improve one's condition" (16b).

This model of the Six Breaths represents a detailed medical method to treat various imbalances of *qi* associated with the five inner organs and the Triple Heater. It follows the standard correspondence system of Chinese medicine, is both therapeutic and preventive, can address many different conditions, and still forms an important part of qigong practice today (Despeux 2006, 59).

Beyond providing a general overview, the *Daoyin jing* also prescribes the different breaths in connection with stretching exercises. It says,

Place both hands on the ground, contract the body, and bend the spine, then lift up. Repeat this move three times. Doing this exercise every day will tonify and increase *qi* and extend your years. The best time to do it is when there is no one around. It also involves holding the breath in, then absorbing it once and exhaling so softly that the ears cannot hear it. If you are exhausted or fatigued, use *si* to exhale. If you have cold-based troubles in the organs, use *chui*. If you have a heat-based condition, use *hu*. (15b–16a)

Other ways of moving *qi* and increasing overall vitality include standing up straight against a wall and holding the breath, then guiding the *qi* from head to feet or feet to head (14b), or lying on the back, closing the mouth, pulsing jaw and belly, and making the *qi* fill the mouth ready for swallowing while intentionally moving it toward the back and around the body (15a). Stretching both arms to the right or left while holding the breath to the count of nine, furthermore, will keep the *qi* firmly within the body and prevent unwanted leakages, while guiding it mentally to the area below the navel and holding it there will release knots and tensions (15a). Overall health, moreover, is promised to anyone regularly practicing one or several of the following exercises:

> Raise both hands as if lifting a thousand-pound rock, right and left moving well together. (15b)
>
> Sit cross-legged, interlace the fingers, reach up above your head, then stretch the head and bring it forward so as to touch the ground. Hold the breath for the count of five.
>
> Kneel upright and bend the arms back so that the hands embrace the nipples. Rock to your right and left while holding the breath. (18a)

Like its forerunners in the medical manuscripts, the exercise involves simple arm movements. Unlike them, it places greater emphasis on holding the breath, thus working with a greater inward focus. Breathing is the key method of working with ailments and has replaced the emphasis on outward bodily movements to a large degree. Although the earlier exercises are still rudimentarily present, the inward shift has altered their composition and execution.

ELIMINATION OF AILMENTS

Beyond these general health-enhancing activities, the *Daoyin jing* also lists a number of practices that are geared to what appear to be dominant ailments at the time. Again, as in the earlier materials, they tend to be either locomotive or gastrointestinal, involving digestive troubles and sexual enhancement as well as joint aches (especially in the hips) often combined with fatigue. In a few cases, the exercises are geared specifically toward discomforts associated with too much food and drink. The following practice, for example, seems to have been quite efficient, since it appears twice in the text:

> Sit or kneel upright, look up at the sky, and exhale deeply to expel all *qi* from being drunk on wine and satiated with food, so that you can again be hungry and sober. If done in the summer months, this will also moderate your body temperature. (15a, 19a)

Just as this exercise obviously addresses an audience that is well off financially and concerned with the ills of civilization rather than with plain survival, so are several techniques geared toward improved digestion and sexual enhancement, described as an "increase in essence" or "aiding yin and yang":

> [Stand up.][4] Lower the head and with both hands hold on to your feet. Hold the breath for a count of twelve. This helps with the digestion of grains, makes people's bodies feel light, and increases essence and *qi*. (17b)
>
> [Sit or kneel.] Slightly incline the head, breathe softly, then interlace the hands and move the arms to the right and left. Hold the breath for the count of twelve. This will help digestion, make people feel light, and increase essence. (15b)
>
> [Sit or kneel.] With your left hand quickly pull your hair while your right hand pulls against the neck. This aids the activity of yin and yang. (18b)
>
> [Stand up.] With the thumbs of both hands pinch your two nostrils. Hold the breath. This keeps people's yin-yang from getting tired. From here, turn the feet in and out ten times. This tonifies all empty or diminished conditions and augments *qi*. (19a)

These exercises all affect the intestines. The one listed first is an intestinal massage, effected by a forward bend and accompanied by a long stretch of the back. The next one works with a twist, engaging the abdominal muscles and turning the torso against the belly, again tightening and squeezing the internal organs. Stretching the neck and pulling on the head, third, forces the torso open and releases tension in the inner organs, while the last one regulates breathing and engages the hip flexors in an effort to open the genital area to greater *qi*-flow.

Besides digestive and sexual problems, people also seem to have suffered from swellings and piles or hemorrhoids, for which two practices are prescribed, both of which involve stretching the lower body and thus increasing blood flow to the hips and pelvis:

> Squat with both hands joined, then stretch the feet up and down. Hold the breath for a count of five. This helps with inflammation and ulcers in the nose and mouth as well as with the five different kinds of piles. (17b)
>
> With one hand raised up and holding onto a hanging rope, take the other hand to touch your feet. This helps with piles and swellings. (18b)

Yet another common problem at the time apparently was arthritis or difficulty in moving the joints, often accompanied by fatigue, for which the same exercises tend to be prescribed. A classic practice is the following:

---

4. Postures are not specified in the text. I supply them either on the basis of the exercise described, which seems to be done best in a certain posture, or because of a preceding exercise in the text where the body position is given, assuming that the instructions were meant to carry over. In all cases, however, postures supplied in brackets remain speculative.

> Squat on the ground leaning against a wall. Hug your knees with both arms, bend
> the head forward, and hold the breath for the count of nine. This cures neck
> pain and problems in the hips and legs. It also helps with fatigue. (15a)

A combination of a huddling, protective position and a releasing stretch of the
neck in a posture of utter surrender, this exercise provides a welcome time-out
for people under pressure or in some discomfort. Holding the pose, not needing
to do anything but let the head hang, allows the person to give in to feelings of
tiredness and fatigue and creates a valuable space for recovery. The problem
seems to have been common, as the text presents the same technique several
times more, once without the wall (19a), using a rope to tie the head to keep it in
place, and again from a sitting rather than squatting position (18a).

Another practice to open the hips, stretch the neck, release the back, and
eliminate fatigue is to bend over one's legs while extended straight out (18b), what
in yoga is called Seated Forward Bend *(paschimottanāsana)*. Its effects, according
to Iyengar, include toning the abdominal organs, rejuvenating the spine, and improving digestion. He even vouches for sexual benefits:

> A good stay in this pose massages the heart, the spinal column, and the abdominal
> organs, which feel refreshed while the mind is rested. Due to the extra stretch given
> to the pelvic region, more oxygenated blood is brought there and the gonads absorb
> the required nutrition from the blood. This increases vitality, helps to cure impo-
> tency, and lead to sex control. (1976, 170)

A slightly different variant is to sit on the floor with legs spread wide, grasp
the feet with the hands, and come forward as far as possible, reaching the head
toward the ground while holding the breath for the count of twelve. "This cures
pain in the head, neck, hip, and back," the *Daoyin jing* notes; "it also makes people's hearing keen and their vision bright" (18a). In yoga, this pose is called Wide
Angle Forward Bend *(upavistha konāsana)*. According to Iyengar, it

> stretches the hamstrings and helps the blood to circulate properly in the pelvic region
> and keeps it healthy. It prevents the development of hernia, of which it can also cure
> mild cases, and relieves sciatic pains. Since the *āsana* controls and regularizes the
> menstrual flow and also stimulates the ovaries, it is a boon to women. (1976, 165)

The *Daoyin jing* proposes yet another way to relieve pelvic and digestive ailments: by "bending both legs and, while either sitting, lying down, or standing,
holding the toes" (18b). In yet another version, practitioners are asked to "sit
cross-legged, interlace the fingers of both hands, place them underneath the head,

and stretch them as far away as possible while holding the breath for the count of six" (18a). A self-massage that helps with joint trouble, moreover, is to "lie down flat on the back and with both hands massage the belly toward the feet, then pull the *qi* up again, still using both hands" or to "rub the belly with both hands, then touch the feet while squatting on the ground," in each case "holding the breath for the count of twelve" (18b).

ANIMAL FORMS

Continuing the earlier tradition, the *Daoyin jing* also presents various practices associated with animals, in this case mostly water-based creatures, such as toad, turtle, and dragon. None match the Five Animals but some already appear in the medical manuscripts. Thus, the *Daoyin tu* mentions a Dragon Rise (#27) and a Turtle Move (#42), the latter depicted as a standing figure with both arms raised forward at shoulder height, while the *Yinshu* notes that Dragon Flourish is to "step one leg forward with bent knee while stretching the other leg back, then interlace the fingers, place them on the knee, and look up" (#19). It also has a form called Leaping Toad (#37), which involves waving the arms up and down in rhythmical movement (Lo 2001a, 73).

None of these have anything in common with the forms outlined in the *Daoyin jing*, which are more introspective and involve holding the breath and guiding the *qi*. Thus, the "Dragon Way of Guiding the *Qi*" focuses on holding the breath. It can be done in various ways:

> Bow the head and look down. Hold the breath for the count of twelve. This relieves wind-induced itches and boils; it also prevents heat from entering the throat. To take best care of an ailment, do the exercises facing the sunlight.
>
> Lie down. With both hands massage from the belly down toward the feet, then with your hands pull the feet under the arms. Hold the breath for the count of twelve. This relieves dampness and rheumatism in the legs and feet, as well as stiffness in the hips and back pain.
>
> Interlace the fingers of both hands at the neck and stretch. This helps with all kinds of poison but will not relieve too much *qi* in the belly, which needs a proper form of exhalation. (4b–5a)

All these are geared toward opening the chest and breathing apparatus by lengthening the neck or massaging the belly. As the windpipe and chest open, breathing deepens and greater amounts of fresh oxygen are taken in while stale carbon dioxide is eliminated, thus achieving the detoxifying and warming effect described in the text.

Similarly, the first exercise listed under the "Turtle Way of Guiding the *Qi*" involves covering the mouth and nose with a garment and holding the breath for the count of nine, then gently releasing the breath through the nose. Or one can raise the head like a turtle and hold the breath for a count of five, then rub the tongue around the mouth and swallow the saliva (4ab; see Maspero 1981, 550). The practice is more reminiscent of the *Baopuzi* story about the little girl who observed the swallowing of the turtle and stayed alive than of ancient medical practice. In addition, the Turtle Way repeats several medical exercises described above,[5] then adds two from a kneeling position:

> Kneel upright and interlace your hands behind your back. This is called the sash tie. It relieves constipation and benefits the belly.
> Kneel on the floor and interlace your hands underneath your shins. This relieves excessive yin. (5b)

Both these exercises serve to tighten the abdominal muscles and lengthen the back, thus massaging the inner organs and releasing tension.

The Turtle Way also has the earliest mention of inverted poses among Chinese healing exercises. It says,

> With both hands holding onto a rope, pull yourself up, then hang upside down, so that the legs are above the torso. This relieves dizziness in the head and craziness due to wind.
> Pull up with both hands and reverse yourself, so you hang from the rope with your back at the top. This relieves lack of concentrated essence and failure to digest properly. (6a)

Both these practices involve placing the head below the heart, thus reversing blood flow to the brain, a fact accounted for in the effect listed for the first pose, a relief of dizziness and mental confusion. They also alleviate heaviness in the legs and lower body, thus aiding digestion and the overall balance of circulation. They are similar to Head Stand in yoga *(sirsāsana),* which

> makes healthy pure blood flow through the brain cells. This rejuvenates them so that thinking power increases and thoughts become clearer. It is a tonic for people whose brains tire quickly. It also ensures a proper blood supply to the pituitary and pineal

---

5. It repeats the exercises that involve holding the hair, pinching the nostrils, stretching against a hanging rope, and executing a seated forward bend (5b–6a).

glands in the brain. Our growth, health, and vitality depend on the proper functioning of these two glands. (Iyengar 1976, 190)

The third aquatic animal in the *Daoyin jing* is the toad, which is the key animal
in the medical work *Hama jing* 蝦蟆經 (Toad Classic), a text related to the *Huangdi
neijing* (Yellow Emperor's Inner Classic) that survived in Japan but probably goes
back to the seventh century, if not before (Lo 2001a, 68–69). The toad, of course, is
not only an aquatic creature but also the mythical animal in the Moon and appears
as the seventh of ten sexual positions in the Mawangdui manuscripts (Lo 2001a,
73). Its practice accordingly serves to improve breathing and open the pelvic area.

One practice of the "Toad Way of Guiding the *Qi*" is to sit or kneel and hold
the breath while moving the shoulders to the right and left or to do the same
while lying down on one side or the other, matching the location of the condition
to be remedied. One can also stand up in the direction of the Sun, hold the breath
for the count of nine, then lift the head and inhale the Sun's light and essence. All
these methods improve energy and enhance well-being (2b–3a).[6] Another practice involves squatting, then "threading both arms under the bent knees to grasp
the toes" (3a). Yet others involve some intricate exercises using the legs:

> Sit with your legs spread wide, then cross the legs up and over to hold them with
> your hands. Interlace the hands within the crossed legs. Stretch as much as you
> can. This relieves irregularities in waking and sleeping and prevents *qi* and
> essence from leaking.
>
> Raise both legs and press them toward the sides of the cheekbones while you press
> your hands down against the floor. This will help cure contractions and
> obstructions.
>
> Hold both feet with your hands, your fingers placed right above the toes. This helps if
> you cannot reach the ground when bending from the hip. It is also good if you
> bruise easily.
>
> Raise the right hand and extend the left hand forward while kneeling on your right
> leg and holding the left leg [with the left hand]. This relieves all pains in the
> tailbone. (3ab)

These exercises are new in the *Daoyin jing* not only in that they use the wide-angled leg position or "winnowing basket," a posture associated with ghosts and

---

6. The same holds also true for the wild goose form, for which only one move is described, others
possibly being lost: "Bow the head and bend the shoulders forward. Hold the breath for the count of
twelve. Mentally push all remaining liquid and food in digestion from the lower body. This will aid
natural healing" (4b).

madness in ancient China, to begin the practice, but also in that they demand quite a bit of gymnastic agility of the practitioner.[7] They open the lower body and stretch the legs and hips in new ways, adding relief of obstructions and tensions to the ailments treated in other forms.

Since toads, moreover, in addition to long flexible legs also have extensive forefeet or arms, the Toad Way has a few ways to open the upper body by moving the arms, neck, and shoulders:

> Raise both hands and interlace them behind the neck. Press them against each other as strongly as you can. This helps with pain below the waist.
>
> Stretch out your left hand with the right hand underneath it. Press the thumb and fingers of the left hand as strongly as you can. Reverse sides. This is good for arthritis in the bones and joints.
>
> If you cannot turn your neck to look backward, raise your right arm above the head and bring it slowly forward and down. Then twist the torso, with the left arm placed on the floor.
>
> Kneel on the floor and raise your left hand while the fingers of the right hand are placed near the left shoulder. Then twist to the right and left. This stretches the sides and releases the knees and hips.

This segment is more traditional, both in posture and in movements, raising the arms and turning the neck in various ways being already part of the medical manuscripts. Developing older patterns, the *Daoyin jing* thus brings together different ways of exercise practice, arranging, organizing, and standardizing the forms.

Integrated Sequences

In accordance with its overall standardizing and systematizing effort, the *Daoyin jing* next presents several integrated sequences to be undertaken in the early morning with the goal of creating an overall balance of *qi*. Some sequences are undertaken from a single position, while others involve all different postures of the body; some are geared toward medical healing, while others are for overall health and the attainment of long life.

One systematic sequence, called "Pengzu's Method of Lying-Down Exercises for Nurturing Immortality," puts the different medical practices into an orga-

---

7. The wide-angled seat, which often also comes with the loosening of the hair—another preparatory measure in Daoist practice—traditionally are signs of unconventionality and the going beyond social boundaries. For discussions on the role and symbolism of hair in Chinese culture, see Ōgata 1995; Dikotter 1998.

nized pattern and treats various physical conditions. Practitioners remain in a supine position; they always undertake the practice between midnight and dawn, and never after a meal or a bath: [8]

1. In your residence, loosen your clothes and lie down on your back. Stretch your hips and lengthen the sacrum. Hold for five breaths. This stretches the kidneys, relieves diabetes, and helps with yin and yang [sexual energy].

2. Stretch out the left leg while holding the right knee and pressing it into the torso. Hold for five breaths. [Repeat on the other side.] This stretches the spleen and eliminates all cold and heat from the heart and belly as well as all wayward and obstructed qi from the chest.

3. [With legs straight up in the air,] pull the toes of both feet with your hands. Hold for five breaths. This eliminates all potential hernias and digestive trouble from the belly. It also benefits the nine orifices.

4. Raise your torso toward your toes. Hold for five breaths. This stretches the hip and the spine, relieves localized pain and stiffness, and improves hearing.

5. Turn your feet so the toes face each other. Hold for five breaths. This stretches the heart and lungs, eliminates coughs, and helps with ailments due to rising or reverse qi.

6. Turn your feet so the heels face each other. Hold for five breaths. This tenses the thighs, thereby cleansing the qi of the five networks. It benefits the intestines and stomach and eliminates wayward qi.

7. Bend your left shin and press it against the right knee [with right leg straight up]. Hold for five breaths. [Repeat on the other side]. This stretches the lungs and eliminates qi-depletions caused by wind. It also sharpens the eyesight.

8. Extend the shins all the way to the toes. Hold for five breaths. This prevents muscle cramps.

9. Grasp the knees with both hands and bend them in so they are directly above your heart. Hold for five breaths. This relieves hip pain.

10. Turn both feet to the outside. Repeat ten times. Then turn both feet to the inside. Repeat ten times. This restores you from fatigue. (6b–7a)

Unlike many medical practices, which use a count to eight or twelve for holding the breath, this sequence works with holding the pose for five breaths in each exercise, thus stretching the part in question for about half a minute. But as the text notes in a supplementary explanation, it also requires that all exercises be repeated

---

8. The numbers of the exercises in the following sequences are not part of the original, which connects the different practices with "next." I have added them for easier access.

five times and thus increases both the duration and the effect of the practice. Although performed while lying down, like those of the Toad Way, the exercises here are quite vigorous. Pushing one's legs up in the air and lifting the torso requires strong abdominal muscles, and turning and bending the legs so that the toes or knees face this way and that demands quite a bit of flexibility. Several of the poses are similar to yoga postures, such as Corpse Pose *(savāsana),* Wind-Relieving Pose *(pavana muktāsana),* and Inverted Frog *(adhamukha mandukāsana).* Again, as in other sequences, the medical benefits are listed, and in this case they cover a wide range of conditions and ailments and do not merely focus on long life and harmonious *qi.* The sequence flows smoothly from one exercise into the next and greatly aids overall energy and muscular strength in different parts of the body.

Unlike this sequence and the multitude of healing practices, the other sequences described in the *Daoyin jing* do not treat specific ailments but are designed for longevity and immortality. As the text says about one of Master Redpine's sequences, "If done regularly, this practice will make your hearing keen, your vision bright, and your years extended to great longevity, with none of the hundred diseases arising" (19b). Since the practices serve a more spiritual purpose, they have to be performed under careful conditions. As the text specifies, the practice platform should be high off the floor "to prevent earth-*qi* from rising up and attacking you as well as to keep demon *qi* from invading your body" (16b); one should never be hasty or aggressive in one's practice, since "haste and aggression are robbers of the entire body" (17a); and one should avoid facing north or practicing while turning the back on the gods or ancestors, violations that could result in a reduced life expectancy. Also, the text requests that the sequence be undertaken "between midnight and noon" (2a) or when getting up early in the morning (1a).

The simplest of these spiritual exercises is associated with Master Redpine. Limited to a seated or kneeling posture, it is called the "Seated Exercises of Master Redpine" and consists of six exercises that use the arms in various ways to open the chest, shoulders, and upper body (fig. 10). There are no specific benefits, medical or otherwise, mentioned for each exercise, but the sequence as a whole is said to increase long life and vigor:

1. First, [sit or] kneel upright and stretch out both arms before you, palms open and fingers turned out.
2. Interlace the fingers, stretch the arms away, and roll the body to the right and left.
3. With the right hand on the hip, reach the left hand up and above the head; repeat on the other side.
4. With the right hand stretched out backwards, use the left hand to grasp the hip from the front; repeat on the other side.

5.   Alternate the right and left arms stretching forward, then bend them back to grasp the hips from the back.

6.   Raise both hands up with vigor. (19ab)

This rather simple sequence looks a bit like a warm-up, but since it is listed separately in the text, it must have been practiced independently for longevity purposes. It may also have been a supplementary practice to other sequences associated with Master Redpine or served as an alternative for followers of the Master Redpine lineage—maybe for people who found it difficult to stand up and bend or get down and stretch. The various movements take the arms and shoulders through their full range of motion and open the upper body and chest quite effectively. There is little doubt that this sequence, short and easy as it may seem, has benefits for health and vigor.

The other major sequence linked with Master Redpine appears right in the beginning of the *Daoyin jing* and is reprinted in its other versions, showing that it was widely known and quite popular. It is an integrated set of exercises that takes the practitioner through all the different postures of the body and flows along nicely to provide an overall expansion of *qi* and the release of tensions and energy blockages in various parts of the body. Like other long-life sequences, it is to be undertaken in the early morning and begins by having the practitioner face east:

1.   When you first get up in the morning, spread your hair and face east. [Standing up] begin by interlacing the fingers of both hands above your head, [stretch up], then bend to the floor. Continue for five breaths. This expands the *qi*.

Fig. 10: A Daoist
sitting up and
stretching his arms.
Source: *Chifeng sui.*

2. Lie down. Supporting your head with the right hand, touch the floor to your left with your left elbow [reaching over as far as you can].[9] Repeat on the other side, with your left hand supporting the head while the right elbow touches the floor. Continue for five breaths [on each side]. This releases muscles and bones.

3. With both hands hold your right knee and pull it toward your waist, raising your head at the same time to meet it. [Repeat with the left knee.] Continue for five breaths [on each side]. This releases the hips.

4. With your left hand push against your left knee as it is raised above the hip. Stretch your right arm up [and back] as far as you can. Repeat on the other side. Do this for five breaths on each side. This releases the chest and belly.

5. With your left hand press against your hip while stretching your right arm up [and back] as far as you can. Repeat on the other side. Continue for five breaths [on each side]. This releases the mid-belly.

6. [Sit up or kneel.] Interlace your fingers in front of the chest. Turn your head to the left and right. Hold your breath for as long as you can. This releases the face and ear muscles, eliminates wayward *qi,* and prevents it from reentering the body.

7. Interlace your fingers [behind your back and] below your hips. Turn your torso to the right and left as far as you can. This opens the blood arteries.

8. Interlace your fingers [in front of your body] and stretch your arms, while turning the torso to the right and left as far as you can. This releases the shoulders.

9. Interlace your fingers, reverse the palms, and stretch your arms above your head. Turn left and right in an easy rhythm. This releases the *qi* of the lungs and the liver.

10. Interlace your fingers in front of the chest. Stretch to the left and right as far as you can. This eliminates tense *qi* from the skin.

11. Interlace your fingers and bring the hands to the shoulders on the right and left. This releases skin-*qi.*

12. Stand up straight. Stretch your calves left and right. This releases leg-*qi.* (1a–2a)

This flow of postures works from a standing through a lying and a sitting posture back up to standing. It uses all the different parts of the body and claims to benefit the entire system but in its actual movements, like Master Redpine's seated sequence, focuses dominantly on the upper body, stretching arms, shoulders, and torso. Like the previous sequences, it requires the continued use of the breath and works dominantly with patterns of five slow, deep breaths, allowing about half a minute for each repetition. Although reminiscent of medical exercises in the *Yinshu* in that it makes heavy use of interlaced fingers and encourages bends and stretches in different directions, the sequence makes no claims about

---

9. Phrases in brackets are based on the *Yunji qiqian* edition.

improved eyesight, hearing, or health. Instead, the sequence focuses on releasing or stretching the different parts of the body to encourage an overall balanced and harmonious *qi*-flow and to serve the continued openness and release necessary for extended longevity.

The last of the structured sequences in the *Daoyin jing* is linked with Master Ning. It focuses strongly on the breath and uses physical movements only as secondary support. Each of its nine exercises requires that the breath be held for one additional count, thus increasing the time of holding and enhancing the stretching and opening effect on the different parts of the body. The sequence is as follows:

1. [Stand up,] loosen your hair, and face east. Make your hands into fists and hold your breath for the count of one. Then raise your arms alternately left and right and stretch them until your hands cover the opposite ear. This will keep your hair black and prevent it from turning white.
2. Lie down and stretch, holding the breath for the count of two. Take the middle fingers of your hands and press them sharply into the channels at the side of your neck. Repeat three times. This will brighten your eyesight.
3. Sit or kneel facing east and hold your breath for the count of three. Take the middle fingers of your hands and moisten their tips with saliva from your mouth. Rub them against each other for two sets of seven. Then gently massage your eyes with them. This will also brighten your eyesight.
4. Sit or kneel facing east and hold your breath for the count of four. Then pinch your nostrils between your fingers. This relieves obstruction of nasal breath due to too much flesh.
5. Sit or kneel facing east and hold your breath for the count of five. Click your teeth a number of times, then bend forward.
6. Lie on your side and hold your breath for the count of six. This relieves deafness in the ears and dizziness in the eyes.
7. Lie on your back and hold your breath for the count of seven. This relieves chest pains.
8. Squat. Embrace your knees with both hands and rise up on your toes. Hold your breath for the count of eight. This relieves all ailments between the chest and head, including those of ears, eyes, throat, and nose, as well as all wayward and hot *qi*.
9. [Lie down.] Remove the pillow. Curl your hands into fists and clasp them behind your head and briefly hold your breath. Rise up on your toes. Hold your breath for the count of nine, still facing east. This causes the *qi* to move up and down smoothly, opens and deepens its passage through the nostrils, and relieves emaciation and weakness. (2ab)

This sequence begins with loosening the hair, a gesture of releasing formality and social convention, thereby opening to one's own deeper energies and to spiritual influences of the cosmos (see Ōgata 1995). It is undertaken in the early morning while facing the rising Sun, allowing adepts to ingest the growing yang energy of the new day. The hands are made into fists to prevent *qi* from leaving the body. Then the breath is held out—the text says "don't breathe" (*buxi* 不息) rather than "enclose the *qi*" (*biqi*), which means holding the breath in—for an increasing number of respirations or heartbeats while different parts of the body are being moved. As the sequence proceeds, it makes use of all the different postures of the body, moving the adept from standing through lying down to kneeling or sitting, then again to lying and through squatting once more to a supine position. The sequence has a clear flow to it, using the body flexibly and with ease. It involves some self-massage, including one of the eyes along the lines of Highest Clarity practice. It also involves some teeth clicking, a practice that is done in religious settings to alert the gods of the body and the universe that devotional activity is about to commence, but that in medical literature is also said to benefit the teeth and through them the essence and marrow of the body.

The claimed effect of the practice is an overall improvement in *qi*-flow and longevity, eliminating the signs of old age, such as the hair turning white, eyesight and hearing diminishing, and the occurrence of chest pains and various other ailments. The focus tends to be on the upper body; there is little to suggest that the exercises are helpful for hips, legs, knees, or feet. However, it encourages the smooth flow of *qi* through the entire body and thus relieves signs of fatigue and weakness. The practice does not take very long and does not require much space. It is simple and easily done, keeping the body active and the mind focused on the varying count of the breath.

A more religious and devotional sequence is called "Ways of Inhaling Lunar Essence." It involves some medical techniques in conjunction with the more meditative absorption of celestial radiance and beams of moonlight. It is undertaken at new moon and full moon (i.e., on the first and fifteenth of the lunar month), in the late evening and early morning, when the Moon rises and sets. To begin,

> stand upright facing the Moon. Hold the breath for the count of eight. Turn the head upward and inhale the essence of the moonlight. Swallow it eight times. This will expand your yin-*qi*. Especially if practiced by a woman, her yin essence will increase to overflowing and she can conceive. (4b–5a)

Not only helping with yin-*qi* (the body's inherent vitality), the practice also affords magical powers over water so that, if a practitioner enters the water, he or she can raise both arms and hold the breath to avoid all harm (5a). Similarly, a variant listed in a different part of the *Daoyin jing* affords exorcistic powers and the prevention of suffering:

> Face east and kneel in the direction of the Sun. With your left hand salute the Moon, raising the whole body. Then look toward the Northern Dipper and mentally absorb the *qi* of the Moon. This prevents all sorts of evils from entering the head and keeps away hardship and suffering. (3b–4a)

Beyond these magical and mystical efforts, Inhaling Lunar Essence also includes two exercises done with legs spread wide, similar to the Toad Way: one involves holding the toes while bending forward; the other has adepts lift the legs, cross them, then with their hands push the tailbone off the floor (5a). It continues with two cross-legged forms that are more medical and less magical:

> With both hands lift the feet as high as you can, bringing the shins to horizontal. This relieves *qi* blockages and hip pain. It also prevents cold disorders from moving up or down and affecting the kidney-*qi*.
> With both hands lift the toes of the feet, then bend to bring the head forward as much as you can. This opens the *qi* of the five organs and aids rejuvenation. (5ab)

The absorption of lunar essence is closely related to similar practices of Highest Clarity, which emphasize the swallowing of the *qi* of the Sun (fig. 11).
One example is found in the *Wozhong jue*. The text says,

> To absorb solar energy, at dawn when the Sun first rises, sit or stand up, concentrate your attention, and click your teeth nine times. Then from the bottom of your heart, invoke the essence of the Sun which shines like a pearl with green reflection and visualize it changing into a red halo, bright and mysteriously flamboyant.
> Next, close your eyes, hold them tightly shut, and visualize the five colors of the Sun spreading into a halo and coming to touch your body. Allow them to sink as far down as the feet and reach as high up as the top of the head. Next, see the center of the brilliant cloud in a purple hue like the pupil of an eye. Repeat this process ten times. Then join the five colors together and let them enter your mouth to swallow them. Do this swallowing of solar energy forty-five times, then swallow the saliva nine times and clap the teeth nine times. (2.19a; Maspero 1981, 514)

This practice is more a visualizing meditation than a form of healing exercises, but the basic concept is still the same as in the absorption of lunar energies: the body of the adept transforms into a more cosmic entity by enclosing and absorbing celestial powers. Its inclusion in a book on healing exercises shows just to what degree the physical release of tension and increase of vital energies has been merged with more spiritual practices and how deeply rooted the unity of the body-mind is in Chinese thinking. Doing physical movements, guiding the *qi,* and visualizing colors and deities form parts of the same overall health improvement regimen, which in turn is the key to enhanced *qi*-power and a key stepping-stone toward transcendence.

Yet another version of this practice appears in the *Dengzhen yinjue* 登真隱訣 (Secret Instructions on the Ascent to the Perfected, *DZ* 421), by Tao Hongjing of the early sixth century (see Strickmann 1981; Cedzich 1987; Schipper and Verellen 2004, 201–205). It reads as follows:

> To absorb solar energies, write the character for "Sun" in a square or circle nine inches in size, using vermilion ink on green paper. Every morning, turn east, hold the paper in the left hand, and concentrate on it until it turns into the resplendent Sun itself. Then swallow it and let it remain in your heart; click the teeth nine times and swallow saliva nine times.
>
> You may also add the absorption of Sun rays to your practice. Do this three times a day, facing east in the morning, south at noon, and west in the afternoon. Visualize a red sun with a bright red radiance as big as a large coin in your heart,

Fig. 11: A Highest Clarity practitioner connecting to the Sun. Source: *Yuyi jielin.*

then allow its nine rays to rise from the heart into the throat and let them reach the
inside of your teeth. However, do not let them pass beyond the teeth but send them
back down into the abdomen. Visualize them distinctly in your heart and belly. Then
let them leave together with the breath and swallow the saliva thirty-nine times.
(2.14a–16b; Maspero 1981, 514–515)

Using these resources and thus increasingly integrating the different modes of
the exercise tradition, the *Daoyin jing* in its organized sequences thus brings together medical, magical, longevity, and visualization practices, expanding the
modes of healing exercises while at the same time standardizing forms and systematizing patterns. The sequences as much as the medical practices actively combine
breath control with movements and stretches of different parts of the body, encourage intention to focus on the part moved or the celestial entity invoked, and link the
practice with heroes of immortality or animals of high flexibility and long life.

Systematic Breathing

Going further beyond bends and stretches, the *Daoyin jing* also prescribes methods of guiding the *qi* through specific breathing techniques. For example, it outlines a preventive method of maintaining inner purity through cleansing and
swallowing *qi*. First prescribed here, these methods later appear as the first steps
to a more complex and systematic *qi*-practice, formulated in detail in the *Huanzhen neiqi fa* of the mid-Tang and reprinted in the *Chifeng sui* of the Ming dynasty (Despeux 1988, 65–84).

Like Highest Clarity forms of Daoyin, the practice should be undertaken upon
waking up in the early morning; it focuses dominantly on the breath and uses
physical movements in support. The basic idea underlying the method is that when
people go to sleep at night, their *qi* is partially enclosed in the body, and the various
digestive fumes of the evening meal are not processed fully. To remove these nox-
ious vapors from the body and open the way for the absorption of pure, fresh *qi*,
practitioners according to the *Huanzhen neiqi fa* should have a quiet, clean, warm,
and well-ventilated room with a bed platform raised above the floor and equipped
with a comfortable mattress. The practice has to be done in the time of living *qi*
between midnight and noon; it is best performed about daybreak. A set of preparatory practices includes exhaling with *chui* nine times to remove stale *qi* from the
bowels, meditating silently to calm one's thoughts, clicking the teeth thirty-six
times to wake up the body gods, gently massaging the face, especially around the
eyes, and stretching to get the joints lubricated (1ab).

Once set up properly, adepts should practice Revolving *Qi* (*zhuanqi* 轉氣) or

Cleansing *Qi* (*taoqi* 淘氣) to release the stale *qi* accumulated in the course of the night and thereby prepare the body for the intake of new vital breath. This breathing exercise is already outlined in the *Daoyin jing*:

> To revolve *qi*, first close your eyes and curl your hands into fists. Lie down flat while looking up, then bend the arms so that the two fists are placed between the nipples. Place the feet on the mat to raise the knees, then lift the back and buttocks [into Bridge Pose]. Hold the breath in, then drum the Ocean of *Qi*, causing the *qi* to revolve from the inside to the outside. Exhale with *he*. Do one or two sets of nine repetitions. (13b–14a; *Huanzhen neiqi fa* 2a)

This practice is very similar to the yoga posture known as Bridge *(setu bandhāsana)*. It opens the chest and bends the back, thereby toning "the cervical, dorsal, lumbar, and sacral regions of the spine" (Iyengar 1976, 251). By having the practitioner place the head lower than the heart, the pose allows the blood to flow from the lower to the upper torso and the head, thus enlivening the thyroid, pituitary, and adrenal glands. In Chinese terms, it encourages an upward flow of *qi*, allowing it to be released from the abdomen and exit through the throat and mouth.

Following this, practitioners go on to Balancing *Qi* (*diaoqi* 調氣), described only in the *Huanzhen neiqi fa*. This essentially means inhaling through the nose and exhaling through the mouth—the gates of Heaven and Earth respectively. The breath should become so soft that it is all but inaudible, allowing for an inner calmness of mind and a steadiness of respiration (2b).

After having cleansed their intestines from dead or stale *qi* and balanced their breathing, releasing all tensions and creating a deep calm in body and mind, practitioners are ready to swallow the *qi*, a method again described in the *Daoyin jing*. It serves to balance the continuous intermingling and separation of earthly or external *qi* and primordial or internal *qi*. The idea here is that every time we inhale, we bring earthly *qi* into the body, where it mingles with primordial *qi* in the Ocean of *Qi* in the abdomen, the energy center commonly known as the lower cinnabar or elixir field. If this process is left unchecked, with every exhalation some portion of precious primordial *qi* will leave the body. To prevent this,

> wait until the very end of the exhalation, then abruptly close the mouth, drum the abdomen, and swallow the *qi* back down. This causes a gurgling sound like water dripping. In men, the *qi* descends on the left side of the body; in women, on the right. It passes the twenty-four articulations [of the esophagus], going drip-drip like water. If you can hear this clearly, the internal and external *qi* look after each other perfectly and will separate as appropriate. Use your intention to send the *qi* along and

with your hands massage its passageway, making it go quickly into the Ocean of *Qi*. (14ab; *Huanzhen neiqi fa* 3a)

Ideally, the *qi* flows smoothly and softly along its prescribed path to enter the Ocean of *Qi* in the abdomen. However, to help the process along, adepts should also use their intention to send the *qi* along mentally or even support it with slight self-massages, rubbing the relevant passageways. Also, beginning practitioners may find that the *qi* flows only haltingly. In that case, they should practice every swallow separately, only moving on to three consecutive swallowings when the flow is open and clear. It may well take a year of practice to get to this level (*Huanzhen neiqi fa* 3b).

Whether moving the *qi* slowly or allowing it to flow freely, the next step—beginning a series of practices that are found only in the *Huanzhen neiqi fa*—is to practice Guiding *Qi* (*xingqi* 行氣). This is a mental exercise that makes the *qi* move around the body. Once swallowed into the Ocean of *Qi*, adepts should visualize two caverns that begin at the back of the cinnabar field and run up toward the Niwan Palace in the head:

Imagine the *qi* in two strands moving up [through these caverns] and entering the Niwan center in the head. From here allow it to steam into the body's palaces, like a dense fog spreading downward, all the way through hair, face, head, neck, and shoulders into the hands and fingers. Once there, it moves further to pervade the chest and the middle cinnabar field, which houses the Heart Palace and thus the spirit. From here, the *qi* drips into the five inner organs and continues to flow once more into the lower cinnabar field. Allow it to continue down along the legs, so that it reaches the Three-mile point [in mid-shin], moving through the thighs, knees, calves, and heels to get all the way to Bubbling Well at the center of the soles. (3b–4a)

This practice, which is very close to a key practice in women's inner alchemy recorded from the seventeenth century,[10] moves the *qi* through the entire body, letting it first rise from the cinnabar field into the head, then allowing it to spread and sink, spread and sink, until it has completly pervaded the body. As adepts find themselves soaked with *qi,* they can also make it flow faster or slower, actively pushing out blockages and obstructions, which they see leaving through the fingers and toes as they perform a long exhalation. They then return to the *qi*

---

10. The text has women perform the same basic guidance of qi while sitting cross-legged and with the left heel pressing against the pelvic floor. Rather than allowing the *qi* to flow into the legs, however, they make it return to the breasts. Practicing "continuously until the body is warm," they will notice that the quantity of menstrual blood gradually decreases, thus leading to the "decapitation of the red dragon" (Valussi 2006, 6).

in the cinnabar field and begin the process anew, starting another cycle and cleansing the body further of ailments and difficulties. It is best to do this with little or no food in the digestive tract, thus enhancing the body's ability to absorb and live on *qi,* expanding the practice to ten rounds or a total of 360 swallowings and cycles of *qi.* More extended practice and increased rounds will eventually lead to a great internalization of nourishment and allow the practice of embryo respiration (*taixi* 胎息), the complete absorption in the greater cosmos as if supported in mother's womb.

This concludes the main cycle of breathing practices, leading to a sense of resting in the process of *qi* and a feeling of oneness with the greater universe. The *Huanzhen neiqi fa* goes on to specify various additional and alternative ways of working with *qi,* supplementing the work outlined so far.

First, there is Refining *Qi* (*lianqi* 鍊氣). As the day breaks, adepts are to lie on their backs, loosen their clothing, release the hair, and open the palms. They balance and swallow the *qi,* then hold it in for as long as possible. "Calm your mind, cut off all thoughts, and follow the *qi* wherever it flows, regulating it in its sealed environment. Now exhale, expel the breath and balance your breathing. Wait until the *qi* is calm, then refine it anew. Do ten rounds" (5a). This is said to enhance vitality and increase life expectancy.

Another variant is Surrendering to *Qi* (*weiqi* 委氣), which essentially means to let the *qi* flow wherever it goes and follow it calmly and smoothly with a detached and serene mind. As the text says,

> whether walking, standing, lying down, or sitting up, enter a state where there is no spirit, no conscious awareness. Deep and serene, you allow the mind to become one with the Great Void. Once there, balance and enclose the *qi* from ten to twenty times, in all cases flowing easily along with it and not letting it get into a struggle with your intention. After some time, the *qi* will emerge from the hundred hair pores of the body and you won't need to exhale any longer, not even as much as two-tenths of your normal rate. Keep balancing it and repeating the practice until you can do this for more than ten breaths. (6a)

A form of insight meditation in conjunction with breath, this too enhances youthful vigor and complexion and extends longevity. It makes adepts feel as if they have just stepped out of a refreshing bath, relaxed and at ease, pure and clean.

Enclosing *Qi* is yet another variant of the practice. It is used particularly if there is a blockage, defined as an obstruction in *qi*-flow, an unexpected ailment, or a difficulty in destiny. In this case, adepts should retire to their practice chamber and practice the various methods of absorbing *qi* with their palms and soles wide open:

Balance the *qi* and swallow it. Think actively of the place of your suffering, enclose the *qi* [hold the breath], and imagine it dripping in there, all the while using your intention to attack the ailment. When the *qi* reaches its height, exhale. Once done, swallow it again in close succession and attack the ailment as described. Do it fast, then stop. Repeat as needed, even as many as fifty times. (6b)

The text continues by giving the example of an ailment in the head or hands. Just hold the breath in and guide the *qi* into the afflicted area, maintaining a steady pressure and working with the intention of eliminating the problem. Once the problem is attacked, allow it to dissolve into the *qi*-flow and move the *qi* out through the open soles and palms, thus alleviating the condition. "It affords a most amazing relief."

Another possibility of using the *qi* for healing is to practice Spreading *Qi* (*buqi* 布氣) or what is today called external *qi* healing. Practitioners obtain cosmic *qi* from the direction associated with the inner organ of the patient's affliction, then guide it through their body and into the palms of their hands. They have the patient face the direction in question and have him or her rest the mind and clear all thoughts, then release the *qi* through the hands into his or her body. After completion, the patient is to practice swallowing *qi* to balance the internal and external energies. The activity combines the help of a trained adept with the personal practice of the patient, not only passively relieving ailments but empowering the person to maintain health on his or her own.

From here, the text moves on to describe the Six Breaths in their classic combination that is already part of the *Daoyin jing*. As in earlier materials, it specifies a variety of symptoms for each:[11]

heart	*he*	oral dryness and roughness, *qi* obstructions, pathogenic *qi*, heat, heart conditions, emotional states
liver	*xu*	inflamed, teary, or red eyes; liver conditions; vision problems; rising *qi*
spleen	*hu*	fast and hot *qi*, abdominal swelling, *qi* obstruction, dry lips, spleen conditions, arm and leg problems
lungs	*si*	temperature imbalance, lung problems, abscesses, skin problems, nasal obstructions, fatigue, exhaustion, oppression
kidneys	*chui*	coldness in the back and joints, genital problems, deafness, ear conditions
heater	*xi*	all conditions associated with the Triple Heater

---

11. The Six Breaths are also outlined in the *Chifeng sui* (Despeux 1988) and the *Xiuling yaozhi* 修齡要旨 (Essential Pointers to Cultivating Long Life) of the late Ming (today found in *Qigong yangsheng congshu*). For details on the historical development of the Six Breaths, see Despeux 2006.

Master Huanzhen's outline of breathing techniques concludes by outlining the best way of supporting *qi* through the control of fluids and food intake. In a section called "Balancing *Qi* and Fluids" (*diaoqiye* 調氣液), he describes two conditions of the mouth, one of dryness, the other of coolness and loss of taste, and recommends balancing measures:

> If the inside of the mouth feels burning and dry, there is a slight pain in the mouth, the tongue is rough and swollen, there is not enough saliva when swallowing, or if the throat hurts upon swallowing so that you have trouble eating, you have a condition of extreme heat. In that case, open the mouth very wide and exhale with *he*. After every swallowing, close the mouth tightly, then release the *qi* with *he*. Do this ten to twenty times, then beat the heavenly drum seven or nine times. (8a)
>
> If the saliva and fluid in the mouth are cold and insipid and you have no sense of taste, or if you have overdone *he* and your chest and head are stuffy, so that you cannot taste your food and receive no water when eating and drinking, then you have a cold condition. For that, use the *chui* breath to warm up. (8b)

In each case, practitioners are to repeat the exercise until the condition has resolved and they feel balanced and comfortable with the amount and quality of saliva in their mouths.

The last section of the text is called "Regulating Food and Drink" (*shiyin diaohu* 食飲調護). It recommends certain types of food, including rice or sesame gruel, soft noodles, and various kinds of buns and cakes made from wheat, buckwheat, or millet. None of them should be strongly flavored or eaten steaming hot, since that would upset the *qi*-balance. Also, they should be varied in accordance with the season to allow maximum attunement with natural changes. After every meal, moreover,

> exhale with *he* to eliminate all poisonous and stale *qi* through the mouth and make sure that there is no residual harm. People practicing *qi*-absorption should keep their stomach and intestines vacant and clean. For this, all things raw, cold, sour, smooth, gooey, greasy, old, hard, rotten, or decayed, or again anything else that is hard to digest must not be taken. (9b)

The account of these various breathing practices first mentioned in the *Daoyin jing* and later expanded in the *Huanzhen neiqi fa* thus presents a systematic overview of the various modalities in working with *qi,* providing clear definition of terms and a logical sequence of practices, as well as offering various alternative and supplementary methods. The text is clear and straightforward: it describes the practices in sufficient detail so they can be pursued even without in-depth oral instruction, and it actively integrates previously known and time-proven methods. Combining these breathing techniques with the seasonal and healing exercises that were also systematized in the *Chifeng sui* and *Neiwai gong tushuo jiyao*, practitioners had a well-organized and clearly presented repertoire of healing techniques to see them through difficult times and prepare them for spiritual attainments.

Visualizations

Beyond the activation of *qi* through breath and mental guiding, the *Daoyin jing* also presents several visualizations to ensure complete harmony of all aspects of the body. One of them is ascribed to Wangzi Qiao and called the Eight Spirit Exercises. Practitioners begin lying on their back, their neck supported by a pillow,[12] their feet five inches apart, and their hands three inches from the body. Relaxing the mind, they inhale through the nose and exhale through the mouth, allowing the breath to become so subtle that it is all but inaudible but remaining aware of movements in the belly as the *qi* is swallowed together with saliva (7b). Next, they engage in a systematic vision of the body, seeing its different parts in different shapes and colors (fig. 12). The text says,

> See the throat as a succession of white silver rings, stacked twelve levels deep. Going downward, you reach the lungs, which are white and glossy. They have two leaves reaching tall in front and two leaves hanging low in back. The heart is connected to them underneath. Large at the top and pointed below, it is shining red like an unopened lotus bud hanging down from the lungs.
>
> The liver is connected to it underneath. Its color is a clear green like a male mallard's head. It has six leaves that envelop the stomach—two in front that reach up tall and four in the back that hang down low. The gallbladder connects to it underneath, like a green silk bag. The spleen is in the very center of the belly, enwrapped from all sides. It is bright yellow like gold, lustrous and radiant.
>
> Behind all this, see the kidneys lying back to back like two sleeping rats, curled up with elbow to navel and as if they wanted to stretch out. Their color is a thick, glossy black. Fat streaks run through them, so that the white and black glow jointly.[13] (8a)

---

12. The height of the pillow, as already specified in the *Jin'gui lu,* varies according to whether and where there is an ailment to be treated: "If the ailment is located in the throat or chest, work with a pillow seven inches high. If it is below the heart, use a four-inch pillow. If it is below the navel, do away with the pillow altogether" (8b).

13. For contemporary practitioners, the image of rats may be offensive or disgusting. It works well to replace them with sleeping kittens, which are also small and furry but provide a better feeling of comfort and well-being.

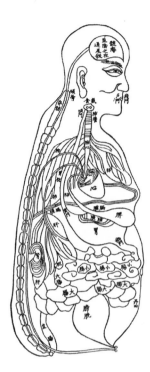

Fig. 12: Organs and energy channels in the
body. Source: *Huangting neijing buxie tu.*

Following this, practitioners are to become aware of the different psychological agents that reside in the various organs, echoing the basic system of Chinese medicine while applying it actively to meditative healing. The five agents are
the spirit souls (liver), the material souls (lung), the spirit (heart), the intention
(spleen), and the essence (kidneys).[14] They should also note whether there are any
areas in the body that are empty or full, that is, suffer from insufficient or excessive *qi*. Should there be places that are empty, it is best to keep the eyes closed
during practice; for full areas, it is best to keep them open (8b). Also, the practice
should be complemented by easy movement, such as walking back and forth for
two hundred steps or doing some gentle stretches of the four limbs.

This version of meditative *qi*-guiding for the first time outlines a detailed
inner vision of the body in the context of healing exercises. It does not quite integrate the Highest Clarity system of seeing body gods and palaces within, but it
shows a creative and potent way of activating the key inner organs of the body. It
can be considered a forerunner of the modern practice of the Inner Smile, which
too has practitioners visualize the organs in their characteristic shape and color

---

14. On the mental agents connected to the five organs, see Porkert 1974, 184–185; Ishida 1989, 52;
Kaptchuk 2000, 59–62.

while releasing negative emotions and inviting advanced virtues into the self (Chia and Chia 1993, 85–102).

Another version of body visualization inspired by Highest Clarity appears toward the end of the *Daoyin jing* and is associated with Master Ning. It consists of eight short instructions on how to visualize the body, including a vision of the five inner organs with their respective colors that will "allow the *qi* to flow evenly through the body" (17a). In addition, the text suggests that one should "visualize the gods of the five organs with their appropriate colors, each in his specific place" or see them "transform into dragons or fish" (17a). Practitioners should envision "the heart radiant as a fire, shining brightly like the Dipper to block out bad *qi*" (17b) and "the kidney-*qi* below the navel in bright red and white, allowing it to move along the spine, up to the head, and back down again to pervade the entire body" (17ab). The latter practice is called "reverting essence." While the expression is commonly used to refer to the refinement of sexual energy, the practice described here is more reminiscent of the Microcosmic Orbit, in which *qi* moves along the central channels up and down the torso.

A highly similar technique that involves breathing in conjunction with visualizing a flow of energy is also found in the *Han Wudi waizhuan* 漢武帝外傳 (Outer Record of Emperor Wu of the Han, DZ 293), a Highest Clarity collection of stories on the famous Han emperor that dates from the fifth century. It says,

> Every evening concentrate on a red *qi* entering through the Heavenly Gate [at the top of the head] and visualize it as it makes the round of the body within and without. At the end, see it transform into fire in the brain that consumes the body, giving a fiery brilliance. This practice is called refining the physical form.
>
> You can also hold the *qi* and swallow it in a practice known as embryo respiration. Or you can make the saliva gush forth beneath the tongue and swallow it in "embryo nourishment." (12a; Maspero 1981, 486–487)

That this is part of early Highest Clarity practice is made clear from the description in the *Zhen'gao* of a method that involves visualizing multicolored rays issuing from the Sun as described in the practice of solar absorption; the rays then, however, move around the body and turn into divine forms of *qi* that give rise to an immortal body within the adept. Called the Method of the Three *Qi*, this practice was revealed to a certain Fan Youchong 范幼沖 and recorded in Tao Hongjing's *Dengzhen yinjue*:

> Constantly visualize the three breaths, one green, one white, and one red. See them like ribbons descending from the sun in the east and let them enter directly into your

mouth. Inhale them consciously ninety times and you will feel naturally full. Stop. After doing this for ten years, three shining *qi* in these three colors are born spontaneously in the body. They will make you immortal. (2.19ab; Maspero 1981, 513; also in *Shangqing wozhong jue* 2.14ab)

Along with integrating these various forms of Highest Clarity energy work, the *Daoyin jing* also presents exercises and methods of guiding the *qi* that have a more devotional component. According to one set, practitioners should focus on a divine radiance standing guard to their left and right or on the Ruler of Fates as he takes up residence in the body with his two acolytes, resting there permanently and keeping the person alive (17a). Another set instructs adepts to "visualize themselves flying about and dividing their bodies" (17b). More than that, as adepts fly, they should always see people like themselves in front or behind. After many years of practice, they may even be able to talk to these divine entities to receive divine guidance and instruction as they traverse the otherworld.

To sum up, the *Daoyin jing* includes it all: from dominantly medical exercises that focus on physical movements and concentrated breathing through Highest Clarity energy work to the devotional practices of envisioning the body inhabited by gods and surrounded by divine entities. Healing exercises as presented here involve a wide-ranging collection of techniques that actively integrate the medical with the magical, the functional with the devotional. The body is no longer merely an assembly of limbs and organs, nor even yet a combination of energy centers and pathways, but a multilayered phenomenon, an intricate network that forms part of the cosmic patterns of the larger universe. Healing exercises and *qi*-practice cure the body, but they also go beyond physical wellness and lead to the wholeness of the Dao.

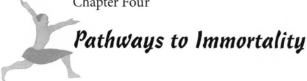

Chapter Four

Pathways to Immortality

Bringing the integrative trend visible in the *Daoyin jing* to full fruition, Daoists and medical masters of the Tang dynasty (618–907) created a highly complex and intricate system whereby to attain immortality that made use of physical practices on various levels. Their work closely reflects the dominant cultural trends of the time.

In general, the Tang dynasty marks a high point in the development of Chinese culture. Reunited under a Chinese ruling house after centuries of division and multiple local kingdoms, the country expanded militarily, earned wide respect, and came to exert a great cultural influence on neighboring cultures. With growing economic prosperity and relative peace and without the need to be defensive at all times, Tang rulers relaxed restrictions and opened the society to a new level of freedom. At the same time, the overall tendency toward unity and integration created political and philosophical visions that emphasized integration and systematization. As a result, the country's major schools of thought—Daoism, Buddhism, Confucianism—strove not only to get along with each other but also to develop organized worldview systems and administrative structures to match the dominant culture.

Daoists in particular came to refine and expand their practices and beliefs into new universalist dimensions. They created a complex ordination hierarchy, joining the three major medieval schools of Celestial Masters, Numinous Treasure, and Highest Clarity into one system. They compiled various comprehensive accounts of their worldview, presenting a coherent system of thought and integrating concepts from all three schools as well as Confucian ethics and Buddhist doctrine. They became part of the political structure, managing state-sponsored Daoist temples in all districts of the empire, serving in key ritual and official functions, and taking an active interest in educating the elite in Daoist ways of long life and transcendence.[1]

As part of this overall effort toward cultural integration and concern with serving the country, several important Daoist masters emerged who presented a systematic account of how best to attain health, long life, and immortality, in the

---

1. For more on the Tang dynasty, see Benn 2002, Twitchett 1979. On Daoism under the Tang, see Barrett 1996; Kirkland 1997; Kohn and Kirkland 2000; Kohn 2001, ch. 7.

process creating an integrated vision of the entire Daoist path and transforming the role and importance of healing exercises into yet new dimensions. Not only unique in their specific effort and vision, they are also well documented biographically, allowing us a first detailed look at the social background, lifestyle, and activities of traditional practitioners. And, of course, they wrote a number of essential works on self-healing and self-realization. These works go beyond the previous literature in that they actively integrate medical techniques, such as diet control and the taking of herbal medicines, with the practices common to healing exercises (moderation, breathing, stretching, guiding the *qi*), then on this basis systematically guide followers to spiritual attainments through more cosmic-oriented exercises, which include talismans, meditations, and *qi*-absorption. The works of the great Tang masters are longer and more intricate, and they place exercise practice firmly in the transition between healing and spiritual transcendence.

Who were these great masters and innovators? What kind of life did they lead? How did they come to the practice, and what did the practice do for them? What system of healing and immortality did they develop? Are their systems compatible, or do they show differences? How are healing exercises changed under the new impact of the systematization and the quest for immortality?

Sun Simiao

The first and maybe most important master of longevity in the Tang is Sun Simiao 孫思邈, born in 581 near the western capital of Chang'an. According to official biographies, which tend to stereotype masters as child prodigies and emphasize personal virtues, such as bone-deep honesty and a hesitation to accept imperial honors, he was a precocious child who studied eagerly from an early age. By age twenty he supposedly not only had an extensive knowledge of the classics and philosophers, but was also familiar with Buddhist and Daoist scriptures. Despite several invitations to serve at the imperial court under the Sui and early Tang dynasties, he went to live in seclusion on Mount Taibai 太白山 in the Zhongnan mountains, about a hundred miles from his ancestral home.[2]

In contrast to the report of this shining and easy childhood that brought forth an upright and noble character, an autobiographical note in the preface to his *Qianjin fang* 千金方 (Priceless Prescriptions) notes that he was a sickly boy who underwent all kinds of treatments, thus inspiring a great interest in medical matters and an inclination toward longevity practices and Daoist seclusion. The text says,

---

2. Details of Sun's early life are outlined in Sivin 1968, 82–96; Engelhardt 1989, 266; Sakade 1992, 2; Chen 2000, 91–94.

In my childhood I suffered from a cold disorder due to winds, and constantly consulted physicians. My family's finances were exhausted to pay for medicine. So it was that during my student years I held the medical classics in special regard, and that even in my old age I have not set them aside.

As to the reading of pulses and other techniques of diagnosis, the gathering of herbs and their compounding, administration and dosage, hygiene and the various precautions associated with health—when I heard of any man who excelled me in any of these, no distance would keep me from him. I would learn what he had to teach and apply it. When I reached maturity, I became aware that I had attained some understanding. (Sivin 1967, 271; see also Engelhardt 1989, 279)

This documents Sun Simiao's early start in medical studies, which resulted from an intense personal need, and his dedication to being the best and knowing the most in this field. To this end he also traveled widely, collecting ancient books and recipes all over the country and, especially between 605 and 615, engaged in various alchemical experiments to find the medicine of immorality, thus entering the realm of religion and going beyond the goals of healing and long life. Most of his case histories, and therefore his main activities as a healer, date from 616 to 626. In 633, it seems, he was in Sichuan, where he conducted various alchemical experiments and contracted "cinnabar poisoning" (*dandu* 丹毒). He reports on the illness in his *Qianjin yifang* 千金翼方 (Supplementary Priceless Prescriptions):

While asleep, I felt pain throughout the flesh and bones of my extremities. By dawn, my head was aching and my vision unclear; there was a blister the size of a crossbow pellet on my left temple, which ached so badly I could not bring my hand near it. By noon the swelling had spread to my right temple, and by night it had become general. My eyes, once closed, could not be reopened. I came very close to death. The county magistrate, Squire Zhou, treated me with every sort of medication, but without remission. After seven days I myself worked out a prescription which was magical in its efficacy. (22.30a; Sivin 1968, 251)

The same text also contains several passages suggesting that Sun Simiao was an ordained Daoist of the Celestial Masters level, that is, the lowest and most popular level of the Tang Daoist hierarchy (Kohn 2004b, 16). He refers to certain exorcistic formulas that were reserved for exclusive recital by Daoist masters, and it seems unlikely that someone uninitiated would have had access to them (Sivin 1978, 312; Engelhardt 1989, 267). Even in his medical function, moreover, he applied Daoist recipes, using the same methods for herbal compounds as for al-

Fig. 13: Sun Simiao, the King of
Medicines. Source: *Liexian
quanzhuan.*

chemical drugs and prescribing remedies that on occasion involved massive
doses of highly toxic ingredients such as mercury (Sivin 1968, 142).

Besides continuing to heal and pursue immortality, Sun apparently did his
main writing between 730 and 760. In 759, having become famous as a physician
and master of long life, he joined the retinue of Emperor Gaozong in an informal
capacity. After about fifteen years, he requested permission to retire from the court
because of illness; he presumably died in 682, a good hundred years after his alleged birth in 581. These dates may well be an exaggeration of the chroniclers, eager
to show him successful in his quest for long life. They also claimed that he attained
immortality, insisting that for one month after his death there was no change in his
appearance and no physical decomposition and that his corpse, when placed in the
coffin, was as light as cloth (Sivin 1968, 130; Engelhardt 1989, 267). Possible exaggeration notwithstanding, the chroniclers made a strong case for Sun's extraordinary powers, leading to his widespread veneration as the King of Medicines
(Yaowang 藥王) in Daoist temples and popular shrines to the present day (fig. 13).

Sun Simiao was a prolific writer. The standard histories of the Tang list
twenty-two works ascribed to him, a number that grew to about eighty over the
centuries (Sivin 1968, 60; Engelhardt 1989, 277). Only a handful of these survive,

the most important among them being the Priceless Prescriptions series, extensive collections of highly technical medical information that date from the 650s and are still actively used by physicians in China today (Sivin 1968, 132).

There is first the *Qianjin fang*, a general outline of medical methods and prescriptions in thirty *juan*, which focuses primarily on pharmacological therapy (chs. 2–25) but also includes chapters on dietetics (ch. 26; see Engelhardt and Hempen 1997), longevity techniques (ch. 27), pulse diagnosis (ch. 28), and acupuncture and moxibustion (chs. 29–30; see Despeux 1987). Then there is the *Qianjin yifang*, which has one chapter on long-life theory. Both were extensively modified in the Song dynasty and exist only in editions from the fourteenth century onward (Sivin 1968, 138).[3]

Among other extant works, Sun is credited with two brief general outlines on how to best live one's life: the *Baosheng ming* 保生銘 (On Preserving Life, *DZ* 835), a concise treatise extolling moderation, a regular lifestyle, and virtuous attitudes; and the *Fushou lun* 福壽論 (On Happiness and Long Life, *DZ* 1426), a presentation of the workings of fate and various ways to enhance it.[4]

Beyond these, two texts survive that specify seasonal methods: a short set of verses describing optimal breathing practice in the four seasons, contained in the Song-dynasty collection *Xiuzhen shishu* 修真十書 (Ten Books on Cultivating Perfection, *DZ* 263, 19.7a); and the *Sheyang lun* 攝養論 (On Preserving and Nourishing [Life], *DZ* 841), an account of dietary and other health methods for each of the twelve months of the year (see Schipper and Verellen 2004, 356).

Two further works are more specialized and religious in nature: the *Danjing yaojue* 丹經要訣 (Essential Formulas of Alchemical Classics, *Yunji qiqian* 71; trl. Sivin 1968), which collects various formulas for preparing immortality elixirs; and the *Cunshen lianqi ming* 存神練氣銘 (On the Visualization of Spirit and Refinement of *Qi*, *DZ* 400, *Yunji qiqian* 33.12a–14b; trl. Kohn 1987), a concise outline of five major stages of the mind in concentrative meditation plus seven stages of the self as it transcends to immortality.

Last but not least, two texts contain comprehensive outlines of long-life methods: Sun's *Zhenzhong ji* 枕中記 (Pillowbook Record, *DZ* 837; *Yunji qiqian* 33.1a–12a), a collection of longevity techniques in five sections; and the *Yangxing*

3. An expanded later version is the *Qianjin yaofang* 千金要方 (Essential Priceless Prescriptions, *DZ* 1163), in 93 *juan* and 232 sections. Part of the Daoist canon, it contains various prefaces and some additions from Song writers. It deals with the full contingent of medical methods, focusing particularly on drug therapy and dedicating three *juan* to long-life practices (81–83). See Schipper and Verellen 2004, 339–340.
4. This is probably the same as the *Fulu lun* 福錄論 (On Happiness and Prosperity), ascribed to Sun in the early bibliographies (Sivin 1968, 132). On these two texts, see Schipper and Verellen 2004, 535, 743.

yanming lu 養性延命錄 (On Nourishing Inner Nature and Extending Life, *DZ* 838; *Yunji qiqian* 32.1a–24b), a summary of nourishing life practices in six sections that is linked with various masters in the bibliographies but may well be a work of Sun or of his disciples. While not all of these texts discuss healing exercises, they do contribute to our understanding of how the practice was viewed in the early Tang dynasty and how it was integrated with other longevity and immortality techniques (Schipper and Verellen 2004, 345–347).

Working toward Long Life

Sun Simiao's basic understanding of the dynamics of long life are described in the *Fushou lun*. Here he notes that health is one among various functions of good fortune, which in turn is directly related to karma and depends on the good and bad deeds one performs in life (1b). The key to being good, aside from accumulating "hidden virtues" by doing good deeds that may not even be recognized, is to appreciate one's standing within the greater scheme of things or to remain within one's allotment, the share (*fen* 分) one has in the world. He defines this in terms of rank and position, carriages and horses, wives and concubines, servants and slaves, houses and residences, silks and brocades, clothes and garments, and food and drink, as well as profit in business (2a–3b).

It is most important to gain a basic understanding of how the Dao works in the world so that one can discern when to move forward and when to retreat, when to accumulate more and when to leave well enough alone. In this context, Sun distinguishes nine different kinds of people: sages who embody the Dao in nonaction; worthies who know misfortunes but do not cheat to avoid them; accomplished ones who obey destiny and do not pursue anything beyond their level; faithful people who guard their faith and rest in calm tranquility no matter what happens; benevolent folks who are modest and diligent, caring and circumspect in their relations with others; knights who are dedicated in service and maintain respect at all times; ordinary people who observe the principles but are careless about their implementation; ignorant ones who are obstinate in their egotism and cannot be convinced to pay attention to the greater flux; and, finally, small men who actively go against the Dao, keeping themselves busy without even thinking about the greater picture (1a).

One should examine oneself to see which category fits, then cultivate the attitude of the next higher level, so that one ends up with clear perception and a dedication to service, benevolence, and destiny. Whatever good fortune one may find, one should keep a sense of detachment: "Reside in wealth and not love it, reside in nobility and not cherish it" (4b). To further enhance long life and good fortune, moreover, one should take certain active steps to preserve life. Only hinted at in the *Fushou lun,* these are spelled out in more detail in the *Baosheng ming* (fig. 14). The full text, in parallel sentences, reads as follows:

> If people exercise their bodies, the hundred ills cannot arise.
> If they never drink to intoxication, the host of ailments stays away.
> After a meal, walk a hundred steps and massage the belly a few times.
> For sleep avoid high pillows, and spit or cry without looking back.
> Cut your nails on *yinchou* days and give your hair a hundred strokes.
> When satiated, urinate standing up; when hungry, pass water squatting down.
> In walking and sitting avoid the wind; in your residence avoid small nestings.
> Never face north to relieve yourself, and throughout life remain obscure and hidden.
> Observe all the taboos on Sun and Moon; stay away from dangerous fire and water.
> Every night wash your feet before retiring, and after dinner don't eat another snack.
> Consideration and forbearance are of highest value, while cheating and gossiping kill family relations.
> Thinking and worrying most harm the spirit, while joy and anger upset your respiration.
> Regularly remove all nasal hairs; always avoid spitting on the ground.
> Rise as soon as the day breaks, and when getting up, put the left foot first.
> Throughout the day avoid disasters, get rid of wayward *qi,* and stay away from evil.
> Focus on performing the Seven-Stars Step, which will let you live a long and happy life.
> Sour flavors harm the muscles and pungent flavors reduce good *qi.*
> Bitter flavors diminish the heart while sweet tastes injure the will.
> Salty flavors hinder your long life, so don't give in to cravings for one or the other.
> In spring and summer, go along with ease; in fall and winter, stabilize your yang.
> Sleep alone to guard perfection and remain cautious and tranquil at all times.
> Wealth and brocades all have their proper lot; know what is enough to find your best advantage.
> Aggressive acquisition is a great affliction, while few desires keep you out of trouble.
> Then *qi* and spirit remain naturally present and you can learn the Dao completely.
> Write this on your wall or door and teach it well to other worthy fellows.

Sun Simiao thus emphasizes that it is best to live in moderation, observe one's proper allotment, stay away from dangers, avoid all stressful speech and thought, balance the five flavors, and observe the taboos of Sun, Moon, and the four seasons. By living calmly and in harmony, *qi* and spirit remain within the body, and one can live in health and happiness for extended years. He recommends that one paste a copy of the text on a wall where one can see it often and spread the good word to others in one's environment (1b).

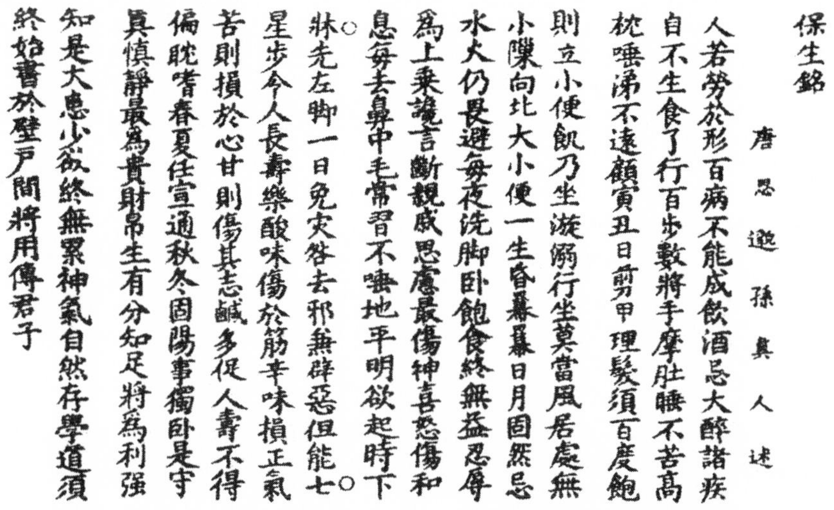

終知真偏苦星林息為水小則枕自人　保
始是慎眈則步先每上陟立唾不若　生
書大慎靜則令左去乘仍小向涕生勞　銘
於患靜最損人脚鼻讒畏便北不食於
壁小最為於長一中言避飲大遠了形
尸欲為貴心壽日毛斷每乃小顧行百　唐
間終貴財甘樂免常親夜坐便實百病　思
將無財帛則酸災習戚洗游一丑步不　邈
用累帛生傷味咎不思腳溺生日數能　孫
傳神生有其傷去唾慮卧行昏剪將成　真
君氣有分志於邪地最飽坐暮甲手飲　人
子自分知鹹筋無平傷食莫暮理摩酒
　然知足多辛辟明神終當日鬢肚忌
　存足將促味惡欲喜無風月須睡大
　學將為人損但起怒益君固百不醉
　道為利壽正能時傷忍處然度苦諸
　須利強不氣七下和辱無忌飽高疾

Fig. 14: The original text of On Preserving Life. Source: *Baosheng ming*.

Further details on how best to align oneself with the rhythm of the Dao in physical practice are spelled out verses on seasonal breathing practice attributed to Sun Simiao according to the *Xiuzhen shishu*. The text says,

> In spring, breathe *xu* for clear eyes and so wood can aid your liver.
> In summer, reach for *he*, so that heart and fire can be at peace.
> In fall, breathe *si* to stabilize and gather metal, keeping the lungs moist.
> For the kidneys, next, breathe *chui* and see your inner water calm.
> The Triple Heater needs your *xi* to expel all heat and troubles.
> In all four seasons take long breaths, so spleen can process food.
> And, of course, avoid exhaling noisily, not letting even your ears hear it.
> This practice is most excellent and will help preserve your divine elixir. (19.7a)[5]

Sun further supplements this with instructions in the *Sheyang lun* that specify for each month how to live and eat correctly. Thus, for example, in the first

---

5. This reflects the standard system of the Six Breaths as it is still practiced under the name Six Healing Sounds. It is probably a later ascription to Sun Simiao, since in his *Qianjin fang* he links *he* with the liver, *si* with the kidneys, *xu* with the lungs, and xi with the spleen (ch. 26). At the same time, the system also appears in the *Yangxing yanming lu*, another text closely associated with Sun. Here the breaths are not linked with specific organs, but serve to remove heat, fatigue, wind, or anxiety. The method was, moreover, not limited to a Daoist or medical environment, but also appears in a Buddhist text, the *Tiantai xiao zhiguan* 天台小止觀 (Lesser Cessation and Observation [Methods] of the Tiantai School), and in a fragmented Dunhuang manuscript (P. 3043). See Sakade 2005, 28–29.

month one should be aware that the kidneys (associated with winter) may be prone to ailing and that the function of the lungs (the organ dominant in the fall) is still reduced. To help with these conditions, limit the intake of salty and sour foods and increase pungent flavors in the diet but still avoid fresh scallions, which reduce body fluids and blood, as well as fresh ginseng, which creates fatigue. Also, do not eat the flesh of hibernating animals, for doing so will lessen your life energy, or the meat of predators, such as foxes, for doing so will agitate your spirit. Generally taking care to balance the diet will support the kidneys and tonify the lungs, calm and balance the spleen and stomach.

Although it is cold outside, being still midwinter, one should not resist or resent it nor should one keep oneself too warm. One should rise and go to sleep early to avoid lingering in the darkness of night. Very specifically, and reminiscent of the farmer's almanacs still in use today, the text notes that one should remove white hair on the fourth day, practice meditations and fast for an increase in good fortune on the seventh, and avoid long journeys on the eighth (1ab).

Similarly, in the seventh month in midsummer, the liver and heart *qi* are lessening, and the lungs are rising as the dominant organ. One should keep calm and at peace in all emotions, increase salty and reduce pungent flavors, thus nourishing the spleen and stomach—which are supported by the changing emphasis in diet in all seasons and not allotted a specific period, such as the Indian summer, to themselves. As in winter, one should balance one's temperature, avoiding heavy sweats without strongly resisting the heat and engaging in extreme cooling measures. One should not eat pork and should avoid thinking evil thoughts. Again, certain days are best for personal hygiene, such as taking baths and cutting hair; others are ideal for devotions and fasting; yet others should not be used for travels or new adventures (3ab).

The pattern here is to provide dietary and health advice in equal measure with concrete taboos and emotional and spiritual suggestions. What we would classify in completely separate categories is conflated into one integrated pattern, giving testimony to the integrated Chinese vision of the person as a physical, emotional, communal, and spiritual being. Also, the key lies in the details of daily life, not in the big gestures or grand retreats that one engages in only once in a while. To be successful in the attainment of extended longevity and perfect health, one needs to take all these different aspects into account.

Medical Exercises

Healing exercises appear in three places in Sun Simiao's work, each in a different collection of long-life methods and each presenting different sets. First, in chapter 27 of his *Qianjin fang*, under the heading "Massages" (*anmo* 按摩), he presents them as part of a medical regimen for the overall extension of life. The regimen is outlined in eight sections: Nourishing Inner Nature, Master Daolin's Methods, Living Quarters, Massages, Harmonizing *Qi*, Food and Diet, Various Taboos of the Yellow Emperor, and Bedchamber Arts.

This entire presentation, as indicated in the heading of the second part, is adapted from the *Daolin shesheng lun* 道林攝生論 (Discourse on Protecting Life by Master Daolin, *DZ* 1427), a short work that discusses the subject in similar terms but in a different order and in only six sections: General Issues, Timing, Taboos, Massages, Breathing, and Residences. The text is ascribed to Daolin 道林, commonly identified as Zhi Dun 支盾 (314–366), one of the earliest aristocratic Buddhists in Chinese history and a popular figure among authors of long-life texts, such as the *Yangsheng yaoji* and the *Daoyin jing* (Despeux 1989, 229, 231). Although mentioned frequently in this context, Zhi Dun is not credited with the practice or the creation of physical regimens in historical sources, and the text associated with his name probably dates from the Tang (Schipper and Verellen 2004, 361–362).

Both the *Qianjin fang* and the *Daolin lun* present two sequences of movements under the heading "Massages" that activate various parts of the body and are, in a different order, recounted in the ninth-century *Zhiyan zong* 至言總 (Collection of Perfect Words, *DZ* 1033, 5.1a–3b).[6] The first sequence is called Brahmanic Indian Massage Techniques, indicating a possible Indian or Buddhist influence that, however, cannot be substantiated from historical sources. It consists of eighteen exercises and takes the practitioner through different positions of the body. The text claims that, if undertaken three times a day, it will "lead to the complete elimination of all ailments within a month. You will be able to walk as fast as a galloping horse, extend your years, eat as you please, and enjoy perfect eyesight. You will feel light and healthy and never get tired" (5.1a).

BRAHMANIC INDIAN MASSAGE TECHNIQUES
1. [Kneel upright.] Bring both hands together, then wring and twist them as if washing.[7]

---

6. This text was written by Fan Youran 范翛然, a native of Kuaiji in Zhejiang. It contains numerous *Yangsheng yaoji* fragments and various citations from the *Daolin lun: Zhiyan zong* 2.8a = *Daolin lun* 23a, 2.11ab=2ab, 2.12ab=4b, 4.9a–10b=16b–17a, 18b–19b, and 5.1a–2b=13b–16a (Despeux 1989, 232). See also Schipper and Verellen 2004, 446–447. For a thorough study of the text in relation to other Tang Daoist scriptures, see Yoshioka 1967. The "Exercise" section is translated in Huang and Wurmbrand 1987, 2:40–46.
7. To make the flow of movements smoother and keep exercises in the same posture together, I have slightly rearranged the original order.

2. Interlace the fingers, reverse the palms, and place them over the chest three times.

3. Both hands joined, press down on the thighs, exerting equal pressure on the left and right.

4. Both hands joined, again press down heavily on the thighs, then slowly twist to the left and right.

5. Lift up both hands as if pulling a bow seventy pounds in weight, repeating it on both sides.

6. Curl the hands into fists and punch forward, exerting equal force on both sides.

7. Raise the hands as if lifting a boulder, exerting equal pressure on both sides.

8. Curl the hands into fists, then pull them back and punch forward alternately to open the chest. Use equal pressure on both sides.

9. Sit up straight with legs extended and lean the body sideways as if pushing against a mountain, exerting equal pressure on both sides.

10. Holding your head with both hands, twist and bring up one thigh at a time. This is to stretch the waist.

11. Sit up straight with legs extended and bring one leg forward and up in the air. Do this equally on both sides.

12. Now, raise one leg and with the hand on the same side hook the extended foot to put it on the opposite knee. Press it down with both hands, then switch to the other side.

13. Reverse the hands, place them on your back, and pound them up and down against the spine, exerting equal pressure on both sides.

14. [Kneel.] Place both hands firmly on the ground and contract the body to round the spine, then lift up the head. Repeat three times.

15. Place both hands firmly on the ground and turn the head to look back like a tiger, moving in both directions.

16. Interlace the fingers tightly and step one foot on the joined palms. Repeat on the other side.

17. Stand upright and bend the body back, then lift up again. Repeat three times.

18. Stand up straight, then step one foot forward and backward, kicking into empty space. Do it equally on both sides.

This sequence works all the different muscle groups in the body and uses three major basic postures: kneeling, sitting, and standing. Moving through the body from top to bottom, it warms up the joints to activate the synovial fluids. It also includes a number of potent bends and twists that will release tensions and open the body. Unlike earlier series, it pays particular attention to the smaller joints, such as the neck, wrists, and ankles, and also emphasizes massages in the form of rubbing and pounding, especially of the extremities. The entire sequence being called "massages" may indicate that its creators thought of the movements as a form of internal rubbing and stimulating, indicating in general the close connection in the medieval Chinese mind of exercises and massages.

Following this, the second sequence in the *Qianjin fang* is called Laozi's Method of Massage. It consists of forty-nine exercises that have no specified postures but can all be performed in a seated position. Like the Brahmanic Techniques, its practice—undertaken in two sets of seven repetitions each—consists more of stretches than massages in the narrow sense and serves to create a greater openness in the muscles and joints. It begins with a series of seated twists of the waist and torso, then stretches the neck in all four directions. Bringing head and knees together in a curl next, it moves on to a series of arm stretches, up and down, right and left, pulled into the chest and punching outward. Following this, practitioners are to shake their wrists and loosen up their fingers, curling them in and out and interlacing them for a greater stretch. The last section of the series works on the feet and thighs, having practitioners twist the feet, move the toes, and bend and stretch the legs. The pattern ends with a group of standing movements, stretching up and bending down, twisting spine and torso.

In many ways similar to the Brahmanic Techniques, Laozi's Method works all the major muscle groups in the body, provides some potent twists and stretches, and pays close attention to the smaller joints. Both sequences together, moreover, appear in the systematic presentation of the text after establishing auspicious residences and before moving into the harmonization of *qi* and the balancing of food, seasonal rhythms, and sexual activities. Exercises here are clearly a primarily medical means to open the body and improve *qi*-flow in preparation for higher attainments, consisting of strictly physical moves without visualization or other spiritual components.

Advanced Practice

In contrast to these medical and mechanical practices, which are addressed largely to a lay audience, Sun's other descriptions of healing exercises integrate a sense of inner harmony and emphasize a meditative focus, reaching beyond health and long life toward the spiritual realm. In his *Zhenzhong ji*, they appear in the third of five sections—Prudence, Prohibitions, Exercises, *Qi*-Guiding, and Meditation. In contrast to the *Qianjin fang*, the focus of the text is more internal and aims to awaken the mind and raise the individual's awareness of internal energy flows.

For this reason, from the very beginning it emphasizes prudence, described—in continuation of an earlier presentation in the *Jin'gui lu*—as a sense of awe and respect, which encourages moral actions and virtuous thoughts. This quality alone creates great benefit. The text says,

> One who is able to understand these things is safe from harm by dragons when traveling on water, and cannot be hurt by tigers or rhinoceroses when traveling on land. Weapons cannot wound him, nor can contagious diseases infect him. Slander cannot destroy his good name, nor the poisonous stings of insects do him harm. (Sivin 1968, 118; see also Engelhardt 1989, 281)

To maintain prudence, moreover, one should avoid overindulgence in food and drink as well as other sensual and sexual pleasures, observing instead seasonal guidelines for healthy living as outlined also in the *Baosheng ming.*

Next, under "Prohibitions," the text encourages closer alignment with the Dao by observing moral precepts, temporal taboos, and dietetic regulations. Similar to rules also described in the *Sheyang lun,* these include conventional taboos concerned with specific days of the month. For example, days including the cyclical signs *jia* and *yin* are considered dangerous because they mark the time when the demons fight each other and people are given to tension and nervousness. The text also proves a set of precepts that has to do with ritual purity. To maintain oneself in good status, one should avoid

1. Debauchery
2. Stealing and doing evil
3. Drinking
4. Uncleanliness
5. Eating the meat of the zodiac animal corresponding to the year of one's father's birth
6. Eating the meat of the zodiac animal corresponding to the year of one's own birth
7. Eating any meat at all
8. Eating anything raw or the five pungent vegetables
9. Killing a sentient being, including even insects and worms
10. Urinating while facing north (33.6a; Engelhardt 1989, 284)

These ten precepts combine the classic five precepts against killing, stealing, lying, sexual misconduct, and intoxication (uncleanliness), which are prevalent in both Daoism and Buddhism and generally form part of the great universal rules, with specific dietary regulations and several concrete taboos against offending the Dao by urinating north or eating animals with specific cosmic connections. They are typical for the intricate mixture in Daoist thinking of behavioral guidelines on all different levels—personal, social, and cosmic—thereby enhancing a more cosmic awareness of the importance of human behavior. In addition, the text says that practitioners should keep themselves and their surroundings scrupulously clean and always maintain emotional harmony. They should move frequently to prevent getting involved with ordinary people and to avoid any deep relationships with the opposite sex. Female adepts should not get pregnant; male practitioners should not approach pregnant or menstruating women. Both should strive for greater self-reliance and venerate the gods and goddesses but not dream of engaging in sexual intercourse with them (Engelhardt 1989, 282).[8]

All this leads to the third section, "Exercises," which specifies concrete daily routines that will help the foundation of immortality. Although the practices here are called exercises, they focus mainly on massages and include instructions for morning stretches, face massages, and eye stimulation. The morning exercises are an adaptation of Highest Clarity practice as outlined in the *Qiju jing* and can also be described as a condensed version of the more extensive routines described in the *Qianjin fang*. They begin with a neck stretch, interlacing the fingers behind the neck and pressing the head against them, then go on to a series of standing bends and stretches in all four directions (8a; *Qiju jing* 6a).

Following these, adepts are to practice face massages:

Massage the entire face with both hands. This will give you radiance and glossiness while preventing wrinkles and discolorations. If you do this for five years, your complexion will be like that of a young girl. Massage the face for two rounds of seven repetitions, then stop.

When you first wake up, rub the neck, the four sections of the face, and the ears with the soft inside of your hand, then cover the entire area with a hot, moist towel. Next, comb your hair and massage the top of your head for a good long time, then move both hands over the face and the eyes, covering them for a good while. This will make your eyes naturally bright and clear and prevent all wayward *qi* from accosting you. (8a)

Next, adepts swallow the saliva thirty times, guiding it deep inside the body, a practice that can also be done at other occasions during the period of rising or living *qi*.

In addition, again as in the Highest Clarity texts, adepts should practice regular eye exercises:

---

8. Sexual relations with divine beings were a common fantasy among Tang seekers, some of whom expressed them in beautiful poetry. See Cahill 1985.

Place your middle fingers on the inner corner of the eyes against the bridge of the nose. [Note: The inner corners of the eyes connect to the brightness of the pupils.] Then hold the breath and allow the *qi* to come through. Once you feel the *qi* [as a pulse], look around to work your eyes, then repeat once more. If you do this regularly, you will be able to see as far as ten thousand miles.

With your hand massage the small hollow behind the eyebrows. [Note: This is where the *qi* flows to the eyes.] Repeat this for three sets of nine. Also, using both palms and fingers, rub from the eyes upward all the way to the forehead and sideways as far as the ears. Do thirty repetitions without losing track of count or time.

After this, stroke the hands upward against the forehead for three sets of nine. Begin by moving from the center of the eyebrows and into the hairline. Prolonged practice will help you attain immortality. When you cultivate this, make sure not to interfere with the Flowery Canopy. [Note: The Flowery Canopy indicates the eyebrows.] (8b–9a; see also *Qiju jing* 4a)

All this, based on a strong awareness of morality and seasonal change, creates the physical basis for immortality practice of ordained Daoists and dedicated hermits. As already subtly indicated in the *Daoyin jing,* healing exercises are now clearly no longer merely a series of bends and stretches that open the body and lubricate the joints, but a way of activating the *qi* in readiness for higher attainments. Once the body is warmed up and the eyes are strong and clear, adepts can move on to practice guiding the *qi,* the subject of the next section. Learning to absorb the *qi* and retain it in the body, adepts can eliminate pain and cure diseases, then begin to practice embryo respiration, where "one does not use the nose or the mouth but instead one breathes in the manner of an embryo inside the womb, thus finding realization and attaining the Dao" (9b; Jackowicz 2006, 76). Supplemented by various techniques of visualizing the Sun and the Moon within the body, as well as by such meditative techniques as Guarding the One (see Kohn 1989c) and the concoction of an alchemical elixir described in the last section of the text, this will eventually lead to a cosmicization of the body, magical powers on earth, and ascension to the immortals above.

Immortality

This same focus on immortality in addition to healing is also present in the other integrated practice text associated with Sun Simiao, the *Yangxing yanming lu.* Arranged in six sections—General Observations, Dietary Precepts, Miscellaneous Taboos, Absorbing *Qi* to Cure Diseases, Exercises and Massages, and Controlling

Sexual Activity[9]—the text covers similar ground as the *Zhenzhong ji*, but does not outline a systematic progress. Rather, it presents different kinds of methods under appropriate headings, suggesting that adepts may find any number of suitable practices for their particular level and goals. The preface to the text, like other of Sun's works, emphasizes the importance of one's allotment and warns people not to "foolishly waste your intention to indulge in sights and sounds, apply your knowledge to scheme for wealth and fame, suffer a loss and harbor it permanently in your chest, rush about so you cannot even keep up with yourself, never heed the rules of rites and deportment, or eat and drink without moderation." It concludes this warming with a note that "if you stumble along like this, how can you possibly avoid the afflictions of harm and early death?" (pref. 1a).

The section on physical practices is titled "Exercises and Massages," resolving the conflict in the other texts where physical practices were described under "Massages" and massages under "Exercises." It contains a few basic explanations of why the practices are undertaken, such as listing six kinds of body fluids—semen, saliva, tears, mucus, sweat, and urine—which should not be lost unnecessarily. "If you can refrain from losing mucus and saliva throughout your life," the text says, "and instead practice rinsing and filling the mouth [with saliva] and swallowing it—steadily holding it as if you were sucking on a date pit—you can support your *qi* and vitalize your body fluids" (2.5a). The same need for containment of internal energies also explains the frequent instructions to curl the hands into fists, which at the same time serves to keep outside influences at bay. As the text says, making fists

> means that you join your spirit and material souls in securing the gates and doors of the body, thereby stabilizing your essence, brightening your eyes, maintaining your years, and reversing any white hair you may have. If you do this, especially in the winter months, all kinds of wayward *qi* and the hundred poisons will not be able to do you harm. (2.4b)

Along the same lines, in its section "Absorbing *Qi*," the text notes that by holding the breath and guiding the *qi* to painful or blocked areas one can "expel the hundred ailments." It says one should

> follow it wherever it is needed and develop clear awareness there. If your head hurts, become aware of your head; if your foot hurts, become aware of your foot, using harmonized *qi* to attack the pain. From one moment to the next, the pain will dissolve by itself. (2.1b–2a; Jackowicz 2003, 2006)

---

9. A Japanese translation of the entire text with extensive annotation is found in Mugitani 1987. Sections 2 and 3 appear in English in Switkin 1987. Section 4 is translated and analyzed in Jackowicz 2003.

Once one has become aware of the *qi* in the body, one can activate and enhance it with various methods, such as massages. One way is similar to a practice outlined in the *Zhenzhong ji*. Called Dry Wash, it consists of the following:

> Rub your hands together until they generate heat, then massage the face from top to bottom, eliminating all wayward *qi*. This will help you to maintain a radiant glow on your face. Yet another way is to rub the hands together for heat, then massage and pound the entire body from top to bottom. This is called Dry Wash. It helps to overcome wind and cold, seasonally hot *qi*, and headaches, as well as drives out the hundred diseases. (2.5b)

This practice is best undertaken in the early morning, again echoing the *Zhenzhong ji*. However, the *Yangxing yanming lu* here has a more intricate and complex morning routine that involves massages together with clicking the teeth, swallowing the saliva, holding the breath, and doing exercises. It says,

> In the early morning, before you get up, first click your teeth for two sets of seven. Then close your eyes, make your hands into fists, move your mouth three times as if rinsing to fill it with saliva, then swallow and hold. Hold the breath until you reach your maximum. When you cannot hold it any longer, let it out very, very slowly. Repeat three times.
>
> Next, rise to do the wolf crouch and the owl turn,[10] shake yourself to the right and left, and again hold the breath until you reach your maximum. Do three repetitions.
>
> Get off the bed. Make your hands into fists and hold the breath in while stomping the heels three times, then raise one arm and lower the other, and again hold the breath in to your maximum. Repeat three times.
>
> Next, interlace the fingers behind the head and twist to your right and left, holding the breath each time. Repeat three times.[11]
>
> Stand up to stretch from both feet, again interlace the fingers, revolve the palms, and press forward. Hold the breath. Repeat three times.

---

10. The "wolf crouch" and the "owl turn" are not described in extant sources. The former may be similar to the "tiger catch" mentioned in Sun's *Qianjin fang*, which involves stepping forward while turning the head back to look over one shoulder (Mugitani 1987, 114). Or it may be like the crouching tiger exercise in the Five Animals' Frolic as described in the *Yangxing yanming lu* (see ch. 5 below). As for the "owl turn," the translation of the world for "owl" follows DeWoskin 1983, 139. The modern master Ni Hua-ching has an exercise called The Immortal Imitating the Owl Turning Its Head, which involves sitting with the foot of one leg pressing into the thigh of the other leg, then leaning forward and turning to look over the extended leg (Ni 1989, 47).

11. The *Zhen'gao* has some additional details on this part of the practice. It notes that the exercise should be done while kneeling upright and that one should lift the gaze upward and put some pressure on the hands at the neck while twisting to the right and left. The practice, it says, stabilizes blood flow and prevents harmful winds from entering the body, thus contributing to a state of "no death and no disease" (9.10a).

Do this entire sequence every morning and evening, for at least three times. If can do more, so much the better. (2.4b)

This pattern integrates the more subtle energy work of swallowing the saliva and holding the breath with physical movements similar to those in the Brahmanic and Laozi sequences. Like the latter, they are repeated three times each. The movements activate the muscles of the face, neck, and upper body and provide basic twists and stretches. Like the simple moves described in the *Zhenzhong ji,* they stimulate the *qi* in the early morning, allowing practitioners to be vibrant and active throughout their day.

In addition, the *Yangxing yanming lu* also has a seated sequence to be executed in "lofty pose" (*junzuo* 峻坐), which the *Ishinpō* explains as follows: "If you sit in the lotus posture when it is cold, you will warm up but then your legs will go to sleep. Sit lofty by opening the legs into a character 'eight' (*ba* 八) position. This will drive out the cold and alleviate the five kinds of piles" (ch. 27). In other words, it is a wide-angled, samurai-style kneeling posture, with thighs opened sideways. In this position, adepts are to perform eight practices, again timed in the early morning. The text says,

1. Sit in lofty pose and support your head with your left hand under your chin and your right hand above the head. Holding the head, shake the body and the hands with vigor. Repeat three times. Reverse sides. This eliminates sleepiness and fatigue.
2. In the early morning, before sunrise, sit in lofty pose facing south and place both hands on your thighs. Shake the body with vigor. Repeat three times. This will help maintain a radiance and glossiness in the face.
3. In the early morning, before you get up to comb and wash, sit in lofty pose and place your right hand covered by your left hand on your left thigh. Lean forward with vigor, pressing into the left thigh. Repeat three times. Reverse and repeat three times on the other side.
4. Interlace the hands, stretch them forward, and push strongly. Repeat three times.
5. Interlace the hands again, press them in toward the chest, allowing the elbows to move forward and pushing them strongly together. Repeat three times.
6. Pull the left shoulder back while curling the right shoulder forward. With the same strength it would take to draw a fifteen-pound bow, draw the bow with the right hand, constantly maintaining the level of exertion. Repeat and reverse.
7. Place your right hand on the floor and raise your left hand up to push strongly against the sky. Repeat and reverse.
8. Curl your hands into fists and punch forward right and left. Do three sets of seven for each side. Curl the left hand into a fist and strongly grip the fingers

while moving the hand up the back. Repeat three times, then do the same with
the right hand. This will help eliminate labored *qi* from the back, shoulder
blades, shoulders, and elbows. The more often you repeat the exercise, the better.

While providing some stretches in the legs through the basic wide-angled
posture, this sequence is mainly an upper body workout, moving down from the
head through the face, shoulders, chest, arms, waist, and back. It includes body
shakes to enhance *qi*-flow and encourages practitioners to bend and twist the different parts, opening the joints and releasing the muscles. In a few instances the
text also notes conditions improved by the practice, such as fatigue, facial complexion, and labored *qi*. In line with the overall tendency to gear healing exercises
toward immortality, however, these are not medical conditions but ways of self-
improvement in preparation for advanced states, which are described in Sun's
Cunshen lianqi ming. A strong focus on the purification and transcendence of
spirit, this text begins by outlining that one first needs to diminish the diet and
come to a point where deep, conscious breathing and swallowing of saliva can
replace all food intake (see Arthur 2006). The text says,

> If you want to learn the technique of refinement of *qi* as described here, you must
> first of all stop eating grains. Then focus your mind calmly on the Ocean of *Qi*, visu-
> alize the spirit in the cinnabar field, control the mind, and purify your thoughts.
> When the Ocean of *Qi* is replenished, you will always feel satiated naturally. (1a)

From here practitioners should focus the mind on one object and gain control
over it, leading it from an initial state of "much agitation and little tranquility"
through five phases to being "turned entirely toward purity and tranquility." Only
when the mind is completely calm and controlled can the higher stages of immortality be entered, which lead through the recovery of a youthful appearance and vigorous body to extended longevity of even a thousand years and eventually to "taking
up residence next to the Jade Emperor of the Great Dao in the Numinous Realm"
(3a). This form of otherworldly existence is thus the ultimate goal of the complex
integrated system of healing, self-cultivation, and transcendence presented in Sun
Simiao's work. Exercises play a crucial role in both the healing and cultivation aspects, supporting the quest for long life and preparing adepts for the higher stages.

Sima Chengzhen

Healing exercises play a similar role in the work of the other major figure in Tang
longevity techniques, Sima Chengzhen 司馬承禎 (647–735), the twelfth patriarch

of Highest Clarity Daoism (see Engelhardt 1987, 35–61; Chen 2000, 94–95). A native of Henan, he was a descendant of the imperial house of the Jin dynasty that ruled China in the third and fourth centuries. Even after losing the throne, the family remained at the top of the official hierarchy: Sima's grandfather served as a senior governor under the Sui, and his father was a high-ranking officer under the Tang. Trained well in the classics and arts of the gentleman, such as calligraphy and poetry, Sima is described in the sources as a highly precocious and very intelligent child. Some even claim he was able to speak at birth.

Still, rather than dedicating himself to standard Confucian service, he opted for a career in Daoism, which in the eighth century had risen to official status and was the main religion as supported by the state. He began his Daoist studies on Mount Song 嵩山, the central of the five sacred mountains, which is near Luoyang in his native Henan. At the age of twenty-one, in 669, he underwent Daoist ordination under Pan Shizheng 潘師正 (d. 684), the eleventh patriarch of Highest Clarity and direct successor of Tao Hongjing, the first official leader and main coordinator of the school. Continuing his climb through the Daoist hierarchy and absorbing all the esoteric rites and scriptures of the different schools, Sima was chosen to succeed his teacher as twelfth patriarch in 684. In this role, he understood himself very much as an heir to Tao Hongjing, whom he sincerely venerated and variously praised in his writings. Moving the headquarters of the school, he settled on Mount Tongbo 桐柏山 in the Tiantai 天台 range in Zhejiang, returning to where "at the beginning of the fifth century, the Highest Clarity texts were propagated for the first time" (Strickmann 1981, 34).

Sima Chengzhen was invited to court four times: first by Empress Wu (r. 690–705), then, in 711, by Emperor Ruizong (r. 710–711). This emperor built a monastery for him in the Tiantai Mountains, and one of his daughters became Sima Chengzhen's disciple. The remaining two invitations were issued by Emperor Xuanzong (r. 712–756) in the years 721 and 727. The emperor, who was also the recipient of a divine sword and mirror cast and engraved by Sima,[12] thought very highly of the Daoist master and ordered him to take up residence on Mount Wangwu 王屋山, which was closer to the capital. It was also one of the ten major grotto heavens of Daoism, thought to connect the world of the living with that of the immortals. The emperor had a large monastery erected there, the Yangtai guan 陽臺觀 (Sunlit Terrace Monastery), and Sima Chengzhen spent the later part of his life there (fig. 15).

Like Sun Simiao, he traveled widely, propagating Daoist teachings and seeking out learned masters. He was well versed in medical knowledge and engaged in the

---

12. The art work and inscriptions on the mirror and sword presented by Sima to the emperor are studied in Fukunaga 1973, Schafer 1979.

various longevity practices, abstaining from grains for extended periods, taking herbal medicines to enhance and transform his *qi,* and undertaking physical and breathing exercises. However, unlike Sun Simiao, who had a predominantly medical focus, Sima's entire practice was steeped in the religious dimension of the teaching: connected at all times with the deities in the body and the heavens and closely interlinked with ritual practices, talismans, and incantations. Within this framework, he became known for his extraordinary powers. For example, a story in his biography in the tenth-century collection *Xuxian zhuan* 續仙傳 (Supplementary Immortals' Biographies, *DZ* 295; Penny 2000, 121; Schipper and Verellen 2004, 429) tells how he and another Daoist celebrated the fall purgation rites and, after a round of lengthy rituals, went to sleep around midnight:

> Suddenly the Daoist heard a sound. It seemed as if a small child was reciting a classical text and as if bells of gold and jade were sounding. He collected his clothes and crept closer to examine the source of the sound. Then he saw a miniature sun on Sima's forehead. It was about the size of a coin and spread a bright radiance. He stepped closer and listened carefully. The sounds came from Sima's head. (1.2a; Engelhardt 1987, 41)

Fig. 15: Sima Chengzhen, the twelfth patriarch of Highest Clarity. Source: *Sancai tuhui.*

That is to say, Sima's Daoist powers were such that the deities were present within his body at all times, even during sleep. They were so prominent that their radiance issued from his head and their chanting could be heard even with ordinary senses.

Not only involved with rituals and devotion, Sima Chengzhen as patriarch of the leading Daoist school also engaged in frequent interactions with the aristocrats of the time. He had many close friends with whom he exchanged poems and learned discussions, and he went out of his way to make Daoist teachings available to lay adepts. His work *Zuowang lun* 坐忘論 (On Sitting in Oblivion, *DZ* 1036; trl. Kohn 1987) is an outline of seven steps that can be attained in Daoist meditation, including the successful interception of karmic causes, control over the mind, a detachment from the affairs of ordinary life, a true vision of what life and death are all about, and a sense of oneness with the Dao. The practices closely echo Buddhist meditation techniques of *samathā-vipasyanā* or insight meditation (see Kohn 1989b) as taught especially in the Tiantai school, centered on the very mountain where Sima spent a good part of his life. The text, which appears in a rudimentary first version in an inscription of the early ninth century, may well go back to lectures Sima gave to an aristocratic audience in hopes of weaning them away from the joys of the senses and guide them toward the delights of the Dao. As he says in his preface,

> People tend to hate the sufferings of life and death, yet they love to be involved in affairs. They honor words dealing with the Dao and its virtue, yet they take any actual practice very lightly. Delighted by colors and flavors, they think they realize their will. At the same time, they demean placidness and plainness as stretching the limits of disgrace. They run after rare treasures and haggle over the happiness of a future life, while by giving rein to defiling passions they waste the Dao they could have now in this very body....
>
> The *Miaozhen jing* [Scripture of Wondrous Perfection] says: "Human beings always lose the Dao, the Dao never loses them. Human beings constantly reject life, life never rejects them." Nourishing life therefore centers around not losing the Dao. Practicing the Dao means mainly to watch out not to lose life. This way one causes life and the Dao to preserve and to guard each other, to never part company. Thus one can live long. (pref. 1ab; Kohn 1987, 83–84)

Rather than emphasizing the ultimate goal of immortality, Sima here advocates Daoist practice as a way to long life and inner tranquility, encouraging his audience to see beyond the affairs and profits of ordinary existence.

This concern with making the teachings accessible is also evident in his major work on longevity practices, the *Fuqi jingyi lun* 服氣精義論 (The Essential Meaning of *Qi*-Absorption), which outlines the different aspects of physical cultivation in nine steps, placing the most advanced first.[13] According to this, and reading the text in reversed order, one should begin by establishing a clear diagnosis, defining one's physical condition and taking special care to spot latent diseases that may erupt in the future. In a second step, one should treat these disease tendencies with various *qi*-balancing methods, then move on to energize the five inner organs, making sure they store ample *qi,* and take care to live in moderation, avoiding excessive strain or emotions.

Moving into the more refined level of practice and starting to engage with immortal dimensions, in step five one can gradually begin to replace ordinary food with herbal concoctions, allowing the body to cleanse and refine itself as it opens up to more subtle states. This, then, can be supplemented with "talisman water" (the remnants of a burnt talisman mixed with water). Taking this, adepts align themselves with the higher energies of the cosmos. The last three steps involve healing exercises, the absorption of *qi,* and the ingestion of the five sprouts, the pure energies of the five directions of the universe, which firmly places the adept into the larger cosmic context of the Dao.

Sima himself engaged in these practices and lived a long and healthy life. What is more, according to the biographers, he bypassed death in a well-orchestrated ceremony of ascension. In June of 735, after announcing his imminent transformation for transfer to an official post in the celestial administration, he sat quietly in meditation and, accompanied by white cranes, purple clouds, and celestial music, ascended to emptiness, vanishing before the astounded eyes of his disciples (Engelhardt 1987, 51). The Daoist master thus returned to his true home above the clouds.

Healing Exercises and the Absorption of *Qi*

Among all Sima's writings, healing exercises appear mainly in the *Fuqi jingyi lun.* Here they are closely connected with the meditative absorption and visualized circulation of *qi.* To begin, in the section on the treatment of diseases he recommends, like the *Yangxing yanming lu,* that one should focus one's attention on the ailing area, following the *qi* as it goes there and using it to dispel the perceived blockage. Sima says,

> If you have an aching or sore head, loosen the hair and comb it with vigor for several
> hundred strokes, then shake the head to the left and right several ten times. Next,

---

13. The complete text is found in *Yunji qiqian* 57. The first two sections also appear in *DZ* 277, while the remaining seven are contained in *DZ* 830 (see Schipper and Verellen 2004, 373–374). The text is studied and translated with ample annotation in Engelhardt 1987.

inhale deeply, place the hands on the neck and hold tight, then lift the head up, pressing against the hands.

Also, visualize the *qi* as it flows into your brain, then let it push all wayward energies out through the top of the head and other body openings, allowing them to dissipate and disperse. Following this, release the hands, move the *qi* evenly through the entire body, and repeat the exercise. Once you feel sweat erupting on the head and notice that the ailing area becomes open and permeable, you have reached your goal. (23b–24a; Engelhardt 1987, 182)

Similar techniques, supplemented with herbal remedies and various bends and stretches, will also work in other parts of the body and the inner organs. However, in the case of chronic conditions they will only alleviate but not cure.

Another healing method with *qi* is to "enclose the *qi*" by holding the breath and keeping it in the body for a prolonged period, until sweat arises, which will purge the system from unwanted influences. Sima mentions this only briefly, but the *Yangxing yanming lu* has some details:

Enclose the *qi* and do not breathe. Mentally count [the heartbeat] to two hundred, then expel the *qi* by exhaling through the mouth. As you breathe like this for an increasing number of days, you will find your body, spirit, and all the five organs are deeply at peace. If you can enclose the *qi* to the count of 250, your Flowery Canopy will be bright. [Note: The Flowery Canopy is the eyebrows (also the constellation Cassiopeia).] Your eyes and ears will be perceptive and clear, and your body will be light and free from disease; nothing wayward will bother you any more. (2.2b)

Assuming about eighty heartbeats per minute, a count of 250 would mean holding the breath for three minutes, which is quite long and can well lead to the healing sweat encouraged by the texts.

On a different note, Sima recommends the absorption of solar energies for healing. He says,

In general, to treat ailments practice right after sunrise and preferably when the weather is calm and mild. Sit up straight, face the Sun, close your eyes, curl the hands into fists, and click the teeth nine times. Then visualize the scarlet brilliance and purple rays of the Sun, pull them into the body as you inhale, and swallow them. Envision this healing energy entering the inner organ or area of the body that is afflicted by the ailment (*Yunji qiqian* 57.23ab; Engelhardt 1987, 181)

Highly similar methods reappear in the *Fuqi jingyin lun* in the section "Healing Exercises," placed between "Talisman Water" and "The Absorption of *Qi*." Here Sima emphasizes that the body needs to be moved to be healthy, just like "a door hinge does not rust" (14b), and that the different parts are closely interrelated, so that sensory faculties connect to skeletal structures and inner organs to body fluids. He says,

> The bones correspond to the eyes; the bone marrow matches the brain; the sinews are related to the joints; and the blood is linked with the heart. All the different kinds of *qi* belong to the lungs. Thus works the interrelated action of the four limbs and the eight major joints. Realizing this, understand the harm done by the five labors and the need for proper movement and rest. (14b)

Rather than an assembly of different parts that are to be healed with the help of concentrated *qi*-movements or holdings, the body here appears as an intricate network that needs to be understood as one whole and moved in close coordination, all the different parts influencing and affecting each other. As he says, "In the human body above and below depend on each other, rise and fall change rhythmically" (15a). He then recommends that one practice exercises regularly in the early morning hours, beginning with the usual preparation:

> Loosen your hair and brush it in all four directions, touching the top of the head 365 times. Then either spread the hair back or tie it into a loose knot. Next, burn incense, face east, and kneel upright. Make your hands into fists, close your eyes, and focus your thoughts on the spirit. Click the teeth 360 times, relax the body, and allow the breath to become even. (15ab)

Following this, he has a series of stretches for the arms and chest, undertaken in either a seated or kneeling position (fig. 16).

1. Hold the breath while interlacing the fingers. Reverse the palms and stretch both arms vigorously forward to full extension, pulling the shoulders and pushing against an imaginary resistance. Hold.
2. Raise the arms, turn the palms out and stretch upward to full extension.
3. Lower the left arm and use it to lift the right elbow strongly, causing the left elbow and shoulder to be pressed back over the top of the head.
4. Lower the left arm and press it downward with force [while still pressing the right arm upward].
5. Push the left hand toward the left, opening the right armpit and lifting the ribs.

Reverse. Lift the left arm back up, then lower the right and perform the sequence [3–5] on the other side.

6. Lower both arms, interlace the fingers behind the head, and lift the elbows, opening the chest and allowing the head to fall back. Alternating the arms and head back and forth, stretch them vigorously in both directions.

7. Keeping the fingers interlaced at the neck, lower the elbows slightly, then twist the torso to the right and left.

8. To close, place the hands on the knees and subtly blow out the *qi,* allowing the breath to flow freely.

Start again from the beginning. Complete a total of three cycles.

The exercises open the upper body, releasing *qi* blockages from the arms, neck, and chest areas and thus readying the practitioner for the more intricate practice of the absorption of *qi,* which can only be undertaken after one has "first healed all bodily ailments and illnesses to allow the organs and viscera to open up in free flow and the limbs to be at rest and in harmony" (5b). While earlier texts tend to include *qi*-absorption in the practice of exercises, for Sima Chengzhen it is a different and more advanced mode of practice, leading to the highest form of body cultivation in the *Fuqi jingyi lun,* the ingestion of the five sprouts.

Like exercises, the absorption of *qi* should be undertaken in a quiet, secluded room that is comfortably warm and well ventilated. Beyond this, however, one needs to purify the *qi* through the gradual elimination of ordinary foods and their replacement with herbal concoctions and celestial energies. To achieve the latter, adepts are encouraged to spend at least three days ingesting talisman water to bring celestial energies into their bodies. They also need to pay attention to the

Fig. 16: A Daoist practicing healing exercises matching Sima Chengzhen's prescription. Source: *Chifeng sui.*

annual cycle of *qi,* and ideally begin their practice in the early part of the month, after the third and before the eighth day. Practitioners enter the chamber around midnight and perform the usual preparation, then open the *qi*-flow by performing a simple sequence.

These preliminaries accomplished, they lie down flat on the back. As the *Fuqi jingyi lun* says,

> For a while sit quietly to stabilize the breath, then lie down on your back with your head pointing west. The mattress should be thick and warm. Cover yourself according to the prevailing temperature so that you are comfortable. It is best if especially the lower body, from hips to feet, is nicely warm on both the right and the left.
>
> If you want your neck support low, make it lower than the back. If you want it high, set it to be in one line with the body so that trunk, head, and neck are on the same level. Loosen your clothes and belt, allowing them to be wide and comfortable. Your hands should be about three inches from the body and curled into fists. Your feet should be about five or six inches apart. (6b)

In this position, practitioners begin by breathing slowly and consciously, inhaling through the nose and exhaling through the mouth. They then visualize the first rays of the Sun, which they face as it rises in the east, entering their bodes like an elixir of flowing radiance. Next, they practice swallowing the *qi.* This involves taking in long, deep inhalations through the nose and allowing the breath to reach the mouth, where it mingles actively with the saliva. This mixture is then consciously swallowed through the gullet and into the lungs, where it is held for a little while. To conclude, practitioners exhale softly through the mouth with lips slightly open.

An alternative is to inhale three, five, or seven breaths consecutively, then mix and swallow these while exhaling only briefly (Maspero 1981, 474). The goal is to enrich the breath with saliva as another potent form of *qi* and enter this mixture into the lungs. With time, practitioners will, as the *Fuqi jingyi lun* says, "feel the lungs expanding and enlarging, and thus know that the right measure has been reached" (7a). The text also admonishes to practice this with due moderation, making sure that inhalation and exhalation are even and harmonious at all times.

To make sure that the *qi* reaches all the different parts of the body, practitioners actively visualize it moving into all its parts. As Sima Chengzhen says,

> First, visualize the *qi* in the lungs for some time, then feel it run along the shoulders and into the arms, until it reaches your hands that have been curled into fists. After this envision it gently moving down from the lungs and into the stomach and spleen area, from where it moves into the kidneys. Allow it to flow through the thighs into

the legs and feet. You will know that you are doing it right when you feel a slight tingling between skin and flesh, sort of like the crawling of tiny insects. (7b)

With prolonged practice, this *qi*-circulation becomes natural. Then there is no more need to hold the *qi* in the lungs and one can direct it immediately into the intestines. "The ideal level is reached when the *qi* moves about with rumbling noises and eventually flows to the area beneath the navel. You will have a feeling of fullness and satiation in your intestines" (7b). The ultimate goal of the practice is to refine the inner functioning of the body to the point where one can "stop eating grain and start living on *qi*." The process requires a gradual adjustment, over a period of about six weeks. As Sima describes it,

> For the first ten days of the practice, essence and *qi* tend to be weak and malleable and your complexion is grayish or yellow. For the second ten days, your movements are stumbling, your limbs and joints are numb, your bowels only move slowly and with great difficulty, and your urine is reddish and yellow. You may also have temporary diarrhea, which is first hard then liquid. After the third ten days of the practice, the body is emaciated and it is very hard to move. However, in the course of the fourth ten-day period, you will find your complexion clearing up and your mind starting to be calm and healthy. (8a; Engelhardt 1987, 105)

It is all progress from here on. One becomes healthier, the body feels lighter and is more radiant, the mind reaches a state of euphoria, and one is generally serene and relaxed. The more the body becomes one with the cosmic flow of *qi*, the more one attains a state of celestial awareness and finds access to immortality.

The Five Sprouts

Immortality is further attained through ingesting the five sprouts (*wuya* 五芽), a Highest Clarity practice that enhances the cosmicization of the body and can be described as a subtler and more refined version of the absorption of celestial energies (see Robinet 1989b). It begins with swallowing the saliva while chanting invocations to the original *qi* of the four cardinal directions. Adepts face the direction in question, usually beginning with the east, and in their minds visualize the *qi* of that direction in its appropriate color. A general mist in the beginning, it gradually forms into a ball, sort of like the rising Sun, then through further concentration shrinks in size and comes closer to the adept. Eventually the size of a pill, the sprout can be swallowed and guided mentally to the organ of its correspondence. A suitable incantation places it firmly in its new receptacle,

and gradually the adept's body becomes infused with cosmic energy and participates more actively in the cosmos as a whole.

The incantations are short and to the point. As the *Fuqi jingyi lun* says,[14]

Green Sprout of the East:
Be absorbed to feed my [internal] green sprout [liver].
I drink you through the Morning Flower [root of upper teeth]. (3a)

Vermilion Cinnabar of the South:
Be absorbed to feed my [internal] vermilion cinnabar [heart].
I drink you through the Cinnabar Lake [root of lower teeth].

Lofty Great Mountain of the Center:
Be absorbed to feed my [internal] essence and *qi*.
I drink you through the Sweet Spring [root of the molars].

Radiant Stone of the West:
Be absorbed to feed my [internal] radiant stone [lungs].
I drink you through the Numinous Liquid [saliva inside the lips].

Mysterious Sap of the North:
Be absorbed to feed my [internal] mysterious sap [kidneys].
I drink you through the Jade Sweetness [saliva on the tongue]. (3ab)

In each case, the text also specifies that adepts should pass the tongue along a
certain part of the lips and teeth (matching the incantation). They should then
lick the lips, rinse the mouth by filling it with saliva, and swallow. The practice is
to be repeated three times for each sprout.

The sprouts, as Isabelle Robinet points out, are originally the "germinal es-
sences of the clouds" or "mist." They represent the yin principle of heaven—that
is, the yin within the yang. They manifest in human saliva, again a yin element in
the upper, yang, part of the body. They help to nourish and strengthen the five
inner organs. They are very tender, comparable to the fresh sprouts of plants, and
assemble at dawn in the celestial capital, from where they spread all over the universe until the sun begins to shine. Turning like the wheels of a carriage, they
ascend to the gates of the nine heavens, from where they continue to the medium
level of the world—to the five sacred mountains ruled over by the five emperors of

---

14. The practice, including the chants, is also presented in the *Taixi qi jing* (Highest Qi Scripture on
Nourishing Life through Embryo Respiration, *DZ* 819), translated and discussed in Jackowicz
2003.

the five directions—and finally descend into the individual adept. They thus pass through the three major levels of the cosmos (Robinet 1989b, 166).

The virtue of these sprouts is twofold. They are "emanations of the highest poles" and as such full of the power of far-off regions (yin), the fringes of civilization where the Dao resides in a rawer state. At the same time, they are "tender like freshly sprouted plants" (yang) and as such contain the entire potential of being in its nascent state. In this growth potential of both yin and yang, the small and imperceptible *qi* in a state of pure becoming, lies their main attraction for the Daoist practitioner. "Sprouting" means inherent creation, purity, newness, return to youth. It also implies the prevalence of the soft over the hard and the power of yin over yang that Laozi describes in the *Daode jing* (see Robinet 1993). The practice is undertaken at dawn, the time when everything awakens to life, yet another symbol of yang and of creative, unstructured potential. By ingesting the sprouts, the Daoist partakes of the inherent power of celestial bodies and feeds on the pure creative energy of the universe in its most subtle form. Becoming increasingly one with the germinal energy of the universe, adepts become lighter and freer, learn to appear and disappear at will, overcome the limitations of this world, and attain immortality in the heavenly realms.

Their very bodies change under the impact of the advanced techniques. As Stephen Jackowicz puts it,

> The individual returns to the primordial state of being and is like the embryo, but instead of being supported by a mother's body, he or she is now nourished in the womb of the universe, the body corrected to be only *zhengqi* [harmonious *qi*]. The universe is *zheng* and the individual partakes of its nature, so that even what was formerly considered *xie* [wayward] is now part of universal correctness. The practitioner in his or her body has returned to the stage of the primordial egg, from which the comic giant Pangu transformed and created the world. Primordial union has been reestablished, and the practitioner partakes of the unlimited supply of original, primordial, ever-circulating *qi*. (2006, 82–83)

To summarize: For both major representatives of the tradition in the Tang dynasty, Sun Simiao and Sima Chengzhen, the ultimate goal of all practices is the complete overcoming of worldly states and the final attainment of immorality, a spiritual state of otherworldly residence. Healing exercises play an important part and appear in various levels of the immortal curriculum, but they are secondary to visualizations, *qi*-absorptions, and ecstatic excursions. In many ways the methods the Tang masters adopt continue the tradition of Highest Clarity, the dominant school of Daoism at the time. Yet they are also very medically aware and make health and wholeness an important part of the process. For the first time in Chinese history, these masters consciously integrate healing, longevity, and immortality into a complete Daoist system of self-realization and spiritual attainment. They thereby lay the foundation for all later methods, patterns, and sequences that have remained standard to the present day.[15]

Ritualized Practice

As healing exercises became part of Daoist practice, they were also formalized in the priestly hierarchy of Tang Daoism, introduced with ritual formalities and transmitted in ordination-type ceremonies. The *Daoshi jushan xiulian ke* 道士居山修錬科 (Rules on Refining Cultivation for Daoist Masters and Mountain Hermits, *DZ* 1272) outlines the basic practices and precepts prescribed for serious Daoists with regard to physical refinement (see Schipper and Verellen 2004, 363). It is divided into ten sections, beginning with a discussion of basic methods of *qi*-absorption and the description of ceremonies involved in the transmission of relevant scriptures, methods, and formulas. It goes on to outline the formal petitions to be submitted to the gods at the time of the transmission and at the time of practice (sects. 3–4), then widens its scope to present information on the concoction of alchemical elixirs, the best ways to abstain from grains, and the formal use of talismans. The last three sections deal with precepts and precautions to be taken for the various self-cultivation practices, preferred times and ways to enter the mountains for the collection of herbs and minerals, and various recipes for the expulsion of intestinal worms and parasites.

The entire text focuses on the physical cultivation of adepts, culminating in the transformation of their bodies into vehicles of pure Dao that are independent of food and drink and can live on *qi* alone. Adepts begin with the absorption of *qi,* to be undertaken at sunrise in a special chamber set up for the practice. They burn incense, face east, and strike the sacred lithophone nine times to announce their intention to practice. Next, to the rhythmic beat of the lithophone they chant an incantation that invokes the deities in charge of *qi* and its cultivation to help them in their effort to gain long life and no-death, activate the twenty-four cosmic energies in their bodies, and provide them with divine guards that will protect them at all times (1a). With divine help, they open the inner palaces in their bodies, strengthen

---

15. Yet another well-known and well-documented Tang master who created a systematization of the immortality process is Wu Yun 吳筠 (d. 778). He wrote several important treatises on the organized attainment of transcendence; however, his overall tendency was to allow physical practices only in the very beginning and to scorn their use in advanced levels. For details of his life and work, see the detailed study by Ian DeMeyer (2006).

their joints and limbs, harmonize the five inner organs, overcome all hunger and thirst, and eventually ascend to heaven as flying immortals (1b).

The actual practice begins with adepts stepping to the bed platform, taking off their outer clothing, and lying down supine, supported by a pillow four inches high. Their feet about one foot apart, their hands rest by their sides and are curled into fists. In their minds, adepts actualize the presence of the Six Jia deities who are responsible for the different aspects of the body in relation to time and space as well as the gods of the Niwan Palace in the head and the cinnabar or elixir field in the abdomen. They feel how these divine agents pull in the living *qi* from Heaven and Earth through the nose and allow stale *qi* from their bodies to be released through the mouth. The rhythm of practice is to inhale in several short gasps—to enhance the absorption of cosmic *qi*—and let the breath out in a single exhalation that is to be long, slow, and complete. At first the ratio is three inhalations to one exhalation; this is gradually increased to a ratio of twelve to one, making the breaths deeper and opening the lungs and thereby enhancing the oxygenation of the body (1b).

Eventually a stage of practice is reached that comes in sets of eight and is described as "pulling out" (*yin*). Adepts practice eight, four, or three pulls, in each case taking a breath for the count of eight, so that they undertake sixty-four, thirty-two, and twenty-four breathings, which add up to the sacred number of 120 (2a). Ideally the breathings are lengthened with each set, so that the count—although remaining at eight—is perceptibly slower as the practice goes on. The goal is to reach a stage of the "long breath" (*changxi* 長息) and continue the practice to the count of 360 and even 1,200. Only when this has been accomplished should adepts begin to hold the breath and make it so subtle that when they exhale slowly, it feels as if the breath is reversing back into the body immediately, creating a continuity of *qi*-flow and a sense of being submerged and immersed in *qi*. With the practice, swallowings of *qi* are recommended, three or four every so often (2a).

Once the breath has become deep and stable, one may proceed to physical stretches. Still lying supine, adepts bend their thumbs into the center of their palms, then lift the arms up toward the ceiling and contract them again. This is repeated for three rounds of seven repetitions, coordinated with slow breathing (2a). Next, they open the hands and lift the palms up to the ceiling, stretching the shoulders and lifting them slightly off the bed for two or three repetitions. After this follows a twist. Placing the thumbs into the opposite elbow crease, adepts hug themselves and turn the torso to the right and left three times, leaving the legs in place and stretching the muscles of the sides and waist. Next, they pull one knee into the chest while stretching the other leg away, toes pointed to the ceiling. After repeating this pose for three sets of nine on both sides, they pull both knees into the chest, hold their feet with their hands, and roll themselves up into a standing forward bend. This is done three times (2b).

Lying down again as before with feet apart, they once more practice breathing the sequence of pulls up to 120. Next, they interlace their hands in three different positions and breathe for a set number of repetitions: across the chest (81 times); around the knees, which are pulled into the chest (21, 25, 19, 17, and 15 times); and behind the head while crunching up to meet the knees (3 sets of 7). This is followed by a resting period of unspecified length. To conclude the session, adepts get up, burn incense, don their garb, strike the lithophone nine times, and chant another incantation. They pray for the *qi* that descended in the beginning to exit again from their bodies and return to Heaven, thus creating an open set of pathways between their bodies and the cosmic spheres. It is optimal, the text concludes, to walk around for 500 or more steps after the practice to allow the *qi* to flow smoothly through the body (3ab).

Greater success is achieved with prolonged practice and extended rounds of breathing, so that during the first year one should work with 120 breathings, then move on to 240 and 360 in the following years (3b). Similarly, adepts should reduce their food consumption as they proceed, taking no more than 2 *dou* (scoops) of liquids plus some grain, rice, fruit, and dates in the course of a day in the first year, then reducing that by half in the second, and by half again in the third. At that point they should be able to survive on nine dried dates per day and drink no more than half a liter (a pint) of water (4b). The body feels light and free, unfettered by aches or sickness; all extraneous matters are eliminated, the various parasites are expelled, and herbs and minerals give strength and vigor. Only at this point is it feasible to stop eating completely and live entirely on *qi*, beginning with shorter periods, then advancing to a hundred days or even a year or two (4b) (see Arthur 2006).

The methods of *qi*-absorption and the liberation from ordinary food are transmitted in a formal ceremony that involves the presence of several masters, the giving of pledges, the swearing of vows, the taking of precepts, the issuing of warnings, and the delivery of petitions to the gods. It is in all respects like an ordination ceremony for beginning Daoists, described variously in Tang literature (Kohn 2003a, 389–392; 2004a, 82–84). The specific ceremony for *qi*-absorption, it seems, was administered to adepts who had reached a stage in their practice that allowed them to focus dominantly on physical cultivation and who would go to live in the mountains for extended periods of time, becoming hermits, alchemists, and herbal masters. Some may have been beginners who had only undergone the first stages of ordination; others may have opted for the physical self-cultivation path later in their careers. Their precepts reflect this, insisting that they remain silent, live in solitude, and avoid all encounters with anything potentially defiling (23b–24a). They should also be very aware of the workings of particular substances, realizing, for example, that certain drugs can create great heat in the body and that sudden cooling, although desirable at the time, could cause injury and even death (24b). The combination of herbs and minerals with certain common foods, moreover, might be detrimental to their efforts. Thus mica should be taken as the dominant mineral supplement only after the ingestion of sesame for a year, and anyone ingesting realgar should avoid all "blood food" (24b). Similarly, mica should be collected only on a cloudy day, and any excursion into the depth of the forest should be preceded by a period of meditation (25a).

In addition to remaining part of the medical tradition, in the Tang dynasty healing exercises and methods of breath control and cosmic qi-absorption have become a firm part of the Daoist pathways to immortality, leading adepts away from their ordinary physicality and providing them with the means to live without food and drink, open their bodies fully to the presence of the Dao, and transform their qi into pure cosmic power. Adepts receive specific scriptures, rules, and instructions on how to work with their bodies, thereby enhancing their lung capacity, increasing the flexibility of their limbs and joints, lessening their food intake, and instructing them on how to collect and apply herbs and minerals for physical transformation. They spiritualize their bodies, activating the gods and palaces within and finding a greater Dao presence with prolonged practice. And they revert in their very physical existence to a level of primordiality at the root of creation. The quest for health and long life, without being lost, is thus superseded in Tang Daoist practice by the urgency to develop a different kind of body, becoming lighter, freer, more spiritual, a part of the flowing Dao.

Chapter Five

Modern Precursors

A complete new chapter of developments in Chinese healing exercises, and one that would lead directly to their modern adaptation into qigong, commenced with the Song dynasty (960–1260). The religious and social environment of this time was very different from that of the Tang, whose political, religious, and cultural structures had been eroded and destroyed over a two-hundred-year period of military fighting and overall decline. With the empire reunited in the mid-tenth century and old aristocratic structures gone for good, a great new upswing began, economically, socially, and culturally. The imperial government built better roads and created a whole new canal system to increase commerce and open up the southern part of the country. The merchant class came to prosper and replace the old aristocracy in the economic field, just as a new, scholarly trained, and officially examined group of bureaucrats took over its role in the imperial administration.

The growth of the merchant class had three major effects on the religious scene. First, there was a great increase in lay organizations and lay-sponsored temples and practices—ordinary people joined together to worship various deities and perform rites and cultivation practices together, sometimes in private homes, sometimes in special community halls. Second, there emerged a much larger market for practical religious aids to daily life, from talismans for building homes and spells for granting a safe passage to exorcisms for healing, funeral rites, and services for the dead. Third, as more and more ordinary people became religiously engaged, they required more direct contact with gods, spirits, and ancestors. As a result, trance techniques increased manifold, either through spirit mediums or by automatic writing with the help of the planchette, a kind of Ouija board (Kohn 2001, 136–138).

In Daoism, the more merchant-oriented culture of the Song found expression in the increased application of popular rites and spells for good fortune, supported both by the importation of Buddhist tantric practices and the growth of new schools. For more specialized Daoist practitioners, the dynasty saw the evolution of inner alchemy (*neidan* 內丹), a complex system that integrated health techniques, meditations, and visualizations with the ideas of transformation expressed in the terms of operative alchemy and the *Yijing*. Numerous new texts were written and collections of Daoist materials undertaken, setting the stage for the modern development of the religion.

Spreading to wider segments of the population while at the same time continuing to play a key role in Daoist cultivation, healing exercises played a key role both in popular efforts to extend life and in the inner alchemical ways of reaching beyond the world. Beginning in the Song and continuing in the following dynasties of the Yuan (1260–1368), Ming (1368–1644), and Qing (1644–1911), several major trends emerged. First, undergoing greater popularization, healing exercises for medical purposes and longevity became standardized in stretch-and-bend sequences such as the Five Animals' Frolic and were expanded in various new patterns, including seasonal systems, immortal practices, and formalized techniques of guiding the *qi*.

Second, in their Daoist application, the exercises came to form part of inner alchemy, a new way of feeling interior energies for the purpose of transforming to subtler levels and the experience of new powers. One exercise sequence that integrates the inner alchemical approach to healing and spiritual attainment is the famous Eight Brocades in their seated version, a systematic meditative refinement combined with body movements. In addition, having reached a very high level of attainment, adepts learned to release the spirit from their body, engaging in a new practice known as sleep exercises, during which they lay motionless on their side while their internal energies mixed and combined to create a more subtle level of being that would eventually create the immortal embryo.

Beyond these two tendencies, in the late Ming and early Qing dynasties, healing exercises also became part of the martial arts as practiced by monks of the famous Shaolin monastery and followers of the newly arising technique of taiji quan. Entering a realm quite separate from either medicine or Daoism, the practices were then used to support workout regimens that required superior strength, powerful coordination, and high-level endurance. It was from here—more so even than from their medical or religious applications—that they eventually reached the imagination of the masses and gained the popularity they have today.

What are some of the major forms of healing exercises that become popular in this period? How do they relate to practices still undertaken today? What are the key medical concerns in this new phase? How similar or different are the methods involved? How does inner alchemy shape the tradition? And how does it work with the various martial arts?

The Five Animals' Frolic

One of the most popular forms that spreads in this period and still plays an active part in qigong today is a sequence known as the Five Animals' Frolic (*wuqin xi*

五禽戲).[1] Developed in its contemporary form in the early 1980s by Jiao Guorui 焦國瑞 and Liang Shifeng 梁士豐 (see Miura 1989), it now has over twenty variations, which the Chinese government hopes to standardize into one officially recognized version. The sequence consists of a mixture of standing and moving exercises associated with the crane, bear, monkey, deer, and tiger. In its modern understanding, each animal is linked with a cosmological entity, an organ and a section of the body, specific qualities, and certain healing effects:

Animal	Cosmos	Organ	Body area	Effect	Quality
crane	Heaven	heart	muscles	breathing	lightness
bear	Earth	kidneys	lower back	inner focus	rootedness
monkey	Humanity	spleen	joints, wrists	openness	agility
deer	Spirit	liver	calm mind	subtlety	patience
tiger	Body	lungs	whole body	awareness	strength

The pattern is quite complex, each animal form involving between five and ten different exercises so that, for example, the bear has eight standing practices, such as Bear Pushes Paws, Bear Pushes Back, Bear Extends Paws, and Bear Double Push, followed by four variations of the Bear Amble that range from a basic form through Bear Ambles with Fists to Pointing to the Sun and Holding the Moon. None of these specific patterns or movements can be traced back to before the 1980s.

Animal practices, on the other hand, go back very far (Lo 2001a, 71). As noted earlier, the ancient medical manuscripts have exercises associated with all five animals. Thus, the *Daoyin tu* contains an illustration of the Bear Amble (#41) that shows a figure walking in a stately fashion with arms swinging. The *Yinshu* already notes that the practice is good for the lower back. Then there is a Bird Stretch (#32), depicted as a figure bending forward with hands on the floor and head raised that is said to benefit the shoulders and muscles. Gibbon Jump (#40) is undertaken by extending the arms diagonally up and down, while Double Deer involves raising both arms and pushing up, then bending forward as far as possible (#34). The *Yinshu*, moreover, has three separate Tiger moves:

Tiger Stretch: place one foot forward, raise one arm and extend (#31).
Tiger Move: align the arms, rotate the shoulders up and back, alternating on the right and left (#35).
Tiger Turn is good for the neck.

---

1. For a recent study that covers the historical precedents and contemporary uses of the Five Animals' Frolic and has alternative translations to the ones offered here, see Wang and Barrett 2006.

While these are individual exercises and not connected in any particular way or systematic pattern, the Five Animals' Frolic as an integrated pattern appears in historical sources for the first time in the official biography of the famous physician Hua Tuo of the second century C.E. According to the *Sanguo zhi* 三國志 (Record of Three Kingdoms), he once said to his disciple Wu Pu,

> The body needs a certain amount of movement. This movement serves to properly balance right and left and to redistribute and assimilate the various grain energies; it also causes the blood to circulate smoothly and prevents the arising of diseases.
>
> The human body is like a door hinge that never comes to rest. This is why Daoists practice healing exercises. They imitate the movements of the bear, which hangs itself head down from a tree, and of the owl, which keeps turning its head in different ways. They stretch and bend the waist, and move all the joints and muscles of their bodies in order to evade aging.
>
> I myself have developed a series of exercises which I name the Five Animals' Frolic. The five animals are tiger, deer, bear, monkey, and bird. The practice of the frolic aids the elimination of diseases and increases the functioning of the limbs and joints. Whenever a disorder is felt in the body, one of the animals should be practiced until one perspires freely. When perspiration is strong, one should cover the affected parts of the body with powder. In due course the body becomes lighter and more comfortable, and a healthy appetite will return. (29.2a; Despeux 1989, 242; also *Hou Hanshu* 82B.2739)

The chronicle then notes that Wu Pu followed his master's advice and even in his nineties enjoyed keen hearing, clear eyesight, and a full set of strong teeth, thus being able to eat like a youngster.

From this record it is clear that by the Later Han dynasty, the Five Animals' Frolic was known and practiced as a set of healing exercises, encouraging perspiration and enhancing the circulation of blood and *qi*. However, the first description of the actual practice does not appear until the Tang dynasty, when it is found in the *Yangxing yanming lu,* associated with Sun Simiao, and again—in exactly the same version—in the *Laojun yangsheng jue* 老君養生訣 (Lord Lao's Instructions on Nourishing Life, *DZ* 821; see Schipper and Verellen 2004, 354).

According to this, the animals' patterns appear in the order tiger, deer, bear, monkey, and bird; they tend to require only one type of movement, which is repeated seven times; and most are done from a squatting position, with only the first part of the bird executed while standing. The practice is vigorous and encourages sweating—as prescribed by Hua Tuo. On the other hand, it is not linked with either cosmological entities or specific organs or sections of the body. It runs as follows:

The Tiger Frolic: Squat on the floor with all four limbs. Move forward for three steps and back for two. In each case, begin by lengthening one hip forward while raising the opposite leg back and up into the air. Then place the leg back into the squatting position, moving forward or back. Do seven complete sets.

The Deer Frolic: Squat on the floor with all four limbs. Extend the neck forward and look back over your shoulder, three times to left and twice to the right. Next, stretch the legs, extending and contracting them also in a rhythm of three and two.

The Bear Frolic: Squat on the floor with your hands wrapped around the legs below knees. Look straight up, then lift your head while stomping down alternately with your feet, completing seven repetitions on each side. Return to a straight squat and lengthen the back with your hands pushing off the floor.

The Monkey Frolic: Holding onto a horizontal bar, hang straight down by the arms and stretch the entire body. Contact and extend for one set of seven repetitions. Next, drape the legs over the same bar, hang down and curl and release your arms to the right and left. Do seven repetitions.

The Bird Frolic: Stand up straight, place both hands on the floor, and lift up one leg at a time, letting it soar upward while stretching the shoulders and lifting the eyebrows. Do it with vigor. Repeat two sets of seven. Then sit down, extend the legs forward, and with your hands grab the heels of the feet. Do seven repetitions. Sit up straight, contract and extend the shoulders seven times each. (*Yangxing yanming lu* 2.7b–8a; *Laojun yangsheng jue* 1a–2a)

As different as these exercises are from the modern version of the Five Animals' Frolic, they still work similar body parts. Thus, the deer involves remaining quiet and turning the neck to look back, the bear stretches the muscles of the lower back, the monkey is playful and vibrant, and the bird involves a lifting motion that radiates lightness.

A more recent form of the Five Animals' Frolic develops the sequence to a pattern that is closer to the one practiced today. It appears first in the *Chifeng sui* 赤鳳髓 (Marrow of the Red Phoenix; trl. Despeux 1988), a collection of longevity methods by Zhou Lüjing 周履靖, dated to 1578. The son of an aristocratic family, Zhou was trained for office and married, but contracted tuberculosis and left the family to reside in a Daoist temple to heal himself. He remained a recluse and developed numerous skills, including sword fighting, paper making, painting, calligraphy, and long-life techniques. He collected prescriptions for healing, including herbs, talismans, rituals, exorcisms, and spells, which he wrote up variously (Despeux 1988, 12–13). His *Chifeng sui* consists of three sections: techniques of breathing and guiding *qi*, exercise sequences, and sleep exercises. The Five Animals' Frolic appears as the first sequence in the second part and is closer

Fig. 17: The Tiger Frolic. Source: *Chifeng sui.*

to what is practiced today. The Tiger Frolic is illustrated here for the first time (fig. 17).[2]

Textually the same version but with illustrations showing female practitioners appears also in the *Wuqin wu gongfa tushuo* 五禽舞功法圖說 (Illustrated Explanation of the Five Animals' Dance Practice). This is a short text, found in the nineteenth-century collection *Neiwai gong tushuo jiyao* 內外功圖說輯要 (Collected Essentials and Illustrated Descriptions of Inner and Outer Practices, *Daozang jinghua* 2.10:183–198). The preface notes that a woman living in the seclusion of the family home who wishes to cultivate herself should begin by setting up a quiet spot for her practice, then create some heat (with unspecified methods) to accumulate *qi*. Next, she should take the *qi* and circulate it through the arteries and meridians of her body until she feels it full and overflowing. Then she can practice the Five Animals' Frolic to eliminate all diseases and allow the emergence of subtler energetic levels. After this, she should pursue more meditative practices that lead eventually to the inner alchemical refinement of the elixir of immortality.

---

2. The same version is also found in the first chapter, "Peaceful Nurturing" (*Anyang pian* 安養篇), of the *Fushou danshu* 福壽丹書 (Elixir Book on Long Life and Good Fortune), dated to 1621. It was translated by John Dudgeon and is today found in Berk 1986, 57–62.

Unlike in the Tang version, all the exercises in this form are practiced standing up; unlike their modern variant, they involve only one or two movements per pattern and place a heavy emphasis on internal awareness and the meditative guiding of *qi*. There are no cosmological connections or links with the five inner organs, but in each case the text specifies medical benefits and areas of the body most affected:

The Tiger Frolic: Hold the breath, lower the head, and make the hands into fists. Assume the fighting stance of a tiger, exuding force and dignity. Now, lift both hands as if you were supporting a thousand pounds of iron, still holding the breath. Straighten the body and swallow the *qi,* feeling it enter the belly. At the same time make the spirit energy descend from above. Do this until you become aware of a rumbling sound like thunder in the belly. Repeat five sets of seven. Through this practice in the entire body the *qi* and meridians will be harmonious, essence and spirit will be lively, and the myriad diseases will be expelled.

The Bear Frolic: Hold the breath and make the hands into fists, then like a bear lean slowly from side to side [turning kidneys], alternating the weight on the right and left foot. Next, gingerly place one foot in front of the other and hold for a moment. Do this in such a way that the *qi* enters deep into the sides of the body and resonates strongly in the waist and joints. Doing this will enhance hip strength and eliminate abdominal distension. Repeat three sets of five, then stop. The practice stretches muscles and joints, calms the spirit, and nourishes the blood.

The Deer Frolic: Hold the breath, lower the head, and make the hands into fists. Stand like a deer turning back its head to look at its tail. Then straighten the body, contract the shoulders, and alternately rise up on the toes and stomp down on the heels, so that the entire body, like an integrated heavenly pillar, shakes and trembles. Repeat three sets of two or practice once a day after getting up in the morning. The more the better.

The Monkey Frolic: Hold the breath as usual when we make a fist. Then, hold a tree branch in one hand and a piece of fruit in the other. One foot lightly lifted in the air, pivot on the heel of the other foot to twist the body backwards. Now tighten the spirit energy and swallow it to guide it into your belly. Do this until you begin to sweat.

The Bird Frolic: Hold the breath and stand as if rising up. Inhale the breath all the way to the coccyx, then move the *qi* up to the top of the head. Next, raise both hands into the air and lean the body forward, lifting the head to receive the spirit as it breaks through the crown. Bow lightly in a formal obeisance, thus showing how your five *qi* pay their respects to the Prime. This will ensure that your six viscera are in harmony and your primordial *qi* will not get less. Thus, the hundred diseases will not arise. (*Chifeng sui* 63–67)

It is obvious from looking at this sequence where the modern version gets its particular shape, and how it came about by working with the traditional pattern and expanding it into various standing and moving aspects. As in the contemporary version, the Ming–Qing practice of the Five Animals' Frolic links the tiger with strength and overall body conditioning, the bear with lower-back stretches and kidney issues, the deer with neck and shoulders and mental calmness, the monkey with agility and twisting branches, and the bird (later to become the crane) with lightness and a lift toward the heavens. At the same time it continues the earlier system in that it prescribes repetitions, often in sets of seven, and encourages people to break out into a sweat. The sequence as a whole, moreover, is a classic example of the exercise tradition in that it works systematically through the different parts and muscle groups of the body and provides relief from tension and alleviates ailments.

Seasonal and Immortal Practices

Two other kinds of healing exercises that have influenced qigong practice today are found in the same texts as the Five Animals' Frolic. One consists of twenty-four simple moves to be practiced as the seasons change (i.e., in accordance with the twenty-four solar nodes or two-week periods that divide the Chinese year).

Fig. 18: The seasonal exercise for
the summer solstice. Source:
Neiwai gong tushuo jiyao.

The other involves brief practices associated with immortals, each geared to alleviate a particular ailment.

The Chinese calendar is a mixture of lunar and solar measuring. The dominant mode is lunar, so that the months begin on the 1st with the new moon, peak on the 15th at full moon, and end at waning moon on the 29th or 30th. On the other hand, the year is determined by solar cycles. It begins about six weeks after the winter solstice, usually in late January or early February, with the seasons measured by the solstices and equinoxes, which—contrary to Western usage—mark their high points rather than their beginnings. To combine seasonal solar changes with the twelve lunar months, moreover, the Chinese have a system of twenty-four two-week periods, named after climate changes and essential for the agricultural rhythm of the year. Each of these, then, has a specific healing exercise to alleviate common complaints. The practices are associated with the immortal Chen Tuan 陳摶 (d. 989), a famous Song-dynasty figure whose main specialty was the practice of sleep exercises as described in more detail below. They are recorded in the *Ershisi qi zuogong daoyin zhibing tushuo* 二十四坐功導引治病圖案 (Twenty-four Illustrated Seated Exercise Practices to Heal Diseases), contained in the *Neiwai gong tushuo jiyao* (133–181).[3]

The diseases they propose to heal tend to be associated with *qi*-blockages, including joint pains, digestive problems, and muscular weakness. Although some texts, following the ancient manuscripts and the recommendations of Sun Simiao, speak in detail about the different organs associated with each season,[4] ailments treated by the Twenty-four Seated Exercises are not classified in this manner. Rather, the exercises tend to work on all the different parts of the body in the course of a few months, providing well-rounded care (fig. 18).

The timing of the practice is in the very early morning hours, around midnight or 1 a.m. in the winter months (11th, 12th, 1st) and after sunrise or 5 a.m. in the height of summer (4th, 5th). During the remainder of the year, it is best to perform them at dawn, around 3 a.m. In each case, after the physical stretch or movement, adepts are to click their teeth and swallow the saliva, guiding it to the area activated. Each exercise is repeated five or seven times. The practices are shown in Table 2.

---

3. The same set is also found in the *Zunsheng bajian* 尊生八牋 (Eight Folios on Honoring Life), in 20 *juan*, by Gaolian Shenfu 高濂深甫 of the late Ming dynasty. Translated by John Dudgeon, it is found today in Berk 1986, 19–47. The same material also appears in the *Wanshou xianshu* (Immortal Book on Longevity of Ten Thousand [Years]). See Berk 1986, 17.

4. A text of this kind is the *Siji diaoshe zhelu* 四季調攝摘錄 (Record of Harmonizing and Balancing in Accordance with the Four Seasons), found in the *Neiwai gong tushuo jiyao* (89–131). It closely resembles the earlier instructions of Sun Simiao on keeping the organs healthy month by month, to which it adds breathing techniques and simple stretches. For example, to maintain the liver in the spring, one should use the *xu* breath thirty times daily and twist the torso to the right and left with the hands placed on the shoulders.

TABLE 2. Seated healing exercises for the twenty-four seasonal energies

Mo.	Period	Practice
1	Spring beginning	Cross-legged, press both hands on R/L knee, turn neck R/L, 15x.
	Rainwater	Press both hands on R/L thigh, turn neck and torso R/L, 15x.
2	Insects stirring	Make tight fists, lift arms to elbow level, turn neck R/L, 30x.
	Spring equinox	Stretch arms forward, turn neck R/L, look over shoulders, 42x.
3	Pure brightness	Pull arms into shooting bow position R/L, 56x.
	Crop rain	Lift arm up, palm out, place other arm across torso, turn shoulders, 35x.
4	Summer beginning	Cross-legged, interlace fingers, hug knee into chest R/L, 35x.
	Slight ripening	Lift arm up, palm out, press other arm on legs, press R/L, 35x.
5	Seeds sprouting	Stand up, lift both arms to ceiling, slight back bend, 35x.
	Summer equinox	Sit with legs out, lift one leg, hold with both hands, stretch R/L, 35x.
6	Slight heat	Kneel on one leg, stretch other leg away, lean back, R/L, 15x.
	Great heat	Cross-legged, lean forward over legs, push floor, turn neck R/L, 15x.
7	Fall beginning	Cross-legged, press both hands on floor, push body up, 56x.
	Last heat	Lifting the chest, turn the head R/L, drum fists on back, 35x.
8	White dew	Press hands on respective knees, turn neck R/L, 15x.
	Fall equinox	Interlace hands behind head, lean sideways R/L, 15x.
9	Cold dew	Lift arms overhead in V position, pressing upward, 35x.
	Frost descending	Sit with legs out, hold both feet, stretch and lift, 35x.
10	Winter beginning	Cross-legged, stretch both arms to one side, turn head to the other, 15x.
	Slight snow	Press one hand on knee, hold at elbow with other hand, R/L, 15x.
11	Great snow	Stand up, cross legs at knees, open arms to the side, press, 35x.
	Winter equinox	Sit with legs straight, press arms on knees with vigor, R/L, 15x.
12	Slight cold	Cross-legged, push one arm up, looking at it, other arm on floor, 15x.
	Great cold	Kneel on one leg, lean back, bend and straighten other leg, R/L, 15x.

Note: R = right side; L = left side; x = number of repetitions on each side

The instructions mention that one should alternate the practices to the right and left and practice them on each side for the given number of repetitions. The practices are gentle, helping people to keep their joints moving and their energies harmonious as the seasons march through their preset path, and, with two exceptions, undertaken while sitting down. They should not take more than ten minutes or so to complete.

In addition to the seasonal exercises, texts of the late Ming also present simple

moves and stretches for specific medical conditions. Associated with famous immortals of various ages and provenance, they specify briefly which symptoms they
are good for, give a concise description of the practice, and illustrate it in a pertinent
ink drawing. They also provide an herbal remedy, usually consisting of five to eight
different ingredients (often including ginseng, *danggui*, China root fungus, and
various animal and mineral substances) to supplement the regimen, and outline a
more metaphorical and symbolic version of the practice—often replete with inner
alchemical imagery—in a practice poem of four lines of seven characters each.

Three variants of these immortals' practices survive. One, consisting of
forty-eight items, appears in the second chapter, "Extending the Years," of the
Fushou danshu, dated to 1621 (Berk 1986, 71–117); a second one, largely identical
with the first in contents, style, and illustrations, but arranged in a slightly different order and minus six items, is found in the *Zhuxian daoyin tu* 諸仙導引圖
(Illustrated Exercises of the Various Immortals), contained in the *Neiwai gong
tushuo jiyao* (1–86); the third, consisting of forty-six exercises that have completely different names and do not present herbal remedies or a poem but—with
the exception of twelve—are identical in symptoms, prescriptions, and illustrations, appears in the *Chifeng sui* (Despeux 1988, 127–221).[5]

The exercises cover all kinds of medical symptoms and conditions. The largest group of thirteen exercises is geared to alleviate conditions of excessive or
blocked *qi* as well as sexual problems, such as insufficient libido, nocturnal emissions, and venereal excesses. Next, eleven practices deal with joint issues of the
neck, shoulders, back, hips, and legs, closely followed by a group of nine that help
with digestive problems, stomachaches, and intestinal ailments. Another ten deal
with more sensory and psychological issues, such as poor eyesight, headaches,
vertigo, depression, melancholy, and anger. Beyond this, two are specifically for
paralysis, one is for cold and its various related disorders, and four serve to benefit the entire body.

By far the largest number of exercises are performed in a seated position,
nineteen cross-legged and six with legs extended. Fifteen are executed standing,
sometimes with legs turned out in the position of the character *ba* 八, sometimes
with legs wide apart, set in stride, or one up against the wall, and sometimes in
character *ding* 丁 position, with the heel of one foot close to the middle of the
other (what ballet dancers call "third position"). One practice is done while squatting, one while kneeling—using some of the postures prominent in the old ver-

---

5. Sixteen of the *Chifeng sui* practices, with illustrations, are also translated in Liu 1990, 129–143. They are
#3, 6, 8, 10, 11, 14, 16, 17, 18, 19, 22, 23, 25, 30, 34, and 44 (following the numbering of Despeux 1988, also
used in table 3). Another presentation of the practices in modern Chinese is found in Ma 1999.

Fig. 19: The immortal Dongfang Shuo grasping his toes. Source: *Neiwai gong tushuo jiyao.*

sion of the Five Animals' Frolic. And six are done while lying down, one each on back and belly, and four on the side. There is no immediate correlation of positions to symptoms, although all practices for headache and vertigo are undertaken from a cross-legged posture and all squatting and lying-down practices are for curing digestive ailments.

Figures associated with the different exercises vary widely. They range from Daoist deities such as Lord Lao through ancient immortals recorded in the *Liexian zhuan,* medieval alchemists such as Ge Hong, and figures from the *Shenxian zhuan* to more recent saints such as the famous Eight Immortals and the Seven Perfected of the Complete Perfection school, all made popular in theater plays and vernacular novels.[6] The association of figure and practice differs widely among the variants. For example, Dongfang Shuo 東方朔, a famous immortal and magician under Emperor Wu of the Han (r. 140–86 B.C.E.) with a biography in the *Liexian zhuan,* according to the *Fushou danshu* represents a cure for blocked *qi* and hernias by "grasping the toes" (fig. 19): "With one hand holding the foot, with the other hand rotate the big toe for the duration of five breaths. Guide the *qi* through the abdomen and the entire body. Do the same for all ten toes" (Berk 1986, 112).

---

6. The Eight Immortals were first constituted as a group in Yuan drama. See Yetts 1916, Yang 1958, Lai 1972. On their prominence in popular novels, see Broman 1978. The Seven Perfected appear in vernacular literature and tales of magic. See Wong 1990.

In the *Chifeng sui*, on the other hand, Dongfang Shuo is associated with relieving wind-induced problems, such as dizziness and vertigo. He sits cross-legged and raises his hands to his scalp, embracing the ears and massaging the top of the head for the duration of twelve breaths (Despeux 1988, 146–147). Similarly, Lü Chunyang 呂純陽, better known as Lü Dongbin 呂洞賓, the leader of the Eight Immortals, is associated with a seated head massage and meditation in one text (Berk 1986, 92) and with a standing manipulation of arm-*qi* in the other (Despeux 1988, 184–185). For a complete list of the practices, see table 3. It uses the number according to the *Fushou danshu* as its baseline, because the practices are available in English translation (Berk 1986) and thus most easily accessible to the modern reader. Next, it gives the corresponding number in the *Neiwai gong tushuo jiyao,* followed by the name of the immortal connected with the practice. After this, the table provides the number of the practice as found in the *Chifeng sui,* again with the associated immortal. Next, the table focuses on the actual practices. It lists the type of posture required, the type of ailment alleviated, and the movement or meditations necessary.

TABLE 3. Immortals' exercises of the Ming dynasty

No.	NW	Immortal	CF	Immortal	Pose	Symptom: move
1	2	Taiqing zongshi	42	Wu Tongwei	X	Digestive: rub belly with hands.
2	1	Li Laojun	23	Gouchun	X	Overall: hands on knees, guide *qi.*
3	3	Xu Shenweng	39	Bai Yuchan	X	*Qi:* hands to opposite shoulder, look L/R.
4	4	Li Tieguai	30	Hanzi	S	Paralysis: extend arms fore and back.
5	5	He Xiangu	46	Qi Xiaoyao	Q	Digestive: hug knees into belly.
6	6	Bai Yuchan	26	Ma Ziran	L	Digestive: lie on belly, lift limbs off ground.
7	8	Han Zhongli	8	Rongcheng Gong	X	Vertigo: heavenly drum, click teeth.
8	29	Cao Xiangu	—		X	Eyes: tongue up, eyes up, guide *qi.*
9	—	Qiu Changchun	18	Wei Boyang	X	Back: extend legs up R/L, guide *qi.*
10	—	Ma Danyang	24	Xie Ziran	X	*Qi:* warm hands, rub eyes, place on chest.
11	—	Zhang Ziyang	37	Xu Qiao	S	Digestive: raise arms up to heaven.
12	—	Huang Huagu	—		L	*Qi:* lie on side, rub abdomen, press legs.

No.	NW	Immortal	CF	Immortal	Pose	Symptom: move
13	30	Yin Qinghe	25	Song Xuanbai	L	Digestive: lie on back, leg over knee, stretch.
14	11	Li Qichan	—		E	*Qi:* rub one foot on other sole.
15	12	Zhang Zhennu	45	Jin Keji	X	Depression: hands on knees, guide *qi.*
16	13	Wei Boyang	7	Juanzi	X	Paralysis: one fist on chest, other press knee.
17	14	Xue Daoguang	27	Xuan Su	X	*Qi:* visualize *qi* in ailing area.
18	15	Ge Hong	—		S	Melancholy: hands at chest, push out/in.
19	16	Wang Yuyang	—		S	Overall: up on toes, press belly with fists.
20	17	Ma Gu	—		S	*Qi:* push weight R/L, guide *qi.*
21	18	Zhang Guolao	19	Zi Zhu	X	Triple Heater: rub belly and inner thighs.
22	19	Chen Ziran	12	Xiuyang Gong	L	Cold: lie on side, knees up, hands on legs.
23	20	Shi Xinglin	31	Pei Xuanjing	X	Digestive: warm hands, rub elixir field.
24	21	Han Xiangzi	20	Gu Qu	S	Hips: bend forward, elbows over head.
25	22	Zhao Lingnü	29	Lü Chunyang	S	Legs: extend arm, massage elbow area.
26	23	Lü Chunyang	33	Han Xiangzi	X	Overall: hands over temples, guide *qi.*
27	24	Chen Xiyi	5	Qiong Shu	L	*Qi:* lie on side, press nostril, press coccyx.
28	25	Fuyu dijun	17	Xu Jinyang	S	Anger: stretch and bend arms to shoot bow.
29	26	Xu Shenzu	21	Fulü	X	Back: twist torso R/L.
30	7	Chen Niwan	10	Dongfang Shuo	X	Head: hands behind ears, rub neck.
31	28	Cao Guoqiu	6	Jieyu Wang	S	Legs: hand at wall, raise leg, push up.
32	9	Zhao Shangzao	16	Shantu	E	*Qi:* hold toes, lift up legs, move R/L.
33	10	Xujing tianshi	9	Zhuangzi	L	*Qi:* lie on side, leg over knee, hand on pubis.
34	31	Su Xuanxu	2	Huangshi Gong	E	Hips: grab toes, move feet up and down.
35	32	Gao Xiangxian	22	Tao Chengyang	S	Hips: cross legs, arms front/back, stretch.
36	33	Fu Yuanxu	—		X	Vertigo: warm hands, rub top of head.

No.	NW	Immortal	CF	Immortal	Pose	Symptom: move
37	34	Li Hongzhi	43	Ziying	S	*Qi:* cross legs, bend forward, cross arms.
38	35	Li Tieguai	15	Donghua dijun	S	Hips: hands on stick, push up on toes.
39	36	Yuzhen shanren	14	Zhongli Yunfang	X	*Qi:* warm hands, rub kidney area.
40	27	Li Yepo	—		E	*Qi:* push on thighs, bend forward.
41	37	Lan Caihe	28	Fuju xiansheng	E	Overall: hands in fists, bend forward.
42	—	Xia Yunfeng	—		K	Back: crawl on all fours, twist R/L.
43	—	He Taigu	36	Xuanzhenzi	X	Digestive: raise arms up to heaven.
44	38	Liu Xigu	1	You Quan	S	Digestive: extend arms back/forth, twist.
45	39	Su Buer	—		S	Digestive: bend, hands at wall, push leg back.
46	40	Chang Tianyang	35	Hou Daoxuan	S	Back: interlace hands, bend head to chest.
47	41	Dongfang Shuo	—		X	*Qi:* massage toes.
48	42	Pengzu	—		E	Eyes: cross legs, arms behind, guide *qi.*

Note: Number in first column is according to the *Fushou danshu* (trl. Berk 1986); *NW* = *Neiwai gong tushuo; CF = Chifeng sui.* X = cross-legged; S = standing; L = lying down; E = seated with legs extended; Q = squatting; K = kneeling.

In whatever framework they appear, these medicinal exercises are simple, easy to perform, and quick to execute. They use twists to limber up the body, bends and stretches to engage the muscles, movements to warm up joints, massages to bring blood flow to desired areas, and various kinds of *qi*-guiding to enhance the flow of energy through the body. They reveal a strong concern with balancing and harmonizing *qi,* preventing excessive loss—through nocturnal emissions and the like—and clearing blockages in various areas. Second to that, ailments tend to be, again as they were in the Han and the middle ages, either of a locomotive or gastrointestinal nature. Arthritis and indigestion loomed large on the horizon of Chinese practitioners and are accordingly well represented in the exercises. In addition, healing exercises also helped with emotional issues such as depression, melancholy, and anger through the release of blocked *qi* from the body, notably the heart area. Taken together with the seasonal practices, these medical methods provide a wide selection of exercises that help people to recover and maintain health.

Inner Alchemy

The more religious or spiritual dimension of healing exercises began to play an active role in the dominant system of Daoist immortality practice at the time: inner alchemy, the meditative transformation of grosser energy cycles into subtle levels of spirit and pure cosmic being. Inner alchemy can be characterized by the active reconciliation of physiological training and intellectual speculation (Robinet 1989a, 300). In particular it combines the system of operative alchemy as described by Ge Hong of the fourth century; the practice of visualizing body gods central to Highest Clarity; the transformation of sexual and other gross energies essential to methods of *qi*-absorption; and cosmological speculation associated with yin and yang, the five phases, lunar and solar cycles, and the *Yijing* (Pregadio 2006b, 210, 219; 2006a, 123). While the earliest inner alchemical text dates from the mid-eighth century (Skar and Pregadio 2000, 475), the fully formulated and recognized system emerges only in the Song dynasty (Baldrian-Hussein 1990, 187).

Over the centuries, several major schools emerged within inner alchemy:

- the Zhenyuan 真元 (Perfect Prime) school of the late Tang, which focused mainly on Highest Clarity visualizations and ecstatic excursions while integrating *Yijing* speculation, herbal remedies from the materia medica, and the insight practice of inner observation (Skar and Pregadio 2000, 468; see also Robinet 1990)
- the Zhong-Lü 鐘呂 school of the tenth century, named after the two immortals Zhongli Quan 鐘離權 and Lü Dongbin 呂洞賓, which focused dominantly on physiological practices, working with energy exercises and embryo respiration, and gaining fame mainly through the accomplishment of miracles (Baldrian-Hussein 1984, 34)
- the so-called Southern school (Nanzong 南宗), centered on Zhang Boduan 張伯端 (984–1082) and Bai Yuchan 白玉蟾 (1194–ca. 1127), which sprang up in southern China in the eleventh century and placed great emphasis on cosmological speculation, also integrating a great deal of Buddhist thought and formal rituals, making heavy use of the newly arising thunder rites (Skar and Pregadio 2000, 470–471; see also Cleary 1987; Wang 2004)
- the Quanzhen 全真 or Complete Perfection school, founded in twelfth-century north China by Wang Chongyang 王重陽 (1113–1170), which was ascetic and monastic in organization and worked dominantly with interior voyages and the inherent transformation of the self into cosmic dimensions (Yao 2000, 586; see also Komjathy 2007)

Each of these schools placed a slightly different emphasis on physical, meditative, ritual, and ecstatic practices and envisioned the process in somewhat different cosmological and psychological terms. As centuries passed, further schools created yet different forms of inner alchemical practice, including entire systems specifically for women,[7] and integrated more traditional Confucian thought in the overall climate of "harmonizing the three teachings." Yet within this great variety, inner alchemy—then and now—typically begins with a preparatory phase of moral and physical readiness, which involves practicing all the various longevity techniques, setting one's mind fully on the Great Work, and learning to control the mind with basic breath observation and other concentration exercises.

Once ready, practitioners typically pass through a series of three transformations: from essence (*jing* 精) to energy (*qi* 氣), from energy to spirit (*shen* 神), and from spirit to the Dao, consciously and actively reversing human gestation and cosmic creation (Robinet 1989a, 317–319; Skar and Pregadio 2000, 488–490). They begin by focusing on essence, the tangible form of *qi* that sinks down periodically from its original center in the Ocean of *Qi* in men and in the Cavern of *Qi* in women, manifesting as semen and menstrual blood respectively. To revert essence back to *qi,* men allow a feeling of arousal to occur, then guide the flowing energy back up along the spine and into the head, thus "subduing the white tiger." Women, when they feel menstrual blood sink down from the Cavern of *Qi,* massage their breasts and visualize it rising upward and transforming into *qi.* Over several months, this will cause menstruation to cease, the "decapitation of the red dragon" (Despeux and Kohn 2003, 221–223). They then circulate the newly purified *qi* in the Microcosmic Orbit, guiding it along the central channels of the torso and opening a series of passes along the way. Not only strengthening the body and enhancing health, this *qi*-circulation eventually leads to the manifestation of a concentrated pearl of primordial *qi*—newly formed in men, latently present from birth in women. The first stage concludes when the pearl coalesces.

The second stage is the same for men and women. It focuses on the transformation of purified *qi* into spirit. The pearl of dew is developed into the golden flower with the help of transmuted *qi.* For this, yin and yang are identified as different energies in the body, each described with different metaphors depending on the level of purity attained. Typically there are the following (Robinet 1989a, 325–326):

---

7. Later developments are documented in a large variety of texts, some of which have been studied and translated. Prominent examples include Lu 1970, Despeux 1979, Cleary 1992, Esposito 1998, Darga 1999, Liu 2001, Mori 2002. For presentations of women's practice, see Despeux and Kohn 2003, Valussi 2003. For a general survey of the tradition, see Needham et al. 1983, Robinet 1995. For modern versions of the practice, see the works by Mantak Chia (1999, 2003, 2005) and Ni Hua-ching (1989). A modern take on the practices, with full translation, is found in Olson 2002.

yang = heart = fire = trigram *li* ☲ = pure lead = dragon = red bird
yin = kidneys = water = trigram *kan* ☵ = pure mercury = tiger = white tiger

The texts describing these advanced practices tend to be obscure and highly metaphoric. As Zhang Boduan says in his poetic cycle *Awakening to Perfection*,

In the crescent-moon furnace, jade blossoms grow;
In the vermilion crucible, mercury flows evenly along.
Only after harmonizing them with great firing power
Can you plant the central pearl to gradually ripen. (Verse 4)

The lightning of true water boils and thunders in the realm of metal and of water;
True fire arises from Mount Kunlun—these are our yin and yang.
The two restored and harmonized in proper ways
Make the elixir grow naturally, pervade the body with its fragrance. (Verse 13)

At each stage of the transmutation process, the energies are given different names, and different metaphors are employed. Eventually adepts learn not only to mix them in the abdomen but also to revolve them through an inner-body cycle that includes not only the spine and breastbone but leads all the way to the feet and is known as the macrocosmic orbit. Gradually one's energies are refined to a point where they become as pure as the celestials themselves. Spirit emerges as an independent entity; the pearl opens up to give rise to the golden flower, the core of the immortal embryo in the lower cinnabar field.

Once the embryo starts to grow, adepts switch their practice to nourish it for ten months with embryo respiration. In addition to nurturing the embryo, this practice also makes the adept increasingly independent of outer nourishment and air. Whereas the first phase is easier for men, this stage is easier for women because they are naturally endowed with the faculty to grow an embryo. After ten months, the embryo is complete.

Adepts then proceed to the third stage. The as yet semimaterial body of the embryo is transformed into the pure spirit body of the immortals, a body of primordial *qi*. To attain its full realization, the embryo has to undergo several phases. First it is nourished to completion and undergoes a spiritual birth by moving up along the spine and exiting through the Hundred Meeting (Baihui 百會) point at the top of the head, which is now called Heavenly Gate (Tianguan 天關). The first exiting of the spirit embryo is known as "deliverance from the womb." It signifies the adept's celestial rebirth and is accompanied by the perception of a deep inner rumbling, like a clap of thunder. When the Heavenly Gate opens, a white smoky essence can be seen hovering above the adept. The spirit passes through the top of the head and begins to communicate with the celestials, thus transcending the limitations of the body (Despeux and Kohn 2003, 237).

Once the embryo has been born, it grows through a further meditative exercise known as "nursing for three years." Gradually getting used to its new powers, the embryo moves faster and travels farther away until it can go far and wide without any limitation. As the spirit enters into its cosmic ventures, the adept exhibits supernatural powers, including the ability to be in two places at once, to move quickly from one place to another, to know past and future, to divine people's thoughts, and so on. Known as "spirit pervasion," this indicates the freedom achieved by the spirit as manifest in the practitioner. Eventually, the enlightenment gets strong, and the adept, whose body is already transformed into pure light, overcomes life and death and melts into cosmic emptiness (Despeux and Kohn 2003, 243).

The Eight Brocades

Besides various physical exercises that serve to heal diseases and prepare the adept for the long haul of the Great Work, there are several prominent Daoyin practices that form part of inner alchemy. A meditation-cum-exercise practice that involves ritual preparation and *qi*-circulation in inner-alchemical fashion is the so-called Eight Brocades (*baduan jin* 八段錦), a sequence of eight seated practices that stimulate *qi*-flow, rotate energies around the body, and encourage alchemical transmutations. The text appears first in the *Xiuzhen shishu* 修真十書 (Ten Books on Cultivating Perfection, DZ 263), an extensive compendium in 10 *juan* that dates from the thirteenth to fourteenth centuries and collects materials associated with the Bai Yuchan 白玉蟾 school of inner alchemy (Schipper and Verellen 2004, 946). Next to an illustration of each Brocade, the written text here consists of two parts, a general description of the exercises in short phrases and a more detailed commentary. The same description and illustrations also appear in the *Chifeng sui* (Despeux 1988, 112–117) and, with more extensive commentary and explanations, in the *Neiwai gong tushuo jiyao* (217–266).[8]

According to this, the Eight Brocades are a mixture of internal *qi*-guiding and

---

8. The same outline is also found in the *Zunsheng bajian*, translated in Berk 1986, 48–56, as well as in *Xiuling yaozhi*. A modern Chinese presentation appears in Ma 1999. Another English version, with a completely different sequencing and a thorough mixture of text and commentary, is found in Yang 1988, 40–51. Yang divides the first Brocade into three separate exercises, then has the second as his fourth. The third he leaves out completely. The fourth becomes his fifth and the fifth his sixth and part of his eighth (done while stretching the legs). The sixth is also left out; the seventh is the same, but combined with the eighth and performed while seated with legs extended, and the meditation practice at the end of the text appears as his eighth. He also provides his own illustrations and

simple physical movements executed on the basis of deep concentrative meditation and serving the purpose of "burning the body" (*fenshen* 焚身), an important practice in inner alchemy, executed on both the second and third levels, that serves to eliminate illnesses or demonic influences that might hinder the entering of the indepth meditations needed for the completion of the immortal embryo (Baldrian-Hussein 1984, 160).

The technique focuses on the breath (dragon) as opposed to the concoction of the elixir that uses the body fluids (tiger). It involves swallowing *qi* in the form of a mixture of breath and saliva and guiding it into the lower cinnabar field where, in conjunction with the fire of the heart, it turns into a wheel of fire that gradually expands and burns throughout the body, eliminating demonic or psychological problems of various kinds: nervous troubles when awake, nightmares when asleep, and hallucinations during meditation. By extension, various negative desires and attachments, such as to worldly wealth and success, passions and love relationships, military and political prowess, and speedy ascension and supernatural attainments, are eliminated, leaving the practitioner free to focus fully on the divine transformation of inner alchemy (Baldrian-Hussein 1984, 162).

THE EIGHT BROCADES
1. Click the teeth and assemble the gods:[9] Click the teeth thirty-six times, then place both hands on your head and beat the heavenly drum twenty-four times.
2. Shake the Heavenly Pillar: Shake the Heavenly Pillar to the right and the left, for a total of twenty-four times on each.
3. The red dragon churns the ocean: Move the tongue around the mouth to the right and left, reaching upward to the gums. Repeat thirty-six times. Swallow the saliva in three gulps like a hard object. After that you can circulate the *qi* in accordance with the proper firing times.
4. Massage the hall of the kidneys: Massage the hall of the kidneys with both hands, rubbing them thirty-six times. The more you do of this, the more marvelous the results.
5. Single-pass rotation: Rotate the torso at the single pass like an axle to the right and left. Repeat this thirty-six times.
6. Double-pass rotation: Rotate the torso at the double pass like a pulley to the right and left. Repeat this thirty-six times.
7. Interlace fingers on top of the head: Rub both hands and exhale with *he*. Repeat five times. Then interlace the fingers, palms facing out, and raise the

---

interpretation, plus an account of the standing sequence, which is not documented well in historical literature and seems to go back to the Shaolin rather than the medical or Daoist tradition.
9. The headings are provided in *Neiwai gong tushuo jiyao*, 218–219.

arms above the head to support Heaven. Then press the hands against the top
of the head. Repeat nine times.

8.   Hands and feet hook together: With both hands formed into hooks bend
      forward and press the soles of the feet. Repeat this twelve times. Next, again
      pull the legs in to sit cross-legged with back straight.

Concluding meditation: Wait as the water reverts to rise. Once more rinse and once
again swallow the saliva in three gulps. Once this is done, you will have swallowed
the divine fluid altogether nine times. As you swallow it down with a rippling,
gurgling sound, the hundred meridians will naturally be harmonized and the River
Chariot [at the base of the spine] will create the perfect circulation [of *qi*]. Thereby
you develop a fire that burns the entire body. (19.1a–6b)

The practice begins with a seated meditation, during which adepts close their
eyes, focus inward, and eliminate all extraneous thoughts. They click their teeth
and snap their fingers against the back of their heads to wake up the gods inside the
body (fig. 20).

Following this, they turn the neck to the right and left to loosen up the muscles of
the throat, so they can swallow the *qi* more easily. The *qi*, next, is collected by moving
the tongue around the mouth and begins to circulate around the body in accordance
with the "firing times" (*huohou* 火候), that is, following a set pattern of yin-yang interchange that facilitates the optimal potency of *qi* (Robinet 1989a, 316). To activate
the lower body, where the *qi* is to center and turn into the wheel of fire, adepts next

Fig. 20: The First Brocade:
Beating the Heavenly Drum.
Source: *Xiuzhen shishu.*

massage the kidney area, the so-called Gate of Essence (*jingmen* 精門), while holding their breath and visualizing a radiant fire descending from the heart area.

In the second half of the practice, adepts first roll their shoulders to cause the *qi* to move upward from the abdomen, then twist the torso to allow it to flow smoothly along the spine toward the head. As the *qi* fills the chest area, they eliminate its fire from the body by focusing on the heart, exhaling with *he*, and raising their hands palms up above their heads. This practice corresponds exactly to the Heart Exercise among the Six Breaths or Six Healing Sounds and as such is still commonly practiced today. It is used to eliminate fire from the body, and with this fire the negative emotions of impatience, arrogance, hastiness, and violence (Chia and Chia 1993, 105). The last Brocade, moreover, is close to the modern Kidney Exercise, where adepts exhale with *chui* and bend forward to open the back of the body. Going into a seated forward bend, they hook their hands around their feet and stimulate the first point of the kidney meridian, Bubbling Well (*yongquan* 涌泉) in the center of the soles.

Having thus balanced the two most fundamental *qi*-powers (fire and water) in the body by allowing them to rise and emit consciously, adepts return to a meditative posture and once more swallow breath and saliva, letting the mixture descend into the abdomen, where it harmonizes the various energy channels and continues to purify the entire person. The effect is an overall cleansing and liberation from negative forces and natural extremes. As the text says,

> Doing this, wayward [*qi*] and demonic forces will no longer dare to approach you. Dreaming and waking will never be confused. Heat and cold can no longer penetrate you. And all kinds of calamities and ailments will stay away. If you practice this method between midnight and noon, the inner transformations will effect a perfect union of Heaven [Qian] and Earth [Kun], establish the internal circulation in its proper stages, and make the eight trigrams revolve properly. The method is most excellent indeed. (19.6b)

Using exercises that also appear among the medical practices described earlier and combining them with the systematic guiding of *qi* and with inner alchemical visualizations, the Eight Brocades provide a powerful means to enhance health and engage in the process of transcendence. They show in a hands-on, practical manner just how Daoists envisioned the transition from health and longevity practices geared to improve the natural functioning of body and mind to immortality meditations that served to create a level beyond the natural. Doing so, the Brocades aid adepts in realizing themselves in both this world and the next, in overcoming the ordinary self and gaining a foothold in the Dao.

Sleep Exercises

A more advanced version of healing exercises in the tradition of inner alchemy is found in the so-called sleep exercises (*shuigong* 睡功), associated most closely with the tenth-century saint and immortal Chen Tuan.[10] Born in Henan in the late ninth century, he spent his formative years wandering around famous mountains, presumably seeking instructions in various Daoist and other arts from learned masters. During this period he stayed for a while on Mount Wudang 武當山 in Hunan, where he practiced Daoist techniques of meditation and healing exercises, as well as dietetics and breathing. He may or may not have been instructed in practices that were later to become famous as the Wudang school of martial arts.

In 937, Chen Tuan apparently was in Sichuan, where he left behind an inscription praising the Daoist meditation and breathing methods he learned from a master there. He then resumed his migrations to settle eventually, probably in the early 940s, on Mount Hua in Shaanxi. Here he took care to restore an ancient Daoist settlement that had fallen into disrepair during the destructive last years of the Tang dynasty. As a result of his efforts, the Yuntai guan 雲臺觀 (Cloud Terrace Monastery) became a flourishing center again. It was here that he spent the rest of his life—a considerable span, since he died only in 989, at the alleged age of 118 *sui*. In between, he visited the imperial court three times and was honored variously with gifts, subsidies, and formal titles. In 984, he was awarded the official honorary title Xiyi xiansheng 希夷先生 (Master of the Invisible and the Inaudible), a reference to chapter 14 of the *Daode jing*.

Chen Tuan is known for three major areas of exploits. First, he was a physiognomist who could predict the fate and fortune of people by looking at their facial features, and he allegedly helped Emperor Taizong select the heir apparent from among his many sons (Kohn 1988, 220). Second, he is credited with formulating the philosophy of Taiji, the Great Ultimate, and creating the diagram that became famous in Neo-Confucian circles and later provided the basis for the ubiquitous yin-yang symbol (Li 1990, 45; Louis 2003, 164).

Third, he was a master of sleep exercises, that is, he practiced a form of inner alchemy that is undertaken while reclining on one side. A number of stories relate exploits that often involved several months of catatonic trance. According to one tale, he once lay like dead in his hermitage in the mountains. Upon being brought back to life by a badly frightened wood gatherer, he glared at him with exasperation and rasped, "Why do you disturb me in my marvelous sleep?"[11]

---

10. For studies on the life and legends of Chen Tuan, see Knaul 1981; Kohn 1990; Russell 1990a, 1990b.
11. This is first reported in 1051 by Wu Yuanxiang and recorded in *Lequan ji* 33.14a. See Knaul 1981, 98.

Other accounts also record songs he composed on the wonder and high quality of the sleep state; supposedly he even explained to the emperor that no palace in the world could compare with his heavenly visions (Knaul 1981, 200).

His biography in the *Lishi zhenxian tidao tongjian* 歷世真仙體道通鑒 (Comprehensive Mirror through the Ages of Perfected Immortals and Those Who Embody the Tao, *DZ* 296) of the early thirteenth century has a discourse that details his view of the practice:

> An ordinary person eats to satiation and then takes plenty of rest. He or she is mainly worried that the food should not be too rich, eating when he feels hungry and sleeping when he feels tired. His snore is audible everywhere. Yet at night when he should be sound asleep, he wakes up unaccountably. This is because fame and gain, sounds and sights agitate his spirit and consciousness, sweet wine and fried mutton muddle his mind and will. This is the sleep of ordinary folk. (47.9b)

In contrast to this, Chen Tuan as the ideal representative of sleep practice has a pure and clear mind that is tranquil and at rest. As he says in the hagiography, he sleeps the sleep of the perfected, keeping the energies tightly locked and continuously circulating in his body, guarded by celestial entities such as the green dragon and the white tiger. He has numinous powers, calling forth the spirits and summoning the gods to support his work, and he can whirl spiritually out of his body to converse with immortals and visit the palaces above. He says,

> Madly I whirl, appear and vanish with the clouds alight,
> Sitting quiet, I well reach the purple Kunlun height.
> With ease I pass through Heaven's caves and power spots of Earth,
> Inhale the flowery essence that Sun and Moon disperse.
> Sporting in the wondrous scenery of vapors and of haze,
> I visit sylphs and talk about the marvels of our days.
> I join immortals in their visits to strange lands,
> And get to see the green sea turning into strands.
> I point at yin and yang and screech with exultation,
> I cease to care about all rules and worldly limitation.
> Like stepping on clear wind my feet rise high and bright,
> As my body floats along with the falling rays of light. (47.9b–10a)

Similarly stylized and legendary is a set of twelve sleep practices associated with Chen Tuan that appears in the *Chifeng sui* (Despeux 1988, 225–269). Called *Huashan shier shuigong zongjue* 華山十二睡功總訣 (Comprehensive Explanation of the

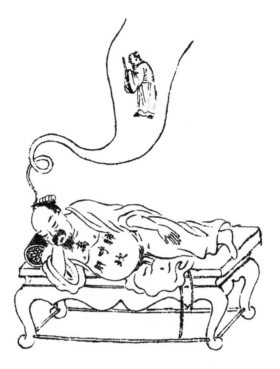

Fig. 21: Mao Xuanhan Conquers the Dragon and Tiger. Source: *Chifeng sui.*

Twelve Sleep Exercises of Mount Hua), it presents twelve pictures of sleeping immortals together with their names and inner alchemical doings. The text for "Mao Xuanhan Conquers the Dragon and Tiger" (fig. 21), for example, runs as follows:

> *The primordial* qi *of the heart is called the dragon.*
> *The original essence of the body is called the tiger.*
>
> Inner nature harnessed, dragon returns to water.
> Emotions forgotten, tiger hides in mountains.
> When the two join in harmony,
> Your name is entered in the ledgers of immortality. (Takehiro 1990, 83; Despeux
>   1988, 142)

This rather obscure passage refers to the inner alchemical practice of revolving the energies of the heart and kidneys, stylized as fire and water, dragon and tiger, through the body to create a subtler level of *qi* suitable for the creation of the immortal embryo. The text in most cases begins by giving two lines of seven characters in definition, such as "Extracting mercury from cinnabar is the task of the spirit soul; extracting gold from water is the act of the material soul" (Takehiro 1990, 84). These are followed by a poem of four lines in five characters that describe the activity in more or less obscure terms, in some cases reaching out to the great realm beyond. For instance,

> Destroy the vast vagueness of the senses
> To know what came before symbols and emperors.
> Only this is true realization and attainment.
> This is the Heaven of Grand Network. (Takehiro 1990, 94)

The goal of the exercise is to eliminate personal cravings and idiosyncratic tendencies in favor of a flowing oneness with the processes of the Dao, processes that in the beginning stages involve the body as multiple merging energies and that in more advanced practice lead to the realization of immortality and ecstatic flight.

Before detailing the practices, the text also has an explanatory introduction that echoes the attitude found in Chen Tuan's hagiography. It starkly contrasts ordinary and perfected sleep:

> In ordinary people, deluded thoughts never cease, passions and desires inflame each other, and their minds are defiled by myriad karmic causes. Their spirit does not have peace or tranquility for an instant. Vague and finicky, they dream during the day and they dream during the night. They dream while they are asleep and they dream while they are awake. When finally their lives come to an end, their incessant passions and desires haul them on without interruption. How could they not be rushed into another path [of reincarnation], not be thrown into another life form? Once deeply mired in the cycle of transmigration, they will never have a chance to break free. (Takehiro 1990, 78)

In contrast to this dire picture of people being thrown from life to life, incessantly pushed about by passions and desires, adepts who practice sleep are set on a path to transcendence, eternal freedom from worldly involvement, and a permanent resting place among the immortals. They focus all efforts on the refinement of the three interior energies: essence, *qi*, and spirit. They begin by subduing evil specters on the inside, using exorcistic and cleansing practices such as the Eight Brocades. Then they work on interior refinement through systematic guiding and revolving of heart- and kidney-*qi*, fire and water, lead and mercury, dragon and tiger.

Like all classical Daoyin exercises, the practice is undertaken at the time of rising yang or living *qi* (i.e., between midnight and noon). It begins with a seated meditation to calm the mind, followed by a ritual that calls the body gods to attention so they can both guard and assist the practitioner.

> Thereafter loosen your robe and belt and enter the position of sleeping on one side. Firmly close the mouth and keep the eyelids lowered halfway. Press the tip of the tongue against the upper palate, bend the knees, and pull in one foot with the toes bent. This helps yin and yang to return to the Prime and Sun and Moon to combine their radiance. (Takehiro 1990, 75; see also Despeux 1988, 225)

Next, adepts are to form their hands into the sacred gesture of the "unsheathed sword," the classic taiji quan gesture of extending the index and middle fingers while bending the others into the palm (Mitamura 2002, 236). One hand is placed under the head to support it atop the pillow, a rectangular object commonly made from porcelain or bamboo; the other hand is placed on the Gate of Life (Mingmen 命門) in the abdomen.

> The eyes should be focused on the nose, which is in direct line to the Gate of Life. Now, close the teeth firmly, open the Gate of Heaven [in the head] and close the Door of Earth [in the lower pelvis]. With the eyes of the spirit, begin to observe within, seeing how the trigrams Kan and Li [Heaven and Earth, heart and kidneys] merge and unify. This is called "the interchange of the interior sun and moon." (Takehiro 1990, 75; see also Despeux 1988, 225–226)

The practice continues with an increasing awareness of interior energies and ways of *qi*-circulation, creating an automatic flow of cosmic patterns and letting go of all thinking, planning, and other conscious activity. It leads, in the long run, to a complete dissolution of sensory attachments and reactions and allows the primordial patterns of *qi* to be reestablished in the adept's interior. As Chen Tuan says according to the hagiography,

> In eternal sleep the world is *qi*—
> The soul all gone, no movement in the body.
> Coming back to consciousness—where is there a self? (47.10a)

> Perfected beings do not dream: they sport with the immortals.
> Realized ones never sleep: they float up with the clouds. (47.10b)

The text does not specify how long the practice should take, but given the stories, it can be anywhere from half an hour to several weeks. After concluding the exercises, "get up and rub your heart area a few times. Then massage your eyes so that body and mind feel comfortable and glowing" (Takehiro 1990, 77). Even when not actively practicing, adepts are to maintain a sense of oneness with the cosmic patterns whatever they do and whatever position of the body they hold. Throughout waking and sleeping, the identity of the person as a separate, working, and clinging entity is lost, replaced by a sense of flowing along with the Dao. At the same time, the ability to be pure spirit also comes with various kinds of supernatural powers. Adepts can be in two places at once, move quickly from one place to another, know the past and the future, divine people's thoughts, procure wondrous substances, overcome all hazards of fire and water, and have powers over life and death. Having found the freedom of mystical union in "spirit pervasion" (*shentong* 神通), they have merged with the divine and are one with the Dao.

Taiji Quan and Shaolin Gongfu

In a separate development of healing exercises in the late Ming and early Qing periods, the exercises also served as the foundation of martial practices, among which the best known are taiji quan 太極拳 (great ultimate boxing) and Shaolin gongfu 少林功夫 (martial practice of Shaolin temple). The heavy reliance of these martial arts on Daoyin is obvious in their emphasis on deep abdominal breathing; their intense, focused movements; their rhythmic alternation of bends and stretches; and the fanciful names of their patterns, which are often associated with animals or supernatural figures. But the influence is not one way. On the contrary, various martial moves and sequences have spilled over into the healing exercises of today, so that modern qigong followers use them to harmonize *qi*-flow, enhance blood circulation, release stress, and improve balance.

Both taiji quan and Shaolin gongfu go back to the need for self-defense among Chinese communities, which caused all kinds of paramilitary organizations and training groups to spring up among villages and temples. The specific feats of religious fighters are recorded first in the early Tang dynasty when Shaolin Buddhists and Louguan 樓觀 Daoists helped the new rulers win the empire: Shaolin monks, residing at the foot of Mount Heng near Luoyang, supporting the conquest of the eastern capital (Shahar 2000, 21); and Louguan Daoists, in the foothills of the Zhongnan mountains near modern Xi'an, helping to secure the front around the western capital (see Kohn 1998, 44–45). Both places, moreover, are associated with deep meditation and self-cultivation and are linked with important legends in religious history. At Shaolin the Chan patriarch Bodhidharma, who had arrived in China from southern India in 520, meditated facing a wall for nine years, cutting off his eyelids so they would not close and stop him from practicing; instead they grew into tea plants, and tea has kept drowsy monks awake ever since. At Louguan, the old home of the border guard Yin Xi, the Daoist founder and ancient saint Laozi recorded the classic *Daode jing* on his way into emigration, thus creating a focal point for the Daoist religion (Kohn 1998, 257–260).

Aside from the early mention of Shaolin and Louguan in the context of the founding of the Tang dynasty, historical records have remained largely silent about military activity at both places. What little information there is, moreover, does not indicate a great fighting spirit so that, for example, Shaolin was easily sacked by Mongol troops in the thirteenth century. This changed in the sixteenth century, when the Ming dynasty was in decline and looting bandits and marauding armies made self-defense a priority. The Shaolin monks became famous for their fighting skills, especially with the staff. Unarmed combat (*quan* 拳, lit. "fist"), on the other hand, became dominant only in the seventeenth century, when the incoming Qing rulers prohibited all use of weapons among nonmilitary fighters. Both monastic and civil militias accordingly developed new techniques, combining defensive moves with the age-old practices of controlled breathing and healing exercises (Shahar 2001, 398). Among monastics, this occurred most prominently at the Buddhist Shaolin temple and the Daoist Mount Wudang. Within civil militias, it was most prominent in the southern part of the country, where it led to the development of taiji quan and other strengthening routines. Both kinds of martial practices, moreover, came to influence the modern tradition of healing exercises, and their patterns still form an active part of qigong.

Shaolin practice involves various kinds of systematic sequences, often in holy numbers such as twelve or eighteen, that are executed in different positions of the body. A lying-down sequence, for example, involves stretching the arms and legs away from each other, rotating the arms up and down, lifting both arms to the ceiling, raising one leg up, then both legs, pulling the knees into the chest, moving over to one side, and again stretching arms and legs in different directions (Shi and Xu 2003, 36–44). Similarly, seated practice involves stretching, rotating, and loosening up the arms, while standing routines include more actively martial positions and movements (Shi and Xu 2003) (fig. 22). A distinction is made between inner practice (*neigong* 內功), harmonizing practice (*taihe* 太和), soft training (*rougong* 柔功), and hard practice (*yinggong* 硬功), the latter often involving kicks and punches as well as more acrobatic feats (Shi and Xu 2003, 139–166).

A popular form of Shaolin practice, much used among qigong practitioners today,[12] is a standing version of the Eight Brocades, associated both with overall

---

12. The practice is also used frequently as a preparation for *qi*-healing, notably in contemporary jujitsu. See Teeguarden 1975.

Fig. 22: A sequence of Shaolin qigong. Source: Shi and Xu 2003.

bodily stamina and specific areas of healing. The practice begins with standing quietly, allowing the *qi* to circulate through the body, then performing twelve repetitions each of eight different movements:

1. Uphold Heaven with Two Hands: Stand with feet parallel, bring the hands to the chest, then stretch them overhead with palms up. Good for digestive organs.

2. Open the Bow: Squat in horse stance with feet wider apart; place the hands at chest level, then turn to the right and left as you open the arms like shooting a bow, punching with the front fist. Good for lungs and shoulders.

3. Raise the Hands Separately: Stand with feet hip-width apart and parallel, hold both hands at stomach with palms up, then raise the right while lowering the left and vice versa. Good for spleen and stomach.

4. Looking Backward: Lift the arms to the chest, then stretch them out and back while lifting the chest and head into a back bend. Good for the entire body.

5. Punch with Angry Eyes: Squat with legs wide, make fists, punch forward to the right and left as the hip turns. Good for spirit, vitality, and vision.

6. Hold the Toes and Stretch the Back: Stand with feet parallel, place the hands over

the abdomen with palms down, lift them to chest level and raise them up above the head with palms up, then bend into a forward bend. Good for kidneys and waist.

7. Swing Torso and Head: Squat with legs wide, move ninety degrees to one side, and bring the arms out straight, then move to the other side. Good for heart, lungs, and blood circulation.

8. Press the Knees: Stand with feet parallel and open the arms wide to the sides, then place the hands on the knees and sink down into a squat. Good for the entire body. (See Shi, Shi, and Shi 1999; Yang 1988, 52–65; Shi and Xu 2003, 101–107)

Practitioners conclude by once again standing in silence and breathing deeply, their mind focused and calm. The entire set is executed while standing and involves some gentle and some rather vigorous moves. Typically for the martial arts, it uses the so-called horse stance, a standing squat with legs spread wide, for some of its exercises; it also involves punches in various directions and encourages practitioners to use their eyes to glare at a potential enemy. Beyond its martial application, the series is helpful in strengthening the body and healing specific areas, and as such is very popular in qigong circles today.

While the Buddhists were developing their practices at Shaolin, Daoists established a similar center of martial arts on Mount Wudang in Hunan. This mountain had become a major Daoist sanctuary in the early Ming dynasty, when it was associated with protecting the imperial house and served as the main worship place of the Dark Warrior (Xuanwu 玄武). Originally a constellation in the northern sky, the Dark Warrior appears first in the Han dynasty as the mythical animal of the north. He is most commonly symbolized by an intertwined turtle and snake, but also appears as a mighty warrior with armor and multiple weapons. His rise to imperial protector began in the Song dynasty, when he was seen as the latent force behind the moving energy of the universe and was associated closely with newly imported, potent protector deities of tantric Buddhist background. A national cult developed, and the Dark Warrior appeared in various manifestations at court and in religious centers. He was honored in several inscriptions and records, his hagiography growing with ever longer accounts of his miraculous lives and military exploits (Kohn 1998, 129–134).

Shortly after the establishment of their dynasty, the Ming rulers set up regular sacrifices for him and between 1405 and 1418 greatly expanded his center on Mount Wudang. Bolstered by imperial patronage, the god was adopted by both leading Daoist schools, Complete Perfection and Celestial Masters, and he grew into a popular figure, as described in the novel *Beiyou ji* (Journey to the North).[13]

13. On the symbolism of the emblems of the Dark Warrior and their starry correlates, see Staal 1984, Major 1986. The history of the Dark Warrior under the Ming is outlined in White 1940, 169; Lagerwey 1992, 299. On his role in popular literature, see Liu 1962, 152. The *Beiyou ji* was written by Yu

Recounting his adventures during several reincarnations, the text shows his progress from human crown prince to divine emperor. It tells how, powerful and intelligent from birth, he grew into a demon queller of the first order. Traveling throughout the world, he obtained a magical sword that contained the essence of the cosmos, perfected himself through personal cultivation, and performed numerous miracles. The god's life story, moreover, became the model for Daoist martial artists, who too expanded their physical skills for the sake of transcendence and immortality as well as to defend their institutions.

While there are no detailed records of what exactly Wudang Daoists practiced, it is clear that the martial image of the ideal Daoist became widely popular at the time. Besides the Dark Warrior's hagiography, it is most obvious in the late-Ming novel *Fengshen yanyi* (Creation of the Gods; trl. Gu 1992). The book describes in mythological fashion the fight of the righteous Zhou against the tyrannical Shang dynasty in the second millennium B.C.E. In each phase, developments on earth are paralleled by activities in the heavens, and the Daoist god Lord Lao appears repeatedly to support the fight of the righteous group against the opposition. This latter group lays various traps for the advancing Zhou army, and time and again Lord Lao is asked to give advice and support, provide weapons and help, mastermind battle plans, or seek truce and adjudication.

For example, called upon to help spring a particularly nasty trap, he joins the battle, becoming manifest as "a saint on a blue fairy ox" and taking an active hand in the fighting (Gu 1992, 1:258). Supported by another powerful Daoist god, the Heavenly Primogenitor, he first tries to parley with the enemy; then, still on his faithful ox, he enters the trap to engage his divine opponent in one-on-one combat. Auspicious lights flash forth, white mists rise up, magical charts turn into bridges, walking sticks become wondrous weapons, and swords glitter with numinous brilliance. Then, in the middle of the battle, "Laozi suddenly pulled in his rein and jumped out of the combat circle. He pushed his fishtail coronet to one side, and three columns of gas released from his head transformed into three immortals, called the Clarities" (Gu 1992, 2:260). The immortals join Lord Lao to attack the enemy from all sides and emerge victorious.

Lord Lao, and with him the ideal Daoist hero of the time, emerges from meditative recluse as a sword-swinging master of magic, a martial hero who masterminds a vigorous campaign to stamp out evil and impediments to rightful cultural progress. He is a fighter and a trickster, a conjurer and a wizard who knows right

---

Xiangdou 余象鬥 in the seventeenth century. The novel was first studied in Grootaers 1952; a complete translation and analysis is found in Seaman 1987. For a discussion of the god's progress in the novel in relation to Mount Wudang's peaks and sanctuaries, see Lagerwey 1992, 315–321.

Fig. 23: The Taiji diagram.

and wrong and never hesitates to fight actively for his goals. He throws talismans and bolts of lightning, brings forth gases and obscuring mists, and performs marvelous feats as a heavenly combatant on the side of the good and the just.

This culture of martial heroes, fighting monks, and Daoist demon quellers is at the root of various self-defense practices that inherited traditional healing exercises and still play an important role in qigong today. The best known among them is taiji quan. It began when, after the end of the Qing conquest in 1644, the military officer Chen Wangting 陳王廷 retired to his hometown and began to teach martial exercises consisting of five routines and a sequence of 108 moves. Transmitted through the family, his methods were organized into a slightly less martial system by his descendant Chen Zhangxing 陳長興 (1771–1853), leading to what is today known as the Chen style, a series of rather simple moves in the four directions. The Yang style, on the other hand, goes back to Yang Luchan 楊露禪 (1799–1872), who originally studied Shaolin boxing, then visited the Chen family and became a student of Chen Zhangxing. His practice is softer and rounder, with wide arm movements, circular patterns, and intricate flexing in the wrists and arms. Spread by his sons and developed further into various sublineages, it is the most popular form of taiji quan today.[14]

In the original creation of this self-defense form, Master Chen used healing exercises in combination with military training. He also followed the dominant thought of the time, which combined Daoist and Neo-Confucian thinking, and picked the popular Taiji diagram to symbolize his practice (fig. 23). This diagram, showing yin and yang in interlocking curves, has roots that go back to Chen Tuan, inner alchemy, and Neo-Confucianism and shows the state of the universe at the time of creation. First published in 1613, it greatly influenced the intellectual world at the time (Louis 2003, 191).

Unlike traditional healing exercises and modern qigong, taiji quan is exe-

---

14. For a survey of the history and features of taiji quan, see Kohn 2005, 195–197; Bidlack 2006, 86–89. On the early history and the written tradition, see Davis 2004; Wile 1983, 1985, 1996.

cuted exclusively from a standing position and involves continuous movements that are choreographed into lengthy and complex sequences. Rather than using the mind to systematically guide *qi,* practitioners keep it open and relaxed, allowing the *qi* to flow smoothly in all directions and the spirit to be receptive to all stimuli. The practice thus combines an open meditative awareness with soft, slow, and focused body movements, preparing adepts for attack and self-defense.

Although taiji quan was not originally designed as a healing technique, it has many beneficial effects. Regular practice increases the circulation, harmonizes the respiration, strengthens the muscles, enhances muscle control, straightens the spine, opens the chest, and improves balance. It can alleviate chronic conditions and helps with weight loss. Its calm and graceful moves reduce stress and nervous dispositions while increasing harmony, providing a sense of wholeness and creating a feeling of inner quiet and equanimity. Like other marital arts it also assists character building, insisting on a strong moral base, a nonviolent outlook, deep respect for others, unfailing obedience to the master, consistent discipline, honorable conduct, inner stillness, single-minded dedication, humility, forbearance, a letting go of ego, and the unfolding of inner calmness and stability (Nelson 1989, 79–80). From this perspective, it also serves as a good foundation for spiritual attainments (Bidlack 2006, 193).

Another special quality of taiji quan, and one way in which it clearly differs from traditional healing exercises, is that, in addition to smooth *qi*-flow and muscular health, it emphasizes the springiness of the tendons, sinews, and ligaments for enhanced internal suppleness. Instead of using muscular strength, practitioners rely on the suppleness and internal tenacity of their tendons and build their power in this manner. The very same tendency is also true for another martial practice that appeared in the seventeenth century (probably created by another former serviceman), was later associated with the patriarch Bodhidharma, and plays a popular part in qigong today: the twelve exercises of the *Yijin jing* 易勁經 (Sinews Transformation Classic).

Published in various editions (and with increasingly more ancient prefaces) since the seventeenth century (Berk 1986, 148–151), the text's Twelve Tendon Exercises enhance internal muscular functioning rather than strength or vigor. Each is called by a mythological or illustrative name and undertaken from a standing position in which practitioners hold certain positions while tensing the muscles to strengthen the tendons. Arms, legs, and torso are engaged, and the entire body is made suppler and more open. The mind is kept calm and relaxed, the breath is deep and slow. Positions should be held for up to nine breaths.

1. Wei Tuo Presents a Club—1. Stand upright, place the palms together in front of the heart, push them together with vigor while keeping the legs tense and grabbing the floor with toes and heels.

2. Wei Tuo Presents a Club—2. Keeping the legs and toes engaged, stretch the arms out to the sides, tensing the muscles. Keep your mind calm and your breath subtle.

3. Wei Tuo Presents a Club—3. Lifting the arms to support heaven with palms facing up, look up. Still keep the legs engaged, the jaw tight, the mind calm.

4. Plucking the Stars to Move the Dipper. Place one hand on the lower back while raising the other above the head, palm facing up and looking up at the extended hand. Press hard in both directions. Change sides.

5. Pulling Nine Bulls' Tails. Take a big step forward with one leg while placing the other in lunge position. With one arm reach forward at shoulder level, with the other reach back in a slight twist, keeping both wrists bent. Push hard. Change sides.

6. Extending Claws, Spreading Wings. With feet parallel and eyes glaring, extend the hands out at shoulder level, then pull them back in. Repeat seven times in and out.

7. Nine Ghosts Pull Swords. Encircle the head with one hand while placing the other hand on the back. Rotate the torso and stretch. Change sides.

8. Three Plates Drop to the Ground. Stand in horse stance, eyes wide open. Push the hands down vigorously and hold; then turn the palms up and slowly raise the arms as if lifting a thousand-pound weight.

9. Green Dragon Extends Claws. Stand up straight. Make a fist with one hand and place it around the back and on the hip. With the other hand swing across the torso, stretching and leaning into it. Change sides.

10. Crouching Tiger Catches Prey. On hands and knees, lift the head, then bend one leg forward and in while stretching the other leg straight back. Hold and stretch. Change sides.

11. Bending in a Bow. Interlace the fingers behind the head, then bend from the waist to bring the head close to the knees. Close the eyes, hold, and stretch.

12. Wagging the Tail. Interlace the fingers in front, then bend from the waist and place the palms on the ground. Lift the head, open the eyes wide and gaze ahead, while stomping the feet. Come back to standing. Repeat twenty-one times.

Conclude by opening the arms wide to the sides seven times, then sit cross-legged and regulate the breath. (Berk 1986, 165–177; Liu 2004, 122–128)[15]

---

15. The practice as described in the historical sources and summarized by modern scholars is quite different from its contemporary qigong version. In preparation for writing this chapter, I participated in a workshop on the *Yijin jing* by Frank Yurasek at the annual meeting of the National Qigong Association in Boulder, Colorado, in 2005. He learned the practice from medical doctors while working as an intern at a traditional Chinese hospital in Guangzhou. It is the same as the sequence described here only for the first five items, then has some that are similar in practice but different in name and a few that are entirely different. For example, number six of his sequence is called Dragon Places Palm. It involves standing in a wide stance with one hand curled into a fist and held at the

Except for the first three, which mention the Buddhist protector deity Wei Tuo 韋馱, chief of the twenty-four heavenly generals and usually depicted as a fierce warrior in full armor,[16] few of the practices' names refer to traditional Chinese life and myth. The exercises engage the spine, rotate the torso, stretch arms and legs, and in general provide an opening and lengthening of the muscles. They have a distinct martial component in the glaring eyes, integrate animal forms in their use of dragon and tiger, and use traditional healing exercises in their overhead stretches, lunges, and forward bends. Their use as a sequence and the emphasis on the tendons and sinews are new, as is the connection to Bodhidharma and the Buddhist tradition.

Overall, the Song, Yuan, and Ming dynasties saw a great expansion and unfolding of healing exercises in the Chinese tradition. They spread more widely through more extended literacy, and among commoners and women; they were integrated into the practice of inner alchemy and used for meditative purposes; and they underwent a radical transformation into martial practices because of the need for self-defense of ordinary people and monastic institutions alike. The vision of what an enlightened master should be like changed as well, bringing folklore and religious doctrine together in the images of the fighting monk, ecstatic Daoist, and female master, all equipped with superior physical strength and impressive magical powers. In many ways, the late Ming and early Qing paved the way for the modern integration of the practices under the heading of qigong and the flourishing of the martial arts in popular movies as well as in Buddhist and Daoist centers.

---

kidneys, the other placed on or toward the floor. One should then look up with a concave spine. It seems to be a mixture of Dragon Extends Claws and Wagging the Tail.

16. There is also a modern practice called *weituo qigong*, which is an adaptation of martial practices that works in eight-minute drills and uses movements named after powerful animals, such as the eagle, crane, dragon, and tiger. See Wei-Tuo Foundation Web site; www.weituoqigong.org.

Chapter Six

Daoyin Today

The most obvious place to look for traditional Chinese healing exercises today is modern Chinese qigong 氣功, a Communist adaptation of ancient practices for public health that developed into a mass movement, supported the quest for supernatural powers, and eventually grew into religious cults—because of which it has been suppressed since 1999. Usually rendered Qi-Exercises but literally meaning the "effort" or "merit" of *qi*, the system includes both martial and restful practices, ranging from boxing through gentle exercise, breathing, and mental guiding of *qi* (as in traditional Daoyin) to visualizations, meditative absorptions, devotional activities, and trance states. Dominantly focused on health improvement in China in the 1970s, it has, since the 1980s, become increasingly well known in the West and is one major venue for the continuation of Daoyin.

Beyond the qigong movement, healing exercises in China have been medicalized and—under the more modern-sounding name Movement Therapies—found a firm place in the official system of traditional Chinese medicine (TCM). They are essential to modern Chinese methods of life cultivation, which combine Western scientific anatomy and physiology with ancient ways of moving the body. Like medieval texts that provide overall guidance to healthy living, modern books on health maintenance create systematic outlines of techniques and emphasize the practice of moderation, emotional balance, sexual hygiene, and exercise. Like their forerunners, they detail all aspects of daily life for the sake of health and harmony and actively adopt and integrate traditional methods. Unlike them, they integrate Western-style physical therapy, use medical technology to measure success, and create one-fits-all systems of health improvement that sweep the country and are even introduced into elementary schools. One side branch of this development appears in several new forms that have the word Daoyin as part of their name and combine parts of the practice with other techniques, such as massage and taiji quan.

In addition to their role in Chinese health practice, healing exercises also have made increasing inroads into the Chinese religious scene as officially recognized by the Party. Besides the well-known martial arts centers of Shaoling and Wudang, Buddhist and Daoist temples throughout China now hold public classes in basic exercises and taiji quan, advise people on self-massages, and offer treatments by trained specialists—altogether turning into modern spalike establishments with hot tubs, computer terminals, and fancy restaurants. Monks and nuns practice healing exercises as part of their daily routine, deities descend to reveal new and more advanced methods, temples publish pamphlets and booklets that praise the importance of the body for spiritual cultivation, and monasteries turn into health centers with all the gadgets and accoutrements of the modern age.

In the West, Daoyin is promoted chiefly—and under its traditional name—by two Daoist masters: Ni Hua-ching in Los Angeles (originally from Taiwan) and Mantak Chia (from Thailand). Both inherit the tradition of inner alchemy and clearly have no connection to the qigong movement. Training people in their world-wide centers according to the ancient system of healing, long life, and immortality, they present body practices that reflect ancient Daoyin in that they are executed in standing, seated, and reclining postures, work with deep breathing, and focus on the conscious guiding of *qi*. Still, despite the masters' claim that their techniques go back tens of thousands of years and are documented in Daoist scriptures, their methods are mostly new and tend to integrate large sections of yoga.

Beyond these two major masters, Daoist associations in the West also promote Daoyin, and certain qigong and Chinese medical associations take recourse in the practices. Already moving the methods out of the strictly Chinese environment, followers of certain new forms of yoga connect asanas with acupuncture points and channels. As energy medicine and energy psychology gain increased acceptance, it is likely that Chinese healing exercises as a traditional form of energy work will spread more widely and influence the way Westerners work with their health.

Qigong

While the term *qigong* in common Western parlance refers to a set of exercises that combine gentle body movements with deep breathing and a mental guiding of *qi*, used predominantly for healing and undertaken by groups of people in parks, in China qigong is very much a social phenomenon, consciously created by the Chinese Communist Party (CCP), that evolved through a series of transformations over the past fifty years.[1]

It all began in 1947 when Party cadre Liu Guizhen 劉貴珍 (1920–1983), suffering from a virulent gastric ulcer, was sent home to recover or die. He went home but refused to die—he was only twenty-seven years old at the time! Instead, he took les-

---

1. On the history of qigong in contemporary China, see Miura 1989, Heise 1999, Hsu 1999, Scheid 2002, Chen 2003, Morris 2004, Kohn 2005, Chau 2005, Palmer 2007. For Western presentations of qigong, see Eisenberg 1985; Cohen 1997; MacRitchie 1997; Jahnke 1997, 2002. On its history in America, see Komjathy 2006.

sons in gentle exercises and breathing from the popular Daoist Liu Duzhou 劉渡舟. After 102 days of faithfully undertaking these practices, he was completely cured.

He returned to his job and described his healing success to Party secretary Guo Xianrui 郭獻瑞, who undertook the methods himself with great success and suggested that these simple exercises might just solve the continuous problem of health care for the masses—at a time when there was one biomedical doctor for 26,000 people in China. The Party adopted the idea and, in a lengthy series of committee meetings, discussed what best to call the practice: adopted from traditional patterns but to be thoroughly cleansed from all ancient cosmology and "superstitions," it needed an appropriate modern name. After discarding the terms "spiritual therapy," "psychological therapy," and "incantation therapy," they settled on "breath exercise therapy" or *qigong liaofa* 氣功療法 (Palmer 2007, 31–32).

In the wake of this politically motivated beginning, qigong has remained very much an artificially constructed phenomenon that has served various social needs in the course of the People's Republic. These needs, and with them the nature and quality as well as the political standing of qigong, have changed essentially with every decade.

Periodic Changes

In the 1950s (until 1964) qigong served as the main vehicle of health maintenance for the cadres of the CCP and was predominantly practiced in a medical setting, both in specialized qigong clinics, such as the sanatoria in Tangshan and Beidaihe, and in general hospitals (Palmer 2007, 34). The practice made few inroads into the larger population, and any research and publications served to make it less traditional and more scientific—removing it from its roots and transforming it into the mind-body system of the future. It also carried a strong nationalist agenda, the hope being that these practices, with their amazing health effects and accompanying enhanced mental powers, would revolutionize medicine and bring forth healthier and more evolved human beings in China—thus setting the stage for superpower status in the twenty-first century.

In the 1960s, notably after the beginning of the Cultural Revolution in 1966, qigong was banished or at least suppressed because it still carried a heavy burden of traditional worldview and culture. Qigong clinics and hospital wards were closed, and practitioners went underground, continuing to perform their exercises and transmitting them in silence. The 1970s saw the emergence of large-scale qigong self-healing by ordinary people—the kind of practice we associate most closely with the term. This new mode was inspired by Guo Lin 郭林, a Beijing artist who had cured herself of uterine cancer in the 1960s. Completely cancer-free in 1969, she started teaching her synthesis of methods (including the Five Animals' Frolic and new modes of breathing) to cancer patients in public parks (Miura 1989, 335). She persisted in the face of police harassment and occasional imprisonment, frequently changing parks while increasing her following. By 1975, her methods had become well known and began to receive the support of Party cadres (Palmer 2007, 48). Others imitated her style, and after the end of the Cultural Revolution and Mao's death in 1976, numerous practitioners came out of the woodwork or, as the Chinese say, "emerged from the mountains" (*chushan* 出山).

About 50 percent of these masters came from a martial background, some 30 percent were trained in the medical field, about 10 percent each were Daoist or Buddhist, and the remainder came to the practice from Confucianism or the study of the *Yijing*. Most were middle-aged, born in the 1930s and 1940s, and few had a valid lineage to past teachings. In fact, 75 percent admit to not having a lineage at all, but picking ideas from various places and creating their own synthesis; of the remaining 25 percent, at least half probably made up their lineages so that, all told, the vast majority of qigong healing practices, notwithstanding the persistent claim of a five-thousand-year history, are newly created (Palmer 2007, 92–95).

As qigong masters engaged in teaching, publications, and healing sessions, the people enthusiastically embraced the practices, and followers came to number in the millions. They experienced qigong as a welcome relief after the forced communal activities and intense persecutions of the Cultural Revolution. Instead of being pushed about and having to engage in various campaigns, people could now voluntarily congregate and work on their bodies in a sphere that remained largely free from Party supervision.

Divine Dimensions
This changed in the 1980s with the establishment of the China Qigong Science Research Society, an academic body that registered the various groups, led conferences on qigong and science, and issued a number of publications in the field (Palmer 2007, 75–76). Together with the State Sports Commission and the State Education Commission, it hoped to control a rapidly expanding scene of practices whose main focus, from the establishment and maintenance of health, had shifted to the acquisition of "Extraordinary Powers," things like clairvoyance, telepathy, psychokinesis, distance healing, and the ability to read with the ears rather than the eyes (Palmer 2007, 106). Promoting their unusual abilities, masters attracted numerous followers and, instead of teaching them to patiently practice breathing and exercise methods, transmitted supernatural powers to them by direct installation.

Some masters became very famous, such as Yan Xin, who established an expansive qigong empire and, in allegedly controlled experiments, was able to influence a building's electrical system and move objects several kilometers away (Palmer 2007,

141). Giving power-inducing lectures to thousands at a time, he became somewhat of a cult figure, with people undertaking pilgrimages to his home village and raising funds for its renovation (Palmer 2007, 145). Both the veneration of qigong masters and the quest for personal powers reflected the need of the Chinese to cope with a massively changing social structure, characterized by the loss of lifelong employment and national health care in an atmosphere of budding capitalism.

The craze for Extraordinary Powers slowed down in the 1990s, when several masters were arrested for fraud and many feats were unveiled as quackery (Palmer 2007, 160). When the state issued more stringent regulations, demanding that qigong leaders be certified doctors or therapists, millions of followers found themselves at a loss. This qigong vacuum was duly filled by new groups that made ethics a fundamental part of the practice. Developing into large-scale organizations, these groups also restored traditional religious patterns, teaching devotion to deities, chanting of sacred scriptures, taking of precepts, and obedience to group leaders (Kohn 2005, 187). The gentle exercises and breathing practices originally at the core of qigong declined further in importance. From having been second-class in relation to the installation of Extraordinary Powers, they were relegated to a minor position in the service of religious cultivation that would lead not only to health but, more important, to transcendent salvation.

Typical groups at the time were Zangmigong 藏密功 (Tantric Qigong), for all intents and purposes a new religion based on Tibetan Buddhism (Palmer 2007, 199); Zhonggong 中功 (Central Qigong), an extensive organization that led practitioners to ultimate liberation through eight levels of increasingly religious practices (Palmer 2007, 208–209); and Falungong 法輪功 (Dharma Wheel Practice), a messianic cult centered on the founder Li Hongzhi 李洪志, who was set to rid the world of demons, both earthly and extraterrestrial, and to prepare a generation of purified and highly empowered followers for the new world to come. To this end, he created a system of strict control, forbidding his followers to read anything except his books (especially *Zhuan Falun* 傳法輪), find healing other than through Falungong practice, enter into mixed marriages, support the autonomy of women, and participate in various other features of modern life (Palmer 2007, 234–236).[2]

While most of the quasi-religious movements in the 1990s made sure to

2. For studies on Falungong or Falun dafa, see Madsen 2000; Schechter 2000; Penny 2002, 2003; Chang 2004; Ownby 2007. As David Palmer correctly points out, its goals, visions, and methods closely resemble other millenarian movements and militant cults in Chinese history, from the early Celestial Masters to the White Lotus Society of the Ming and the Great Peace Movement in the nineteenth century (2007, 289). Since these sects have tended to rise in rebellion, creating major upheaval in the country, the government had every reason to react with radical suppression. Since its expulsion from the Chinese mainland, moreover, Falungong has mutated into a political movement that, as can be clearly seen in its publication *Epoch Times*, openly works for the demise of the

comply with state regulations and cultivated friends in high places, Falungong went on a collision course with the Party. After being expelled from the official qigong association for noncompliance with its rules, it was outlawed in 1996 and only continued to exist because it had many Party cadres among its members. In the following years, members continued to engage in various large-scale demonstrations, usually to coerce various media to rescind or apologize for negative publicity. In April of 1999 it went one step too far by engaging in nationwide protests against bad publicity, a campaign probably undertaken with the knowledge and sanction of the leader. Since then Falungong has been severely persecuted, its leader living in the United States and its overseas followers actively and openly pursuing the downfall of the Chinese Communist government.

Qigong Today

The fallout from all this is that qigong in China in the first decade of the twenty-first century has come to a complete stop. Subjected to strict controls, the various organizations are not able continue their work, and only four forms are still officially accepted, all part of traditional Daoyin: the Five Animals' Frolic, the Six Healing Sounds, the Sinews Transformation Classic, and the Standing Eight Brocades (Palmer 2007, 280). In contrast to this, taiji quan has been systematically raised as a sport, structured according to accomplishment levels along the lines of judo and karate, and is getting ready for Olympic participation. The need for religious expression, moral grounding, and personal leadership expressed in the qigong cults of the 1990s has given way to a more realistic way of life among the people. They still exercise in parks, but aside from many forms of taiji quan, they play badminton or other ball games and work out with Western-style aerobics and ballroom dancing. Also, yoga is making great headway in China, where it is seen entirely as a physical workout to the exclusion of all spirituality or religious contexts.[3]

Qigong now mainly survives in the West. Free from Communist ideology and the social pressures of an authoritarian society, it retains the spirit it had in China in the 1970s and serves the traditional goals of Daoyin: healing, long life, and spiritual attainments. Unfortunately, Western practitioners tend to overlook the social role and aberrations of qigong in China. As noted by Louis Komjathy, they tend to buy

---

Communist leadership. The social alternative it proposes, however, is probably worse, matching the Taliban and other current fundamentalists in severity and restrictions.

3. For the new yoga craze in China, see Yogi-Yoga Center, "Yoga in China," Figures: Yin Yan, founder and general manager; www.yogiyogacenter.com. The movement began in 2003, when Yin Yan, a young woman journalist who had studied in France and worked as editor at *Elle China*, traveled to Rishikesh in northern India and encountered yoga. Benefiting from the practice, she invited several Indian masters to China and had them teach classes. The organization now has an extensive and rather gorgeous headquarters in Beijing and affiliated studios in all major Chinese cities.

into qigong myths, accepting claims of great age and venerating Chinese masters in a kind of reverse Orientalism (2006, 211). Without completely discarding the achievements and techniques of modern masters, they are well advised to go back to the historical roots of the practice and experiment with techniques on their own. Also, it might in the long run serve them better to replace the name qigong with something along the lines of "energy exercises," more expressly and consciously connecting to the unfolding Western fields of energy medicine and energy psychology.

Nourishing Life in Modern China

Similarly bringing Daoyin into contemporary mainstream, Chinese doctors have adopted the practices under the name Movement Therapies as part of preventive medicine nourishing life. Thus Wang Xudong, the editor of the bilingual *Life Cultivation and Rehabilitation in Traditional Chinese Medicine*, begins his work with two chapters on life cultivation, first presenting the theoretical concepts of essence, *qi,* and spirit, then outlining historical highlights of the practice (2003, 4–14). He describes its key efforts as learning to "conform to nature, match the seasons, change with geography, and adapt to society" and calls the Chinese vision a holistic model (22).

After this he turns to the actual practices, which he divides into five sections: (1) regulating emotions; (2) environment, daily life, and clothing; (3) dietary practices; (4) sexual life; and (5) movement therapies.

The first involves examining oneself for imbalances in the emotions, such as anger or depression. Wang recommends that one use the different emotions to hold each other in check and to work with colors to balance them (2003, 22–28). The second works with feng shui and encourages people to seek housing in fresh air and avoid pollution; they should also balance their time of work and rest. Next, it outlines Western sleep studies, reporting how much is needed, what types there are, and what brain activities occur, and recommends lying on one's right side as the optimal sleep posture. Pillows should be narrow and long, somewhat hard and slightly elastic; they can be filled with medicinal herbs to help with various conditions, such as tea leaves for the prevention and treatment of high blood pressure, neurasthenia, and dizziness (35–36). Clothing is best made from natural fibers and should leave one neither too warm nor too cold. Ideally, one should have two bowel movements every day to keep the *qi* moving, and one's urine should be clear and smooth (41–42). Following this, the book has twenty pages on dietary methods, including a discussion of warming and cooling foods as well as various herbal remedies. Like earlier texts, it recommends that one should eat only to 70 or 80 percent capacity and provides specific prescriptions for certain conditions (43–60). A similar attitude is also present in the next section, on sexual activity, which should be undertaken in moderation and without extreme emotions or physical stress (61–63). After all these regulations for daily living, the final section focuses on healing exercises. The section begins with general instructions on mental concentration for the purpose of balancing *qi* and creating a unity of body and spirit. In accordance with current Party directives, it then describes the classic Five Animals' Frolic, Eight Brocades, and Sinews Transformation practice, as well as the basics of taiji quan. It concludes the discussion of life cultivation with a presentation of art and music, singing and dancing, chess playing and painting as useful practices for maintaining a harmonious *qi* and encourages people to take regular hot and cold baths to keep their biomagnetic energy moving (63–78).

In many ways this presentation echoes the *Yangsheng yaoji* of the early middle ages and the *Yinshu* of the Han manuscripts. It sees life cultivation as an all-encompassing effort that includes living quarters, daily routine, diet, breathing, movement, and sexual relations. Doing just one thing is not sufficient. To extend life and preserve health into old age one has to arrange oneself completely in alignment with, and to the best benefit of, the *qi*.

A similar outline is also found in *The Mystery of Longevity* by Liu Zhengcai, who is less a medical doctor than a modern student of longevity. He describes seasonally appropriate ways of dressing, moving, and eating, emphasizing the alternation of yin and yang and advising people to avoid too much cooling in summer and remaining too warm in winter. Focused breathing and meditation are recommended to balance the natural patterns of *qi*. "Just rest calmly without any perplexing thoughts, and one will arrive at refreshing mountains" (Liu 1990, 7).

Health Preservation

The same also holds true for *China's Traditional Way of Health Preservation* by Zeng Qingnan and Liu Daoqing (2002), which in many ways replicates the recommendations made in *Life Cultivation*. In addition, however, the book distinguishes "Traditional Health Protection Exercises" (ch. 11), where it describes taiji quan, the Five Animals' Frolic, the Eight Brocades, and the Sinews Transformation Classic, from "Qigong Exercises" (ch. 12). Qigong, according to this, is more mind-focused and centered on the inner guiding of *qi* as activated during various activities such as sitting and walking; it also includes a series of eye exercises, breathing practices, and practices to promote internal energy circulation. In this section, the book presents several new practices based on exercises that formed an important part of traditional Daoyin: a version of the Seated Eight Brocades in twelve steps (348–349), the Six Breaths (349–360), and a breathing practice said to be based on the *Daoyin tu* chart from Mawangdui. The latter involves seven steps and should take about half an hour:

Be in Silent Pose: Stand, sit, or lie down; place the tongue against the upper palate and the hands on the elixir field, breathe nine times with complete focus, then circulate the *qi* along the channels in front and back of the torso.

Complete the *Qi* Cycle: Expand the cycle of *qi* to run through the entire body, moving back to front for men, and front to back for women.

Swing the Heavenly Column: Focus the mind on the elixir field, turn the head right and left, then bring hands and body into the movement, gradually raising the palms to the top of the head.

Imagine a Snow Fountain: Visualize a fountain of drops washing down from the top of the head to the soles of the feet; repeat three times.

Repeat a Silent Saying: Imagine a spring morning, sunshine, breeze, flowers, birds, restful time, then say to yourself: "All worries disappear in deep silence, my body is relaxed and soft and sways with the wind. I am happy and pleased as if flying through the sky."

Relax and Let Go: Do not try to control the body, but let the *qi* go wherever it moves, let the body move if it does or enjoy its quiet.

Conclude the Practice: Focus on the Bubbling Well point at the soles of the feet and say to yourself: "I wish to conclude the practice. I wish to stop." Open your eyes, raise your hands in spirals along your body to massage its parts, rubbing the top of the head nine times; then concentrate on the middle fingers and mentally let the *qi* rise and fall nine times. Rub the face and head; then get up and walk 30 to 50 steps. (Zeng and Liu 2002, 360–364)

Although it is impossible to say how the authors came to derive this complex sequence from the mere pictures of the *Daoyin tu,* the practice works on opening the *qi*-channels in the body while encouraging the mind to be relaxed and envisioning joyful things. It uses few body movements but integrates breathing and conscious guiding of *qi* into release of stress and relaxation.

Another practice listed in the chapter "Qigong Exercises" is geared to improve the eyesight, in many ways continuing the concerns of Highest Clarity practitioners of old. It involves the mental guiding of *qi* through the liver meridian and the systematic movement of the pupils with closed eyes. It also includes the systematic massage of various points around the eyes with the aim of stimulating blood and *qi*-flow in this area (Zeng and Liu 2002, 323–328), echoing the daily eye exercises prescribed for elementary- and middle-school children:

1.   Massaging the Inner Eyebrows (Heavenly Accord Point): Place the tip of the thumbs into the fleshy part in the upper corner of the eyes, right underneath the eyebrows, then rub both sides equally, gently pressing upward and in toward the

nasal bone. The other four fingers of the two hands rest lightly on the forehead. Make calm, circular movements with all fingers and lightly massage the area, not pressing too hard. One massage circle is one round. Repeat eight times eight rounds for a total of sixty-four turnings, going in both directions.

2. Squeezing the Inner Corners of the Eyes (Pupil Point): With the thumb and index finger of either the right or the left hand gently squeeze the right and left inner corners of the eyes on the sides of the nose. First push down, then squeeze up. One push and squeeze make one round. Repeat for eight times eight rounds, going in both directions.

3. Massaging the Upper Cheekbones (Four Whites Point): Place the index and middle fingers of both hands on the bony hollow of the upper cheekbones right underneath the eyes and to the right and left of the nostrils. Place the thumbs on the mandibles, that is, the bones to the right and left of the chin. Now, release the middle fingers and bend them together with the other fingers to rest lightly against the lower cheeks. Gently circulate the index fingers to massage the bony hollow of the upper cheekbones. Massaging once up and down is one round. Repeat for eight times eight rounds.

4. Rubbing the Temples and Upper Eye Sockets (Great Yang and Related Points): Place the tips of the thumbs on the temples and use the knuckles of the index fingers to rub all around the eyes. Rub first up, then down, lightly massaging both above and below the eyes to hit the various pressure points in the area. Count to four as you do one full up and down circle. Repeat for eight times eight counts or a total of sixteen circles. (Chart obtained at Panliu Village Elementary School, Shaanxi, China)

Beyond this, the book presents medical exercises and self-massages for various conditions, ranging from stiff neck through white hair, sudden chest pain, insomnia, sciatica, and lumbago to digestive problems, hemorrhoids, and sore knees. For white hair, for example, the authors recommend a series of standing and seated forward bends coupled with a thorough scalp massage (fig. 24). All of this will "promote blood circulation to enable the hair papilla to get more nutrients and increase the production of melanin, while at the same time removing obstructions from the channels for the transmission of melanin, thus turning white hair black again" (Zeng and Liu 2002, 193–195).

Similarly, lumbago is treated with walking backwards, a gentle practice based on the taiji quan move Repulse Monkey that engages the muscles of the lower back and can be executed with arms on the hips or swinging by the sides. The practice should be continued for a total of twenty minutes or six hundred steps (Zeng and Liu 2002, 215–217). For sciatica the book recommends leg lifts

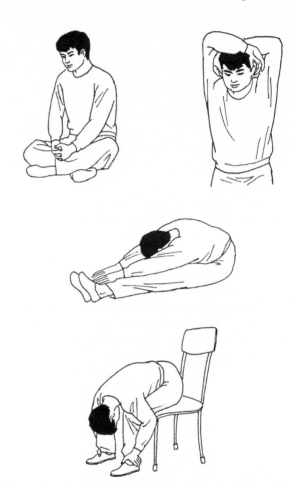

Fig. 24: The white hair
sequence. Source: Zeng
and Liu 2002.

while lying down and side lunges while standing; for digestive trouble it has an
abdominal massage; and for sore knees it suggests gentle knee bends—into the
chest while lying down and into a squat while standing. It also recommends the
pressing of specific acupuncture points, such as Meeting Valley at the thumb and
forefinger, to enhance *qi*-flow and reduce pain and stiffness (229–233).[4] It is interesting to note that, besides the obvious belly massage and knee bends, none of
these medicinal practices can be found in traditional literature; rather, they seem
to reflect both more modern symptoms or concerns (such as the white hair) and
more modern ways of moving and looking at the body.

4. For similar sequences that combine simple movements, activation of pressure points, and breathing in a Western setting, see Li 1990.

Overall, however, the medical community in China is aware of traditional exercises and follows the overall tendencies of its medieval forerunners, emphasizing a holistic approach to well-being and encouraging gentle but regular movements for overall flexibility and well-being. The rationale of the practices follows Western scientific thinking, and the Chinese see no conflict with modern medical theory or practice. Healing exercises, while being revised and reorganized as movement therapy, have thus successfully made the transition into the modern world.

New Daoyin Forms

A side effect of the medical application of Daoyin is its appearance in various new practices that actually use the word as part of their name. A recent example, which developed in England and was officially recognized as an alternative treatment in 2002, is Daoyin Tao, an in-depth massage of face, neck, and shoulders that combines various Chinese and Western techniques. It was developed by Anna-Louise Haigh, a long-term practitioner of reflexology and aromatherapy, and claims to "relax, release, rebalance, revitalize, and rejuvenate" (Anna-Louise Haigh, "What Is Daoyin Tao?"; www.DaoyinTao.com).

Another is Daoyin Yangsheng, developed by Zhang Guangde 张广德, a Beijing academic who developed serious health problems and in 1974 was diagnosed with heart disease and tuberculosis. Then, as the workshop flyer of Red Lotus Tai Chi Qigong in New Hampshire says,

> In an effort to heal himself, he undertook an extensive research of traditional Chinese body-mind exercises, particularly the ancient practice of Dao Yin (ancient name for Qigong) and Yang Sheng (health preservation), utilizing energy circulation to promote health. From this huge wealth of knowledge, he developed a comprehensive system of exercise to which he credits the full restoration of his health and vitality. (Red Lotus flyer, 2005)

Zhang's system, which is quite popular in China and practiced variously in the West,[5] is documented in his book *Daoyin yangsheng gong* 导引养生功 (2001). Acknowledged officially as a form of qigong and recognized by various martial arts and sports organizations in China, it involves moves that are adapted from taiji quan but that are gentler and more medically focused. Its sequences tend to specialize in different areas of ailments. The Dynamic Meridian Form, the Health

---

5. For practitioners and classes of Zhang Guangde's system in various countries of the West, see www.taichinetwork.org; www.dyysg.net; www.daoyin.it; www.daoyin.nl; www.dyysg.co.uk; www.taichiwales.com.

Preservation Form, and the Cardiovascular Form are some examples offered through Red Lotus. Zhang's book describes four forms to improve general health and longevity and four that are directed more specifically toward medical conditions, such as cardiovascular, bone, and nerve problems. Executed either standing or sitting in a chair, they all require relatively simple moves that are easy to learn and repeated in variations. More important, they involve a strong concentration of mind and the guiding of intention to the area in question.

While the medical forms tend to work with specific meridians to increase energy flow, the longevity forms for the most part involve stretches, bends, and squats, executed in a smooth flow as known from taiji quan. One form, Increase Long Life through Nourishing the Blood and Supplementing the Qi, is a series of breathing and qi-guiding exercises, not unlike Master Huanzhen's system of qi-practice. It ends with "drumming and rinsing," consciously guiding the qi through the body (Zhang 2001, 131–140). There are clear traces of ancient Daoyin practice in Zhang Guangde's system, and as is made clear in his introduction, he knows the traditional sources well. However, the forms with their specific execution and contemporary rationale are a new creation that actively continues the tradition in a modern, medical way.

Yet another Daoyin spinoff appears in the work of Jerry Alan Johnson, a medical qigong practitioner in California who was trained in both China and the United States. His version of Daoyin is described in his book *Chinese Medical Qigong Therapy* (2000). It does not involve any movements, focusing instead on breathing exercises ("Respiratory Dao Yin," ch. 16) and meditation ("Mental Dao Yin Training," ch. 17). Under the first heading, he describes seven breathing methods, from deep abdominal breathing through long, reversed, interrupted, and windy forms, adding the Six Breaths as well as several regulatory methods, such as counting or carefully observing the respiration (349–356).

He describes the mental aspects of Daoyin in terms of methods of concentration and inner awareness of thoughts and mental functions to learn about the functioning of the different layers of the conscious and subconscious minds. One can practice with outer, inner, or combined objects, working mainly with concentration or moving on to a more open awareness or insight practice. Ultimately, one will create the so-called Bridge of Light that connects the different aspects of the mind with more cosmic forms of qi, such as the Thread of Life in the heart and the Thread of Creativity in the throat (Johnson 2000, 359–369). Either method is to be prescribed by the qigong physician to enhance the healing effect of other applications. Neither has much to do with healing exercises as found in historical sources, although both breathing and mental awareness are of course part of the practice.

Religious Forms

The religious dimension of healing exercises is a bit more complex. For one, the Chinese Communist government outlawed all religious activity for about fifty years, so there has been a general hiatus of ordinations, rituals, and transmissions in major religious institutions, a hiatus that created a great opportunity for reinvention and the integration of modern concepts and practices. For another, all temples and monasteries today are state owned and require a politically correct justification of their activities; consequently, temple visits for sightseeing, historical study, or health purposes are in general much more respected than visits for devotional activities.

The result of these circumstances is that Daoist (and to a lesser degree Buddhist) temples are becoming major health centers, teaching martial arts and qigong, providing apothecary and massage services, and encouraging both their monastics and their lay followers to be physically fit. Although Daoists already in the middle ages had adopted physical practices into their ecstatic and immortality practices, this is a new trend that stands in stark contrast to the activities of Daoist monks and nuns before the Communist takeover, as documented by various outside observers, notably Heinrich Hackmann (1920; see also Kohn 2003b), Yoshioka Yoshitoyo (1979), and Peter Goullart (1961). Even today, Daoists in their official documents do not place a great emphasis on health activities. Thus, as Louis Komjathy points out, Min Zhiting 閔智亭 (1924–2004), former chairman of the Chinese Daoist Association, in his manual on Daoist monastic life (Min 1990) makes no mention of Qigong. *Taoism,* published in 2002 by the Chinese Daoist Association, depicts Daoism as a monastic, ritualistic, and meditative tradition and contains only two photographs of physical practice (Komjathy 2006, 206). And the recent *Daoism in China: An Introduction* (Wang 2006) focuses to a large extent on devotional and social activities, barely mentioning physical practice.

An example of a Daoist spa is the Shaolong guan 紹龍觀 in the southwestern metropolis of Chongqing. A vast complex of various buildings, nicely refurbished in traditional style, it contains not only worship, lecture, and meditation halls, but also extensive areas dedicated to massages, physical treatments, medical diagnoses, herbal prescriptions, and exercise. It has modern hotel facilities for visitors, with spacious rooms and up-to-date kitchen and dining areas, a computer room so people can stay in touch with their families and connect to their businesses, hot tubs and pools to languish in after working out, and all other sorts of amenities commonly associated with pricey retreats.

Its infomercial, shown by Abbot Li Jun 李俊 at the end of the Third International Conference on Daoism in 2006, presents the monastery entirely as a center for the unique acquisition of Daoist secrets of long life, following the ancient model of the Yellow Emperor, who, about five thousand years ago, concocted his cinnabar elixir right here on this mountain. Its monks appear as model healers, serving as grand masters of qigong and performing acrobatic moves of taiji quan and other martial arts. They perform a new version of religious service to society, teaching the newly wealthy and accordingly stressed-out class of upscale Chinese businessmen how to relax and keep themselves fit.

New Daoist Doctrines

The emphasis on physical fitness not only appears in modern Chinese Daoist practice but is also reflected in its doctrine. Integrating the traditional emphasis on moderation and healthy living with contemporary bodybuilding and health awareness, this new Daoist thinking also fortuitously connects with the Communist emphasis on physical fitness and the importance of movement. As Mao Zedong said in the 1920s,

> Human beings are active animals and they love to be active. Human beings are also rational animals and thus they need a reason for their activity. Why is this? Because activity secures survival. Yes, but that is an easy explanation. Because activity secures the fortune of the homeland. Yes, and that is a weighty explanation. Neither reaches the basis of the matter. Activity is ultimately what nourishes life and satisfies the mind. This and none other is the truth. (Mao 1972, 39)

An example of a Daoist doctrinal statement on the importance of physical practices and the body is found in a small pamphlet that I collected at the Great Clarity Temple (Taiqing gong 太清宫) on Mount Qingcheng 清城山 in Sichuan in 2004. The booklet is titled "Daojiao yangsheng quanxiao geyan" 道教养生功孝格言 or "Pertinent Words on Daoist Long Life and Filial Piety." After a short preface, it contains three treatises on nourishing life and behaving with proper filial piety, among them the "Yangsheng baojian geyan" 养生保健格言 or "Pertinent Words on Nourishing Life and Preserving Health." Written in an easygoing, popular style and rhythmic verses that are easy to remember, the text is highly reminiscent of Sun Simiao's *Baosheng ming* in that it covers a large variety of activities and aspects of daily living in a rather haphazard order.

Right at the start, the text says categorically,

> Work the body and live long;
> Enjoy your pleasures and cut life short.
> Rest in quietude to nurture spirit;
> Move with vigor to exercise the body.

If you can rest and move in equal measure,
You can extend your destined years.
And if you really want health,
Then practice every day.

It then recommends that one should get up early and work one's body with enthusiasm, avoiding laziness and indolence that "will produce old age." Just as unpolished metal will not shine, so the body will not be fit unless one works on it regularly and with dedication. "Let the hands dance and the feet be hopping, and even ninety will not seem like old," the text claims, thereby assuring the reader that one can not only have strength and health at one's current level but can even return to youthful vigor. Suggesting variation to avoid boredom, it leaves the exact form of exercise to the individual, giving just a few pertinent examples:

Practice self-massage.
Study fist or sword,
Kick a ball,
Or go for a walk,
Maybe bathe in sunlight—
But never cease your efforts.

In addition, the text stresses the need for a healthy diet, limiting the intake of fat, sugar, and salt while eating greens and other vegetables. "It's o.k. to drink a little wine, but tea is better—and don't smoke!" Also, not unlike the health texts of old, it recommends that one never completely fill the stomach but leave it about 20 percent empty and that one walk a few hundred steps after every major meal. "And when you eat," it says, "start with a nice, hot soup; then even in old age you won't be tired." The only "religious" note in this otherwise entirely health-centered booklet is an encouragement to "accumulate merit" by doing good deeds and behaving ethically. But again, it is not morality for its own sake. Instead, such moral behavior will aid the attainment of long life by keeping one's conscience clean and one's mind pure.

Exercise Practice

Daoist institutions in China today appeal to the public (and the government) not only as centers of cultural preservation but very strongly through catering to the increasingly powerful health industry that demands easily accessible and effective practices to keep people well and fit. The traditional exercises of Daoyin fit right into this scheme, just as they were easily integrated into the modern qigong movement. Their importance in the Daoist context—and the fact that contemporary Daoists are quite aware of their history—is documented in the book *Zhong-guo daojiao yangsheng mijue* 中国道教养生秘诀 (Secret Essentials of Chinese Daoist Ways to Long Life) by Ma Daozong 马道宗, published in 1999. In this book, Daoyin and *qi*-guiding come in the first of ten chapters, followed by different forms of meditation (stillness, visualization, inner awareness), embryo respiration, inner alchemy, elixir transformation, and sleep exercises. As if in an afterthought, the book also discusses methods of medical relief and the best harmony to be attained through daily activities.

Within its chapter on Daoyin, moreover, it covers sixteen exercise sequences on the basis of traditional literature, including not only the classics still officially permitted (Five Animals, Eight Brocades, Six Breaths) but also uncovering less well known historical forms, such those associated with Master Redpine, Ningfengzi, Pengzu, and Wangzi Qiao in the *Daoyin jing* as well as later sequences of both movement and *qi*-guiding, mostly taken from the late Ming *Chifeng sui* and the Qing-dynasty collection *Neiwai gong tushuo jiyao*. In an effort to revitalize the body-cultivation scene on the basis of ancient works, the book reveals a thorough knowledge and clear awareness of the richness of the tradition and documents that Daoists today, while catering to the new fads and finding their place in a new health conscious and scientifically thinking world, still preserve the traditions of old.

Beyond mainland China, too, healing exercises are alive and well in a Daoist context. Most Daoist temples in Hong Kong—which are run by lay followers and do not house monastics—offer regular free classes in qigong and taiji quan, usually on Sunday mornings, when people have time to participate (fig. 25). More than that, and following in the footsteps of Highest Clarity and Ming-dynasty Daoists, Hong Kong Chinese receive new forms of healing exercises through transmission from the beyond, usually via the planchette, a tray of sand in which a medium in trance writes characters dictated by the gods. Various deities are being channeled, most commonly the immortal Lü Dongbin, but the one revealing healing exercises is Jigong 濟公 (1162–1194), the so-called mad monk who allegedly lived during the Song dynasty and was famous for his unconventional behavior (see Shahir 1998).

Flouting the monastic rules against meat and wine, he was expelled from his temple and went begging through the country, always laughing and bringing kindness to the people. He became well known as a trickster who played all sorts of pranks but also as a healer who had the magic touch and could slay both internal and external demons. Today, Jigong is venerated as a deity who can help overcome problems and relieve difficulties. His most common depiction has him seated on a rock with his feet up, a funny hat on his head and holding a cup of wine (fig. 26). His role as helper with everyday problems fits in nicely with his transmission of healing exercises.

The practice that goes back to him is called Formless Meditation in Motion

Fig. 25: Getting ready for Sunday qigong practice at a Hong Kong Daoist temple.

(*wuxiang xinfa donggong* 無相心法動功). It appears in a booklet with the title "Wuxiang ji" 無相集 (Formless Collection), which I picked up in 2005 at the Yuen-Yuen Institute (Yuanxuan xueyuan 圓玄學院), a major Daoist ritual and research center in Hong Kong. The exercises are easy and straightforward and take ten to fifteen minutes to complete. They consist of seven subtle moves executed from a standing position and geared to enhance the functioning of the inner organs. Combined with deep, abdominal breathing in through the nose and out through the mouth, full mental concentration, and an intentional absorption and guiding of *qi*, Jigong's essential health practice goes as follows:

1. Massage the belly to protect the inner organs. Standing in a slight horse stance, begin with the hands lightly folded at the abdomen, then bring them up to the chest, stretch them away from each other to the right and left, and bring them back to the abdomen.

2. Close the seal to warm the heart. Beginning in the same fashion, after the hands have reached the chest, stretch the arms overhead, then complete the circle back to the abdomen.

3. Rotate the hip to support the kidneys. From horse stance with hands at the

Fig. 26: A statue of Jigong, the mad monk, at the Five Dragons Mountain –
Phoenix Mountain Temple in Gaoxiong County, Taiwan. Photo by Meir Shahar.

abdomen, bring the right hand to the kidneys, then make a circle with the left
hand going out and around, following it with your eyes and rotating the hip
accordingly. Bring the left hand around in a front circle and place it on the
kidneys while moving the right hand forward to repeat the practice on the
other side.

4. Raise the *qi* to strengthen the gallbladder. From the hands at the abdomen,
    make inward-moving circles to chest level and up while lifting the elbows to
    horizontal.

5. Extend right and left toward Heaven and Earth. From the hands at the
    abdomen, look up as you lift the left hand up toward Heaven, palm facing up,
    and press the right hand down toward Earth, palm facing down. Repeat on the
    other side.

6. Lift the legs to step on Bubbling Well. Place both hands on the kidneys, then
    lift the left leg to be at right angle at the knee, then point and flex the foot. Place
    the foot back down and repeat on the other side.

7. Inhale *qi* and return it to the elixir field. With hands closed over each other at
    the abdomen and slowly rotating, inhale deeply and visualize the *qi* returning
    to the elixir field. (Hang Sin Tong 2002, 62–78)

According to the book's supplementary explanation, the practice should be done once a day and—as all Daoyin moves—is best undertaken in times of rising yang. However, even at night is better than not at all. To enhance it further, practitioners can follow it with a seated meditation, their eyes closed and hands placed at the abdomen, with thumbs touching in a circle. If undertaken daily for a mere ten days, it will create a great openness of *qi*-flow and energetic awareness as well as an overall sense of well-being. Easy to learn and executed in little time and with little space, it is said to be very effective and to offer a quick release of tensions and obstructions. It will help with all sorts of symptoms, from joint problems through digestive difficulties to psychological issues. If continued beyond the healing stage, moreover, it will calm the mind, balance the body's energy, and greatly enhance one's life expectancy.

Altogether, this survey of the different manifestations of healing exercises in a Chinese Daoist environment shows that Daoists, in a development not unlike the religious adaptation of healing exercises in the middle ages, once again integrate dominantly medical practices into their repertoire and use them to create a new form of contemporary spirituality. While in some ways this development can be seen as a return of old patterns, it is also new in various ways. Daoists take the practices and adapt them and their setting to the new cultural and political environment; they use a completely new language that integrates Western biomedicine and contemporary worldview; they apply new technologies, such as computers; they actively enter the health maintenance market by creating new kinds of retreat centers that include health spas with modern facilities; they engage in publicity and advertising to make their product known within the market; and they develop new forms of the practices that suit the modern business world—whether guided by experience or received in revelation. It is fair to say, overall, that healing exercises in the Chinese religious scene are alive and well and that they will continue to evolve—be it through further creation of new forms, through recovery of ancient materials and patterns, or through the adaptation of yoga practices.

Western Daoyin

As noted earlier, in the West Daoyin is propagated under this name predominantly by Ni Hua-ching and Mantak Chia. Each has developed his own form of Daoyin, which combines ancient practices with medicine and qigong (and to a certain degree also with yoga), thus both continuing the tradition and giving it new life in the twenty-first century.

Ni Hua-ching

Ni Hua-ching was born in Wenzhou, a coastal city in Zhejiang province, no-
body knows quite when.[6] After training as a physician of traditional Chinese medicine, he fled the Communists and moved to Taiwan in 1949, where he continued his
medical practice and began to study Daoism. In 1976, two students of the Los Angeles Taoist Sanctuary who had been training in Taiwan brought Ni to California.
They installed him in a house in Malibu, where he opened a shrine called the Eternal
Breath of Tao and began teaching classes privately in a venue he named the College
of Tao. Over the years, Ni-sponsored organizations have multiplied. His private acupuncture clinic was known as the Union of Tao and Man. He also founded Yo San
University of Traditional Chinese Medicine in 1989, an accredited degree-granting
college. Both the clinic and the university are now headed by his sons, Maoshing and
Daoshing, while Master Ni lives in semiseclusion when not traveling.

Some aspects of his biography are controversial: reports are contradictory,
his own story changes, and opinions vary wildly. One of several official biographical statements about Ni has it that

> as a young boy he was educated in spiritual learning by his family, and was then
> chosen to study with Taoist masters in the high mountains of mainland China.... After
> more than 31 years of intensive training, he was fully acknowledged and empowered
> as a true master of the traditional Tao, including all aspects of Taoist science and
> metaphysics. In Taiwan for 28 years, Master Ni taught and practiced Taoist arts such
> as Tai Chi Chuan, Kung Fu, Taoist meditation and internal alchemy. (Seven Star
> Communications)

This statement suggests that Ni was born in the early twentieth century, something he neither confirms nor denies. He began publishing books in English in
1979, and today, with the help of his students who worked as volunteer editors,
designers, and publishers, has some sixty self-published books in print. Among
these is a volume titled *Attune Your Body with Dao-In: Taoist Exercises for a Long
and Happy Life* (1989). It presents a general description and outline of Daoyin
and contains a series of sixty-four exercises, divided into four sections—preliminary, central, concluding, and optional.

Ni's Daoyin

According to Ni, Daoyin has a very ancient history indeed, going back to prehis-
tory, when "about 10,000 years ago the ancient Yellow River people who lived in wil-

---

6. I am indebted to Elijah Sieger for this concise biography of Ni. Personal communication, June 2006.

derness and simplicity" discovered Daoyin to treat arthritis and other ailments (1989, 1). Defining healing exercises as a way to "conduct physical energy," he acknowledges that they are similar to hatha yoga; however, he sees the latter as being more for public show, while Daoyin is for spiritual cultivation. He further asserts that the exercises were passed down for tens of thousands of years and then were formalized in the Daoist canon, from which he claims to take most of his practices (3).

The essence of healing exercises, which form part of Daoist medicine—defined as the holistic approach to health through herbs, exercise, and meditation—is the practice of rhythmic movements to adjust and attune one's health; the movements also generate, strengthen, and invigorate personal energy. After doing the exercises, one should ideally spend an equal amount of time sitting in meditative stillness, matching practices that are even more ancient and go back one million years (Ni 1989, 5). In addition to improving health, the practices, which are suitable for all different ages, will also eradicate emotional problems and increase overall happiness (6). They will eliminate all sorts of negative patterns and emotions, such as bitterness, pride, rigidity, fear, melancholy, jealousy, self-obsession, and the like (30–31), and eventually lead people back to the awareness that they are in essence spirit beings who are only on a short sojourn on earth (10). With the help of Daoyin, practitioners can open each cell of the body to fresh air and learn to use different ways in their interaction with society and the natural environment. With prolonged practice, they can reach spiritual immortality, attained through a process of sublimation and the refinement of energy and defined as spiritual independence, when there is no more need for the senses and one instead experiences direct perception (12).

In more concrete terms, Ni provides some general rules: practice around sunrise to match the time of rising *qi;* practice in a clean and quiet indoor location; allow enough time and do not hurry; wear loose, natural clothing; eat less and take lighter foods; empty bladder and bowels before the practice; moderate sexual activity and strive to refine sexual energy into *qi;* calm the mind and let go of all urgent business; do as much of the exercises as you can, being mindful of particular needs and physical abilities; practice in total relaxation and with ease; and do the whole set rather than repeating just a few of the exercises (Ni 1989, 17–18, 32–36).

Ni's Daoyin system consists of sixty-four exercises divided into nine sections: three preliminary series (fifteen moves), four main ones (thirty-four moves), one concluding (ten moves), and one optional (five moves). Almost all called Immortal [Doing This or That], they are undertaken in either a seated or lying posture. The first preliminary sequence begins by lying on one's back to execute a pelvic tilt and pull one's knees into the chest. Lifting the legs, one comes to a seated position, then stretches the neck by holding opposite shoulders, lifting the torso, and bringing the chin toward the chest. The first section ends with Immortal Lifting the Mountain, a lift of the torso while lying on one's back or what yoga practitioners call Bridge Pose (Ni 1989, 45). The other preliminaries are similar in that they provide overall stretches and loosening of the joints. The second is executed while seated; the third contains various back bends undertaken while lying face down. All of the first fifteen practices have matches in Indian yoga (47–60).[7]

The four main sections move beyond the yoga model. They involve self-massages, torso twists, arm movements, and various seated forward bends. While in essence all found in ancient texts, the sequence is completely new and does not match any of the ancient sources, nor do the names relate to historical precedents. There is, though, a distinct connection to inner alchemy when practitioners undertake Immortal Sitting in Meditation to conclude the main section. Seated comfortably with buttocks slightly raised and hands on their thighs, thumbs and index fingers joined, they visualize a fire at the base of the spine that spreads warmth throughout the body. Gradually penetrating everywhere, it burns away negative thoughts, foolishness, and egoism and opens the path for complete self-forgetting in deep trance. After staying there for a while, adepts slowly and gently rub the face or belly to emerge back to waking consciousness (Ni 1989, 94–106).

The concluding section, which is recommended as an initial practice for people who have trouble getting up in the morning (Ni 1989, 32), includes a series of head and face massages and stimulation of the sense organs, such as the eye exercises for school children described earlier, and ends with a three-minute resting meditation executed while lying down (107–112). The optional section, finally, involves abdominal massages plus the conscious guiding of qi while pressing specific energy points. Three of its five exercises call for "immortal strengthening" of the abdomen, vital energy, and self (111–116).

Overall, Ni Hua-ching's version of Chinese healing exercises combines modern patterns adapted from yoga with traditional Chinese moves, massages, and meditations, while at the same time giving the practices new names and creating a yet different system of health improvement that can serve as a foundation for more advanced practices of inner alchemy and immortal transformation, as taught in his Daoist seminars.

---

7. The connection to yoga here is obvious but not explicit. In contrast, Daniel Reid, in *The Tao of Health, Sex, and Longevity,* presents a version of "Taoist exercises" that claims to go back to "therapeutic dances called *dao-yin*" (1989, 197) but in fact—and quite openly—includes a series of yoga poses, such as Plow, Cobra, Forward Bend, and Splits in conjunction with various martial arts moves, executed in horse stance and using twists and bends (205–212). His longevity practices include softer stretches, such as of the neck, in conjunction with various self-massages, back bends, and taiji push hands moves (213–225). He concludes the series, again in yoga fashion, with complete relaxation in the Corpse Pose (226–228).

Mantak Chia

Mantak Chia has a very similar take on Daoyin. He, too, was trained traditionally, came to the West to start a Daoist system—called Healing Dao—and uses healing exercises, again in a new and transformed way, both for health improvement and
as a foundation of his ultimate practices, which are an adaptation of inner alchemy.

Mantak Chia was born in Thailand in 1944. Recognized early for his spiritual
potential, he began the practice of Buddhist insight meditation at age six. During
his teens, he went to live in Hong Kong, where he learned taiji quan, aikido, and
kundalini yoga. There he met the Daoist master Yi Eng (One Cloud), who report-
edly died at the age of 168 and ate hardly any food for the last five years of his life.
From him Chia learned the practices of inner alchemy over five years. Achieving
expertise in these methods, he decided to integrate them with Western thinking to
enhance health, reduce stress, and open higher spiritual awareness.

In 1978, Chia established a first Western foothold in Huntington, New York;
in 1983, he opened a center in New York City. Today he resides in northern Thailand but travels widely to give lectures and workshops. The main Western teacher
trained by Chia is Michael Winn, who founded the Healing Dao University in
upstate New York and supports local centers that can be found in all metropoli-
tan areas (www.healingdao.com).

The general theory of Healing Dao matches inner alchemy and Daoist meditation. It sees the unfolding of spirituality in three levels: (1) create healing energy, and strengthen and calm the body; (2) change negative emotions into strong,
positive energy; (3) develop creative and spiritual practices. On the first level,
practitioners engage in qigong and taiji quan. They begin their practice by shak-
ing all parts of the body to loosen up and release toxins. Then they undertake
deep breathing together with qigong standing meditations and qi-collecting
techniques as well as a long and a short form of taiji quan. In all cases, muscles are
consciously contracted and relaxed to gain maximum flexibility and control. The
pelvic area is opened, and practitioners learn to tighten the perineum and feel the
qi move up along the spine. All this serves to open the body and strengthen the
qi-flow, greatly enhancing health and well-being.

Daoyin exercises provide an alternative method to attain this fundamental
opening part of the practice. Described in Chia's book *Tao Yin: Exercises for Revitalization, Health, and Longevity* (1999; reedited in Chia 2005) and visually documented
on a CD by Mantak Chia and Maneewan Chia (1994) and by Karin Sörvik (2001),
they serve to increase qi-flow and internal awareness in the practitioner. Undertaken
with similar preparation and in similar settings as those prescribed by Ni Hua-ching,
they yet require a more detailed knowledge of the internal functioning of the body in
terms of Chinese medicine and Daoism, an awareness of the overall yin-yang struc-

ture, the organs, meridians, and major acupuncture points, and awareness of the three elixir fields and notions of essence, *qi,* and spirit. All these are explained in detail and with frequent recourse to Western science in the five chapters of the first part of Chia's book. After this, he presents healing exercises in five sets.

Chia's Healing Exercises

The first set of exercises begins in a lying-down posture with full-body breathing, gentle self-massages, a raised awareness of *qi*-flow, the activation of specific energy points (such as Laogong in the center of the palm), and the conscious warming of the Triple Heater with the *xi* breath (one of what Chia calls the Six Healing Sounds). This is followed by two supine stretches that closely match yoga poses (Chia 1999, 65–68): Grab Knees and Rock (Spinal Rocking) and Crocodile Lifts Head (Wind-Relieving Pose). After this, adepts hug their knees into the chest and press their elbows between the lifted knees for an increased lengthening of the spine. The set ends with Twist like a Snake (Knee Down Twist) and Monkey Flaps Legs (Supine Bound Angle Pose) (1999, 68–75).

The purpose of this initial set is to open the body for the various exercises to come and to create an initial awareness of the back and stomach muscles as well as of the meridians that will be energized in the following sets. While the poses may match what yoga practitioners do, there is much less holding of poses and instead a much greater awareness of energy points and channels. Also, conscious and active breathing, often with the help of one or the other of the Six Healing Sounds, transforms the body postures into a more Daoist-style practice.

The next set combines an initial strengthening of the abdominals with some serious back bends, a match also commonly found in yoga classes. The first three poses are as follows (Chia 1999, 76–80):

Chia's practice	Yoga pose	Description
Stretch the Bow	Boat with Oars	seated, with legs and arms raised
Mountain Rises from the Sea	Bridge Pose	lying, with buttocks and back raised
Cricket Rests on Flower	Wheel Pose	back bend, with hands and feet on the floor

Following this, four poses work on the back: an abdominal crunch with twist, a lifting of legs and arms into the air, and a hugging of the knees into the chest (1999, 81–87). The goal of this stage of the practice, as explained in some detail, is to engage and strengthen the ring or sphincter muscles that surround the orifices or openings of the body. Both external and internal, these muscles form "the prime mover, the substratum, the source which activates all the body's processes. All the organs, muscle systems, the blood circulatory system, lymphatic system and digestive system—everything in the body owes its functionality to the sphincter muscles" (1999, 87). The key to health and vigor is the harmonious functioning of their rhythmic opening and closing. Thus, as practitioners perform the exercises, they are to consciously tighten the perineum and—as specified in the instructions—variously make fists or open the hands and squeeze the mouth shut or open it wide.

Set 3 is mostly executed on the belly and consists fully of poses also found in yoga (Chia 1999, 95–119):

Chia's practice	Yoga pose	Description
Dolphin Lifts Tail	Locust Pose	on belly, both legs raised
Flying in Dreams	Supine Boat Pose	on belly, legs and arms raised
Cobra's Ritual of Love	Cobra Pose	on belly, arms and chest raised
Peacock Looks at His Tail	Pigeon Pose	on belly, one leg bent under, chest raised
Monkey Rotates Spine to Leg	Head to Knee Pose	seated, one leg tucked in, forward bend

This set serves to strengthen the back and open the hips, as well as further activate the inner connections and enhance the dynamics of *qi*. The practice of Cobra at various height levels is supplemented with holding the breathing, rolling the eyes up, stretching out the tongue, and vigorously and completely expelling the breath with a growl. It ends with a rest with buttocks on ankles and forehead on the ground, in what yogis call Child's Pose, then moves through a chest-to-floor stretch into the next round (1999, 100). All poses are repeated several times, allowing a dynamic sense of flow in the practice.

The next set, executed from a seated position, begins with the internal rotation and guiding of *qi*, aided by the gentle passing of the hands over belly, arms, and legs (Chia 1999, 121–123). It then moves on to the activation of the kidney meridian through a leg stretch and massage of the soles of the feet. After that practitioners open the bladder meridian in a move called Rowing a Boat, which in yoga is known as Seated Forward Bend, and the stomach meridian through Arch from Knees (Camel Pose). The last five poses of this set, variations of seated forward bends and twists, involve the so-called Empty Forth Breath (Udayana in yoga), which serves to increase oxygen in the body. As Mantak Chia describes it,

It is performed by fully exhaling, emptying the air out of the body and then holding the breath out. It is completed by drawing the organs up into the rib cage "dome" and

then expanding them back down consciously, repeating this up and down movement
a few times before inhaling. This creates a force, a strong vacuum suction, in the abdomen. Hence the abdominal vacuum can draw air directly into the abdominal digestive tract to oxygenate the blood, thereby enhancing the level of overall body
functioning. (1999, 132)

The fifth and last set focuses almost entirely on the arms. It involves raising
the arms and twisting them at the wrist, lifting the elbows out to the side and
placing the hands in the armpits, stretching the shoulders, and opening the fingers, wrists, and elbows. Called Dragon Stretches Tail or Dragon Stretches Claws,
they particularly activate the meridians that run through the arms. When joined
by forward bends and twist, executed from a cross-legged position, they also
work on the meridians of the back and legs. This part of the practice, which ends
with Snake Coils around Tree, a seated twist, is probably closest to traditional
healing exercises as they are described in the historical literature. But, as noted
earlier, even poses commonly undertaken in yoga can form an active part of
Daoyin when undertaken with the right breathing and deep *qi*-awareness.

In addition to these major masters, several Western Daoist associations promote the practice of Chinese healing exercises, offering training in retreats. For
example, the British Taoist Association has a Daoyin workshop that includes self-
massages, gentle stretches, focused breathing, and the meditative guiding of *qi*. It
claims to go back to the origin of the ancient tradition and to convey its methods
accurately and to practitioners' benefit (fig. 27). All these different masters and organizations promote new versions of healing exercises that help people access their
energy body, enhance their overall health, and open themselves for spiritual practices of internal cultivation. Leaders provide an integrated structure to the practices, and although they claim that their origins go back for millennia, do not
overemphasize their use or misrepresent their ultimate purpose. Daoyin here serves
as a healing stage in the preparation of the great inner alchemical work to come.

Other Venues

There are a few other venues in which Daoyin appears in the West today. Still
under the name Daoyin, but in its Japanese form *dōin,* the practice has made its
way into macrobiotics, a diet based on the Chinese yin-yang division of food, but
developed in early-twentieth-century Japan.

No longer called Daoyin, but representing the same basic principles and
strongly working within the traditional Chinese medical system, are some gentle
Western qigong exercises that serve in healing and are increasingly brought into

Dao Yin Retreat

Led by Shi Jing

1 - 3 July 2005, Hourne Farm

This retreat will look into *dao yin* system in depth and explore the origin of this ancient tradition. *Dao yin* is a yoga practiced by Daoist sages over thousands of years in their quest for longevity and immortality. It is an integral part of the ancient Daoist cultivation called *yang sheng* (nourishing life), which also includes meditation, diet and emotional hygiene. The cultivation of softness and receptivity are the key qualities of *dao yin*, which involves purifying and invigorating our *qi* to restore vitality and well-being. This is done, firstly, by way of self-massage to warm the body and smooth the circulation of body fluids. Secondly, the sequence of simple stretching movements of the body helps to establish the inner circulation of *qi* and gently release the blockages that inhibit the flow and flexibility. Easy and undemanding, the movements are done in a soft and slow rhythm to ensure the breathing becomes relaxed and natural.

Cultivation of *dao yin* comes to fruition in meditation, which seamlessly integrates all the aspects of *dao yin*. This is expressed in the meditation posture which is stable, aligned and relaxed, allowing the *qi* to follow its natural pattern. To help internalise this cultivation and facilitate an understanding that goes deeper than just the physical level, meditation will be introduced on the retreat.

Shi Jing is an English daoshi (Daoist adept) with thirty years experience of cultivation. He first studied the Dao in the seventies with Giafu Feng, a Chinese Daoist well known for his translation of the Daode jing. Later he travelled to China and in 1995 he became the disciple of Feng Xingzhao, who initiated him as a 31st generation daoshi of the Dragon Gate tradition.

The Dragon Gate is a sect of the Quanzhen school and in present day China it is one of the most prominent. Deeply rooted in the ancient traditions of Daoism, its teachings have been handed down through many generations of hermits and adepts. They offer a clear, authentic path of self cultivation, presenting it as a natural process that is accessible to anyone.

Cost: £130 (BTA members) £150 (non members)
If you have any further enquiries please contact Justyna Gorska: 020 8 516 5244 retreats@taoists.co.uk

To book a place on the retreat please complete the booking form on page 19 and return it to:
British Taoist Association, PO Box 2274, Buckhurst Hill, IG9 5YQ

Fig. 27: Advertising a Daoyin retreat through the British Taoist Association.
Source: *Dragon's Mouth* 2005 (No. 2).

hospitals and health maintenance organizations and thereby to the attention of Western physicians and physicists. The main organizations working in this context in the United States are the National Qigong Association, the National Expert Meeting on Qigong and Tai Chi, and the Institute for Integral Qigong and Tai Chi.

Last but not least, practices highly similar to Daoyin and body energy maps derived from the Chinese system are at the foundation of several new forms of yoga. Both in Acu-Yoga and Yin Yoga, practitioners use yoga poses that closely resemble Daoyin forms to open up meridians and stimulate energy points. Unlike the more conventional forms, asanas here are not strenuous or acrobatic, nor are they done in an integrated sequence *(vinyasa)*. Rather, simple poses are assumed, often with considerable props, and held for as long as five to ten minutes, allowing channels to release.

Macrobiotics

Macrobiotics is a whole-grain, all natural diet developed by George Ohsawa (1893–1966), who in 1909 contracted tuberculosis and was told that he would die soon. Trying to avoid this, he studied a book by Sagen Ishizuka called *The Curative Method of Diet* and began to eat accordingly. He consumed only natural foods and beverages and made whole grains the backbone of his diet. After he cured himself, he taught the method to others. His main disciples were Herman Aikawa and Michio Kushi.[8]

In 1949, Kushi brought the practice to the United States, where he gave lectures, conducted workshops, wrote books, and founded centers in Boston and San Francisco. He educated wide segments of the population on the relationship between diet, lifestyle, and disease, and with his whole-food nutrition method was successful in curing numerous degenerative diseases, including terminal cases.

Macrobiotics is based on the cosmology of yin and yang in relationship to the Dao, which here is described as Infinity. Infinity manifests itself in the complementary forces yin and yang, which are endless in change and transformation. Yin represents centrifugality; yang represents centripetality. Together they produce energy and all phenomena. They both attract and repel each other and constantly change into one another. Nothing is ever solely yin or solely yang, and one has to maintain the proper balance between them for continued health and prosperity.

To find this balance, one should eat organically and locally grown whole foods that are in season. One should keep stress levels low, listen to the body, and undertake regular exercise. In his work *The Book of Dō-In* (1979), Kushi describes Daoyin as an

---

8. There are numerous publications and cookbooks by Michio Kushi and his wife Aveline—for example, Kushi and Jack 1985, Kushi and Esko 1993. See also www.macrobiotics.org.

ancient practice that is complete in itself, does not require the help of others or use specialized instruments, works toward physical improvement but also has a mental and spiritual effect, and understands human beings as "manifestations of vibrational and spiritual movements" (1979, 95). He then goes on to outline four different kinds of practices: special exercises that serve individual purposes; spiritual exercises for enhancing harmony with the cosmos; daily exercises to keep energies moving smoothly; and general exercises that include self-massages and deep breathing.

Special exercises are all undertaken in a seated or kneeling posture and involve gently holding certain energy points or slowly moving the arms while mentally opening the related area. They are centered on yogic chakras and serve to create an intimate connection to Heaven and Earth while stabilizing emotions, enhancing intuition, bringing forth insight, and strengthening goodwill toward all. They have cosmic names, such as Heavenly Foundation, Ascending to Heaven, and Spiritual Worship (Kushi 1979, 97–127).

Spiritual exercises are a close adaptation of the Seated Eight Brocades. Adepts begin by sitting upright and regulating their breathing, then offer a prayer of oneness and purify themselves through clapping, chanting, and beating the heavenly drum. After that, they swallow saliva and guide it into their organs as spiritual light while making a sound that will open the organs. The exercise concludes with Pacification of the World, a sending of good vibrations in all directions (Kushi 1979, 130–131).

Slightly more physical are the daily exercises, divided into sets for morning and evening. Morning exercises involve lying on the back while massaging one foot with the other, flexing the ankles and knees, then raising the legs to open the hips and strengthen the abdominal muscles. From here practitioners move the legs to the right and left and extend the thighs. This is followed by an abdominal massage and various sit-ups and twists, to conclude with arm and neck stretches (Kushi 1979, 141–152).

Evening exercises begin in a standing pose with raising the arms and bending forward. Kneeling next, one leans back to open the front of the torso, then brings the ankles together to stretch the inner thighs and bends forward with feet stretched out to lengthen the back of the body. Next there are side bends, further forward bends, and the yoga pose called Plow, where one lies down and rolls the legs over the head to open the upper back. Further bends and twists in a kneeling position follow, gradually moving adepts into a face-down posture to perform Cobra and Boat poses, from where they roll over to enter deep relaxation in Corpse Pose (Kushi 1979, 153–160). While the morning set has much in common with sequences associated with Pengzu and Master Redpine in the *Daoyin jing,* the evening section seems largely an adaptation of yoga poses.

The so-called meridian exercises, each of which focuses on a specific energy channel, comprise another set of daily practices. The lung meridian, for example, is aided by a standing forward bend, the spleen is opened by stretching backward from a kneeling position, the liver channel is activated in a forward bend with legs spread wide, and so on (Kushi 1979, 162–165). Kushi's last group, general exercises, serves to smooth energy flow through the entire body. It consists of self-massages of various areas, from the face through the hands, abdomen, and legs to the feet (173–205). It also involves breathing exercises that include deep abdominal and reversed breathing together with different kinds of holding the breath and moving it around the body (167–171). Kushi's regimen thus combines a number of different techniques from both the Indian and Chinese traditions with the customary Japanese kneeling posture with the goal of enhancing personal energy and establishing a conscious connection to Earth as provider of natural nourishment, to Heaven as the governing force of one's internal being, and to Humanity as universal community.

Medical Qigong

Only occasionally speaking explicitly of Daoyin but mostly using the term qigong, various organizations in the United States actively promote Chinese healing exercises and increasingly bring them to the attention of medical institutions and body-mind researchers. Most notable among them is the National Qigong Association (NQA), the largest, most representative, and most influential organization of Chinese exercises practitioners. Founded in 1995, it is a grassroots, nonprofit organization that counts most prominent qigong teachers in America among its members. According to its Web site, NAQ seeks to integrate qigong into all aspects of mainstream culture, healing, science, and education; to encourage self-healing and spiritual self-development through daily practice; and to create a forum and network for sharing information about qigong (www.nqa.org; Komjathy 2006, 225).

NQA currently has about seven hundred members, organizes an annual conference, and provides online assistance for locating qigong teachers and organizations. It has also sponsored an online qigong journal, *The Journal of Qigong in America*, first issued in 2004 under the editorship of Michael Meyer. Besides teaching in their local communities and bringing healing exercises to hospitals and senior centers, members also write books and distribute videos on classical forms, such as the Five Animals' Frolic (John DuCaine, Paul Gallegher), the Six Healing Sounds (Michael Will, Caryn Diel), and the Sinews Transformation Classic (Frank Yurasek).

Some actively experiment with various healing modalities, such as using simple body movements in conjunction with active visualizations to alleviate or cure asthma (Cibik 2003); others present integrated outlines of the complete way to health, like Chinese books on nourishing life describing all kinds of body practices, from general moderation through diet and sexual control to breathing, exercises, and meditations (Cohen 1997, MacRitchie 1997). Yet others actively promote the spread of the practices within the medical establishment in the hope of inciting a health revolution. As Roger Jahnke says, if everyone learns simple health enhancement and self-healing methods along the lines of Daoyin,

> diseases that have been hard to cure, like cancer, heart disease, HIV, and diabetes, will become less devastating. Economies that have been terribly damaged by the cost of medicine will be rehabilitated.... A dynamic, widespread change will occur—a virtuous, wholesome, desirable, positive change. (1997, xix–xx)

Jahnke also has been active in translating the inner workings of the methods into the language of modern science, presenting papers at scientific conferences and writing about the connections between *qi* and quantum physics (e.g., 2002, 237–266). He also works with the National Expert Meeting on Qigong and Tai Chi and the Institute for Integral Qigong and Tai Chi, groups that not only train teachers who serve community centers, schools, social service agencies, and senior centers but also collaborate in measured health studies with the medical schools of various respected universities and strive to spread energy awareness and healing practices to the wider populace. Part of the growing fields of energy medicine and energy psychology, these organizations continue the tradition of Daoyin in a new and modernized way, connecting the practices and their effects to contemporary science and technology.

Yogic Adaptations

A completely different venue for the practice and spread of Daoyin in the modern West are two new forms of yoga that actively combine asana practice with the activation of acupuncture meridians to stimulate and harmonize energy flow in the body. Acu-Yoga, the earlier of the two, was founded by Michael Reed Gach with the express purpose of creating greater efficiency of health maintenance by combining the two methods (Gach and Marco 1981, 15; www.acu-yoga .com). The theory behind the practice is that tension accumulates in certain typical acupuncture points. As it blocks energy from flowing freely, people become unbalanced, having excess energy in certain body parts and deficiencies in others and, as a result, experience sickness and fatigue. To remedy this, Acu-Yoga postures stimulate and open certain nerves, muscles, and acupuncture points, "awakening the meridians and releasing tension," thereby nourishing all systems of the body and leading to "radiant health" (Gach and Marco 1981, 17).

The exercises, which are not strenuous and should be undertaken daily, begin with a centering meditation and energetic balancing through deep breathing. They then divide into several sets: to increase spinal flexibility, to open the seven chakras, to activate the eight extraordinary vessels (called "regulator channels"), and to stimulate the workings of the twelve organ meridians. In all cases, certain postures are assumed that open the area in question and certain acupuncture points are pressed, such as the first point of the kidney channel on the sole of the foot. The mind actively connects to the practice, guiding *qi* to the points and along the channels, fostering a growing awareness of the subtle energy body and creating a sense of well-being and self-integration. Many poses are adapted from both yoga and Daoyin. For example, Bridge Pose, used in the *Daoyin jing* and *Huanzhen neiqi fa* to release stale *qi* from the body, appears here as activating the fifth chakra in the chest, the center housing "the power of communication and the ability of self-expression" (Gach and Macro 1981, 71).

Other Acu-Yoga practices serve to treat specific ailments, both physical and mental. They are listed alphabetically from abdominal weakness to spinal disorders (Gach and Macro 1981, 124–232). To give one example, to release frustration practitioners should lie on the back, interlace the fingers behind the neck, inhale and bend the left leg up, then exhale and roll to the right side while exhaling with *aaahh*. On inhalation, they return to their back, then repeat on the other side (169). These guidelines are similar to practices outlined in ancient Chinese texts, such as the *Jin'gui lu* and *Daoyin jing*. Specific moves are combined with particular exhalations and mental visualizations. Involving body, mind, and breath, the techniques look deceptively simple yet have a powerful effect on the energetic constellation of the person and thus contribute significantly to healing.

The other major new form of yoga that integrates the Chinese medical system is Yin Yoga, developed by Paul Grilley, who started yoga practice in 1979 after reading Paramahansa Yogananda's *Autobiography of a Yogi*. He trained in the more vigorous forms of Ashtanga and Bikram while studying anatomy and gaining strength and flexibility. In the 1980s, he came in contact with Paulie Zink, a martial arts practitioner who had begun practicing under the tutelage of a Chinese master as a teenager and had, aside from numerous martial techniques (notably of the Monkey Gongfu style), also received instruction in limbering exercises allegedly transmitted to his master by a Daoist. Working with these under the name Taoist Yoga, Zink achieved a great deal of flexibility and learned to open the energy body.[9] Paul Grilley was delighted to have found these methods

---

9. He lives today in a Montana homestead and, in addition to teaching qigong healing moves to hospital patients, teaches his techniques locally and in workshops. He also sells a set of five CDs on Taoist Yoga; these target the different areas of the body and explain the underlying concepts of Chinese body geography. His *Taoist Yoga for Beginners*, in particular, arranged according to the Five Phases, revives ancient patterns of Daoyin, using forms such as the Toad and Dragon that are already described in the *Daoyin jing*. For more on his work, see www.pauliezink.com.

and absorbed them rapidly, finding himself limbering up even more. In 1990, he also became a student of the acupuncturist Hiroshi Motoyama and thus deepened his understanding of traditional Chinese body energetics.

Putting all this together, Grilley created Yin Yoga, which is a meditative, restful practice where students place themselves into certain postures that open the body but are not strenuous and can be supported by a variety of props, such as pillows, blankets, straps, and bolsters. Students stay in a pose for five to twenty minutes to allow the tendons and nerves to release tension and renew themselves. Mental engagement through the detached observation of various body sensations and active visualization of the flow of healing energies are key to the practice. As in Acu-Yoga, the main work is in the release of blockages and the opening of flow (Grilley 2002, 12).

The Yin Yoga Web site lists only twenty-five postures from which to choose. In fact, in accordance with its yin principles, Yin Yoga masters find that less is more and that one should rather practice a few poses in depth than a lot superficially. Although essentially the same as classic yoga asanas, many have names different from the standard nomenclature, so that, for example, Cobra is now called Sphinx. Each pose is, moreover, linked with one or more acupuncture channels and explained with regard to its healing properties—the latter drawing heavily on Iyengar's *Light on Yoga* (www.yinyoga.com). Several also have matches in ancient Daoyin, the most obvious being a dragon series, which consists of a variety of holds in lunge position, closely resembling Dragon Flourish and Snapping Yin from the ancient *Yinshu*.

The name of the practice—which Grilley claims is the most ancient and the very original form of asana practice (www.yinyoga.com)—contrasts the restful, yielding, and softening approach with the more active or yang styles of yoga. Also, while the latter exercise muscles through repeated movement and intense stretching, Yin Yoga targets the connective tissue, not only the main object of practice according to the Sinews Transformation Classic, but also nowadays understood to be at the root of the workings of acupuncture. The connective tissue pervades the entire body; in addition to the outer sheath of the muscles known as the myofascia, it surrounds the nerves, the blood vessels, the lymphatic system, and the bones. It holds the skeleton together, connects muscles to bone, and keeps the organs in place. It not only conducts energy, but it also produces it. As James Oschman notes,

The connective tissue fabric is a semi-conducting communication network that can carry signals between every part of the body and every other part.... Each movement and each compression of the body causes the crystalline lattice of the connective tissue to generate bioelectronic signals. (2000, 49)

As practitioners of Yin Yoga hold one or the other of the prescribed poses, their main task is to remain calm and in a state of simple being, relaxing into the present and letting go of all urgency and tension. This aspect of the practice closely reflects a key characteristic of the internal martial arts: *fangsong* 放送, the letting go of all extraneous zeal as one applies only the amount of effort necessary. Practitioners in this state feel relaxed but are alert and active (Cohen 1997, 98), thus allowing the *qi* to move through areas that were otherwise blocked by tension (Bidlack 2006, 183). Yin Yoga thus has many connections with and overlaps the worldview and practice of traditional Chinese healing exercises.

Overall, Daoyin today is present in a variety of forms and venues and continues to evolve as a healing modality and foundational practice for spiritual attainment, in both China and the West.

In terms of healing, after the decline of the qigong movement in mainland China, doctors and longevity practitioners are turning to the exploration of historical forms other than the four basic patterns still officially allowed. Sometimes engaging quite a bit of creativity, they are developing new patterns that serve overall wellness or the healing of specific ailments and engaging in systematic presentations and clinical studies. Along the same lines, Western qigong masters bring the practice into heath organizations and cooperate with medical institutions on scientific research. At the same time, the Japanese diet master Michio Kushi uses the techniques to enhance the overall effect of macrobiotic eating, mixing it freely with Indian chakra meditation and yoga poses. Practitioners of yoga, finally, are picking up the body geography of traditional China and, in some cases learning from masters trained in Chinese practices, developing new forms of a more meditative and energy-oriented practice.

In terms of spirituality, Daoyin is present in Chinese Daoist temples and mediums continue to receive new methods—inheriting a tradition of divine connection as old as the Highest Clarity revelations. Masters of inner alchemy (such as Ni Huaching and Mantak Chia) of Chinese origin but active also in the West, moreover, work with Daoyin to prepare students for the subtler energetic transformations required in their systems. Daoist associations offer workshops in healing exercises, following the traditional pattern and placing healing at the basis of long life and the ultimate effort of transcendence.

Conclusion

Over six chapters and many pages we have now pursued the history and unfolding of Chinese healing exercises or Daoyin. The tradition is long and varied, ranging from the earliest traces in the late Zhou dynasty to the modern West. Its first documentation shows the centrality of slow, gentle movements in conjunction with deep, intentional breathing and the conscious guiding of *qi*, thus activating the body's energetic substructure while moving its limbs and joints. Next, the various detailed outlines found in Han-dynasty manuscripts make it clear that healing exercises formed part of the medical tradition, serving rehabilitation, prevention, and the overall enhancement of health, and were mainly practiced by the aristocratic elite, who had the necessary leisure and resources.

Our next cluster of written documents dates from the fourth century when, because of political pressure, many northerners emigrated to the south, displacing southern officials and local leaders. The exercise tradition then evolved into three distinct forms: medical, magical, and spiritual. While medical Daoyin continued, serving to maintain and enhance health, magical Daoyin focused on overcoming physical needs such as hunger, attaining supernatural powers, performing exorcism, and protecting the practitioner from demonic forces. It was predominantly used by seekers in the alchemical tradition who had to venture deep into the wilderness, where dangerous beasts and specters abounded, where edible food was scarce, and where getting lost was a constant threat. Spiritual Daoyin, finally, was the domain of the newly emerging Daoist school of Highest Clarity, whose adepts combined healing exercises with ritual procedures, devotional obeisances, the chanting of incantations, and the activation of potent talismans. The goal, although always connected to health and long life, shifted accordingly to the attainment of high mystical states and the eventual transfer into the otherworldly administration.

It should be made clear at this point that although we have clear documentation of these three dimensions of the Daoyin tradition only from the fourth century, it is more than likely that exercises were used for both the attainment of supernatural powers and spiritual transcendence before then. In fact, the recorded Chinese hermit tradition goes back to the end of the Shang dynasty, when Boyi and Shuqi refused to submit to the new Zhou rulers and took off for the wilderness. It has remained an active part of Chinese culture ever since.[1] Similarly, Han accounts of immortals record their moving into the mountains and learning to survive, acquiring lighter bodies and various magical powers in the process.

Along the same lines, the spiritual use of exercises is apparent in the Zhou-dynasty *Chuci,* whose shamanic songs speak about movements to entice the gods to descend or to induce a trance in the seeker. Just as these early forms of Daoyin are not fully documented until the fourth century C.E., so there are only small hints of a possible Indian influence on the tradition from around this period, when there was for the first time a greater presence of Buddhists from Central Asia who may well have brought physical practices along with meditation techniques, precepts, and new doctrines.

In the late middle ages and the Tang dynasty, the Daoyin tradition underwent further expansion and increased systematization. Not only did the first fully dedicated "Daoyin scripture" appear in the late Six Dynasties, but the two leading Daoist and medical masters of the Tang, Sun Simiao and Sima Chengzhen, created integrated paths of the different longevity and immortality methods, placing healing exercises both at the foundation of physical health and at the higher levels of activating the energy body. The continuum of healing, long life, and immortality, always key in all longevity and Daoist practices, for the first time is fully formulated, theoretically underscored, and outlined in distinct and streamlined practices.

In the later dynasties, Song through Qing, practitioners continued the different dimensions of the tradition, creating new forms of practices for healing, integrating Daoyin into the practice of inner alchemy and connecting it with self-defense in the newly arising martial art of taiji quan. Many of the forms then developed are still practiced today and play an important role in modern health and longevity teachings. The modern age, finally, has seen the spread of Chinese healing exercises into the politically stimulated mass movement of qigong and from there into new forms of energy healing in the West. Numerous new practices, sequences, and forms appeared, and—interestingly enough—the tradition in China once more went through all its major dimensions: healing in the first few decades, then magical powers, and finally religious spirituality and sectarianism. In the West Daoyin has remained mainly in the realm of healing, with some Daoist masters advocating it as a foundation for subtler alchemical transmutations. Increasingly understood in scientific terms and linked with the emerging fields of energy medicine and energy psychology, Chinese healing exercises are here to stay. Transmitting the legacy of an ancient culture, representing

---

1. On the hermit tradition in ancient China, see Li 1962; Vervoorn 1983, 1984; Berkowitz 1989; for modern hermits, see Porter 1993.

millennia of body-cultivation experiences, they have much to contribute to people's health and well-being in the modern age.

How then, to conclude, are Daoyin exercises unique? How are they different from other methods that share the same basic characteristics of slow, gentle movements in conjunction with deep, intentional breathing and conscious mental awareness? In other words, if you were to see someone doing taiji quàn, qigong, yoga, or Daoyin, how would you know which is which?

Well, if you only look very briefly, you couldn't probably tell the difference. With prolonged watching, however, you could tell. Taiji quan is a martial art: practitioners move slowly but continually, never stopping and rarely repeating a movement; they never lower their head lest an enemy comes to chop it off; and they do not engage in internal visualizations but keep their eyes open and their mind in a state of alert awareness, ready to jump into martial action at all times. Also, taiji quan practitioners may use a weapon (sword, stick, pole, fan) and engage in partner work known as push-hands. They use traditional Chinese exercise moves and deep breathing and they gain the health and longevity effects, but they are not doing Daoyin.

Yoga, in contrast, comes from the Indian tradition, where complete physical stability and stillness are the prerequisites for successful meditation practice, which alone will uncover the true self and lead to the ultimate goal of oneness with Brahman. Practitioners hold poses for extended periods; they engage in inversions and balancing postures not found in Daoyin; and they work with breathing techniques that involve rasping in the throat *(ujjayi)*, short and gasping breaths *(kapalabhati)*, and the alternate closing of the nostrils *(nadi shodana)*. Also, they tend to focus on single or a few poses, working with proper alignment and detailed awareness of joints and muscles. They do not develop a dance-style continuity, nor do they wave their arms about to create circles of *qi* or connect to the energies of Heaven and Earth. The mind in yoga, moreover, stays focused on the particular body part that is being opened, allowing the breath to work in the area with clear awareness. There is little guiding of *qi* and no active visualization of energies.

Qigong practitioners, on the other hand, do a lot of arm waving and body swinging, engage in deep abdominal breathing, and do much guiding of *qi* and inner visualization. They are the most direct heirs of the ancient exercise tradition. In fact, the only kinds of qigong still allowed in China today are four forms of Daoyin. The distinction in actual practice is minimal, although since qigong in China has generally been undertaken in parks, where lying down is not practical, most new forms tend to be executed while standing. Followers rarely work with the reclining and seated parts of the practice and—with the exception of the sectarian groups of the 1990s—for the most part relegate the restful, calm, and meditative dimension of traditional Daoyin to a minor position.

If one sees one person practicing qigong and another doing Daoyin, the likelihood is that one practitioner will work more from a standing position than the other, but there really is very little obvious difference in practice and execution. The lines are likely to blur even further. As qigong, after its excursions into extraordinary powers and religious cults, comes back to being mainly a healing modality and as it is increasingly integrated into modern institutions that have warm and carpeted facilities, more traditional forms are recovered while new patterns evolve that work specifically with the ailments of intense, high-tech societies—lower-back pain, tension headaches, mental stress, and the like. This is already the case in China, where TCM doctors and longevity followers are going back to ancient Daoyin texts and creating forms connected to manuscript charts. It is increasingly the case in the West, where Daoist and other masters present their unique version of exercises, often combining *qi*-awareness with yoga, and where all kinds of specialized practices are emerging: for liver ailments, for eye trouble, for weight loss, and many more. All these forms, then, are gradually making their way into the medical establishment, offering the public new healing modalities and contributing to the active continuation of the age-old tradition of Chinese healing exercises.

Original Sources

Baopuzi neipian 抱朴子內篇 (Inner Chapters of the Master Who Embraces Simplicity, *DZ* 1185), by Ge Hong 葛洪 (283–343), southern aristocrat and would-be alchemist who provided the first and most comprehensive account of Chinese alchemy. For a study, see Needham and Lu 1974; Pregadio 2000. The text is translated in Ware 1966. The "Outer Chapters," which focus more on traditional thought and social issues, are translated in Sailey 1978.

Baopuzi yangsheng lun 抱朴子養生論 (Nourishing Life According to the Master Who Embraces Simplicity, *DZ* 842), short spin-off of the fourth-century *Baopuzi* (chs. 13, 18) for a general readership on the benefits of moderation and basic longevity practices.

Baosheng ming 保生銘 (On Preserving Life, *DZ* 835), a concise treatise extolling moderation, a regular lifestyle, and virtuous attitudes.

Beiyou ji (Journey to the North), seventeenth-century novel by Yu Xiangdou 余象鬥 on the adventures and divine progress of the Dark Warrior (Xuanwu 玄武) over several reincarnations. It is translated and discussed in Seaman 1987.

Chifeng sui 赤鳳髓 (Marrow of the Red Phoenix; ed. Xinwenfeng, 1987; trl. Despeux 1988), a collection of longevity methods by Zhou Lüjing 周履靖, dated to 1578. The text contains most of the practices still undertaken today, such as the Five Animals' Frolic, the Eight Brocades, and the Six Breaths.

Cunshen lianqi ming 存神練氣銘 (On the Visualization of Spirit and Refinement of *Qi*, *DZ* 400; trl. Kohn 1987, 119–124), a concise outline of five major stages of the mind in concentrative meditation plus seven stages of the self as it transcends to immortality.

Danjing yaojue 丹經要訣 (Essential Formulas of Alchemical Classics, *Yunji qiqian* 71; trl. Sivin 1968), by Sun Simiao (581–682), a report on alchemical experiments that also presents various formulas for preparing immortality elixirs;

Daolin shesheng lun 道林攝生論 (Discourse on Protecting Life by Master Daolin, *DZ* 1427), a short work that provides a general outline of longevity practice in six sections: General Issues, Timing, Taboos, Massages, Breathing, and Residences. The text is ascribed to Daolin 道林, commonly identified as Zhi Dun 支盾 (314–366), one of the earliest aristocratic Buddhists in Chinese history and a popular figure among authors of long-life texts.

Daoshi jushan xiulian ke 道士居山修鍊科 (Rules on Refining Cultivation for Daoist Masters and Mountain Hermits, *DZ* 1272), a Tang-dynasty outline of basic practices and precepts prescribed for ordained Daoists who wish to specialize in physical refinement.

Daoyin jing (Scripture on Healing Exercises, *DZ* 818), partly reprinted in *Yunji qiqian* 雲
  笈七籤 (Seven Tablets in a Cloudy Satchel, *DZ* 1032, ch. 34) of the eleventh century;
  and in *Daoshu* 道樞 (Pivot of the Dao, *DZ* 1017, ch. 28) of the twelfth century. The
  latter version is translated in Huang and Wurmbrand 1987, 2:134–143). Mentioned
  in various Song bibliographies and cited in various Tang sources, the text may well
  go back to the fifth or sixth century. For a discussion, see Despeux 1989, 230–231.

Daoyin tu 導引圖 (Exercise Chart), a Mawangdui manuscript that contains forty-four
  color illustrations of human figures performing therapeutic exercises together with
  brief captions. The chart is reprinted in Wenwu 1975 and translated in Harper
  1998, 310–327. For a study, see Engelhardt 2001; Leong 2001.

Dengzhen yinjue 登真隱訣 (Secret Instructions on the Ascent to the Perfected, *DZ* 421),
  by Tao Hongjing of the early sixth century. For studies and partial translations, see
  Strickmann 1981; Cedzich 1987.

Ershisi qi zuogong daoyin zhibing tushuo 二十四坐功導引治病圖說 (Twenty-four Illustrated Seated Exercise Practices to Heal Diseases, ed. *Neiwai gong tushuo jiyao,* pp.
  133–181), a short illustrated treatise on seated exercises undertaken in the rhythm
  of the solar nodes. Associated with the Song immortal Chen Tuan, the text probably goes back to the late Ming.

Fengshen yanyi (Creation of the Gods; trl. Gu 1992), by Xu Zhonglin (d. 1566) or Lu Xix-
  ing (ca. 1520–1601), a fictional account of the fight of the Zhou against the last ty-
  rant of the Shang with many martial scenes and active celestial involvement.

Fulu lun 福錄論 (On Happiness and Prosperity, lost), a text on long life by Sun Simiao
  (581–682) according to early bibliographies. Probably identical with the *Fushou lun*
  (see below).

Fuqi jingyi lun 服氣精義論 (The Essential Meaning of *Qi*-Absorption), by Sima Chengzhen (641–735), patriarch of Highest Clarity under the Tang. The text outlines the
  different aspects of physical cultivation in nine steps beginning with healing and
  ending with the absoption of *qi*. It is studied and translated with ample annotation
  in Engelhardt 1987.

Fushou danshu 福壽丹書 (Elixir Book on Long Life and Good Fortune), dated to 1621, an
  collection of longevity practice and immortality recipes. It was translated by John
  Dudgeon in the nineteenth century and is today found in Berk 1986, 57–62.

Fushou lun 福壽論 (On Happiness and Long Life, *DZ* 1426), a presentation of the workings of
  fate and various ways to enhance it that was probably written by Sun Simiao (581–682).

Han Wudi waizhuan 漢武帝外傳 (Outer Record of Emperor Wu of the Han, *DZ* 293), a
  Highest Clarity collection of stories on the famous Han emperor and his various
  immortal advisers that dates from the fifth century. A translation and study is
  found in Smith 1992.

He yinyang (Harmonizing Yin and Yang), a Mawangdui medical manuscript on sexual
  cultivation. It is translated in Harper 1998, 412–422. For a study, see Engelhardt
  2000. As all Mawangdui manuscripts, the text was reprinted in *Wenwu* once it had
  been rendered legible by archaeologists.

Huainanzi 淮南子 (Book of the Master of Huainan, *DZ* 1184), an important Daoist collection of the mid-second century B.C.E. On the origin and editions of the text, see Roth 1992. Partial translations appear in Kraft 1957; Larre 1985; Major 1993; Larre, Robinet, and de la Valle 1993. For studies of its thought, see Ames 1983; LeBlanc 1985; LeBlanc and Mathieu 1992; Vankeerberghen 2001.

Huangdi Hama jing 蝦蟆經 (Toad Classic of the Yellow Emperor), a text related to the *Huangdi neijing* that survived in Japan but probably goes back to the seventh century, if not before. For a study and analysis, see Lo 2001a.

Huangdi neijing 黃帝內經 (Yellow Emperor's Inner Classic; ed. Renmin weisheng), main source of traditional Chinese medicine, extant in several versions: (1) *Huangdi neijing suwen* (Simple Questions; trl. Veith 1972; Lu 1987; Ni 1995), edited by Wang Bing in 762; (2) *Huangdi neijing lingshu* (*Divine Pivot*; trl. Ki 1985; Wu 1993), edited by Yang Shanshan around the year 600; (3) *Huangdi neijing taisu* (Great Simplicity), also edited around the year 600 but not translated to date; (4) *Huangdi bashiyi nanjing* (Eighty-one Difficult Issues; trl. Unschuld 1986), which also goes back to around 600, was transmitted as a key manual to Korea and Japan and has remained popular among acupuncturists there.

Huangting jing 黃庭經 (Yellow Court Scripture, *DZ* 332), fourth-century scripture on visualization of body gods and interior cultivation, closely associated with Highest Clarity but in its older (outer) form preceding the revelations. On the nature and date of the text, see Robinet 1993, 55–56; Mugitani 1982; Schipper 1975a; Schipper and Verellen 2004, 96–97. For partial translations and studies, see Kohn 1993, 181–188; Kroll 1996; Saso 1995.

Huanzhen neiqi fa 幻真內氣法 (Master Huanzhen's Method of Internal *Qi*, *DZ* 828, *YJQQ* 60.14a–25ba), a text on breathing that contains a preface that mentions the Tianbao reign period (742–755) of the high Tang. For a brief discussion, see Maspero 1981, 460–461.

Huashan shier shuigong zongjue 華山十二睡功總訣 (Comprehensive Explanation of the Twelve Sleep Exercises of Mount Hua; ed. *Chifeng sui*, pp. 133–153), a presentation of twelve pictures of sleeping immortals together with their names and poems on their inner alchemical trance activities.

Ishinpō 醫心方 (Essential Medical Methods, ed. Xinwenfeng, 1976), an important medical compendium by the court physician Tamba no Yasuyori 丹波瀨康 (912–995). The text was presented to the Japanese emperor in 984. Especially its later chapters focus on nourishing life: chapter 26 is on facial treatments, magical methods, and grain abstention; chapter 27 deals with breathing techniques, mental cultivation, healing exercises, clothing, and the arrangement of living quarters; and chapter 28 presents materials on sexual practices (trl. Ishihara and Levi 1970; Wile 1992). Chapters 29 and 30 treat diets and the way of healthful eating. The text is translated in Hsia, Veith, and Geertsma 1986. For its role in the Japanese longevity tradition, see Sakade 1989.

Laojun yangsheng jue 老君養生訣 (Lord Lao's Instructions on Nourishing Life, *DZ* 821), a late Tang text that contains instructions on physical exercises such as the Five

Animals' Frolic and visualization practices, such as surrounding oneself with the
four heraldic animals. For a brief summary, see Kohn 1998, 130–131.

Laozi zhongjing 老子中經 (Central Scripture of Laozi, *DZ* 1168), fourth-century manual
on the visualization of body gods. On the origin and history of the text, see Schipper 1979.

Liexian zhuan 列仙傳 (Immortals' Biographies, *DZ* 294), a collection of seventy short accounts of the practices and lives of early immortals, associated with Liu Xiang 劉向
(77–76 B.C.E.). A complete translation with detailed annotation is found in Kaltenmark 1953.

Maishu 脈書 (Channel Book), manuscript unearthed at Zhangjia shan from a tomb closed
in 186 B.C.E. It outlines the major energy channels as known at the time. A full translation will appear in Lo forthcoming. The text is edited in Wenwu 1989; Ikai 2004.

Neiwai gong tushuo jiyao 內外功圖說輯要 (Collected Essentials and Illustrated Descriptions of Inner and Outer Practices, *Daozang jinghua* 2.10), a Qing-dynasty collection of various texts on physical cultivation, including regular exercises for the
seasons, the Five Animals' Frolic, and methods attributed to various immortals.

Pengzu shesheng yangxing lun 彭祖攝生養性論 (Preserving Life and Nourishing Inner
Nature as Practiced by Pengzu, *DZ* 840), short summary of key attitudes and practices for long life similar to the *Yangsheng yaoji* and accordingly dated to the fourth
century.

Qianjin fang 千金方 (Priceless Prescriptions, ed. Renmin weisheng, 1992), a general outline of medical methods and prescriptions in thirty *juan* by Sun Simiao (581–682).
It discusses pharmacological therapy (chs. 2–25), dietetics (ch. 26), longevity techniques (ch. 27), pulse diagnosis (ch. 28), acupuncture and moxibustion (chs. 29–30).
A general outline of the book is found in Unschuld 1985, 18–24. The last two chapters are translated in Despeux 1987. For a discussion of its dietetics, see Engelhardt
and Hempen 1997.

Qianjin yaofang 千金要方 (Essential Priceless Prescriptions, *DZ* 1163), in ninety-three
juan and 232 sections, a major medical compendium by Sun Simiao (581–682). The
text contains various prefaces and some additions from Song writers. It deals with
the full contingent of medical methods, focusing particularly on drug therapy and
dedicating three *juan* to long life practices (chs. 81–83).

Qianjin yifang 千金翼方 (Supplementary Priceless Prescriptions; ed. Renmin weisheng,
1983), by Sun Simiao (581–682), another detailed medical collection, with one
chapter (ch. 12) on "Nourishing Inner Nature." It was edited and revised in the
Song dynasty (Sivin 1968, 138).

Quegu shiqi 卻穀食氣 (Eliminating Grains and Absorbing *Qi*), a Mawangdui text on fasting by means of breathing exercises. Edited in *Wenwu,* it is translated in Harper
1998, 305–309.

Shangqing wozhong jue 上清握中訣 (Highest Clarity Instructions to Be Kept in Hand, *DZ*
140), a set of instructions on physical practices and visualization associated with the
Highest Clarity revelations. Many passages appear also in chapter 10 of the *Zhen'gao.*

Shenxian shiqi jin'gui miaolu 神仙食氣金櫃妙錄 (Wondrous Record of the Golden Casket on the Spirit Immortals' Practice of Eating *Qi, DZ* 836), ascribed to Master Jingli 京里 or Jinghei 京黑 who supposedly lived in the fourth century. The text may be a Tang compilation but in contents predates the Sui. See Loon 1984, 130; Schipper and Verellen 2004, 355. A modern Chinese presentation of its practices is found in Ma 1999.

Shesheng zuanlu 攝生纂錄 (Comprehensive Record on Preserving Life, *DZ* 578), a collection of longevity methods by Wang Zhongqiu 王仲丘 of the mid-Tang. The text is translated partly in Huang and Wurmbrand 1987, 2:75–90.

Sheyang lun 攝養論 (On Preserving and Nourishing [Life], *DZ* 841), by Sun Simiao (581–682), an account of dietary and other health methods for each of the twelve months of the year.

Shiwen 十問 (Ten Questions), a Mawangdui medical manuscript on longevity practices. It is translated in Harper 1998, 385–411. For a study, see Engelhardt 2000.

Siji diaoshe zhelu 四季調攝摘錄 (Record of Harmonizing and Balancing in Accordance with the Four Seasons; ed. *Neiwai gong tushuo jiyao,* pp. 89–131. Closely resembling earlier seasonal instructions by Sun Simiao, it outlines how to keep the organs healthy month by month.

Taishang yangsheng taixi qi jing 太上養生胎息氣經 (Highest Qi Scripture on Nourishing Life through Embryo Respiration, *DZ* 819), a Tang text on *qi* absorption and visualization of energies in accordance with daily cycles. It is translated and discussed in Jackowicz 2003.

Taiwu xiansheng fuqi fa 太無先生服氣法 (Master Taiwu's Method of *Qi*-Absorption, *DZ* 824, *Yunji qiqian* 59.8b–10a), allegedly by Master Taiwu, otherwise unknown, who met an immortal from Mount Luofu during the Dali period (766–779). It contains similar methods as the *Huanzhen neiqi fa.*

Tianxia zhidao tan 天下至道談 (Discussion of the Perfect Way in All under Heaven), a Mawangdui medical text on ways to align oneself with the Dao. It is translated in Harper 1998, 425–438.

Wuqin wu gongfa tushuo 五禽舞功法圖說 (Illustrated Explanation of Five Animal Dance Practice; ed. *Neiwai gong tushuo jiyao,* pp. 183–198), an illustrated outline of the Five Animals, Frolic especially for women.

Xiuzhen shishu 修真十書 (Ten Books on the Cultivation of Perfection, *DZ* 263), an extensive compendium in ten *juan* that dates from the thirteenth to fourteenth centuries and collects various materials on the practice of longevity and inner alchemy,

Xiwangmu baoshen qiju jing (The Queen Mother's Scripture on Treasuring the Spirit Whether Rising or Resting, *DZ* 1319), and early Shangqing document that matches certain passages in the *Zhen'gao*. It focuces on health maintenance and outlines daily regimens and self-massages. For a brief description, see Despeux 1989.

Xuxian zhuan 續仙傳 (Supplementary Immortals' Biographies, *DZ* 295), by Shen Fen 沈汾 of the Five Dynasties (tenth cent.), a collection of thirty-six immortals' biographies arranged according to their ascension method. For more details, see Penny 2000, 121.

Yangsheng fang 養生方 (Recipes for Nourishing Life), a Mawangdui medical text on various longevity techniques. It is translated in Harper 1998, 328–362.

Yangsheng yaoji 養生要集 (Long Life Compendium; lost), attributed to the *Liezi* commentator Zhang Zhan 張湛 of the fourth century. Already listed by title in Ge Hong library catalog, the text was lost after the mid-Tang. A main source of fragments is the Japanese medical compendium *Ishimpo*. For studies, see Sakade 1986a, Despeux 1989. A complete compilation and translation of fragments is found in Stein 1999.

Yangxing yanming lu 養性延命錄 (On Nourishing Inner Nature and Extending Life, *DZ* 838; *Yunji qiqian* 32.1a–24b), a collection of long-life practices in six sections associated either with Tao Hongjing (456–536) or Sun Simiao (581–682). From references in the text and overall style, it is likely of the early Tang and may well have been compiled by Sun's disciples. Its sections on diet and general precautions are translated in Switkin 1987. A complete annotated Japanese rendition is found in Mugitani 1987.

Yanshou chishu 延壽赤書 (Red Book of Master Yanshou, *DZ* 877), a set of instructions on physical practices and visualization associated with the Highest Clarity revelations.

Yijin jing (Sinews Transformation Classic, ed. *Neiwai gong tushuo jiyao*, pp. 267–292), a treatise outlining twelve exercises to strengthen tendons and ligaments. The text has appeared in various editions (and with increasingly more ancient prefaces) since the seventeenth century. It is translated in Berk 1986, 148–151.

Yinshu 引書 (Stretch Book), manuscript unearthed at Zhangjia shan from a tomb closed in 186 B.C.E. It outlines the major energy channels as known at the time. A full translation will appear in Lo forthcoming. The text is edited in Wenwu 1989; Ikai 2004.

Zhen'gao 真誥 (Declarations of the Perfected, *DZ* 1016), a major collection of Highest Clarity documents and revelation by the first patriarch of the school, Tao Hongjing (456–536), dated to 500. The text has has been studied extensively by Japanese scholars. See Ishii 1990; Kamitsuka 1999; Mugitani 1991; Yoshikawa 1992, 1998. For Western studies, see Robinet 1984.

Zhenzhong ji 枕中記 (Pillowbook Record, *DZ* 837, *Yunji qiqian* 33.1a–12a), a collection of longevity techniques in five sections by Sun Simiao (581–682). For a study, see Engelhardt 1989.

Zhiyan zong 至言總 (Collection of Perfect Words; *DZ* 1033), by Fan Youran 范脩然, a late Tang work on nourishing life, containing numerous fragments and citations or earlier works. A thorough study is found in Yoshioka 1967. The "Exercise" section is translated in Huang and Wurmbrand 1987, 2:40–46.

Zhubing yuanhou lun 諸病源候論 (Origins and Symptoms of Medical Disorders; ed. Weisheng chubanshe), compiled upon imperial command by Chao Yuanfang et al. and presented to the emperor in 610. It is the first Chinese medical text to include longevity methods for various diseases, which are classified according to symptoms. A recent Chinese study is found in Ding 1993. A translation into French appears in Despeux and Obringer 1997.

Zhuxian daoyin tu 諸仙導引圖 (Illustrated Exercises of the Various Immortals, ed. Nei-wai gong tushuo, pp. 1–86), a series of immortals showing healing exercises with explanations.

Zunsheng bajian 尊生八牋 (Eight Folios on Honoring Life), a longevity manual by Gaolian Shenfu 高濂深甫 of the late Ming dynasty. Translated by John Dudgeon, it is found today in Berk 1986, 19–47.

Zuowang lun 坐忘論 (On Sitting in Oblivion, *DZ* 1036), by Sima Chengzhen (641–735), a formal text based on an inscription dated 829. It presents an outline of seven steps that can be attained in Daoist meditation, including the successful interception of karmic causes, control over the mind, a detachment from the affairs of ordinary life, a understanding vision of what life and death are all about, and a sense of one-ness with the Dao. A translation and study is found in Kohn 1987.

Bibliography

Allan, Sarah, and Crispin Williams, eds. 2000. *The Guodian Laozi.* Berkeley: Society for the Study of Early China and Institute of East Asian Studies, University of California.

Ames, Roger. 1983. *The Art of Rulership: A Study in Ancient Chinese Political Thought.* Honolulu: University of Hawai'i Press.

Andersen, Poul. 1980. *The Method of Holding the Three Ones.* London and Malmo: Curzon Press.

Arthur, Shawn. 2006. "Life without Grains: *Bigu* and the Daoist Body." In *Daoist Body Cultivation,* edited by Livia Kohn, 91–122. Magdalena, N.M.: Three Pines Press.

Baldrian-Hussein, Farzeen. 1984. *Procédés secrets du joyau magique.* Paris: Les Deux Océans.

———. 1990. "Inner Alchemy: Notes on the Origin and the Use of the Term *neidan.*" *Cahiers d'Extrême-Asie* 5:163–190.

Barrett, T. H. 1980. "On the Transmission of the *Shen tzu* and of the *Yang-sheng yao-chi.*" *Journal of the Royal Asiatic Society* 2:168–176.

———. 1996. *Taoism under the T'ang: Religion and Empire during the Golden Age of Chinese History.* London: Wellsweep Press.

Becker, Robert O., and Gary Sheldon. 1985. *The Body Electric: Electromagnetism and the Foundation of Life.* New York: William Morrow.

Benn, Charles. 2002. *China's Golden Age: Everyday Life in the Tang Dynasty.* New York: Oxford University Press.

Berk, William R. 1986 [1895]. *Chinese Healing Arts: Internal Kung-Fu.* Burbank, Calif.: Unique Publications.

Berkowitz, Alan J. 1989. "Patterns of Reclusion in Early and Medieval China." Ph.D. Diss., University of Washington, Seattle.

Bidlack, Bede. 2006. "Taiji Quan: Forms, Visions, and Effects." In *Daoist Body Cultivation,* edited by Livia Kohn, 179–202. Magdalena, N.M.: Three Pines Press.

Broman, Swen. 1978. "Eight Immortals Crossing the Sea." *Bulletin of the Museum of Far Eastern Antiquities* 50:25–43.

Cahill, Suzanne. 1985. "Sex and the Supernatural in Medieval China: Cantos on the Transcendent Who Presides Over the River." *Journal of the American Oriental Society* 105:197–220.

Campany, Robert F. 2002. *To Live as Long as Heaven and Earth: A Translation and Study of Ge Hong's* Traditions of Divine Transcendents. Berkeley: University of California Press.

Cedzich, Ursula-Angelika. 1987. "Das Ritual der Himmelsmeister im Spiegel früher Quellen." Ph.D. Diss., University of Würzburg.

Chan, Alan. 1991. *Two Visions of the Way: A Study of the Wang Pi and the Ho-shang-kung Commentaries on the* Laozi. Albany: State University of New York Press.

Chang, Maria Hsia. 2004. *Falungong: The End of Days*. New Haven, Conn.: Yale University Press.

Chau, Adam Yuet. 2005. *Miraculous Response: Doing Popular Religion in Contemporary China*. Stanford, Calif.: Stanford University Press.

Chen Banghuai 陳邦准. 1982. "Zhanguo 'Xingqi yuming' kaoshi" 戰國行氣玉銘考試. *Guwenzi yanjiu* 古文子研究 20:485–576.

Chen, Ellen Marie. 1974. "Tao as the Great Mother and the Influence of Motherly Love in the Shaping of Chinese Philosophy." *History of Religions* 14:51–65.

Chen, Nancy N. 2003. *Breathing Spaces: Qigong, Psychiatry, and Healing in China*. New York: Columbia University Press.

Chen Yingning 陈撄宁. 2000. *Daojiao yu yangsheng* 道教与养生. Beijing: Huawen.

Chia, Mantak. 1999. *Tao Yin: Exercises for Revitalization, Health, and Longevity*, edited by Dennis Huntington and Lee Holden. Chiang Mai: Universal Tao Publications.

———. 2003. *Taoist Cosmic Healing: Chi Kung Color Healing Principles for Detoxification and Rejuvenation*. Rochester, Vt.: Destiny Books.

———. 2005. *Energy Balance through the Tao: Exercises for Cultivating Yin Energy*. Rochester, Vt.: Destiny Books.

———, and Maneewan Chia. 1993. *Awaken Healing Light of the Tao*. Huntington, N.Y.: Healing Tao Books.

———. 1994. "Tao-In: Regaining a Youthful Body." Video presentation. 2 cassettes. Dunsmore, Penn.: International Healing Dao.

Chiu, Martha Li. 1986. "Mind, Body, and Illness in a Chinese Medical Tradition." Ph.D. Dissertation, Harvard University.

Chopra, Deepak. 1993. *Ageless Body, Timeless Mind: The Quantum Alternative to Growing Old*. New York: Harmony Books.

Chu, Valentin. 1993. *The Yin-Yang Butterfly*. New York: Putnam.

Cibik, Ted J. 2003. *Air Passages: Surviving Asthma Naturally*. Leechburg, Penn.: Oak Tree Productions.

Cleary, Thomas. 1987. *Understanding Reality: A Taoist Alchemical Classic by Chang Po-tuan*. Honolulu: University of Hawai'i Press.

———. 1992. *The Secret of the Golden Flower: The Classic Chinese Book of Life*. San Francisco: Harper.

Cohen, Kenneth S. 1997. *The Way of Qigong: The Art and Science of Chinese Energy Healing*. New York: Ballantine.

Cope, Stephen. 2000. *Yoga and the Quest for True Self*. New York: Bantam.

Darga, Martina. 1999. *Das alchemistische Buch von innerem Wesen und Lebensenergie: Xingming guizhi*. Munich: Diederichs.

Davis, Barbara. 2004. *The Taiji quan Classics: An Annotated Translation.* Berkeley, Calif.: North Atlantic Books.

DeMeyer, Jan. 2006. *Wu Yun's Way: Life and Works of an Eighth-Century Daoist Master.* Leiden: E. Brill.

Despeux, Catherine. 1979. *Zhao Bizhen: Traité d'alchimie et de physiologie taoïste.* Paris: Guy Trédaniel.

———. 1987. *Préscriptions d'acuponcture valant mille onces d'or.* Paris: Guy Trédaniel.

———. 1988. *La moélle du phénix rouge: Santé et longue vie dans la Chine du seiziéme siècle.* Paris: Editions Trédaniel.

———. 1989. "Gymnastics: The Ancient Tradition." In *Taoist Meditation and Longevity Techniques,* edited by Livia Kohn, 223–261. Ann Arbor: University of Michigan, Center for Chinese Studies Publications.

———. 1995. "L'expiration des six souffles d'après les sources du Canon taoïque: Un procédé classique du Qigong." In *Hommage a Kwong Hing Foon: Etudes d'histoire culturelle de la Chine,* edited by Jean-Pierre Diény, 129–163. Paris: Collège du France, Institut des Hautes Etudes Chinoises.

———. 2004. "La gymnastique *daoyin* dans la Chine ancienne." *Etudes chinoises* 23:45–86.

———. 2006. "The Six Healing Breaths." In *Daoist Body Cultivation,* edited by Livia Kohn, 37–67. Magdalena, N.M.: Three Pines Press.

———, and Livia Kohn. 2003. *Women in Daoism.* Cambridge, Mass.: Three Pines Press.

———, and Frederic Obringer, eds. 1997. *La maladie dans la Chine médiévale: La toux.* Paris: Editions L'Harmattan.

DeWoskin, Kenneth J. 1983. *Doctors, Diviners, and Magicians of Ancient China.* New York: Columbia University Press

Dien, Albert E. 1995. "Instructions for the Grave: The Case of Yan Zhitui." *Cahiers d'Extrême-Asie* 8:41–58.

Dikotter, Frank. 1998. "Hairy Barbarians, Furry Primates, and Wild Men: Medical Science and Cultural Representations of Hair in China." In *Hair: Its Power and Meaning in Asian Cultures,* edited by Alf Hiltebeitel and Barbara D. Miller, 51–74. Albany: State University of New York Press.

Ding Guangdi 丁光迪. 1993. *Zhubing yuanhou lun yangsheng fang daoyin fa yanjiu* 諸病源候論養生方導引法研究. Beijing: Weisheng chubanshe.

Eberhard, Wolfram. 1949. *Dao Toba-Reich Nordchinas.* Leiden: E. Brill.

Eisenberg, David. 1985. *Encounters with Qi: Exploring Chinese Medicine.* New York: Norton.

Eliade, Mircea. 1969. *Patanjali and Yoga.* New York: Funk and Wagnalls.

Engelhardt, Ute. 1987. *Die klassische Tradition der Qi-Übungen. Eine Darstellung anhand des Tang-zeitlichen Textes Fuqi jingyi lun von Sima Chengzhen.* Wiesbaden: Franz Steiner.

———. 1989. "Qi for Life: Longevity in the Tang." In *Taoist Meditation and Longevity Techniques,* edited by Livia Kohn, 263–294. Ann Arbor: University of Michigan, Center for Chinese Studies Publications.

———. 1996. "Zur Bedeutung der Atmung im Qigong." *Chinesische Medizin* 1:17–23.

——. 1998. "Neue archäologische Funde zur Leitbahntheorie." *Chinesische Medizin* 3:93–100.

——. 2000. "Longevity Techniques and Chinese Medicine." In *Daoism Handbook*, edited by Livia Kohn, 74–108. Leiden: E. Brill.

——. 2001. "*Daoyin tu* und *Yinshu*: Neue Erkenntnisse über die Übungen zur Lebenspflege in der frühen Han-Zeit." *Monumenta Serica* 49:213–226.

——, and Carl-Hermann Hempen. 1997. *Chinesische Dietaetik*. Munich: Urban and Schwarzenberg.

Esposito, Monica. 1998. "The Different Versions of the *Secret of the Golden Flower* and Their Relationship with the Longmen School." *Transactions of the International Conference of Eastern Studies* 43:90–109.

Farhi, Donna. 1996. *The Breathing Book*. New York: Henry Holt.

——. 2000. *Yoga Mind, Body, and Spirit: A Return to Wholeness*. New York: Henry Holt.

——. 2003. *Bringing Yoga to Life*. San Francisco: Harper.

Feinstein, David; Donna Eden; and Gary Craig. 2005. *The Promise of Energy Psychology*. New York: Penguin.

Feldenkrais, M. 1970 [1949]. *Body and Mature Behavior*. New York: International Universities Press.

——. 1972. *Awareness through Movement*. San Francisco: HarperCollins.

Feuerstein, Georg. 1998. *The Yoga Tradition: Its History, Literature, Philosophy and Practice*. Prescott, Ariz.: Hohm Press.

FitzGerald, C. P. 1965. *Barbarian Beds: The Origin of the Chair in China*. London: Cresset Press.

Fried, Robert. 1999. *Breathe Well, Be Well*. New York: John Wiley and Sons.

Fukunaga Mitsuji 福永光司. 1973. "Dōkyō ni okeru kagami to ken" 道教における鑒と檢. *Tōhō gakuhō* 東方學報 45:59–120.

Gach, Michael Reed, and Beth Ann Henning. 2004. *Acupressure for Emotional Healing*. New York: Bantam.

——, and Carolyn Marco. 1981. *Acu-Yoga: Self Help Techniques to Relieve Tension*. New York: Japan Publications.

Galambos, Imre. 2006. *Orthography of Early Chinese Writing: Evidence from Newly Excavated Manuscripts*. Budapest, Hungary: Eötvös Loránd University .

Gallo, Fred, ed. 2004. *Energy Psychology in Psychotherapy*. New York: Norton.

Gao Dalun 高大倫. 1995. *Zhangjiashan hanjian yinshu yanjiu* 張家山漢簡引書研究. Chengdu: Bashu shushe.

Gerber, Richard. 1988. *Vibrational Medicine: New Choices for Healing Ourselves*. Santa Fe, N.M.: Bear and Company.

Goullart, Peter. 1961. *The Monastery of Jade Mountain*. London: John Murray.

Graham, A. C. 1960. *The Book of Lieh-tzu*. London: A. Murray.

——. 1986. *Chuang-tzu: The Inner Chapters*. London: Allen and Unwin.

Granet, Marcel. 1926. *Danses et legendes de la Chine ancienne*. 2 vols. Paris: F. Alcan.

Grilley, Paul. 2002. *Yin Yoga: Outline of a Quiet Practice*. Ashland, Ore.: White Cloud Press.

Grootaers, Willem. 1952. "The Hagiography of the Chinese God Hsüan-wu." *Asian Folklore Studies* 11:139–382.

Gu, Zhizhong, trans. 1992. *Creation of the Gods*. 2 vols. Beijing: New World Press.

Güntsch, Gertrud. 1988. *Das Shen-hsien-chuan und das Erscheinungsbild eines Hsien*. Frankfurt: Peter Lang.

Hackmann, Heinrich. 1920. "Die Mönchsregeln des Klostertaoismus." *Ostasiatische Zeitschrift* 8:141–170.

Hang Sin Tong 恆善堂, ed. 2005. *Wuxiang ji* 無相集. Vol. 2. Hong Kong: Han Sin Tong Publications.

Hanna, Thomas. 1970. *Bodies in Revolt: A Primer in Somatic Thinking*. Novato, Calif.: Freeperson Press.

———. 1980. *The Body of Life*. New York: Alfred A. Knopf.

———. 1988. *Somatics: Reawakening the Mind's Control of Movement, Flexibility, and Health*. Cambridge, Mass.: Perseus Books.

———. 1990. "Clinical Somatic Education: A New Discipline in the Field of Health Care." *Massage Therapy Journal*, Fall, 3–10.

Hansen, Valerie. 1995. "Why Bury Contracts in Tombs?" *Cahiers d'Extrême-Asie* 8:59–66.

Harper, Donald. 1982. "The *Wu Shih Erh Ping Fang*: Translation and Prolegomena." Ph.D. Diss., University of California, Berkeley.

———. 1985a. "The Bellows Analogy in *Laozi* V and Warring States Macrobiotic Hygiene." *Early China* 20:381–391.

———. 1985b. "A Chinese Demonography of the Third Century B.C." *Harvard Journal of Asiatic Studies* 45:459–498.

———. 1998. *Early Chinese Medical Manuscripts: The Mawangdui Medical Manuscripts*. London: Wellcome Asian Medical Monographs.

Hawkes, David. 1959. *Ch'u Tz'u: The Songs of the South*. Oxford: Clarendon Press.

Heise, Thomas. 1999. *Qigong in der VR China: Entwicklung, Theorie und Praxis*. Berlin: Verlag für Wissenschaft und Bildung.

Henricks, Robert. 1989. *Lao-Tzu: Te-Tao ching*. New York: Ballantine.

———. 2000. *Lau Tzu's Tao Te Ching: A Translation of the Startling New Documents Found at Guodian*. New York: Columbia University Press.

Holzman, Donald. 1967. "A propos de l'origine de la chaise en Chine." *T'oung Pao* 53:279–292.

Hsia, Emil C. H.; Ilza Veith; and Robert H. Geertsma, trans. 1986. *The Essentials of Medicine in Ancient China and Japan: Yasuyori Tamba's Ishimpō*. 2 vols. Leiden: E. Brill.

Hsu, Elisabeth. 1999. *The Transmission of Chinese Medicine*. Cambridge: Cambridge University Press.

———, ed. 2001. *Innovation in Chinese Medicine*. Cambridge: Cambridge University Press.

Huang, Jane, and Michael Wurmbrand. 1987. *The Primordial Breath: Ancient Chinese Ways of Prolonging Life Through Breath*. 2 vols. Torrance, Calif.: Original Books.

Ikai Yoshio 豬飼祥夫. 1995. "Kōryō Chōkasan kanken Myakusho to Insho no seikaku"

江陵張家山漢簡脈書と引書の性格. In *Shin shutsudo shiryō ni yoru Chūgoku kodai igaku no kenkyū* 新出土資料による中國古代醫學の研究, edited by Yoshinobu Sakade 扳出祥伸, 26–38. Osaka: Kansai daigaku kenkyū hōkō.

———. 2002. "Chōkasan kanbo kanken Insho ni miru *ki* ni tsuite" 張家山漢墓漢簡引書に見る氣について. *Itan* 醫譚 78:30–32.

———. 2003. "Chōkasan kanbo kanken Insho ni miru *dō* to *in* ni tsuite" 張家山漢墓漢簡引書に見る導と引について. *Itan* 醫譚 79:33–35.

———. 2004. "Kōryō Chōkasan kanken Insho yakuchūkō" 江陵張家山漢簡引書釋註. Draft paper. Used by permission of the author.

Ishida, Hidemi. 1989. "Body and Mind: The Chinese Perspective." In *Taoist Meditation and Longevity Techniques,* edited by Livia Kohn, 41–70. Ann Arbor: University of Michigan, Center for Chinese Studies Publications.

Ishihara, Akira, and Howard S. Levy. 1970. *The Tao of Sex.* New York: Harper and Row.

Ishii Masako 石井昌子. 1990. *Shinkō* 真誥. Tokyo: Meitoku.

Iyengar, B. K. S. 1976. *Light on Yoga.* New York: Schocken Books.

Jackowicz, Stephen. 2003. "The Mechanics of Spirit: An Examination of the Absorption of *Qi.*" Ph.D. Diss., Boston University.

———. 2006. "Ingestion, Digestion, and Regestation: The Complexities of the Absorption of *Qi.*" In *Daoist Body Cultivation,* edited by Livia Kohn, 68–90. Magdalena, N.M.: Three Pines Press.

Jahnke, Roger. 1997. *The Healer Within: Using Traditional Chinese Techniques to Release Your Body's Own Medicine.* San Francisco: HarperCollins.

———. 2002. *The Healing Promise of Qi: Creating Extraordinary Wellness through Qigong and Tai Chi.* New York: Contemporary Books.

Johnson, Jerry Alan. 2000. *Chinese Medical Qigong Therapy: A Comprehensive Clinical Text.* Pacific Grove, Calif.: International Institute of Medical Qigong.

Kaltenmark, Max. 1953. *Le Lie-sien tchouan.* Peking: Universite de Paris Publications.

Kamitsuka Yoshiko 神塚淑子. 1999. *Rikuchō dōkyō shisō no kenkyū* 六朝道教思想の研究外. Tokyo: Sōbunsha.

Kaptchuk, Ted J. 2000. *The Web That Has No Weaver: Understanding Chinese Medicine.* New York: Contemporary Books.

Khalsa, Dharma Singh, and Cameron Stauth. 2001. *Meditation as Medicine: Activate the Power of Your Natural Healing Force.* New York: Fireside.

Ki, Sunu. 1985. *The Canon of Acupuncture: Huangti Nei Ching Ling Shu.* Los Angeles: Yuin University Press.

Kieschnick, John. 2003. *The Impact of Buddhism on Chinese Material Culture.* Princeton, N.J.: Princeton University Press.

Kirkland, Russell. 1997. "Dimensions of Tang Taoism: The State of the Field at the End of the Millenium." *T'ang Studies* 15–16:79–123.

Knaster, Mirka. 1989. "Thomas Hanna: Mind over Movement." *Massage Therapy Journal,* Fall, 46–62.

Knaul, Livia. 1981. *Leben und Legende des Ch'en T'uan.* Frankfurt: Peter Lang.

Kohn, Livia. 1987. *Seven Steps to the Tao: Sima Chengzhen's Zuowanglun.* Monumenta
    Serica Monograph 20. St.Augustin/Nettetal: Monumenta Serica.
———. 1988. "A Mirror of Auras: Chen Tuan on Physiognomy." *Asian Folklore Studies*
    47:215–256.
———. 1989a. "Guarding the One: Concentrative Meditation in Taoism." In *Taoist Medi-
    tation and Longevity Techniques,* edited by Livia Kohn, 123–156. Ann Arbor: Uni-
    versity of Michigan, Center for Chinese Studies Publications.
———. 1989b. "Taoist Insight Meditation: The Tang Practice of *Neiguan.*" In *Taoist Medi-
    tation and Longevity Techniques,* edited by Livia Kohn, 191–222. Ann Arbor: Uni-
    versity of Michigan, Center for Chinese Studies Publications.
———, ed. 1989c. *Taoist Meditation and Longevity Techniques.* Ann Arbor: University of
    Michigan, Center for Chinese Studies Publications.
———. 1990. "Chen Tuan in History and Legend." *Taoist Resources* 2.1:8–31.
———. 1991. *Taoist Mystical Philosophy: The Scripture of Western Ascension.* Albany: State
    University of New York Press.
———. 1993. *The Taoist Experience: An Anthology.* Albany: State University of New York
    Press.
———. 1998. *God of the Dao: Lord Lao in History and Myth.* Ann Arbor: University of
    Michigan, Center for Chinese Studies.
———. 2001. *Daoism and Chinese Culture.* Cambridge, Mass.: Three Pines Press.
———. 2003a. "Medieval Daoist Ordination: Origins, Structure, and Practices." *Acta Ori-
    entalia* 56:379–398.
———. 2003b. "Monastic Rules in Quanzhen Daoism: As Collected by Heinrich Hack-
    mann." *Monumenta Serica* 51:367–397.
———. 2004a. *Cosmos and Community: The Ethical Dimension of Daoism.* Cambridge,
    Mass.: Three Pines Press.
———. 2004b. *The Daoist Monastic Manual: A Translation of the* Fengdao kejie. New York:
    Oxford University Press.
———. 2005. *Health and Long Life: The Chinese Way.* In cooperation with Stephen Jacko-
    wicz. Cambridge, Mass.: Three Pines Press.
———, ed. 2006a. *Daoist Body Cultivation: Traditional Models and Contemporary
    Practices.* Magdalena, N.M.: Three Pines Press.
———. 2006b. "Yoga and Daoyin." In *Daoist Body Cultivation,* edited by Livia Kohn,
    123–150. Magdalena, N.M.: Three Pines Press.
———. Forthcoming. "Body and Identity." In *New Studies of the Liezi,* edited by Ronnie
    Littlejohn. New York: Oxford Univesity Press.
———, and Russell Kirkland. 2000. "Daoism in the Tang (618–907)." In *Daoism Hand-
    book,* edited by Livia Kohn, 339–383. Leiden: E. Brill.
Komjathy, Louis. 2002. *Title Index to Daoist Collections.* Cambridge, Mass.: Three Pines
    Press.
———. 2006. "Qigong in America." In *Daoist Body Cultivation,* edited by Livia Kohn,
    203–236. Magdalena, N.M.: Three Pines Press.

———. 2007. *Cultivating Perfection: Mysticism and Self-Transformation in Quanzhen Daoism*. Leiden: E. Brill.

Kraft, Eva. 1957. "Zum *Huai-nan-tzu*: Einführung, Übersetzung (Kapitel I und II) und Interpretation." *Monumenta Serica* 16:191–286 and 17 (1958): 128–207.

Krippner, Stanley, and Daniel Rubin, eds. 1974. *Galaxies of Life: A Conference on Kirlian Photography, Acupuncture, and the Human Aura*. Garden City, N.J.: Anchor Books.

Kroll, Paul W. 1996. "Body Gods and Inner Vision: *The Scripture of the Yellow Court*. In *Religions of China in Practice*, edited by Donald S. Lopez Jr., 149–155. Princeton, N.J.: Princeton University Press.

Kuriyama, Shigehisa. 1999. *The Expressiveness of the Body and the Divergence of Greek and Chinese Medicine*. New York: Zone Books.

Kushi, Avaline, and Alex Jack. 1985. *Avaline Kushi's Complete Guide to Macrobiotic Cooking*. New York: Warner.

Kushi, Michio. 1979. *The Book of Dō-In: Exercise for Physical and Spiritual Development*. Tokyo: Japan Publications.

———, and Edward Esko. 1993. *Holistic Health through Macrobiotics*. New York: Japan Publications.

Lagerwey, John. 1987. *Taoist Ritual in Chinese Society and History*. New York: Macmillan.

———. 1992. "The Pilgrimage to Wu-tang Shan." In *Pilgrims and Sacred Sites in China*, edited by Susan Naquin and Chün-fang Yü, 293–332. Berkeley: University of California Press.

Lai, T. C. 1972. *The Eight Immortals*. Hong Kong: Swinden.

Larre, Claude. 1985. *Le traite VII du Houai-nan-tseu*. Taipei, Paris, Hong Kong: Institut Ricci.

———, Isabelle Robinet, and Elisabeth Rochat de la Vallee. 1993. *Les grands traités du Huainan zi*. Paris: Editions du Cerf.

Le Blanc, Charles. 1985. *Huai-nan-tzu: Philosophical Synthesis in Early Han Thought*. Hong Kong: Hong Kong University Press.

———, and Remi Mathieu, eds. 1992. *Mythe et philosophie a l'aube de la Chine imperial: Etudes sur le Huainan zi*. Montreal: Les Presses de l'Universite de Montreal.

Lee, Michael. 1997. *Phoenix Rising Yoga Therapy: A Bridge from Body to Soul*. Deerfield Beach, Fla.: Health Communications.

Leong, Patricia. 2001. "The *Daoyin tu*." Paper presented at the conference "Daoist Cultivation: Traditional Models and Contemporary Practices." Camp Sealth, Vashon Island, Washington.

Lewis, Mark E. 1990. *Sanctioned Violence in Early China*. Albany: State University of New York Press.

Li, Chi. 1962. "The Changing Concept of the Recluse in China." *Harvard Journal of Asiatic Studies* 24:234–247.

Li, Hongzhi. 1999. *Zhuan Falun*. Taipei: Universe Publishing Company.

Li Ling 李零. 1993. *Zhongguo fangshu kao* 中國方術考. Beijing: Renmin Zhongguo chubanshe.

Li, Ling, and Keith McMahon. 1992. "The Contents and Terminology of the Mawangdui Texts on the Arts of the Bedchamber." *Early China* 17:145–485.

Li, Xiuling. 1990. *Healing with Ki-Kou: The Secrets of Ancient Chinese Breathing Techniques*. Baltimore: Agora Health Books.

Li, Yuanguo. 1990. "Chen Tuan's Concepts of the Great Ultimate." *Taoist Resources* 2.1:32–53.

Liu, Ts'un-yan. 1962. *Buddhist and Taoist Influences on Chinese Novels*. Wiesbaden: Harrassowitz.

Liu, Xun. 2001. "In Search of Immortality: Daoist Inner Alchemy in Twentieth-century China." Ph.D. Diss., University of Southern California.

Liu, Zhengcai. 1990. *The Mystery of Longevity*. Beijing: Foreign Languages Press.

Lo, Vivienne. 2000. "Crossing the *Neiguan*, 'Inner Pass': A *Nei/Wai* 'Inner/Outer' Distinction in Early Chinese Medicine." *East Asian Science, Technology, and Medicine* 17:15–65.

———. 2001a. "*Huangdi Hama jing* (Yellow Emperor's Toad Canon)." *Asia Major* 14.2:61–99.

———. 2001b. "The Influence of Nurturing Life Culture on the Development of Western Han Acumoxa Therapy." In *Innovation in Chinese Medicine*, edited by Elisabeth Hsu, 19–50. Cambridge: Cambridge University Press.

———. Forthcoming. *Healing Arts in Early China*. Leiden: E. Brill.

Loehr, James E., and Jeffrey A. Migdow. 1986. *Breathe In, Breathe Out: Inhale Energy and Exhale Stress by Guiding and Controlling Your Breathing*. Alexandria, Va.: Time Life Books.

Loewe, Michael. 1979. *Ways to Paradise: The Chinese Quest for Immortality*. London: George Allan and Unwin.

Loon, Piet van der. 1984. *Taoist Books in the Libraries of the Sung Period*. London: Oxford Oriental Institute.

Louis, Francois. 2003. "The Genesis of an Icon: The Taiji Diagram's Early History." *Harvard Journal of Asiatic Studies* 63:145–196.

Lu, Henry C. 1987. *The Yellow Emperor's Book of Acupuncture*. Blaine, Wash.: Academy of Oriental Heritage.

Lu, Kuan-yü. 1970. *Taoist Yoga: Alchemy and Immortality*. London: Rider.

Ma Daozong 马道宗, ed. 1999. *Zhongguo daojiao yangsheng mijue* 中国道教养生秘诀. Beijing: Zongjiao wenhua chubanshe.

MacRitchie, James. 1997. *The Chi Kung Way*. San Francisco: HarperCollins.

Madsen, Richard, 2000. "Understanding Falungong." *Current History* 2000:243–247.

Major, John S. 1993. *Heaven and Earth in Early Han Thought: Chapters Three, Four, and Five of the* Huainanzi. Albany: State University of New York Press.

Major, John. 1986. "New Light on the Dark Warrior." *Journal of Chinese Religions* 13–14:65–87.

Mao Zedong 毛泽东. 1972 [1917]. *Mao Zedong ji* 毛泽东集. Vol. 1. Beijing: Jinghua.

Maspero, Henri. 1981. *Taoism and Chinese Religion*. Translated by Frank Kierman. Amherst: University of Massachusetts Press.

Mather, Richard. 1976. *A New Account of Tales of the World*. Minneapolis: University of Minnesota Press.

McCall, Timothy. 2007. *Yoga as Medicine: The Yogic Prescription for Health and Healing*. New York: Bantam Dell.

McDermott, Ian, and Joseph O'Connor. 1996. *NLP and Health: Using NLP to Enhance Your Health and Well-Being*. San Francisco: HarperCollins.

Miller, Richard. 2000. *Breathing for Life: Articles on the Art and Science of Breathing*. Sebastopol, Calif.: Anahata Press.

Min Zhiting 閔智亭. 1990. *Daojiao yifan* 道教儀範. Beijing: Zhongguo daojiao xueyuan bianyin.

Mishra, Rammurti S. 1987. *Fundamentals of Yoga: A Handbook of Theory, Practice, and Application*. New York: Harmony Books.

Mitamura, Keiko. 2002. "Daoist Hand Signs and Buddhist Mudras." In *Daoist Identity: History, Lineage, and Ritual*, edited by Livia Kohn and Harold D. Roth, 235–255. Honolulu: University of Hawai'i Press.

Miura, Kunio. 1989. "The Revival of *Qi*: Qigong in Contemporary China." In *Taoist Meditation and Longevity Techniques*, edited by L. Kohn, 329–358. Ann Arbor: University of Michigan, Center for Chinese Studies Publications.

Mori, Yuria. 2002. "Identity and Lineage: The *Taiyi jinhua zongzhi* and the Spirit-Writing Cult to Patriarch Lü in Qing China." In *Daoist Identity: History, Lineage, and Ritual*, edited by Livia Kohn and Harold D. Roth, 165–184. Honolulu: University of Hawai'i Press.

Morris, Andrew D. 2004. *Marrow of the Nation: A History of Sport and Physical Culture in Republican China*. Berkeley: University of California Press.

Mugitani Kunio 麥谷國雄. 1982. "Kōtei naikeikyō shiron" 黃庭內景經試論. *Tōyōbunka* 東洋文化 62:29–61.

———. 1987. "Yōsei enmei roku kunchu" 養性延命錄訓註. *Report of the Study Group on Traditional Chinese Longevity Techniques*, no. 3. Tokyo: Mombushō.

———. 1991. *Shinkō sakuin* 真誥索引. Kyoto: Dōhōsha.

Nadeau, Robert, and Menas Kafatos. 1999. *The Non-Local Universe: New Physics and Matters of the Mind*. New York: Oxford University Press.

Nathan, Peter. 1969. *The Nervous System*. Harmondsworth: Penguin.

Needham, Joseph, and Lu Gwei-Djen. 1974. *Science and Civilisation in China*. Vol. 5: *Chemistry and Chemical Technology*. Part 2: *Spagyrical Discovery and Invention: Magisteries of Gold and Immortality*. Cambridge: Cambridge University Press.

Needham, Joseph; Ho Ping-Yu [Peng-Yoke]; and Lu Gwei-djen. 1976. *Science and Civilisation in China*. Vol. 5. Part 3: *Spagyrical Discovery and Invention: Historical Survey, from Cinnabar Elixir to Synthetic Insulin*. Cambridge: Cambridge University Press.

Needham, Joseph, and Lu Gwei-djen. 1983. *Science and Civilisation in China*. Vol. 5. Part 5: *Spagyrical Discovery and Invention: Physiological Alchemy*. Cambridge: Cambridge University Press.

Nelson, Randy F., ed. 1989. *Martial Arts Reader*. Woodstock, N.Y.: Overlook Press.

Ngo, Van Xuyet. 1976. *Divination, magie et politique dans la Chine ancienne*. Paris: Presses Universitaires de France.

Ni, Hua-ching. 1989. *Attune Your Body with Dao-In: Taoist Exercises for a Long and Happy Life*. Malibu, Calif.: Shrine of the Eternal Breath of Tao.

Ni, Maoshing. 1995. *The Yellow Emperor's Classic of Medicine*. Boston: Shambhala.

Ōgata Tōru 大形徹. 1995. "Hihatsu kō: Kamikatachi to reikon no kanren ni tsuite" 被髮考—髮型と靈魂の關連について. *Tōhō shūkyō* 東方宗教 86:1–23.

Olson. Stuart Alven. 2002. *Qigong Teachings of a Taoist Immortal: The Eight Essential Exercises of Master Li Ching-yün*. Rochester, Vt.: Inner Traditions.

Oschman, James. 2000. *Energy Medicine: The Scientific Basis*. New York: Churchill Livingstone.

Ownby, David. 2007. *Falun Gong and China's Future*. New York: Oxford University Press.

Palmer, David. 2007. *Qigong Fever: Body, Science, and Utopia in China*. New York: Columbia University Press.

Penny, Benjamin. 2000. "Immortality and Transcendence." In *Daoism Handbook*, edited by Livia Kohn, 109–133. Leiden: E. Brill.

———. 2002. "Falungong, Prophecy and Apocalypse." *East Asian History* 23:149–168.

———. 2003. "The Life and Times of Li Hongzhi: Falungong and Religious Biography." *China Quarterly* 175:643–661.

Pert, Candace. 1997. *Molecules of Emotion: Why You Feel the Way You Feel*. New York: Scribner.

Porkert, Manfred. 1974. *The Theoretical Foundations of Chinese Medicine*. Cambridge, Mass.: MIT Press.

Porter, Bill. 1993. *The Road to Heaven: Encounters with Chinese Hermits*. San Francisco: Mercury House.

Pregadio, Fabrizio. 2000. "Elixirs and Alchemy." In *Daoism Handbook*, edited by Livia Kohn, 165–195. Leiden: E. Brill.

———. 2006a. "Early Daoist Meditation and the Origins of Inner Alchemy." In *Daoism in History: Essays in Honour of Liu Ts'un-yan*, edited by Benjamin Penny, 121–158. London: Routledge.

———. 2006b. *Great Clarity: Daoism and Alchemy in Early Medieval China*. Stanford, Calif.: Stanford University Press.

Puett, Michael. 2002. *To Become a God: Cosmology, Sacrifice, and Self-Divinization in Early China*. Cambridge, Mass.: Harvard University Press.

Reid, Daniel P. 1989. *The Tao of Health, Sex, and Longevity*. New York: Simon and Schuster.

Robinet, Isabelle. 1984. *La révélation du Shangqing dans l'histoire du taoïsme*. 2 vols. Paris: Publications de l'Ecole Française d'Extrême-Orient.

———. 1989a. "Original Contributions of *Neidan* to Taoism and Chinese Thought." In *Taoist Meditation and Longevity Techniques*, edited by Livia Kohn, 295–238. Ann Arbor: University of Michigan, Center for Chinese Studies Publications.

———. 1989b. "Visualization and Ecstatic Flight in Shangqing Taoism." In *Taoist Medita-*

tion and Longevity Techniques, edited by Livia Kohn, 157–190. Ann Arbor: University of Michigan, Center for Chinese Studies Publications.

———. 1990. "Recherche sur l'alchimie interieure *(neidan)*—L'école Zhenyuan." *Cahiers d'Extrême-Asie* 5:141–162.

———. 1993. *Taoist Meditation.* Translated by Norman Girardot and Julian Pas. Albany: State University of New York Press.

———. 1995. *Introduction a l'alchimie interieure taoïste: De l'unité et de la multiplicité.* Paris: Editions Cerf.

———. 1997. *Taoism: Growth of a Religion.* Translated by Phyllis Brooks. Stanford, Calif.: Stanford University Press.

Roth, Harold D. 1992. *The Textual History of the Huai-Nan Tzu.* Ann Arbor, Mich.: Association of Asian Studies.

Russell, Terence C. 1990a. "Chen Tuan at Mount Huangbo." *Asiatische Studien/Etudes Asiatiques* 44:107–140.

———. 1990b. "Chen Tuan's Veneration of the Dharma: A Study in Hagiographic Modification." *Taoist Resources* 2.1:54–72.

Sailey, Jay. 1978. *The Master Who Embraces Simplicity: A Study of the Philosophy of Ko Hung (A.D. 283–343).* San Francisco: Chinese Materials Center.

Sakade Yoshinobu 扳出祥伸. 1986a. "Chō Tan 'Yōsei yōshu' itsubun to sono shisō" 張湛養生要集逸文とその思想. *Tōhōshūkyō* 東方宗教 68:1–24.

———. 1986b. "Kaisetsu dōin no enkaku" 解釋。導引|の沿革. In *Dōin taiyō* 導引|體要, edited by Kitamura Toshikatsu 喜田村利且, 1–41. Tokyo: Taniguchi shoten.

———. 1989. "Longevity Techniques in Japan: Ancient Sources and Contemporary Studies." In *Taoist Meditation and Longevity Techniques,* edited by Livia Kohn, 1–40. Ann Arbor: University of Michigan, Center for Chinese Studies Publications.

———. 1992. "Son Shibo to bukkyō" 孫思邈と佛教. *Chūgoku koten kenkyū* 中國古典研究 37:1–19.

———. 2005. "Daoism and the Dunhuang Regimen Texts." In *Medieval Chinese Medicine: The Dunhuang Medical Manuscripts,* edited by Vivienne Lo and Christopher Cullen, 278–290. London: RoutledgeCurzon.

Saso, Michael. 1995. *The Gold Pavilion: Taoist Ways to Peace, Healing, and Long Life.* Boston: Charles E. Tuttle.

Schafer, Edward H. 1979. "A T'ang Taoist Mirror." *Early China* 4:387–398.

Schechter, Danny. 2000. *Falun Gong's Challenge to China: Spiritual Practice or "Evil Cult"?* New York: Akashic Books.

Scheid, Volker. 2002. *Chinese Medicine in Contemporary China: Plurality and Synthesis.* Durham, N.C.: Duke University Press.

Schipper, Kristofer M. 1975a. *Concordance du* Houang-t'ing king. Paris: Publications de l'Ecole Française d'Extrême-Orient.

———. 1975b. *Concordance du Tao Tsang: Titres des ouvrages.* Paris: Publications de l'Ecole Française d'Extrême-Orient.

———. 1979. "Le Calendrier de Jade: Note sur le *Laozi zhongjing*." *Nachrichten der deutschen Gesellschaft für Natur- und Völkerkunde Ostasiens* 125:75–80.

———, and Franciscus Verellen, eds. 2004. *The Taoist Canon: A Historical Companion to the Daozang*. Chicago: University of Chicago Press.

Seaman, Gary. 1987. *Journey to the North: An Ethnohistorical Analysis and Annotated Translation of the Chinese Folk Novel* Pei-you chi. Berkeley: University of California Press.

Seem, Mark D. 1987. *Acupuncture Energetics*. Rochester, Vt.: Healing Arts Press.

———. 1989. *Body-Mind Energetics: Toward a Dynamic Model of Health*. Rochester, Vt.: Healing Arts Press.

Seidel, Anna. 1982. "Tokens of Immortality in Han Graves." *Numen* 29:79–122.

———. 1985. "Geleitbrief an die Unterwelt. Jenseitsvorstellungen in den Graburkunden der Späteren Han Zeit." In *Religion und Philosophie in Ostasien: Festschrift für Hans Steininger*, edited by G. Naundorf, K. H. Pohl, and H. H. Schmidt, 161–184. Würzburg: Königshausen and Neumann.

Shahar, Meir. 1998. *Crazy Ji: Chinese Religion and Popular Literature*. Harvard Yenching Monographs No. 48. Cambridge, Mass.: Harvard University Press.

———. 2000. "Epigraphy, Buddhist Historiography, and Fighting Monks: The Case of the Shaolin Monastery." *Asia Major*, 3rd s., 13.2:15–36.

———. 2001. "Ming-Period Evidence of Shaolin Martial Practice." *Harvard Journal of Asiatic Studies* 61:359–413.

Shi Deqian 释德虔, Shi Yanxiao 释延孝, and Shi Dexiang 释德相. 1999. *Shaolin baduan jin tujie* 少林八段锦图解. Beijing: Renmin tiyu.

Shi Deyu 释德虞 and Xu Qinyan 徐勤燕. 2003. *Shaolin qigong miji* 少林气功秘集. Beijing: Renmin tiyu.

Sivin, Nathan. 1967. "A Seventh-Century Chinese Medical Case History." *Bulletin of the History of Medicine* 41.3:267–273.

———. 1968. *Chinese Alchemy: Preliminary Studies*. Cambridge: Harvard University Press.

———. 1978. "On the Word 'Daoist' as a Source of Perplexity." *History of Religions* 17:303–330.

Skar, Lowell, and Fabrizio Pregadio. 2000. "Inner Alchemy (Neidan)." In *Daoism Handbook*, edited by Livia Kohn, 464–497. Leiden: E. Brill.

Smith, Thomas E. 1992. "Ritual and the Shaping of Narrative: The Legend of the Han Emperor Wu." Ph.D. Diss., University of Michigan.

Sörvik, Karin. 2001. "Tao Yin Exercises." Video presentation. Dunsmore, Penn.: International Healing Dao.

Staal, Julius. 1984. *Stars of Jade: Calendar Lore, Mythology, Legends, and Star Stories of Ancient China*. Decatur, Ga.: Writ Press.

Stein, Stephan. 1999. *Zwischen Heil und Heilung: Zur frühen Tradition des Yangsheng in China*. Uelzen: Medizinisch-Literarische Verlagsgesellschaft.

Sterckx, Roel. 2002. *The Animal and the Daemon in Early China*. Albany: State University of New York Press.

Strickmann, Michel. 1978. "The Mao-shan Revelations: Taoism and the Aristocracy." *T'oung Pao* 63:1–63.

———. 1979. "On the Alchemy of T'ao Hung-ching." In *Facets of Taoism,* edited by Holmes Welch and Anna Seidel, 123–192. New Haven, Conn.: Yale University Press.

———. 1981. *Le taoïsme du Mao chan: Chronique d'une révélation.* Paris: Collège du France, Institut des Hautes Etudes Chinoises.

Switkin, Walter. 1987. *Immortality: A Taoist Text of Macrobiotics.* San Francisco: H. S. Dakin.

Taimni, I. K. 1975. *The Science of Yoga.* Wheaton, Ill.: Theosophical Publishing House.

Takehiro, Teri. 1990. "The Twelve Sleep Exercises of Mount Hua." *Taoist Resources* 2.1:73–94.

Targ, Russell, and Jane Katra. 1999. *Miracles of Mind: Exploring Nonlocal Consciousness and Spiritual Healing.* Novato, Calif.: New World Library.

Tart, Charles T.; Harold E. Puthoff; and Russell Targ, eds. 1979. *Mind at Large.* New York: Praeger.

Teeguarden, Iona. 1975. *Acupressure Way of Health: Jin shin do.* Tokyo: Japan Publications.

Twitchett, Denis, ed. 1979. *The Cambridge History of China.* Vol. 3: *Sui and T'ang China, 589–906.* Cambridge: Cambridge University Press.

Unschuld, Paul U. 1985. *Medicine in China: A History of Ideas.* Berkeley: University of California Press.

———. 1986. *Nan-ching: The Classic of Difficult Issues.* Berkeley: University of California Press.

Valussi, Elena. 2003. "Beheading the Red Dragon: A History of Female Inner Alchemy in China." Ph.D. Diss., School of Oriental and African Studies, University of London.

———. 2006. "Female Alchemy and Paratext: How to Read *Nüdan* in a Historical Context." Paper presented at the International Conference "Daoism in the Twentieth Century." Stanford Center, Harvard University, Cambridge, Mass.

Vankeerberghen, Griet. 2001. *The* Huainanzi *and Liu An's Claim to Moral Authority.* Albany: State University of New York Press.

Varela, Francisco; Evan Thompson; and Eleanor Rosch. 1991. *The Embodied Mind: Cognitive Science and Human Experience.* Cambridge, Mass.: MIT Press.

Veith, Ilza. 1972. *The Yellow Emperor's Classic of Internal Medicine.* Berkeley: University of California Press.

Vervoorn, Aat. 1983. "Boyi and Shuqi: Worthy Men of Old?" *Papers in Far Eastern History* 29:1–22.

———. 1984. "The Origins of Chinese Eremitism." *Xianggang zhongwen daxue Zhongguo wenhua yanjiu suo xuebao* 15:249–295.

Wang, Li. 2004. "A Daoist Way of Transcendence: Bai Yuchan's Inner Alchemical Thought and Practice." Ph.D. Diss., University of Iowa.

Wang, Shumin, and Penelope Barrett. 2006. "Profile of a *Daoyin* Tradition: The 'Five Animal Mimes.'" *Asian Medicine: Tradition and Modernity* 2.2:225–253.

Wang, Xudong, ed. 2003. *Life Cultivation and Rehabilitation in Traditional Chinese Medicine.* Shanghai: Shanghai University of Traditional Chinese Medicine.

Wang, Yi'e. 2006. *Daoism in China: An Introduction.* Warren, Conn.: Floating World Editions.

Ware, James R. 1966. *Alchemy, Medicine, and Religion in the China of AD 320.* Cambridge, Mass.: MIT Press.

Warshaw, Stephen. 1987. *China Emerges: A Concise History of China from Its Origins to the Present.* Berkeley, Calif.: Diablo Press.

Watson, Burton. 1968. *The Complete Works of Chuang-tzu.* New York: Columbia University Press.

Wenwu 文物. 1975. "Mawangdui sanhao Hanmu bohua daoyin tu de chubu yanjiu" 馬王堆三號漢墓帛畫導引圖的初步研究. *Wenwu* 文物 7:72–74.

———. 1989. "Jiangling Zhangjia shan Han jian Maishu shiwen" 江陵張家山漢簡脈書釋文. *Wenwu* 文物 7:72–74.

———. 1990. "Zhangjia shan Hanjian Yinshu shiwen" 張家山漢簡引書釋文. *Wenwu* 文物 10:82–86.

White, William Charles. 1940. *Chinese Temple Frescoes: A Study of Three Wall-paintings of the Thirteenth Century.* Toronto: University of Toronto Press.

Wile, Douglas. 1983. *T'ai-Chi Touchstones: Yang Family Secret Transmission.* New York: Sweet Chi Press.

———. 1985. *Cheng Man-Ching's Advanced Tai-Chi Form Instructions.* New York: Sweet Chi Press.

———. 1992. *Art of the Bedchamber: The Chinese Sexology Classics.* Albany: State University of New York Press.

———. 1996. *Lost Tai-Chi Classics from the Late Ching Dynasty.* Albany: State University of New York Press.

Wilhelm, Hellmut. 1948. "Eine Zhou-Inschrift über Atemtechnik." *Monumenta Serica* 13:385–388.

Winn, Michael. 2006. "Transforming Sexual Energy with Water-and-Fire Alchemy." In *Daoist Body Cultivation,* edited by Livia Kohn, 151–178. Magdalena, N.M.: Three Pines Press.

Wong, Eva. 1990. *Seven Taoist Masters.* Boston: Shambhala.

Worthington, Vivian. 1982. *A History of Yoga.* Boston: Routlege and Kegan Paul.

Wu, Jing-Nuan. 1993. *Ling Shu or The Spiritual Pivot.* Washington, D.C.: Taoist Center.

Yang, F. S. 1958. "A Study of the Origin of the Legend of the Eight Immortals." *Oriens Extremus* 5:1–20.

Yang, Jwing-ming. 1988. *The Eight Pieces of Brocade: Improving and Maintaining Health.* Jamaica Plain, Mass.: Yang's Martial Arts Association.

Yao, Ted. 2000. "Quanzhen—Complete Perfection." In *Daoism Handbook,* edited by Livia Kohn, 567–593. Leiden: E. Brill.

Yasudian, Selvarajan, and Elizabeth Haich. 1965 [1953]. *Yoga and Health.* New York: Harper and Row.

Yetts, Percifal. 1916. "The Eight Immortals." *Journal of the Royal Asiatic Society*, 773–807.

Yoshikawa Tadao 吉川忠夫, ed. 1992. *Chūgoku ko dōkyō shi kenkyū* 中國古道教史研究. Kyoto: Dōhōsha.

———, ed. 1998. *Rikuchō dōkyō no kenkyū* 六朝道教の研究. Kyoto: Shunjusha.

Yoshioka Yoshitoyo 吉岡義豐. 1967. "Zaikairoku to Chigonsō". 齋戒籙と至言總 *Taishō daigaku kenkyūjo kiyō* 大正大學研究所紀要 52:283–302.

———. 1979. "Taoist Monastic Life." In *Facets of Taoism*, edited by Holmes Welch and Anna Seidel, 220–252. New Haven, Conn.: Yale University Press.

Zeng, Qingnan, and Daoqing Liu. 2002. *China's Traditional Way of Health Preservation*. Beijing: Foreign Languages Press.

Zhang Guangde 张广德. 2001. *Daoyin yangsheng gong* 导引养生功. Beijing: Beijing tiyu daxue.

Zhou Xiaolan 周筱兰. 2000. *Liangong shiba fa* 练功十八法. Beijing: Renmin tiyao chubanshe.

Zhu Yueli 朱越利. 1986. "*Yangxing yanming lu* kao" 養性延命錄考. *Shijie zongjiao yanjiu* 世界宗教研究 1:101–115.

———. 1992. *Daojiao yaoji gailun* 道教要籍概論. Vol. 2. Beijing: Yenshan chubanshe. Daojiao wenhua congshu.

Zohar, Dana, and Ian Marshall. 1994. *The Quantum Society: Mind, Physics, and a New Social Vision*. New York: William Morrow.

Index